Global English and Politi Economy

In this book, John O'Regan examines the role of political economy in the worldwide spread of English and traces the origins and development of the dominance of English to the endless accumulation of capital in a capitalist world-system.

O'Regan combines Marxist perspectives of capital accumulation with world-systems analysis, international political economy, and studies of imperialism and empire to present a historical account of the 'free riding' of English upon the global capital networks of the capitalist world-system. Relevant disciplinary perspectives on global English are examined in this light, including superdiversity, translanguaging, translingual practice, trans-spatiality, language commodification, World Englishes and English as a Lingua Franca. *Global English and Political Economy* presents an original historical and interdisciplinary interpretation of the global ascent of English, while also raising important theoretical and practical questions for perspectives which suggest that the time of the traditional models of English is past.

Providing an introduction to key theoretical perspectives in political economy, this book is essential reading for advanced students and researchers in applied linguistics, World Englishes and related fields of study.

John P. O'Regan is Professor of Critical Applied Linguistics at UCL Institute of Education, University College London, UK. He is co-editor of *Education and the Discourse of Global Neoliberalism* (Routledge, 2021).

Language, Society and Political Economy
Series editor: David Block
ICREA & Universitat Pompeu i Fabra

This series aims to publish broadly accessible monographs which directly address how theoretical frameworks in political economy can directly inform the critical analysis and discussion of language in society issues. Contributions to the series include extensive theoretical background, dealing with an aspect or area of political economy, before moving to an application of this theoretical discussion to a particular language in society issue. The series takes up the challenge of interdisciplinarity, linking scholarship in the social sciences in general (and political economy in particular) with the kinds of issues which language in society researchers have traditionally focused on. The series also aims to publish books by authors whose ideas fall outside the mainstream of language in society scholarship and by authors in parts of the world which have traditionally been underrepresented in relevant international journals and book series.

Titles in the series:

Language Textbooks in the Era of Neoliberalism
Pau Bori

Language and Neoliberal Governmentality
Edited by Luisa Martín Rojo and Alfonso Del Percio

The Commodification of Language
Conceptual Concerns and Empirical Manifestations
Edited by John E. Petrovic and Bedrettin Yazan

Global English and Political Economy
John P. O'Regan

For more information on any of these and other titles, or to order, please go to www.routledge.com/Language-Society-and-Political-Economy/book-series/LSPE

Additional resources for Language and Communication are available on the Routledge Language and Communication Portal: www.routledgetextbooks.com/textbooks/languageandcommunication/

Global English and Political Economy

John P. O'Regan

> To Norman,
> CDA scholar, inspiration and friend.
> This work owes much to you.
> With compliments,
> J⊴—
> 30 April 2021

LONDON AND NEW YORK

First published 2021
by Routledge
2 Park Square, Milton Park, Abingdon, Oxon OX14 4RN

and by Routledge
605 Third Avenue, New York, NY 10158

Routledge is an imprint of the Taylor & Francis Group, an informa business

© 2021 John P. O'Regan

The right of John P. O'Regan to be identified as author of this work has been asserted by him in accordance with sections 77 and 78 of the Copyright, Designs and Patents Act 1988.

All rights reserved. No part of this book may be reprinted or reproduced or utilised in any form or by any electronic, mechanical, or other means, now known or hereafter invented, including photocopying and recording, or in any information storage or retrieval system, without permission in writing from the publishers.

Trademark notice: Product or corporate names may be trademarks or registered trademarks, and are used only for identification and explanation without intent to infringe.

British Library Cataloguing-in-Publication Data
A catalogue record for this book is available from the British Library

Library of Congress Cataloging-in-Publication Data
A catalog record for this book has been requested

ISBN: 978-1-138-81111-9 (hbk)
ISBN: 978-1-138-81112-6 (pbk)
ISBN: 978-1-315-74933-4 (ebk)

Typeset in Sabon
by Apex CoVantage, LLC

Contents

Acknowledgements   viii

1   **The political economy of English in a capitalist world-system**   1
English and capital 1
Capital and capital accumulation 9
Capital circulation and the free riding of English 12
Capital as part of an expanding world-system 16
Capital as a dialectical process 18
Accumulation and classical imperialism 22
The development of underdevelopment 25
Endless accumulation in a capitalist world-system 27
Structural power in international political economy 31
*Accumulation as the endless repetition of the
    original sin 36*
*Capital and normative English across the
    longue durée 41*

2   **English and the political economy of informal empire, 1688–1850**   44
The development of informal empire 44
The imperialism of free trade 49
Gentlemanly capitalism 54
The intrusion of capital, 1688–1815 58
*Capital export and the opening to free trade,
    1815–1850 62*

3   **The political economy of global English, 1850–1914**   69
The intrusion of capital post-1850 69
*The hinge of empire: India and the diffusion
    of English 73*

The social diffusion of English: Shanghai 79
The expansion of English in Africa 84
Railway imperialism and the transportation of English 89
Railway imperialism and the structuring of English in China 92
Invisible chains of English across the longue durée 100

4 **The political economy of global English, 1918–1979** 102
Handing over the baton: transition, 1870–1918 102
Networks of English and the rise of US capital, 1918–1945 106
English and the institutional structuring of the world-economy, post-1945 109
Cold War and the structuring of English in East Asia 113
Communist containment and English incorporation 118
US post-war capital networks: Europe, Latin America and the Middle East 123
US linguistic seignorage and the transnationalization of English, 1968–1979 126
1974 oil crisis and debt structuring in the capitalist world-economy 132

5 **Capital-centric English and the modern world-system, 1979–2008** 135
Capitalist crisis management and the structuration of English 135
Standard English as the capital-centric lingua franca of the capitalist world-system 141
Sub-prime, the derivatives revolution and capital-centric English 148
Language as a dialectical practical consciousness and the financial crisis of 2007–8 153

6 **The decline of the US world-hegemony** 158
US hegemonic decline and the rise of China 158
China's structural power 160
Hegemonic transition in a world-system 164
US economic nationalism and the challenge of China 168
US destabilization of the international trading system 171
Impediments to the Chinese global hegemony 174

7 Superdiverse translingualism, commodification
and trans-spatial resistances   181
  *The multi/plural turn and the persistence of the normative
    form 181*
  The ownership of English 186
  Language commodification 189
  Resistance and superdiverse translingualism 195
  Phonocentrism in superdiverse translingualism 200
  *The normative form as a social relation of capital and
    capitalism 205*

8 The demise of capitalism and the end of the hegemony
  of English   209
  Capitalist crisis and the normative hegemony 209
  *Immiseration, inequality and anti-systemic
    assimilation 211*
  Ideological endism and the collapse of capitalism 214
  *Capitalist disintegration and the end of the English
    hegemony 218*

References   221
Index   254

Acknowledgements

This book has been a long time in the making, and but for the belief, encouragement and patience of others it might not have come to fruition. The topic for this book was first suggested to me by David Block, the editor of the present series. I do not have the right words to be able properly to express the extent of gratitude that I owe David for continuing to have faith in this project, even as it grew far beyond what we originally envisaged it would be. In the same context, I owe an enormous debt to Routledge, and in particular to Louisa Semlyen and Eleni Steck, who have been a most excellent editorial team, and who have shown great forbearance and support in helping me to pursue this book to its completion. As a book about the political economy of English as a global language, it required a good deal of reading. But with this topic, the more I read the more it became apparent that the answer I was seeking as to why English was such a dominant language, and why in particular that it was the structural dominance of the normative standard that was at issue, was located in a much longer time period, and *durée*, than the one I had started out with, such that it was necessary to reach back to the beginnings of capital and of capitalism itself in order to be able to make sense of it. As I explain in the first chapter of the book, the project in its complexity became something of a 'desk clearing' exercise, which made it both necessary and possible for me to engage in a range of disciplinary areas and historical perspectives which have for the most part been absent from debates about the global dominance of English. These include classical and contemporary studies of imperialism and empire, world-systems analysis, dependency theory, and issues around structural power in international political economy.

Deep critical insight on the question of the global dominance of English was provided by the Marx reading group to which I belong at the UCL Institute of Education (IOE). All of the members of this group are either applied linguists or sociolinguists, and we have been reading Marx for about ten years. Including myself, they are David Block, John Gray, Catherine Wallace, Melanie Cooke and Siân Preece. We decided to embark upon a more methodical reading of Marx because, outside of the dedicated left, very few others appeared to be doing so, and yet in 2009–10 we found ourselves in the midst of a profound systemic crisis to which the world's most powerful governments', including the then UK government's, only answer were swingeing austerity measures and the mindless pursuit of the very same economic policies that had created the crisis in the first place. Even amongst mainstream political and economic commentators at the time, in the wake of the 2007–8 financial crash, Marx with his take on systemic capitalist crisis was experiencing something of a revival. Within applied linguistics and sociolinguistics there was also much greater attention being paid to the connection between political economy and language, particularly from the directions of anthropology and sociology. Moreover, the key thinkers we were familiar with in the group, such as Foucault, Habermas, Bourdieu, Bhaskar and Derrida, in one way or another all appeared to define themselves and their work according to a relationship with modernity, and also with Marx. It seemed to us that it would not only be educative to read Marx, but that it was absolutely necessary to do so if one had any real ambition to engage with the unequal political economy of English in the world and also with the intellectual debates which were preoccupying the academy at the time, particularly around poststructuralism and the social turn. We therefore started by reading *Capital Volume I*, and in the years which followed we read all the major works. I owe a considerable debt to Marx and to Engels in this book, but I owe an even greater debt to the members of the Marx reading group, without whom such a systematic reading of Marx and of capitalism would not have occurred. Apart from the critique of capitalism which Marx and his long-time collaborator Engels present, what is most notable about Marx's analysis is its great historicity. Capitalism very specifically begins in the sixteenth century, and it is crucially important to the account which Marx gives that it is possible to pinpoint when and how this evolution commences. Similarly, such historicity is also critical to world-systems analysis and dependency theory perspectives, both of which were also greatly influenced by Marx. But historicity is not unique to Marx and Marxism, it is also central to Foucault and constructivism, for which there is also no understanding of the present in the absence of an archaeology of the past. All the more reason then that any account of the global dominance of English should include the past of capital and of capitalism, because it was from this that the global dominance of English and discourses around English emerged.

My profound thanks also go to all the students on the MA Applied Linguistics module English in Diverse World Contexts at the IOE, who with enthusiasm and good humour have over the years willingly submitted themselves to my theorizing on the global dominance of English, in addition to reading emerging section and chapter drafts. I believe I have learned at least as much from them as I hope they have learned from me. Another group of persons I wish to thank are IOE research students, past and present, whose intellectual engagement has always given me cause for productive reflection and thought, and who in their own ways have also been a great support to me throughout the writing of this book. My heartfelt thanks go out to all of them. I am fortunate to have been surrounded by such excellent interlocutors. A number of people were also kind enough to read draft chapters of the book while it was in preparation. They are Marnie Holborow, Christian Chun, John Gray, Catherine Wallace, William Simpson and Karin Zotzmann. David Block also read a full draft of the manuscript. I am greatly indebted to them all for their incisive critical commentary and also their encouragement. The advice they gave was warmly received and whatever flaws remain they are of course my own. I am also grateful to Jin Tinghe and Sharon Chu for their kind assistance with the Chinese text in the book.

Many of the ideas in this book would not be there but for the engagement and support of past and present colleagues in the Centre for Applied Linguistics at UCL. I wish to thank them all. I feel fortunate indeed to be amongst such a brilliant group of scholars. In addition, the following persons through their generous time and critical inspiration over the years have influenced me in ways they can only guess at, and I would like to mention them here as well: Norman Fairclough, Catherine Wallace, David Block, Alison Phipps, Malcolm MacDonald, Jan Blommaert, Adam Jaworski, Alastair Pennycook, Robert Phillipson, Li Wei, John Gray, Ben Rampton, Joseph Lo Bianco, Jan Nederveen Pieterse, Karin Zotzmann, Robert Skidelsky, Mervyn Hartwig, Phan Le Ha, Gao Yihong, Bob Adamson, Tim McNamara, Zhu Hua, Nicolina Montessori, Paul Wickens, Mike Robinson, and also the much missed Anne Betzel, Dave Hughes, Mo Price, Alex Teasdale, Tope Omoniyi, Jagdish Gundara, Geoff Whitty, Roy Bhaskar and Gunther Kress. I owe them all my gratitude. Lastly, this book could not have been written without the love and support of my wife Paula. I respectfully dedicate this work to her.

1 The political economy of English in a capitalist world-system

English and capital

On June 27, 1615, Richard Wickham, the English East India Company's Factor at Firando [Hirado] in Japan, wrote to his fellow Company agent, Mr Eaton, in Macao. In his letter Wickham begs Eaton to send him 'a pot of the best sort of chaw' (Ukers, 1935: 71–72). Wickham was referring to tea, and the mention of it is thought to be the first written reference to tea in the English language. We do not know if Wickham received his tea, but in addition to the interest of tea being known to English persons some decades before it first arrived in England, the communication also serves as an indication of the formal presence of English, and resident speakers of that language, in East Asia in the early seventeenth century. It may not have been a particularly significant presence of the language, but a presence it was nevertheless. It is now four hundred years since Wickham wrote his letter, and in that time English has advanced its position to become the most sought after and dominant language in the world (Choi, 2002; Reksulak, Shughart & Tollison, 2004; Piller & Takahashi, 2006; Ives, 2006; Chowdhury & Phan, 2014; Ricento, 2015b; Phan, 2017; Lemberg, 2018). It is also the language which, in a global context, appears to arouse the most passion and controversy, particularly amongst scholars of language and linguistics whose interests are with English and Englishes in the world. Here are some indicative alignments [other more recent ones are referenced later]: first, those that take an openly anti-imperialist stance towards global English (e.g. Phillipson, 1992, 2008; Phillipson & Skutnabb-Kangas, 1996; Canagarajah, 1999); second, those that take a postcolonialist and to varying degrees [or not] a poststructuralist stance (e.g. Blommaert, 2010; Canagarajah, 2013; Pennycook, 1998, 2007, 2010a, 2010b, 2020; Mazrui, 2004, 2016; Thiong'o, 1987, 1991; Rajagopalan, 2004, 2012; Kumaravadivelu, 2008); third, those who take a more-or-less Marxist stance (e.g. Block, Gray & Holborow, 2012; Holborow, 1999, 2015a; O'Regan, 2014); and lastly, those who take an English as a Lingua Franca (ELF), World Englishes (WE), translingual practice, translanguaging or superdiversity stance – although these are by no means identical perspectives (Jenkins, Cogo & Dewey,

2011; Jenkins, 2006, 2007; Seidlhofer, 2009, 2012a; Mauranen, 2015; Kachru, 1985, 1996; Bhatt, 1995, 2001; Brutt-Griffler, 2002; Bolton, 2013; Sadeghpour, 2019; Sridhar, 2019; Canagarajah, 2013; García & Li, 2014; Li, 2018a, 2018b; Blommaert & Rampton, 2012; Arnaut & Spotti, 2014).[1] It is perhaps no exaggeration to state that for at least some of these scholars English in its 'ideologized' standard inner-circle form (Kachru, 1985; Ives, 2010: 528; see also Bailey, 2017; Peters, 2017) is one which is deserving of little praise or welcome, and in some corners is even met with outright disdain, for English is seen to come with a considerable social [in]justice burden attached to its history as well as to its present use. This is due, as might be expected, to the indubitable historical association of English with British colonialism and US imperialism on the one hand (Phillipson, 1992; Pennycook, 1998) and its routinely negative association in the literature with the dominance of 'native-speakerism' or 'native-speakerist' ideologies on the other (*passim*). As many reading these lines will know, this refers to the widespread and for the most part instinctive conception that the English(es) of the anglophone core – that is, of the United States, Britain, Canada, New Zealand, Australia, Ireland etc. – and the standard grammatical systems and enunciations on which these are based – somehow represent the most correct models of English in the world and are the forms which ought to be followed in the teaching of English in a largely taken-for-granted globalized age (Kachru, 1990; Quirk, 1989/1990). This book assumes a reasonable familiarity with these arguments and the associated scholarly debates.

While some of these perspectives will be referred to in the course of this book, and indeed are returned to specifically in Chapter 7 when I consider what has usefully been referred to as the 'multi/plural turn' in applied linguistics (Kubota, 2016), it is not my intention to rehearse these different positions here at the outset, or to engage in an in-depth critical overview of them though the book, as this has been more than adequately done elsewhere (Blommaert, 2010; Holborow, 1999, 2015; Jenkins, 2009; Kubota, 2015, 2016; Kirkpatrick, 2010a; Park & Wee, 2012; Pennycook, 1994, 2001; Saraceni, 2015; Saxena & Omoniyi, 2010; Seargeant, 2012; Sowden, 2012; Grin, 2018; Ricento, 2018). A positional account which takes on these perspectives is *not* the main purpose of this book. Rather, I think of this book as more of a 'desk clearing' exercise in which I attempt to fill in a number of the historical and economic lacunae which have existed for me in applied linguistic and sociolinguistic accounts of the spread of English as a global language, and which I hope may show this spread in a different and more historical political-economic light. It has been an unfortunate absence as Block (2017a), Ricento (2015b) and others have suggested, that many applied linguists do not consider the economic dimension of language.

---

1 There are of course many who would not readily be accommodated to such groupings, but this is meant to be more illustrative than prescriptive.

As Bruthiaux has said, 'In the end, it undermines the credibility of applied linguists and makes it unlikely they will play a significant role in solving the social injustices they so rightly deplore' (Bruthiaux, 2008: 20). But as the growing body of work on language and political economy shows, this is now changing (see McGill, 2013; Block, 2017a, 2017b; Simpson & O'Regan, 2018, for overviews). In the course of this book, and particularly in Chapter 7 when the discussion is opened up to include approaches such as superdiversity, translanguaging and language commodification (Arnaut & Spotti, 2014; Blommaert & Rampton, 2012; Budach & de Saint-Georges, 2017; García & Li, 2014; Li, 2018a, 2018b; Heller, 2010; Duchêne & Heller, 2012; Boutet, 2012; Kelly-Holmes, 2016), these and some of the other positions mentioned earlier will be contested or 'stressed' to an extent; and it may be that the reader of these pages will wish to read the last few chapters first before proceeding to the rest of the book, since these are concerned with the current era and address directly more recent debates and concepts as these affect conceptualizations of English in the world today.

To reiterate then, this is a book about the *political economy* of English in relation to capital and the development of the capitalist world-system. That is, as a political economy, it is concerned with 'the interrelatedness of political and economic processes and phenomena' (Block, 2017a: 35) as these are implicated in the global dominance of English. But political economy, while central to this book, is not the whole of the story. The main issue as I see it, and which I wish to foreground in this book, is with the political and economic *historiography* of the global spread of English, which lacks historical as well as political-economic depth and *duration* (Braudel, 1980 [1958], 2012 [1958]; Wallerstein, 2000 [1974], 2011a, 2011b, 2011c, 2011d; O'Regan, 2021), although in the critical sociolinguistic tradition, scholars such as Bolton (2003), Blommaert (2010), Pennycook (1994, 1998, 2007), Phillipson (1992, 2008), Holborow (1999, 2015), Fairclough (2006), Seargeant (2012), and more recently Ricento (2015a) and Saraceni (2015) have each made important contributions. Blommaert indirectly points to this issue in his *Sociolinguistics of Globalization* (2010), when he refers to the 'stereotyping [in the literature] of contemporary globalization processes as fundamentally and shockingly new things' (p. 16). Blommaert notes an over-preoccupation with the recent past, as though globalization only dates to the late 1970s and the birth of modern neoliberalism and the Internet (Blommaert, 2010: 16), or to the collapse of the Soviet Union in 1991 (Gilpin, 2001: 8). Block (2012a: 63) refers to it as a *presentist* outlook on the world (see also O'Regan, 2014, 2016; Simpson & O'Regan, 2018). These events certainly represent new 'moments' in recent historical globalization processes (Harvey, 1996, 2010), but the time which has elapsed since they occurred is too short to be able to draw substantive conclusions about the kind of world that we now find ourselves in, or in the context of this book, about the seeming universalization of English as the world's dominant language. It also quite possibly leads us down erroneous paths. For others, and that includes scholars of global English, historians and political economists alike, 1945 is also often – not unreasonably – cited as *the* watershed moment for modern-day globalization processes and for the indelible hyper-centralization of English amongst the languages of the world (e.g. Calvet, 1998; Castells, 2006; De Swann, 2001; Fukuyama, 1992; Ritzer, 1993; Giddens, 1990, 2002; Held, McGrew, Goldblatt & Perraton, 1999; Gilpin, 2001; Nederveen Pieterse, 2009; Fairclough, 2006; Saxena & Omoniyi, 2010),[2] although common use of the term only came much later. As Gilpin has recorded, 'The term "globalization" came into popular usage in the second half of the 1980s in connection with the huge surge in foreign direct investment (FDI) by multinational corporations (MNCs)' (Gilpin, 2001: 7). Further to this, Gilpin identifies the collapse of the Soviet Union in 1991 as providing 'the necessary political condition for the creation of a truly global economy' (ibid: 8). The popularization of the term 'globalization' in combination with the global communications revolution which also exploded at just about this time seem to have been responsible for locating much of the debate about global English [and Englishes] within the timeframe of the relatively recent past, and rarely earlier than 1945; that is, unless it is to give an account of the history of English in a particular place or region, such as India (Roy, 1993, 1994; Evans, 2002), China (Adamson, 2002, 2004; L. Pan, 2015; Z. Pan, 2015; Gao, 2018) or Iran (Borjian, 2013; Rahimi, 2017; Goodrich, 2020).

It is my purpose in this book to show that a historiography of global English, whose principal focus is the post-1945 or, still more recent, post-Cold War era is not entirely satisfactory either. I believe that it is necessary to start much earlier, that is, with the rise of capitalism and of capital accumulation as an end in itself (Marx, 1976 [1867]; Luxemburg, 1951 [1913]; Sweezy, 1972; Wallerstein, 2000 [1974]; Fine, 1978; Arrighi, 2010; Nichols, 2015). As Blommaert (2010) has commented, 'one has to be precise with respect to the historical framing of the phenomena one examines' (p. 16). This book thus represents an attempt – from a mostly [but not only] Marxist perspective – to put in one place a historically framed account of the global spread of English as this is connected to the global spread of *capital*, and to do this in the context of the rise of a *capitalist world-system* which has been in existence since the sixteenth century, although some place it a century earlier than that (Sweezy, 1972; Wallerstein, 2004; Arrighi, 2010). Marx, on the other hand, goes a little later: 'World trade and the world market date from the sixteenth century, and from then on the modern history of capital starts to unfold' (Marx, 1976 [1867]: 247). It is from around 1600 that we begin to see the rise of England, and subsequent upon this the gradual unfolding of English as the *lingua franca* of global commerce and

---

2 I also wish to acknowledge that for several of these authors globalization is certainly not a process which only begins after 1945.

finance. The historical account shows that the feature peculiar to the world-system as this was managed by the British[3] from the mid-1600s down to at least 1914 was the fact of the movement of British capital, commercial and financial capital in particular, and in association with this movement, that of English as a language of trade and investment. In this context, as is argued in Chapter 2, the British world-system, or 'empire', and the accompanying global spread of English was not only a territorial matter of the *formal* expropriation of foreign lands, but also one of *informal* assimilation to a capitalist world-economy that was founded upon commerce and finance and which extended well beyond the swathes of red ink with which British-produced maps of the world were, by the late nineteenth century, routinely daubed (Gallagher & Robinson, 1953).

My basic premise is that the global spread of English and its ongoing dominance as a *normative form* needs to be understood in relation to the global spread of capital and capitalism, in which capital may be conceived in general terms as referring to the *accumulation* of trade relations and of commercial investments, including in the later twentieth century investments in financialized products (see Chapter 5). In this respect, I wish to argue that English has acted as a vehicular *free rider* (Olsen, 1965; Tuck, 2008; Fontaine, 2014; Calvet, 1998; Lemberg, 2018) upon capital, and that by means of capital's global spread English has become in an almost default manner 'structured in dominance' (Althusser, 1996 [1965]: 200–202; Hall, 1996: 325) in the world-economy and system. It achieved this dominance long before 1945, and it is the historical connection to capital which explains in the present day the ongoing *hegemony* of English (Gramsci, 1971; Taylor, 1996; Wallerstein, 2011b; Ives, 2019)[4] as the most favoured 'global vehicular language' and 'network good' of most of the nation-states and international organizations of the world (Lemberg, 2018: 561; Reksulak et al., 2004: 273) and the 'best candidate to become a universal language' (Choi, 2002: 275). It is moreover a *normative form* which is referenced; that is, as an ideologically idealized but also historically evolving core grammar or code. In the words of Antonio Gramsci, the normative grammar is 'a governing stratum [*ceto*] whose function is recognized and followed' (Gramsci,

---

3 The appellation 'British' is used here to refer collectively to the peoples of England, Wales, Scotland and – somewhat problematically – Ireland. 'Britain' as a political entity, however, did not come into existence until 1707 with the union of England and Wales with Scotland, so there is an anachronism involved in using it prior to then. Ireland, for its part, was incorporated into the 'Union' in 1801 but retained a political and geographical status that distinguished it from the area known as Britain or Great Britain. When I use 'British' or 'Britain' in this chapter and in this book, unless otherwise stated, I am including the strong likelihood that persons from Ireland were amongst this group (cf. Morgan, 1994).

4 'The mechanism of hegemony allowed the modern world-system to become the first world-economy in the history of humankind to survive, flourish, and expand to encompass the entire globe. Without it, capitalism as a historical system would not have been able to survive, and thereby transform the world' (Wallerstein, 2011b: xxvii).

1975: 2343, cited in Ives, 1998: 40),[5] but is also flexible enough that it can change and adapt itself over time, while still retaining its governing hegemony. It is as a normative grammar in Gramsci's sense that English as a global language in this book is understood; that is, as the *grammatical* form which is structurally dominant within the world-system and which stands apart from, and hierarchically 'above', all other realizations because of its relation to capital – in its economic form as related to wealth accumulation and growth, and by extension, in its symbolic form as related to social status and prestige (Bourdieu, 1977, 1984, 1986, 1991). To be clear then, the concern in this book is *not* with what might be called 'normative accents' [e.g. British, American, Australian, Irish etc.] or, to put this another way, with the 'native-like' reproduction of English-language 'authenticity' in pronunciation. Rather, it is with the adherence in both speech and in writing to *grammatical practices* which reproduce, and appear identical to, those which in English are associated with 'ideologized' or 'normative' standard forms and which are widely taken to be representative of authenticity and accuracy in formal contexts of use. It is this understanding which informs the references to *normative standard English* that occur in this book (cf. Milroy, 2000; Wright, 2000; Stein & Tieken-Boon van Ostade, 2012; Chang, 2016; Bailey, 2017; Peters, 2017).

This form is social in character, being connected with capital and power and with the construction of particular kinds of human subjectivities. As Marx observes, 'Capital is a social relation of production' (1976 [1867]: 932n). As a social relation, whether of production, circulation or accumulation, capital is also a relation of language, because without it, capital is unable to expand. Whether we are making reference to the sixteenth century or to the twenty-first, the spread of capital requires language, and preferably a language which is widely understood. In the sixteenth century and later, capital relied amongst other things on ships, 'factors' [commercial representatives], and bills of trade, all of which needed language: for shipboard commands, the verbal conduct of business, and the production of written invoices. Today, it relies on high-speed super-information highways, transnational brokers and printed legal contracts. Everything, and nothing, has changed. Capital can now be transposed at the click of a mouse, but language is still required for the *semiotic mediation* of the capital so transposed (cf. Althusser, 1971; Bakhtin, 1981; Mertz, 1985). Notwithstanding the technological advances of capitalism, the application of meaning to the procession of capital remains a necessary procedure, just as it was four hundred years ago. It is this which has made it possible for English to act as a free rider upon capital and to become a vehicular and 'capital-centric' language of note. This is with

---

5 Gramsci contrasts 'normative grammar' with what he refers to as 'spontaneous' or 'immanent' grammar (Gramsci, 1975: 2343; Ives, 1998: 40, 2010: 528, 2019: 69).

the understanding that as a free rider, the agency of English is provided by the human activity of its users, for without this activity, English could not of itself free ride. That is not to say that English does not have causal powers and effects (Bhaskar, 2008 [1975]: 50). On the contrary, it does. Only that the act of free riding on capital is not undertaken by English of itself but refers to the process of the circulation of the language as this is propagated by its users and is determined by the proximity of capital, whether understood as economic or symbolic, or both. In the case of normative standard English, which is the principal subject of this book, its historical determination by capital has been particularly strong, and it is this which has made this form structurally hegemonic in the world-system (for further discussion see later).

In this book, the concept of the free rider has been translocated from the fields of economics and international political economy, except that in these contexts free riding is defined as 'the action or practice of benefiting (or seeking to benefit) in some way from the effort, sacrifice, financial outlay, etc., of others, without making a similar contribution' (cited in Fontaine, 2014: 361). In economics it often refers to profits which are made in the absence of any financial outlay, but a more everyday understanding would be the use of public services while avoiding or evading the taxes which fund those services, for example watching television without a TV license, or travelling on a train without having paid for a ticket. There are many kinds of free riding that can occur in the economic sphere, and what is and is not free riding may well be a question of perspective. Is the billionaire who pays no personal tax on his income in a country where he resides, but who employs thousands of people in the same country who do pay tax, a free rider or not? Whatever one's view, free riding is considered a 'problem' in economics and in international political economy and is often referred to in those terms (Fontaine, 2014). The problem of free riding is still more heightened in the global context of cooperation between states and can often lead to disputes, for example when one state feels that its efforts are being taken advantage of by another.[6] This is not precisely the conception of free riding which I am working with in this book. I see the free riding of English on capital more as a type of *symbiosis* or even *parasitism*. English as a language and the English-speaking nations have taken advantage of capital. English has given succour to the expansion and accumulation of capital, and capital has given succour to the expansion and accumulation of English. It is in these circumstances that English has gained global acceptance and 'edge' as the dominant language of international communication.

---

6 Donald Trump's approach to international security was based on this assumption. His administration (2016–20) considered, for example, that the nations of Western Europe did not pay their fair share for the security arrangements which NATO provided and into which the US paid. They were therefore accused of free riding on US largesse.

I wish to explore why this is so, and as a secondary objective also to understand why other approaches appear to have overlooked this. This book is therefore offered as a complement and corrective to such perspectives. I would like to fill in some narrational spaces with regard to the history and political economy of English as a global language and the circumstances of its hegemony.

In the remaining sections of this chapter, I outline the theoretical parameters of this study. Being a periodized account of the global spread of capital over the past four centuries and of the relationship of English to this [see Chapter 2 for the periodization that is applied], it seems right to begin with Marx, for the reason that Marx is probably the foremost theorist of *capital* and of *capital accumulation* for the period under discussion. Others might choose Hume (1711–76), Smith (1723–90) or perhaps Ricardo (1772–1823), but it is really with Marx (1818–83) that the analysis of capital properly begins, even as he builds upon the work of those who came before him. Marx also provides the historical basis for the account of capital accumulation which was to inform the perspectives on global capitalism and imperialism which appeared in the work of thinkers such as Hilferding, Lenin, Luxemburg and Bukharin in the later nineteenth and early twentieth centuries (Brewer, 1990; Howard & King, 1985; Callinicos, 2009). Marx's extended historical purview was also to be influential for the *Annales* school of history, particularly as personified by Fernand Braudel, whose notion of the *longue durée* as 'the endless, inexhaustible history of structures and groups of structures' (Braudel, 1980 [1958]: 75) was in turn instrumental for world-systems analysis and dependency theory perspectives (Lee, 2012; Wallerstein, 2000 [1974], 1983, 2004; Arrighi, 2010; Frank, 1969a [1967], 1969b; Sweezy, 1972). In order to trace the journey of capital and of English from the late sixteenth century to the present day, it seems that the best and most obvious place to begin therefore is with Marx, as providing the foundational basis in political economy for the existence and persistence of 'global English' within a capitalist world-economy. Whether this makes this a Marxist account, I will leave for the reader to decide. Certainly, the ideas of Marx and of Marxists have been influential in causing me to think about this question, but so has the work of others such as Foucault, Said and Braudel, who would distance themselves from any such labelling. This book thus draws on theories, histories and perspectives which I have found useful for understanding the global spread of English. As such, it does not rigidly subscribe to any one intellectual position or to the dogmatic application of theory, although some positions and theories have carried more import than others. In this book, the work of scholars and intellectuals of diverse persuasions in political economy, social theory, history, anthropology, and applied linguistics and sociolinguistics have often proved to be as important to me as have the ideas of Marx, and I am grateful to the 'non-Marxist' critical scholarship which exists (see further in this chapter and Chapters 2 and 7).

Capital and capital accumulation

Marx's approach to capital and to capital accumulation was initially developed through his writings of the 1840s and 50s. The prominent texts are the *Economic and Philosophic Manuscripts* (1844), *The German Ideology* (1845) and the *Manifesto of the Communist Party* (1948 [1848]), the latter two being co-written with his collaborator Friedrich Engels. In these early works, Marx had an overriding concern to determine what distinguished capitalism from previous historical epochs. In addition to determining what this difference was, he was also struggling with identifying the correct conceptual point of departure from which to commence his definitive critique, which he isolated as being a choice between *capital* and *production* (Nicolaus, 1973). The thought process which eventually led him to capital was poured into a voluminous series of notebooks, known collectively as the *Grundrisse der Kritik der Politischen Oekonomie (Rohentwurf)*, or *Grundrisse* for short, compiled in 1857–8 for the purposes, as he put it, of 'self-clarification' (Marx, 1976 [1859]: 1).[7] These then formed the basis for volumes I–III of *Capital*, particularly *Volume I* (1867). Some elements of the notebooks also appeared in a condensed form as *A Contribution to the Critique of Political Economy* (1859).[8] In order to develop the conception presented earlier that English has historically acted as a free rider on capital, in what follows I give a brief overview of Marx's conception of capital and of capital circulation.

In the *Economic and Philosophic Manuscripts* (1844), Marx engages in an interrogation of the nature of capital based primarily on Adam Smith's *Wealth of Nations* (1999a [1776], 1999b [1776]). Here Marx begins by defining capital in terms of possession; that is, as 'private property in the products of other men's labour' (1964 [1844]: 78). He quotes Smith as saying that capital is 'the *power of purchasing*; a certain command over all the labour, or over all the produce of labour which is then in the market' (Smith quoted in Marx, ibid: 78; emphasis original in all quotes throughout the volume unless stated otherwise). Marx concludes that capital is 'the *governing power* over labour and its products' (ibid). This then, is an early intimation of Marx's concern with distinguishing capital from the mere possession

---

[7] The notebooks as a whole were not published in Marx's lifetime, but were finally issued as a limited edition by Foreign Language Publishers in Moscow in two volumes in 1939 and 1941 respectively. A complete German edition appeared in Berlin in 1953, and the English edition, translated by the radical German-American émigré Martin Nicolaus, was first published in 1973. The *Grundrisse*, alongside the first volume (1867), and the posthumously-published third volume of *Capital* (1894) are probably the key texts for Marx's treatment of capital and of capital accumulation, although the earlier material also contains much that is of interest to the student of capital and its spread.

[8] See also Pradella (2015) on the notebooks which Marx kept between 1843–8, 1850–3 (aka *The London Notebooks*), 1857–8 (*Grundrisse*), and 1861–3. Many of these have not been published in English.

of money, or wealth. Capital, in this initial iteration, is related to labour by means of the products which labour has created, in which the outcome is a value that is in excess of the initial sum expended, such that value, now as capital, magically appears to grow. In this sense, money is transformed into capital within the production process, although the mechanism by which this occurs is still not entirely clear. Reinforcing the distinctions which accompany capital is that competition is only possible if capital accumulates:

> Accumulation, where private property prevails, is the *concentration* of capital in the hands of the few, it is in general an inevitable consequence if capital is left to follow its natural course, and it is precisely through competition that the way is cleared for this natural destination of capital.
>
> (ibid: 83)

In other words, accumulation is a product of capitalist competition. A further important distinction which arises is that between *fixed capital* and *circulating capital*. Again, this is one which Marx derives directly from Smith, whom he quotes at length. In summary, fixed capital consists of 'capital invested in the improvement of land, the purchase of useful machines, instruments of trade, and such like things' (Smith quoted in Marx, ibid: 85). Circulating capital, on the other hand,

> is a capital which is employed in manufacturing or purchasing goods, and selling them again. The capital employed in this fashion yields no revenue or profit to its employer while it either remains in his possession or remains in the same shape. It is continually going from him in one particular shape in order to return to him in another, and it is only by means of such circulation, or such successive exchanges and transformations that it yields any profit.
>
> (Smith quoted in Marx, ibid: 85)

In other words, circulating capital is capital which is 'on the move', and it is only through this *movement* [and accompanying metamorphosis] that it is able to grow. This theme is pursued with greater specificity in the first volume of *Capital* (see further discussion later). The notion of capital being mobile is also to be found in *The German Ideology*. Here Marx and Engels give an account of the rise of a world market. Beginning in the fifteenth century, they note how

> Manufacture and the movement of production in general received an enormous impetus through the extension of intercourse [commerce] which came with the discovery of America and the sea-route to the East Indies. The new products imported thence, particularly the masses of gold and silver which came into circulation and totally changed the

position of the classes towards one another, dealing a hard blow to feudal landed property and to the workers; the expeditions of adventurers, colonisation; and above all the extension of markets into a world market, which had now become possible and was daily becoming more and more a fact, called forth a new phase of historical development.
(Marx & Engels, 1998 [1845]: 78)

In addition, 'The expansion of commerce and manufacture also accelerated the accumulation of movable capital' (ibid: 78), or 'capital in the modern sense' (p. 77).

The mobility of capital is further pursued in the *Communist Manifesto*. Here, in addition to the connection to wage labour, capital, as in *The German Ideology*, is similarly situated in relation to the creation of a world market. In this text, Marx and Engels give what are in effect some early definitions of globalization, but without employing the term.

Modern industry has established the world market, for which the discovery of America [in 1492] paved the way. This market has given an immense development to commerce, to navigation, to communication by land. This development has, in its turn, reacted on the extension of industry; and in proportion as industry, commerce, navigation, railways extended, in the same proportion the bourgeoisie developed, increased its capital, and pushed into the background every class handed down from the Middle Ages.
(Marx & Engels, 1948 [1848]: 10)[9]

A singular concern for Marx [and Engels] was how the capitalist era distinguished itself from previous historical periods, and this came to dominate Marx's later thinking. One aspect of this difference was the overriding need for capital accumulation. In between the well-known lines of radical polemic in the *Manifesto*, Marx and Engels set out the theoretical bases for capital accumulation and expansion on a world scale.

The need of a constantly expanding market for its products chases the bourgeoisie over the whole surface of the globe. It must nestle everywhere, settle everywhere, establish connections everywhere. The bourgeoisie has through its exploitation of the world market has given a cosmopolitan character to production and consumption in every country. . . . In place of the old wants, satisfied by the production of every country, we find new wants, requiring for their satisfaction the products

---

9 It is noticeable in the passing reference to America that the beginning of a world market – and by implication the transfer from feudalism to capitalism – is thereby dated to around the end of the fifteenth century.

of distant lands and climes. In place of the old local and national seclusion and self-sufficiency, we have intercourse in every direction, universal interdependence of nations.

(Marx & Engels, 1948 [1848]: 12–13)

The necessity of capital accumulation is what drives capitalism to expand.[10] It has to find new outlets for the capital that has been accumulated, or indeed *overaccumulated* (Harvey, 2004: 66). Capital cannot stand still; it is always in search of new spaces in which to accumulate. If capital cannot move, a crisis of accumulation can occur because more capital has been accumulated than can readily be re-absorbed. The resolution to crises of overaccumulation can be one of state-instigated 'creative destruction' (Schumpeter, 2010 [1943]), for example of the landscape, of local industry, or of the built environment in order to create new conditions and spaces for renewed private accumulation (see later). Another alternative is to export the 'surplus capital' to new geographical locations overseas. The export of capital as trade in goods and private speculation became a marked feature of British commerce from about 1600 (see this chapter and Chapter 2).

Capital circulation and the free riding of English

The perorations on capital and capital accumulation in the *Economic and Philosophic Manuscripts*, *The German Ideology* and the *Manifesto* set the scene for Marx's later studies on the subject in *Capital Volumes I–III*. They show that for Marx there are two overarching categories of capital [within which multiple distinctions exist]. These are capital as related to the products of labour; that is, capital as a social relation embodied in commodities [i.e. exploited labour], and capital as mobile money and products, or accumulated capital. Both involve qualitatively different forms of circulation. On the one hand, circulating capital refers to the mechanism and 'movement' of buying something in order to sell it on at a higher price. On the other, it refers to the geographical and 'spatial' movement of capital from one region to another in order to create new opportunities for capital to accumulate and make a profit. In *Capital Volume I*, Marx gives the first type of circulating capital the formula M-C-M, whereby money is exchanged for commodities which are then sold again for money. He contrasts this with the simple circulation of commodities to which he gives the formula C-M-C.

> The direct form of the circulation of commodities is C-M-C, the transformation of commodities into money, and the re-conversion of money back again into commodities: selling in order to buy. But alongside

10 'It is not the individuals who are set free by free competition; it is, rather, capital which is set free' (Marx, 1973: 650).

this form we find another form, which is quite distinct from the first: M-C-M, the transformation of money into commodities, and the reconversion of commodities into money; buying in order to sell. Money which describes the latter course in its movement is transformed into, becomes capital, and from the point of view of its function, is already capital.

(Marx, 1976 [1867]: 247–248)

For money to become capital, the movement M-C-M must lead to the return of more money for C than was originally advanced. In other words, it is an incremental circulation process. In order to indicate that the M which is the outcome of M-C-M has been incrementally enhanced, Marx adjusts the presentation of the formula to M-C-M', 'where M'=M+ΔM, i.e. the original sum advanced plus an increment . . . and this movement converts [money] into capital' (ibid: 251–252). Marx wishes to draw our attention to 'a palpable difference between the circulation of money as capital, and its circulation as mere money' (p. 250); that is, that in the circulation of money as capital its value is enhanced. But it is not only money which acts as capital in this way. By virtue of commodities being changed back into money, commodities also represent value [and capital] as well: 'If we pin down the specific forms of appearance assumed in turn by self-valorizing value in the course of its life, we reach the following elucidation: capital is money, capital is commodities' (p. 255). In other words, M-C-M' is a relationship of both *money capital* and *commodity capital*, whose purpose is the generation of an incremental value: 'This increment or excess over the original value I call "surplus value"' (p. 251; see also Engels, 1981 [1894]: 100–101). However, commodities only exist as *capital* in the circuit M-C-M', that is, when buying in order to sell. In the circuit C-M-C, when selling in order to buy, commodities are not sold in order to enhance their value; they are sold in order to be able to purchase other commodities which are necessary or useful for one's needs, such as food, clothing and the implements of work. In other words, it is a qualitative circulation process in which goods of one kind are exchanged for goods of another kind. With regard to the *quantities* to be exchanged, Marx refers to these as *exchange values*: 'the quantitative relation, the proportion, in which use-values of one kind exchange for use-values of another kind' (Marx, 1976 [1867]: 126). Commodities in the circuit C-M-C, while involving the exchange of quantities of one commodity for quantities of another commodity [i.e. as *exchange values*], have as their outcome the generation of *use values* which meet their conclusion in the satisfaction of human needs.

> The simple circulation of commodities – selling in order to buy – is a means to a final goal which lies outside circulation, namely the appropriation of use values, the satisfaction of needs. As against this, the circulation of money as capital is an end in itself, for the valorization of

> value takes place only within this constantly renewed movement. *The movement of capital is therefore limitless.*
>
> (Marx, 1976 [1867]: 253; emphasis added)

But in M-C-M' – buying in order to sell – the circulation of money capital and commodity capital has no end, but is constantly renewed – value leads to more value, which in turn leads to yet more value. With this gesture, Marx may be said to cross from the limitless circulation of capital as money and commodities *within* a geographical area to the potentially limitless circulation of capital for accumulation globally: 'The tendency to create the *world market* is directly given in the concept of capital itself' (Marx, 1973: 408). It is at this juncture in the process of value valorization that the notion of English as a free rider on capital may be introduced.

> Value therefore now becomes value in process, money in process, and, as such, capital. It comes out of circulation, enters into it again, preserves and multiplies itself within circulation, emerges from it with an increased size, and starts the same cycle again and again. M-M',[11] 'money which begets money', such is the description of capital given by its first interpreters, the Mercantilists. Buying in order to sell, or, more accurately, buying in order to sell dearer, M-C-M',[12] appears certainly to be a form peculiar to one kind of capital alone, *merchants' capital*. But *industrial capital* too is money which has been changed into commodities, and re-converted into more money by the sale of these commodities. Events which take place outside the sphere of circulation, in the interval between the buying and selling, do not affect the form of this movement. Lastly, in the case of interest-bearing capital, the circulation M-C-M' presents itself in abridged form, in its final result and without the intermediate stage, in a concise style, so to speak, as M-M', i.e. money that is worth more money, value that is greater than itself. M-C-M' is in fact therefore *the general formula for capital, in the form in which it appears directly in the sphere of circulation*.
>
> (Marx, 1976 [1867]: 256–257; emphasis added)

If M-C-M' is the general formula for capital in circulation, then we may propose that M^E-C^E-M'^E is the general formula for the free riding of English on capital – where superscript 'E' stands for English, since this highlights its presence at every point in the capital circuit; that is, in investment [the

---

11 In the 1976 Penguin English edition this is rendered as M-M in this passage. This differs from the first English edition of 1887, which was edited by Engels, where it is presented as M-M'. I have preferred the earlier rendering here.

12 Again, in the 1976 Penguin edition this is rendered as M-C-M. In the 1887 English edition it is rendered M-C-M'. I find this to be much clearer, so I have retained it here.

raising of money], in trade [the sale of products], and in the processing of profits from trade [returns on money originally invested]. Not only that, but English 'grows' over time too, as increased numbers of speakers, as new lexical items in the language, as network effects and as symbolic capital (see for example Reksulak et al., 2004).[13] In the previous passage Marx also extends M-C-M' from pre-existing *merchants' capital* to the *industrial capital* of capitalism, for example as money needed for investment in plant machinery for the manufacture of goods, which can then be sold. Merchants' capital is for Marx an 'antediluvian' capital (Marx, 1976 [1867]: 266). That is to say, it is a form of capital which belongs to the pre-history of capitalism, and by being so is not fully integrated into the type of commodity exchange that is peculiar to capitalism. Marx places alongside merchants' capital another form of antediluvian capital, which he refers to as *usurers' capital*. This follows the formula M-M', 'money which is exchanged for more money' (p. 267). He also refers to this as 'interest-bearing capital'. This is the capital which in the pre-history of capitalism was typically associated with moneylending. Marx notes that 'merchants' capital and interest-bearing capital are derivative forms, and . . . appear before the modern primary form of capital' (ibid). In sketching out forms of capital which belong to the pre-history of capitalism, Marx is also at pains to point out that in the relationship of M-C-M' the monetization and commoditization of exchange relations pre-existed the rise of capitalism proper (Harvey, 2010: 146). In *Capital Volume III*, Marx dissolves the distinction between merchants' capital and usurers' capital by incorporating the latter within the former. He also refers to merchants' capital as being the same as *trading capital*. He states that '"Merchants" or trading capital is divided into two forms, or sub-species, commercial capital and money-dealing capital' (Marx, 1991 [1894]: 379). Commercial capital is the movement captured in M-C-M': 'Commercial capital thus simply mediates the exchange of commodities' (ibid: 443). Money-dealing or interest-bearing capital, on the other hand, dispenses with the mediation of commodities in order to exchange money for money: M-M'. But even with M-C-M', 'The driving motive and determining purpose here is the transformation of M into M+ΔM' (ibid), with M+ΔM indicating an incremental gain on the initial advance of M, so that the effect is the same as for M-C-M'; that is, money advanced at one point in the circuit has realized an increased value at another point in the circuit. If in commercial capital the free riding of English is M^E-C^E-M'^E, then in money-dealing or financial capital the free riding of English would be M^E-M'^E, whereby money invested or loaned in the market and the processing of the profits which accrue are accompanied and facilitated by the use of English as a *transactional lingua franca*, in which the movement of money is mediated by English at various points along the circuit – in the act of the

---

13 I am grateful to Will Simpson for this connection.

initial investment, in the management of the investment, and in the collection and processing of the return.

Capital as part of an expanding world-system

The idea that Marx incorporated the notion of an expanding world-economy, or *system*, as part of his analysis of capital circulation is not widely accepted, even by Marxists. According to Lucia Pradella (2015: 2), 'Marxist debates . . . assume that Marx concentrated on a self-enclosed national economy in his main work' (Harvey, 2003: 143–144, 2004: 73; Rosenberg, 2006: 308). There is no doubt a good deal of truth in this insofar as the theorization of capital which appears in *Capital I–III*, and also that which is present in the preparatory notebooks and in the works which preceded it, Marx placed British and European capitalism at the forefront of his thinking. Even so, from the short summary given previously, there is clearly a great deal in the early work – and in *Capital* itself – which points to a more global interpretation and application, which is indeed Pradella's argument.[14] Despite these differences, there is no doubt that capital did circulate and did accumulate in increasing global measure from this time, as development- and world-systems theorists have at length shown (Frank, 1969a [1967], 1969b; Wallerstein, 2000 [1974], 2004; Arrighi, 2010; see later), and as Marx himself states at several points in his work. This is also maintained by empire historians such Gallagher and Robinson (1953) and Cain and Hopkins (1980, 1986, 1987, 2013), who reject the Marxist theory of over-accumulation and advance alternative explanations for capital's spread (see Chapter 2). Moreover, it is a process of capital circulation and accumulation which is as much international as it is within the borders of capitalist nation-states, and it need not circulate overseas only as a result of overaccumulation: 'If capital is sent abroad, this is not because it absolutely could not be employed at home. It is rather that it can be employed abroad at a higher rate of profit' (Marx, 1991 [1894]: 365). It was also simultaneously employed abroad in the company of other languages, English in particular. In general terms, in the period from 1600 to 1850 the dominant form of this relationship was $M^E\text{-}C^E\text{-}M'^E$. In other words, it was one based on mainly British commercial or trading capital (see Chapter 2). After 1850, with the increased dominance of financial capital,[15] led by the City of London, the algorithm shifted more towards $M^E\text{-}M'^E$ as trade in goods – while still substantial – was overtaken by finance as the leading means of British global capital accumulation. This was even as most human experience has to this

---

14 She authenticates this by reference to material and notebooks which have only recently become accessible in what she refers to as *MEGA2* (Karl Marx and Friedrich Engels, *Gesamtausgabe* Berlin, Dietz/Akademie Verlag 1975–).
15 Hilferding (1981 [1910]) preferred to call this 'finance capital'.

day continued to be in terms of the relationship that is M-C-M', either as commodity or service production.

It is the specific nature of capital and capital accumulation in capitalist society which leads Marx to the conclusion that the place to start his study of capitalism is with capital and the circulation of commodities rather than with production, and in the sixteenth century rather than with the dawn of human history. The *Grundrisse* notebooks reveal Marx's thinking on this. He chooses capital over production because he reasoned that if he started with the latter, then there was no historical limit to when the narrative should begin. In the words of Nicolaus,

> if one begins with a category such as 'material production', must one not therefore begin with neolithic man and his flint tools, and then, step by step, wind one's way laboriously up to the intended subject proper, namely material production in the capitalist form of society?
>
> (1973: 37)

Marx argues this through over several pages of his introduction to the *Grundrisse* (1973: 100–108). He finally determines that 'Capital is the all-dominating economic power of bourgeois society. It must form the starting-point as well as the finishing point' (ibid: 107). This theme is returned to in the final section of the last notebook, where he states, 'The first category in which bourgeois wealth presents itself is that of the *commodity*' (p. 881). It also re-surfaces as the first line of *Capital Volume I*.[16] Since production in one form or another applies to all the ages of history, it is the 'commodity' which sets capitalist society apart because its nature is specific to capitalism. Again, it is how value, or better still, how *surplus value* is created which is at issue for Marx. The notion of exchange presupposes that *equal values are exchanged*. Exchange for the derivation of use values and of exchange values – C-M-C – is this type of exchange. But, as we have seen, and as Marx is at pains to point out, in capitalism there is another type of exchange whereby a surplus value in excess of the value originally advanced is the result – M-C-M'. How this surplus value is produced is critical for Marx. It is not simply profit produced as the result of a 'free exchange' in the market as the 'vulgar economists' would have it (Marx, 1976 [1867]: 174n). Rather, it is an opposite process, which by being other than equivalence, 'stands directly opposite exchange' (ibid: 275). That is, it is a process of exploitation *masquerading as exchange*.

> In present bourgeois society as a whole, this positing of prices and their circulation etc. appears as the surface process, beneath which, however,

---

16 'The wealth of societies in which the capitalist mode of production prevails appears as "an immense collection of commodities"' (Marx, 1976 [1867]: 125).

in the depths, entirely different processes go on, in which this apparent individual equality and liberty disappear.

(Marx, 1973: 247)

The exchange between the worker and the capitalist is an exploitative exchange because of the extraction of surplus value. This at length immiserates the worker, while also alienating him from the products of his labour: 'capital . . . realizes itself through the *appropriation of alien labour*' (ibid: 307). Wage labour is distinct from other modes of labour because wealth confronts labour as capital. Under conditions of slavery, on the other hand, 'Wealth confronts direct forced labour not as capital, but rather as [a] *relation of domination* . . . thus the relation of domination is the only thing which is reproduced on this basis' (p. 326). Surplus value is consequently not reproduced, and without this it cannot be capitalism. What this goes to show is that the capital relation – and capitalism as a *world-system* – belongs to a particular historical period, and it is from the commencement of this period, that is, in the sixteenth century, that capitalism can properly be said to have begun, even as alongside the wage relation pre-capitalist forms continued to exist. This history is neatly summed up by the US Marxist Paul M Sweezy.

Capitalism as a world system had its origins in the later fifteenth and early sixteenth centuries when Europeans, mastering the art of long-distance navigation, broke out of their little corner of the globe and roamed the seven seas, conquering, plundering, and trading. Ever since then capitalism has consisted of two sharply contrasting parts: on the one hand a handful of dominant exploiting countries and on the other hand a much larger number of dominated and exploited countries. *The two are indissolubly linked together, and nothing that happens in either part can be understood if it is considered in abstraction from the system as a whole.*

(Sweezy, 1972: 5)

Although history did not entirely bear this out – the Asian Tiger economies and more recently China most notably bucking this trend – the general tenor of Sweezy's observation has been accurate enough as a summary of capitalism's past four hundred years (see also Chapter 2). The world remains as economically divided today as it has ever been with global income inequalities on the rise. That some nations, such as China, South Korea and Taiwan, have moved into the position of being capital accumulators and exporters in their own right does not greatly alter this picture, or that of a global circulating capital which is dominated by English.

Capital as a dialectical process

Marx's method is *dialectical*, for which insight his debt is first to Hegel (1770–1831), who in Marx's words, viewed 'every historically developed form to be in a fluid state, *in motion*' (Marx, 1976 [1873]: 103; emphasis added). What Hegel understood is that the world is not to be grasped as a static thing, but is always in a state of motion. Marx applies this logic to capital: 'Capital is not a simple relation, but a *process*, in whose moments it is always capital' (Marx, 1973: 258). In other words, the movement of M to C to M' are 'moments' of capital which are always on the move; and by being constituent parts of capital are in themselves capital too. From a dialectical perspective, since all things are always in motion, to analyze them it is necessary to hold them still: 'only by holding them fast . . . is their development possible without confounding everything' (ibid: 817). Marx's choice of 'moment' like the choice of 'process' is deliberate, since capital is not a system at rest (Nicolaus, 1973: 29; Harvey, 2010: 12). Dialectics is an attempt to understand the motion behind the settled superficiality – the 'fetish' – of what appears on the surface of things (Marx, 1976 [1867]: 163–165). As we have seen with the exchange of commodities, what appears as a 'free' relation is in fact its opposite – a relation of exploitation that masquerades as exchange. What one sees on the surface 'is therefore pure semblance. *It is the phenomenon of a process taking place behind it*' (Marx, 1973: 255; see also Chapter 7). This process is the depth reality of capital [and of commodities] which Marx wishes us to understand; and it is the acknowledgement of continual movement, as well as that of all historical things, which makes Marx's analysis of capital dialectical.

Marx extends this understanding to his account of society and its history. Marx's is a 'stadial interpretation' of history (Nichols, 2015: 18) in which each historical epoch has its own peculiar character that differentiates it from another: 'In broad outline, the Asiatic, ancient, feudal and modern bourgeois modes of production may be designated as epochs marking progress and the economic development of society' (Marx, 1970 [1859]: 21; see also Avineri, 1969, for a critique).

> My view is that each particular mode of production, and the relations of production corresponding to it at each given moment, in short 'the economic structure of society', is 'the real foundation, on which arises a legal and political superstructure and to which correspond definite forms of social consciousness', and that the 'the mode of production of material life conditions the general process of social, political and intellectual life'.
> (From the 1859 Preface to *A Contribution to the Critique of Political Economy*, cited in Marx, 1976 [1867]: 175n)

The *1859 Preface* is one of Marx's most widely cited texts, on the one hand because it gives a concise summary of historical materialism, and on the other because of the latitude with which it has enabled Marx to be accused of economic determinism (see for example Gal, 2016; Heller & McElhinny, 2017; Del Percio, Flubacher & Duchêne, 2017). While it is possible to appreciate why many – including the scholars just mentioned – have reached this conclusion, it is not one that I readily share, partly because this estimation is often based upon a negligible reading [e.g. the *1859 Preface* and nothing else], or, as Will Simpson and I have suggested, in some cases no reading of Marx at all (Simpson & O'Regan, 2018). Absent, too, is any consideration [or awareness] of the dialectical approach which is central to Marx's thinking, and without which a more insightful understanding of Marx is not to be found. Informed considerations of Marx's dialectic may be discovered elsewhere (see Williams, 1977; Harvey, 2010; Holborow, 1999, 2015; Block, 2017a; Chun, 2017; Simpson, 2020, for good accounts). In the space I have here, I will confine myself to some key points as these relate to economic determinism and to language.

Thus far, we have seen that Marx distrusts appearances. What lies on the surface should not be accepted at face value but be rigorously questioned. The dialectic 'does not let itself be impressed by anything, being in its very essence critical and revolutionary' (Marx, 1976 [1873]: 103; see also Marx, 1978 [1843]).[17] We have also seen how in the *1859 Preface* Marx posits a relationship between an economic 'foundation' or base, and 'a legal and political superstructure . . . to which correspond definite forms of social consciousness'. In this relation Marx informs us that 'the mode of production of material life *conditions* social, political and intellectual life' (emphasis added). Immediately following this in the same text Marx adds, 'It is not the consciousness of men that determines their being, but on the contrary their *social being* that determines their consciousness' (1976 [1859]: 3; emphasis added). It is worth noting here that Marx has opted for an understanding of the mode of production that 'conditions' rather than 'determines' social, political and intellectual life, and that when he does select 'determines' it is in connection with 'social being' rather than simply 'being'. I have always considered these deliberate selections to be indicative of the working of the dialectic in Marx's thinking. It is one's *social being* that determines one's consciousness. Which is to say that Marx understood being as a social construction having a multiplicity of determining influences, and was therefore 'overdetermined' (Althusser, 1996 [1965]: 101; see also Marx, 1991 [1894]: 927–928).[18] As Raymond Williams has noted, 'the concept of "overdetermination" is more useful than any other as a way of understanding historically

---

17 This reminds me of Derrida: 'The only attitude . . . I would absolutely condemn is one which, directly or indirectly, cuts off the possibility of an essentially interminable questioning, that is, an effective and thus transforming questioning' (Derrida, 1995: 239). It is striking how poststructuralism and Marxism seem to connect in this way (see also Derrida, 1994).

18 And Engels' letter to Bloch of September 1890: 'The economic situation is the basis, but the various elements of the superstructure – political forms of the class struggle, and its results, to wit: constitutions establishes by the victorious class after a successful battle, etc., juridical forms, and even the reflexes of all these actual struggles in the brains of the participants, political, juristic, philosophical theories, religious views and their further development into systems of dogma – also exercise their influence upon the course of the historical struggles and in many cases preponderate in determining their form' (cited in Williams, 1977: 79–80).

lived situations and the authentic complexities of practice' (1977: 88). Similarly, the relationship between the base and the superstructure [which is best understood as an heuristic] is also dialectical, and overdetermined, as has been suggested by Harvey (2010: 193, 199). He directs us to a footnote in Chapter 15 of *Capital Volume I*, where Marx states,

> Technology reveals the active relation of man to nature, the direct process of the production of his life, and thereby it also lays bare the process of the production of the social relations of his life, and of the mental conceptions that flow from those relations.
>
> (Marx, 1976 [1867]: 493n)

Harvey delineates six conceptual 'moments' here: (i) technology, (ii) the relation of human beings to nature, (iii) modes of production, (iv) the production and reproduction of daily life, (v) mental conceptions of the world, and (vi) social relations. Here we have again mental conceptions that flow from social relations, but we also seem to have many other determinations as well, of which technology is only one. Again, the choice of language is important. Marx does not say that technology 'causes' or 'determines' the active relation of human beings to nature, only that it 'reveals'. Harvey takes this further by encouraging us to consider this dialectically:

> What Marx is saying . . . is that technologies and organizational forms internalize a certain relation to nature as well as to mental conceptions and social relations, daily life and labor processes. By virtue of this internalization, the study of technologies and organizational forms is bound to 'reveal' or 'disclose' a great deal about all the other elements. Conversely, all these other elements internalize something of what technology is about. A detailed study of daily life under capitalism will, for example, 'reveal' a great deal about our relation to nature, technologies, social relations, mental conceptions and the labor processes of production.
>
> (Harvey, 2010: 193)

Harvey suggests that the six moments, which are all in motion, are in an 'intense interrelation' (p. 194) in which no one moment is dominant. Rather they should be understood as constituting an 'ensemble' or 'assemblage' (p. 196) that is in a dialectical relation, as befits the method of Marx. In this conception economic or technological determinism is eschewed in favour of a relation of overdetermination and multiple connectivity between moments. Language enters into this relationship through our mental conceptions and our social relations, as ideologies and as discourses, as knowledge and also as power (Foucault, 1980). In the words of Marx and Engels (1998 [1845]: 49), language is a *practical consciousness* – a 'practical, constitutive activity' (Williams, 1977: 29), and so takes its place in the dialectical nature of all

Accumulation and classical imperialism

Despite the innumerable references to the global spread of capital and the establishment of a world market which are to be found in Marx's writings, a more systematic treatment of international accumulation processes was left to a later generation of Marxists and non-Marxists to theorize. Of these, the most important contributions were made in the early twentieth century by J A Hobson, Rudolf Hilferding, V I Lenin, Rosa Luxemburg and Nikolai Bukharin. It is with them that modern theories of imperialism originate. It is also with these authors that for example the origins of Robert Phillipson's seminal text *Linguistic Imperialism* (1992) properly lie. Hilferding's *Finance Capital* (1910) was particularly influential for Marxist theory, and when it came out was seen by some as being the fourth volume of *Capital* (Bottomore, 1991: 198). The main intervention of Hilferding was to isolate the concept of *finance capital* as being a further development of Marx's *commercial capital*, but for a new capitalist imperialist age. The concept of finance capital was also enthusiastically embraced by Lenin, for whom 'finance capital, literally, one might say, spreads its net over all countries of the world' (Lenin, 1975 [1917]: 78).

Pre-dating Lenin's discussion was Rosa Luxemburg's *The Accumulation of Capital* (1913). In it, Luxemburg takes Marx's originating concept of capitalist primitive accumulation and transposes it to a colonial age. Like Hilferding and Lenin, in her historical account she locates this age as being principally between 1850 and 1914 and mainly involving the capitalist assimilation and pillage of India, Africa and China by the European colonial powers (see Chapter 3). Luxemburg portrays the non-capitalist regions of the world as a necessary market for capital accumulation: 'The existence and development of capitalism requires an environment of non-capitalist forms of production' (Luxemburg, 1951 [1913]: 368). For Luxemburg, there always had to be non-capitalist regions alongside capitalist regions for capitalism to expand into, although the logic she employed for this is criticized (Bukharin, 1972 [1925–6]; Tarbuck, 1972; Brewer, 1990; Callinicos, 2009).[19] For Luxemburg (1972 [1921]), a non-capitalist outlet or 'third market' for the surplus was essential: 'there is no way that the capitalists as a class can get rid of the surplus goods in order to change the surplus value into money, and thus accumulate capital' (p. 58). Her point being that accumulation in 'an exclusively capitalist environment' was an impossibility (p. 145). Although her critique on this point was not accepted, her analysis

---

19 Her logic appeared to suggest that the driving motor of capitalism was the existence of pre-capitalist regions and forms and not the exploitation of wage labour.

of capital export for accumulation was highly original in being focused on capitalist and non-capitalist sectors of production globally and not on relations between individual nation-states, thus giving a much more systemic orientation to her critique (Brewer, 1990: 71).

Bukharin does not bring a great deal more to capital expansion than that which is provided by Hilferding and Luxemburg. His *Imperialism and World Economy* (1915) followed Luxemburg's *Accumulation* and preceded Lenin's *Imperialism*, and the latter evidently owed a debt to Bukharin's work. Bukharin later wrote a detailed – if often tasteless – riposte to Luxemburg in *Imperialism and the Accumulation of Capital* (1925–6).[20] In general terms, Bukharin found himself profoundly persuaded by Hilferding's theory of finance capital and in deep disagreement and antagonism towards Luxemburg. Where there is no disagreement, however, is that during the classical free trade age of nineteenth-century colonial imperialism, that is, between 1850 and 1914, capital was exported in vastly increasing quantities (see Chapters 2 and 3). In this, Hilferding, Lenin, Luxemburg and Bukharin were also in agreement with the premier non-Marxist historian of imperialism, J A Hobson, whose influential *Imperialism* had been published in 1902. All of the classical Marxists owed a debt to this work, but particularly Lenin and Bukharin. Hobson's was principally a theory of capital overaccumulation, although the term he used for this was 'underconsumption' (Hobson, 2011 [1902]: 104), which he defined in the following manner.

> Everywhere appear excessive powers of production, excessive capital in search of investment. It is admitted by all business men that the growth of the powers of production in their country exceeds the growth in consumption, that more goods can be produced than can be sold at a profit, and that more capital exists than can find remunerative investment.
> (Hobson, 2011 [1902]: 103)

In Hobson's account this leads to the necessity for capital to be exported overseas so that it can be expended in new territories and markets. The economic rationale is therefore not so different to that identified by Marx. But Hobson adds a further dimension of conspiratorial coordination to the account, in which a venal alliance of nationalist politicians, City financiers and industrial manufacturers, vociferously cheered on by a shallow and racialist press, 'are united in strong sympathy to support every new imperialist exploit' (ibid: 80). In particular, where public money can be brought to bear in the furtherance of private interests, 'These men are Imperialists by conviction; a pushful policy is good for them' (ibid: 81). Where Marx and

---

20 In places, Bukharin's essay, which was written a few years following Luxemburg's murder by German reactionaries, is profoundly sexist in the manner of his refutation of her thesis. Bukharin is by turns arrogant, mocking and patronizing.

Luxemburg leave capital export and imperialism to the inexorable dynamics of expansionary capitalism, Hobson sees both the economic and the conspiratorial in the desire of well-placed elites to take advantage. Despite criticisms of Hobson's lack of specificity, his account of public mendacity and greed as a means to political and economic ends stands up well in an era of widespread 'fake news' and xenophobic economic nationalism. There is indeed truth in both positions, and Hobson anticipates Cain and Hopkins' (1986, 1987) theory of *gentlemanly capitalism* by nearly a hundred years in pointing to it, although he overlooks the *informal empire* of capital spread (see Chapter 2). Hobson's theory – and that of Luxemburg too – gains most traction in the hands of David Harvey (2003, 2004), but as a theory of overaccumulation – that is, 'the lack of opportunities for profitable investment' (ibid, 2003: 139) – and not as one of underconsumption or a lack of demand. Again, it is not the export of capital itself which is in question, but the cause. Harvey comes closest to the diagnosis which Hobson and Luxemburg do not allow themselves, that the export of capital 'resulted not from absolute economic imperatives but from the unwillingness of the bourgeoisie to give up on any of its privileges and thereby absorb overaccumulation internally through social reform at home' (2003: 126).

The classical Marxists, Hobson included, framed the historical height of capital-export imperialism as being from 1850 to 1914. In making this period their focus they were responding to the tumults of their time. They each wished to understand the inter-imperialist rivalry of the times they were living through in terms of the major events and changes which had occurred in European political economy in the preceding fifty years, and which they understandably saw as being the significant timescale, since it was in the 'free trade' decades after 1850 that imperial acquisition had appeared to speed up, culminating in the infamous 'Scrambles' for Africa in the 1880s and then China in the 1900s; to be subsequently followed by the cataclysm of 1914 (see Chapters 2 and 3). If the classicists focused on 1850 to 1914, the dependency and world-systems schools followed the Marx of *Capital* in reaching much further back. In the 1960s, amongst intellectual circles on the left there was now a much greater sense of attempting to understand why the auto-destruction of capitalism as predicted by Marx had not occurred but had rather climaxed in two brutal world wars, with the rise of genocidal German Nazism in the West and an equally genocidal Japanese-militarist-hyper-nationalism in the East, both of which made no difference to the survival of capitalism. Rather, led by the United States, global capitalism made a resurgent return after 1945, while 'degenerated' one-party socialist states having only tenuous – and often mainly rhetorical – links to socialism established themselves in Russia, Eastern Europe, Vietnam, North Korea, China and Cuba (Hughes & Main, 2012). Some, such as Horkheimer and Adorno (1997 [1944]) in the Frankfurt School, became increasingly disillusioned and gravitated towards a more theoretical – as well as somewhat isolated – critical interrogation of capitalism and of the entire enlightenment tradition [in which they included Marx] by means of the practice of immanent critique (Jay, 1973: 259). Foucault's disaffection with Marxist main currents led him along similar paths towards a genealogical and archaeological mapping of truth as a construct of power and discourse (Foucault, 1980, 1981, 1989, 1991). What seemed clear was that capitalism possessed a resilience which pre-war intellectuals on the left – with possibly the single exception of Gramsci[21] – had not foreseen. This caused many to look to more historical and globally systemic explanations for the durability of capitalism. The dependency and world-systems theorists fell into this category (e.g. Frank, 1969a [1967], 1969b; Emmanuel, 1972; Wallerstein, 2000 [1974], 2000 [1988]; Amin, 1977; Arrighi, 2010). In the following paragraphs I briefly consider the contributions of two representatives of these schools of thinking, Andre Gunder Frank and Immanuel Wallerstein.

The development of underdevelopment

Drawing on the work on monopoly capitalism of the Marxist economist Paul Baran in the 1950s, it is Andre Gunder Frank who announces the arrival of dependency theory proper with his book *Capitalism and Underdevelopment in Latin America* (1969a [1967]). Frank opens his book by declaring, 'I believe with Paul Baran that it is capitalism, both world and national, which produced underdevelopment in the past and which still generates underdevelopment in the present' (Frank, 1969a [1967]: xi). Moreover, Frank insisted that the underdeveloped regions of the world were 'just as capitalist' (ibid: 240) as the developed regions. In other words, they were components of the same 'system' – a *capitalist world-system*: 'Capitalism is embodied and developed as one single capitalist system: "Brazilian" or "Paulista" or "American" capitalism are but sectors of this single world-embracing system' (ibid). In Frank's account, principally of Latin America (Frank, 1969a [1967], 1969b), the less-developed regions of the world are already a combination of both capitalist and pre-capitalist forms of production *in a dialectical relation* (1969b: 221), but within a world-system which has existed 'on this planet for the past five centuries or more' (1969a [1967]: 242). From this perspective, one might say that economically underdeveloped nations are in an intermediate stage of accumulation, such that some pre-capitalist forms remain extant. While Marx recognized that capitalism had to emerge from and alongside pre-capitalist relations, Frank's conception of capitalism as a system of global exploitation *internalizes pre-capitalist forms within it*.

---

21 This was due to his theory of hegemony. He refers to this as 'the spontaneous consent given by the great masses of the population to the general direction imposed on social life by the dominant fundamental group; thus consent is "historically" caused by the prestige (and consequent confidence) which the dominant group enjoys because of its position and function in the world of production' (Gramsci, 1999: 306–307).

The exploitative relation of underdevelopment is characterized as being in the form of a chain which extends from an advanced capitalist 'core' to an underdeveloped satellite 'periphery', and along which surplus value is transferred from the periphery back to the core.

> Indeed, it is this exploitative relation which in chain-like fashion extends the capitalist link between the capitalist world and national metropolises to the regional centres (part of whose surplus they appropriate) and from these to local centres and so on to large landholders or merchants who expropriate surplus from small peasants or tenants, and sometimes even from these latter to landless labourers exploited by them in turn. At each step along the way the relatively few capitalists above exercise monopoly power over the many below, expropriating some or all of their economic surplus, and to the extent that they are not expropriated in turn by the still fewer above, appropriating it for their own use. Thus at each point, the international, national and local capitalist system generates economic development for the few and underdevelopment for the many.
> (Frank, 1969a [1967]: 7–8)

Although Frank is quick to acknowledge the export of capital from the core to the periphery, the flow in 'capital profits' in the opposite direction generally exceeds the flow from the core (Frank, 1969b: 49); this ensures that the periphery becomes caught in a cycle of relative economic decline. The periphery economies do not completely collapse, but nor do they develop either – they are for Frank condemned to subsist somewhere in between. Class- and ethnically-based elites also operate as agents of the core in ensuring that local political, legal, economic and educational – including language policy – arrangements work in their interests. They do this by dominating politics, the judiciary and business, and by monopolizing to themselves select [i.e. private] education provision. The local elites are thus a further link in a chain which runs from centres of industrial and agricultural production in the periphery through the major cities of each periphery nation back to the central metropolis, or core (see also Harvey, 2003: 40, 55, 186).

Despite some criticism concerning the theoretical fidelity of Frank's conception to Marxism (see Laclau, 1979 [1977]; Brenner, 1977; Brewer, 1990; Callinicos, 2009), the historical alignment of Frank with Marx is unmistakeable, since they both look to a similar period for the start of the world capitalist era and to accumulation as its driving force. Frank's theory of capital export leading to underdevelopment is also noticeably at a midway point between Luxemburg's theory of accumulation (1913) and David Harvey's more recent concept of *accumulation by dispossession* (Harvey, 2003, 2004, 2010). If there is a pressing critique of Frank, and of the dependency school as a whole, it is that the core/periphery model did not seem to allow for the possibility in the developing regions of capital accumulation enabling more advanced capitalist development to occur. This has been disproven by its failure to predict or account for the rise of the 'Tiger' economies in South-East Asia in the 1970s and 80s, as well as for the meteoric rise of China since the onset of the 'open door' policy in 1978–9. But then again, it is unclear why the dependency model should account for *everything*. Its purpose was to critique underdevelopment as it appeared in the 1960s and 70s. This it did to good effect. Moreover, as a point of struggle within the academy against worldwide capitalist exploitation and inequality it was hugely influential, and has been so since, even among non-Marxist realists (Buzan & Little, 2000). As for Frank, his main contribution was twofold. Firstly, he provided an articulation of capitalism as a *world-system* well before the globalization theorists of the 1980s and 90s adopted the same idea, but he called it *globalization* instead (e.g. Cox, 1987; Lash & Urry, 1987; Appadurai, 1990; Giddens, 1990; Harvey, 1990; Ritzer, 1993; Held et al., 1999; Hardt & Negri, 2000; see also Rosenberg, 2005; Robinson, 2007, for good overviews). In the same vein, he and the dependency theorists also anticipated the theories of capital export and accumulation associated with the more recent leftist critiques of global neoliberalism (Harvey, 2003, 2004; Panitch & Gindin, 2012; Mirowski, 2014). Further, Frank was amongst the first to explode the myth of capitalist developmentalism, which Nederveen Pieterse describes as 'the truth [of capitalist development] from the point of view of the centre of power' (2010: 19). In this narrative, nations in the global South are 'underdeveloped' or 'developing' because they have not yet passed through the necessary economic stages as did the developed nations of the core. In Frank's words, 'our ignorance of the underdeveloped countries' history leads us to assume that their past and now indeed their present resembles earlier stages of the history of the now developed countries. This ignorance and this assumption leads us into serious misconceptions about contemporary development and underdevelopment' (Frank, 1969b: 3); not least the deception – largely derived from Rostow (1966) – that advanced capitalist development is within the reach of all nations if only the correct economic strictures are applied (Polanyi, 2001 [1944]: 136–140; Dussel, 1996: 4; Taylor, 1996: 283; Harvey, 2003: 55, 58; Hartwig, 2011: 500). In the international arena the developmentalist fallacy remains strong to this day and finds realization in the English-mediated structural adjustment programmes which are imposed upon debtor nations by the International Monetary Fund (IMF) and the World Bank (see Chapters 4 and 5).

Endless accumulation in a capitalist world-system

The core/periphery model takes on a slightly modified articulation in the hands of Wallerstein (2011a) since he introduces the *semi-periphery* as an intermediate level in the vertical hierarchy of the capitalist world-system: 'There are also semiperipheral areas which are in between the core and the periphery on a series of dimensions' (ibid: 349). Like Frank, he also dates this relationship to the sixteenth century. The semi-periphery is thus deeply historical as well as being integral to the world-system. According to Wallerstein, 'The semi-periphery is needed to allow the world capitalist system to run smoothly' (Wallerstein, 2000 [1974]: 89). The states of the semi-periphery are historically located on a continuum between the core and the periphery and in the global trading system act as a filter, or in his words as 'middle trading groups' (ibid: 2011a: 349), for the interests of the core. They also act as a valve for the pressures which affect the world-system by balancing out the polarizations which exist (Brewer, 1990: 177). Importantly, states may move from one level to the next. States in decline, for example, may slip from the core into the semi-periphery – as Portugal and the Netherlands did in the seventeenth and eighteenth centuries when they ceded their global seafaring dominance to England – and nations in the semi-periphery may in turn slip into the periphery. A major concern of the nations of the semi-periphery 'is to keep themselves from slipping into the periphery and to do what they can to advance themselves toward the core' (Wallerstein, 2004: 29). In general terms, in the modern era the nations of the semi-periphery are more economically advanced than those in the periphery and tend to have stronger state systems, but they also have their own cycle of relative underdevelopment in comparison with the core. Income inequalities, for example, are much larger than in the core, and state authoritarianism is often more prevalent. They may be said to include, in recent years, the economically stronger nations of Latin America, such as Chile, Brazil, Peru, Uruguay and Argentina. In the rest of the world, they also include states such as India, China, Indonesia, Iran, the United Arab Emirates, Malaysia and Russia – middle-income nations, in other words. From our perspective, by being economically closer to the core, they also have more developed education systems and reserves of capital with which to access as well as to promote English. Wallerstein no doubt had additional theoretical reasons for introducing the semi-periphery as 'a necessary structural element in a world-economy' (Wallerstein, 2000 [1974]: 349). But amongst these was that the bi-polar model probably just seemed a bit too *polarized*. However, somewhat akin to Kachru's circles of Englishes (Kachru, 1985), the model as utilized by Frank is better understood as an heuristic rather than as an absolute. It is also relational in the sense of being a representation of how nations and blocs are dialectically positioned rather than being self-enclosed and separate categorizations (for critiques, see Brenner, 1977; Brewer, 1990).

If Frank's contribution is the understanding of the world-economy as a system, Wallerstein's is the account he gives of the system's structural form and the emphasis he places on capital accumulation within it. A primary issue is the historicity of the system: 'I assume that there exists a concrete singular historical system which I shall call the "capitalist world-economy," whose temporal boundaries go from the long sixteenth century to the present' (Wallerstein, 2000 [1983]: 253). The raison d'être of the system is the accumulation of capital: 'In my view for a historical system to be considered a capitalist system, the dominant or deciding characteristic must be the persistent search for the endless accumulation of capital – the accumulation of capital in order to accumulate more capital' (ibid, 2013: 10; see also Arendt, 1968; Emmanuel, 1972; Harvey, 2003, 2004, 2010; Bhaskar, 2002).[22] Capital expansion shows itself again to be the common denominator in all accounts. The next issue is that of the system's periodicity and form (see also Chapter 2). Let us first take the form of the system. As a world-system it exists as 'a unit with a single division of labour and multiple cultural systems' (ibid: 2000 [1974]: 75). The division of labour is based on the production for profit in a world market, where some nations benefit at the expense of other nations within the frame of the core/periphery relationship. Of especial significance is that Wallerstein identifies two types of world-system, one with a common political system and one without. A world-system which also has a common political system is a *world-empire*, and one which does not is a *world-economy*. World-empires had existed historically within geographically defined regions, such as the great empire civilizations of Rome, Greece and China. They grew out of the wreckage of world-economies which were inherently unstable for the reason that no single power was in overall control – either a world-economy is transformed into a world-empire or it falls into disintegration (Wallerstein, 2000 [1973]: 56). This leads Wallerstein to the compelling observation that the nineteenth-century empires of the European colonial powers, such as Britain and France, 'were not world-empires at all, but nation-states with colonial appendages operating within the framework of a world-economy' (ibid). Rather than dealing with *empire*, or when dealing with the *British Empire* – and after 1945, the *US Empire* [if it is possible to go along with such a thing][23] – the proper reference point is the *world-economy*; that is, the capitalist world-economy as a system in which Britain in the nineteenth century was the dominant

---

22 '[T]he real force underpinning [the Philosophical Discourse of Modernity] was nothing else than the remorseless logic of the nascent capitalist mode of production and exploitation of nature and human beings alike, a dynamic and self-expanding form of exploitation without precedent in human history, in which an unconstrained and unconscious conatus or drive to accumulation is hurtling humanity (and with it the planet) into crisis at all four planes of social being' (Bhaskar, 2002: 172n; and also p. 64: 'Simply put, I think modernism is a very pure ideology of the capitalist mode of production'; cited in Hartwig, 2011: 486n).
23 In this book, I have tried to avoid using the descriptors *America*, *American* or *Americans* to refer either to the geopolitical entity that is the United States or to those who are view themselves as being from this region, unless unavoidable. Exceptions to this are *American English*, and where the term used is clearly unambiguous, as in *Latin America* or *North America*. Other circumstances where exceptions occur is when the term is a named entity, such as the 'American concession' in Shanghai, or seems to have greater sociocultural resonance, as in the 'American century'. The rationale for being selective comes from Kenneth Lehman's observation that 'The people of the United States have commandeered the name "America" from their hemispheric neighbors, illustrating the universalist assumptions of their *Weltanschauung* [world view]' (Lehman, 2016: 19; parenthesis added).

exporter of capital and had been so since long before 1850. It was this, in combination with Britain's agricultural, industrial and military might, which made Britain the dominant hegemonic power of a deeply historical capitalist world-system up until at least 1914 (see Chapter 3).[24]

For Wallerstein and Frank then, as well as for others in the dependency and world-systems schools, this is as much a history of continuity as it is one of periodic crisis, cataclysm and change. The accumulation and export of capital for further accumulation was not unique. It had been occurring since the 1500s, but on a cline which increased decade by decade as advances in the capitalist mode of production occurred (see also Chapter 2). The periodicity of the world-system when these factors are taken into consideration suggests a historical teleology or demarcation of global-centric capital accumulation and export which occurs in phases. The first phase lasts from 1600 to 1850 and is the phase of mercantilism and protectionism, when nations erected barriers to trade in order to protect local markets. The second phase is from 1850 to 1945 and is the phase of free trade. The third phase is the phase of the US world-economy and is from 1945 to the present day, although there is a period of hegemonic transition between 1919 and 1956 – bookended by the Treaty of Versailles and the Suez Crisis. Arguably, there is a fourth phase which begins in 1991 with the collapse of the Soviet Union and the full coming of neoliberalism, although the global hegemon does not change. Cutting across these phases are advances in the capitalist mode of production. In Britain and Europe, the period from 1600 to 1750 is dominated by commercial capital based on an agrarian economy (see Chapter 2). The period from 1750 to 1850 witnesses a transition to the domination of industrial capital based on a manufacturing economy, particularly in Britain. In the period from 1850 to 1945, it is finance-based investments together with industrial capital [cf. Hilferding's finance capital], emanating principally from the City of London and later Wall Street, which dominate (see Chapters 3 and 4). The mercantilist era although an era of protectionism in Europe and elsewhere was nevertheless accompanied by the export of capital, particularly from Britain as the world-dominating power. It also witnessed the steady expansion of Britain's formal possessions in India, Southern Africa and East Asia (Chapter 2). Both developments were accompanied by the free riding of English within the world-system [M^E-C^E-M'^E; M^E-M'^E] as the British made their capital-presence ever more globally felt.

---

24 In this book, I still occasionally make reference to a British empire and also to an American empire, as these are well-known terminologies. But in keeping with world-systems analysis, I also refer to a *British world-economy* and a *US world-economy*, while also recognizing that both are referenced to the same capitalist world-system which has existed since the sixteenth century.

Wallerstein describes mercantilism as 'a defensive mechanism of capitalists located in states which are one level below the high point of strength in the system' (2000 [1974]: 87). Between 1660 and 1715 the struggle for hegemony was between England as the rising hegemon and the Netherlands as the waning hegemon. Between 1715 and 1815 the struggle was between France and England, in which France was defeated. After 1815, Britain was unrivalled until the later nineteenth century when Germany and then the United States began to catch up industrially. Germany's attempt to displace Britain as the global hegemon ended in defeat in 1918 and again in 1945. After 1945 a new hegemon had arrived, and with it the Cold War and the struggle between the United States and the USSR. Now at the time of writing, and given increased intensity by the financial crash of 2007–8, the latest struggle is that between an increasingly protectionist United States and a guardedly open, if globally reticent, People's Republic of China (see Chapter 6). The historical account reveals that since at least 1715, the dominant hegemonic power, and so also the dominant source of global capital export and accumulation in the world, has been an English-speaking nation. This has given to global capital and to global capital networks a particular linguistic hue and 'edge' which they would otherwise not have had. According to Wallerstein, in a world-system, the character of a global hegemon or *hegemony* is that it should exhibit *edge* in a minimum of three areas; it should have edge in agro-industrial production, in commercial trade, and in finance: 'Hegemony thus refers to that short interval in which there is simultaneous advantage in all three areas' (Wallerstein, 2000 [1983]: 257). A fourth edge is the *military edge*, which the industrial complexes of Britain in the eighteenth and nineteenth centuries and the United States in the twentieth century both possessed. In the capitalist era since at least 1750, a fifth edge exists which is also not accounted for by Wallerstein. This is the *linguistic edge* of having the default language of the world-system as one's own. The Canton Trade which commences in the early 1700s in China is a good exemplar of this kind of linguistic edge (Cranmer-Byng, 1965; Van Dyke, 2005, 2017; Si, 2006). Not only were most of the bills of trade rendered in English, but the Canton system also relied principally upon Chinese linguists who were at a minimum proficient in Canton Pidgin English. That English achieved a linguistic edge in China and in the global economy is because it was able to free ride on commercial and financial capital movements. It is an edge which English retains today.

Structural power in international political economy

For this book, an important complement and coda to Wallerstein's account – but from a non-Marxist perspective – is Susan Strange's theory of structural power in international political economy (IPE). In a seminal paper written thirty years ago, Strange (1989) challenged the idea that the US was a power in terminal decline as a number of contemporary writers and commentators in IPE were arguing at the time.[25] She based her argument upon the concepts of structural power and hegemony [which owed a good deal to Gramsci and also to world-systems analysis, although this is not readily acknowledged].[26] In Strange's view, the claims of US hegemonic decline were premature and overdone: 'the United States has more structural power than any other political authority in the international system, its power in the system is undiminished' (Strange, 1989: 164). She identifies four interrelated dimensions of structural power. These are production, credit, knowledge, and security. A change in power in one dimension tends to have an effect on power in the other dimensions (ibid: 165). Of especial concern to Strange was how power could be exercised in a world-system in the absence of coercion, whereby

> the price of resistance is determined more by the system than by any other political authority. . . . In short, it embraces customs, usages, and modes of operation rather than the more narrow definition that stays closer to state-state agreements and state-centred institutions.
>
> (p. 165)

Structural power thus appears as a hegemonic power which is sedimented within the world-system and which is determining of the particular complexion and practices of the system, such that while political and economic circumstances in the world may change and even lead to turbulence and regional geopolitical reverses for the dominant global power – as for example happened to the US in Vietnam and Iran in the 1970s – the underlying structure of the system remains as before, dominated by the nation which has depth-preponderance in each of the four dimensions of structural power. In the 1980s, and still now for all its declinist travails, this nation is the United States (see also Chapters 6 and 8 for further discussion). Strange's theory is in these terms a reformulation of Wallerstein's conception of hegemonic *edge*. In addition, even though her concern is the structural power of the United States, her theory is also of relevance to an understanding of British hegemony, particularly during the long nineteenth century from 1789 to 1914.

In production, Strange observes a marked lessening in the power of nation-states in determining what is to be produced, at what market price, and under what local regulatory conditions: 'The technological imperative

---

25 May (1996: 167) refers to this as 'the declinist school of American hegemony' and cites scholars such as P Kennedy and R O Keohane as being representative of this perspective (p. 167n). For more recent rebuttals of US declinism see Tooze (2019) and Sharma (2020). See also Chapter 6 of this book.
26 There is an unreferenced mention of Wallerstein in relation to his contention that 'hegemony does not mean the total power to command' (p. 169).

to sell on a world market reduces the areas common to all states over which national governments are able to exercise exclusive regulatory power' (p. 167). National controls over production in raw materials, in manufacturing and in services were being supplanted by the activities of transnational corporations (TNCs), of which the largest and most numerous were based in the United States (p. 167). This had the consequence that if companies in other parts of the world wished to operate in a global market, 'they will find it increasingly necessary in the future to pay close attention to what goes on in Washington' (p. 167). State actors who flout the will of the hegemonic power are not so much coerced by force as sanctioned through the exercise of implicit and explicit threats as to the consequences of non-compliance. We saw this in the 1980s when the US government sought to restrict world trade with the USSR by pressurizing foreign companies and governments not to do business with communist states. We see it today in the trade war between a petulant and puerile Trump administration in the White House and the autocratic China of Xi Jinping 习近平.[27] We also see it in the intense pressure being placed on foreign companies and states by the US government not to buy oil from Iran, which in the Trump era has become a primary object and vehicle for the populist demonization of Islam and for the apportioning of blame for Islamist-inspired acts of terror globally.

The production structure is underpinned by the financial structure which provides credit for the production structure to go about its business (p. 167). The world financial structure is dominated by the US Federal Reserve as the supreme arbiter of the world reserve currency, the US dollar. It is the Fed through its control of US interest rates which determines whether the global economy inflates or deflates. For example, it was the Fed's decision to increase interest rates sharply in 1979 as a means of bringing down US inflation which led to the Latin American debt crisis (see Chapter 5). The international monetary structure is also based on institutions and systems which were designed under US tutelage after 1945, such as the IMF, the World Bank and the General Agreement on Tariffs and Trade. The Fed in combination with the world's financial institutions gives the US a position of *seignorage* in the world financial structure in respect of its policy interests and needs (see Chapter 4).

In her paper, Strange treats the knowledge structure prior to the security structure, but I have decided to reverse this order for reasons which will soon become apparent. When Strange was writing, the Soviet Union had yet to collapse and China was only in the beginnings of its opening up period. It was very much a bi-polar world in which the security concerns of the US were determined by the Cold War and a nuclear arms race with the Soviets, one which the US administration of Ronald Reagan (1981–9) was unaware

---

27 Since the time of writing, the Democrat Joe Biden defeated the incumbent Trump in the US presidential election of November 2020.

it was winning. Such was the US preoccupation with the spread of communism that its security net spread across the entire non-communist world by means of strategic alliances, such as the North Atlantic Treaty Organization (NATO), security pacts with nations such as Japan, South Korea and Taiwan, and the occupation of over a thousand extraterritorial military bases, many on US-designated islands and atolls in the Pacific. In the words of Strange (ibid), as a result of the security structure, 'U.S. structural power reaches deeply into the developing continents of Africa and South America, into Asia and the Middle East, and relentlessly even into Eastern Europe and China' (p. 169), while also being reinforced by US dominance over the structures of production, finance and knowledge.

The knowledge structure, like the linguistic edge, is a significant one in the context of this book. It is of interest that Strange identifies the knowledge structure as 'the least familiar concept to scholars in international relations' (p. 168). This is because the knowledge structure is perhaps the most obvious of all the structures, and so like the English language in the historiography of empire, it is made invisible by being hidden in plain view. For Strange, the knowledge structure incorporates the types of knowledge to be valued [e.g. technological knowledge vs. historical or social knowledge]; the modes in which it is accumulated and applied [e.g. empirically or theoretically]; how it is stored [e.g. open access or behind a paywall]; and to whom and by what means such knowledge is to be communicated [e.g. to which groups and in what language]. The knowledge structure, in the words of Strange, 'constitutes another kind of structural power in world society and in the world-economy' (p. 168). It is a premise of this book that the knowledge structure permeates the other structures in a fundamental manner which places it in a position of privilege in relation to the other structures. Knowledge is indeed power, but it is power because the other structures are rendered much less effective without it. This is because the other structures in a hegemonic world-system must be mediated according to the language needs of the hegemonic power, and which in turn also mediate the knowledge structure. Since 1945 these needs have been serviced primarily through the medium of standard American English (cf. Bailey, 2017), and prior to that in the medium of standard British English (cf. Peters, 2017). Whatever the priorities of the hegemonic power, whether Britain in the eighteenth and nineteenth centuries or the United States in the twentieth and twenty-first centuries, the cleaving of the world-system to a *lingua franca* which is referenced to a normative standard form (Gramsci, 1975: 2343; Ives, 1998: 40, 2010: 528; Park & Wee, 2012: 109) has been a constant of at least the last three centuries.

In respect of the epistemological priorities which exist within the present knowledge structure, it is technological knowledge over social knowledge, empirical knowledge over theoretical knowledge, and paywalled knowledge over free knowledge, which in a US-configured capitalist world-system is the most valued (Blommaert, 2016; O'Regan & Gray, 2018). The eventual hounding to his death of the activist hacker Aaron Swartz by the US justice system in 2013 for his attempt to make paywalled knowledge freely accessible is indicative of this reality. The knowledge which Swartz attempted to make free was entirely written in standard English, being the accumulated output of several million English-medium journal articles housed in the JSTOR repository at the Massachusetts Institute of Technology. The conclusion which Strange draws from her overview of structural power is salutary and seems as relevant today as it was thirty years ago. It is that 'the decline of U.S. hegemony is a myth – powerful no doubt, but still a myth. In every important respect the United States still has the predominant power to shape frameworks and thus to influence outcomes' (Strange, 1989: 169; see also Tooze, 2019; Sharma, 2020). It may not feel that way, especially since the 2007–8 financial crash, the ascendancy in 2016 of Donald Trump, or the onset of the COVID-19 pandemic in 2020, but US structural power is still a force to be reckoned with across all the dimensions of power which Strange identifies. Not least in terms of the global *lingua franca*, which in language learning practice worldwide and in the discursive output of international institutions, TNCs, and the world's leading research universities persists as a mode of English which is referenced to a normative standard form. This point was also not lost on Strange, even from the purview of 1989.

> Some of the illustrations of American dominance in the global knowledge structure that may be cited are the continued dominance of U.S. corporations in most of the high-technology industries; the dominance of U.S. banks in transborder data flows; the dominance of U.S. media organizations in news and entertainment; the outward spread from the United States to the rest of the world of management, marketing, and advertising techniques; the dominance of U.S. banks and consultancy enterprises in debt management; the dominant position of U.S. government and U.S. corporations in satellite communications; and the ability of U.S. universities to attract and use scientists from the rest of the world, drawing them not simply by better salaries but by better opportunities for research and exchange of information and ideas with their peers. *Above all, perhaps, it is evident in the use of the American version of the English language as the world's lingua franca even for the French, the Russians, and the Chinese.*
>
> (Strange, 1989: 168–169; emphasis added)

The upsurge in approaches to linguistic diversity and in the documentation of that diversity in applied linguistics over the last twenty years as represented by perspectives such as ELF, World Englishes, superdiversity, translanguaging, translingualism and trans-spatial assemblage (see Chapter 7) has to be set against the much longer reality – and *longue durée* (Braudel, 1980 [1958], 2012 [1958]; Lee, 2012) – of British and US structural power over the last four centuries (see Chapters 2–6). During this time English has acted as a free rider on capital, thus facilitating its global spread [M^E-C^E-M'^E; M^E-M'^E]. It is capital which from this perspective is responsible for the dominant linguistic structuring of the world-system and which ultimately provides the foundation for the global persistence of English in its standard form. This can be seen in the language policies of national governments and in the discourse of international institutions, global financial networks, English-medium academic journals and TNCs. It is also to be found in the mindsets of parents who desperately wish for their children to have English in their language repertoires (Block, 2012b: 278). Capital and its accumulation are not especially emphasized by Strange, although she points to it indirectly in her consideration of the production and credit structures and in the management of the international banking system (Strange, 1989: 176). More direct interventions which fill this gap are provided by Arendt (1968) and by Harvey (2003, 2004, 2010) through their respective notions of *superfluous capital* and *accumulation by dispossession*.

Accumulation as the endless repetition of the original sin

In *Part Two of the Origins of Totalitarianism* (1968), Hannah Arendt reaches back to Marx's theory of *primitive accumulation* in order to explain the phenomenon of endless capital accumulation and the rise of European imperialism between 1884 and 1914. Primitive accumulation refers to the 'economic original sin' of 'divorcing the producer from the means of production' (Marx, 1973 [1867]: 874, 875). This kind of accumulation is described as primitive by Marx because 'it forms the pre-history of capital, and of the mode of production corresponding to capital' (p. 875). It was also for Marx a dispossession dating from the sixteenth century whose defining characteristic in Europe was the violent expropriation and 'theft' by private interests of land which was held in common (p. 884).

> The different moments of primitive accumulation can be assigned in particular to Spain, Portugal, Holland, France and England more or less in chronological order. These different moments are systematically combined together at the end of the seventeenth century in England. The combination embraces the colonies, the national debt, the modern mode of taxation, and the system of protection. These methods depend in part on brute force, for instance the colonial system. But they all employ the power of the state, the concentrated and organized force of society, to hasten, as in a hot-house, the process of transformation of the feudal mode of production into the capitalist mode, and to shorten the transition.
>
> (Marx, 1976 [1867]: 915–916)

Through various official edicts, 'Thus were the agricultural folk first forcibly expropriated from the soil, driven from their homes, turned into vagabonds, and then whipped, branded and tortured by grossly terroristic laws into accepting the discipline necessary for the system of wage labour' (ibid: 899). Leap forward another two hundred years [from the later 1600s] to the height of the imperialist 'Scramble for Africa' (see Chapter 3) and we find Hannah Arendt claiming of this period,

> The decisive point about the depressions of the [eighteen] sixties and seventies, which initiated the era of imperialism, was that they forced the bourgeoisie to realize for the first time that the original sin of simple robbery, which centuries ago made possible the "original accumulation of capital" . . . and had started all further accumulation, had eventually to be repeated lest the motor of accumulation die down.
> (Arendt, 1968: 28; see also Harvey, 2003: 142)

Thereafter, Arendt follows the tack of Luxemburg's thesis of domestic underconsumption leading to imperialism, but instead of calling it this she places the emphasis on the lack of opportunities for domestic investment of *superfluous capital*, which is forced to flee abroad in search of expansion and profit. In parallel with superfluous capital there was also *superfluous labour* made up of English-speaking workers with no means of employment on the British domestic market because of economic recession: 'The new fact in the imperialist era is that these two superfluous forces, superfluous capital and superfluous labour, joined hands and left the country together' (ibid: 30). They did so particularly to the diamond and gold mines of Southern Africa. The difference that arises with Arendt and with Luxemburg before her is that primitive accumulation is no longer treated as the opening act in the stadial development of capitalism, as it was with Marx, but as a process of never-ending capital expansion involving forcible expropriation and the subjugation of non-capitalist regions to the interests of capital. Harvey (2003, 2004, 2010) takes Arendt's notion a step further to include the dispossession, expropriation or appropriation – depending on one's preference – of other sectors of the economy in addition to land. This involves, in the modern era for example, the opening up of public resources such as water, gas and electricity to processes of privatization and the handing over of state assets and infrastructure such as national railways and telecommunications to private contractors. Capital accumulation requires that spaces for investment continually have to be 'cleared', or destroyed and created anew, so that a relation of M-C-M' can be established within them. If there are spaces which are as yet not open to private capital, then it is necessary that they be opened up, and that processes of 'creative destruction', as Joseph Schumpeter (1943 [2010]: 73) termed them, be applied so that new cycles of accumulation can begin (see also Harvey, 2003: 101). At a local level for example, through these processes, greenbelt land may be encroached upon for the building of industrial plant, national parks opened to fracking operations, new high-speed rail lines carved out of the countryside, and airport footprints expanded. This is what Harvey (2003, 2004, 2010) refers to as *accumulation by dispossession* because it invariably involves the 'enclosure' and colonization by private capital of space that was once held in common, mostly in the form of assets held by national governments on behalf of 'the people'.

The dispossession, expropriation and appropriation of space indexes that accumulation is not only about the acquisition of land, as it seemed principally to appear in nineteenth-century colonialism, but also about the acquisition of new spaces for capital to enter into and accumulate. On a world scale, accumulation by dispossession, then and now, indexes the requirement of global capital that there exists no impediment to its movement across borders or obstacles placed upon its repatriation, and that legal guarantees are in place which protect it from local expropriation. This is the structural dynamic which the US has sought to impose upon the world-economy since 1945, particularly through the monetary policy of the Federal Reserve, US government-to-government loans, and the lending conditionalities of the IMF and the World Bank (see Chapters 4 and 5). The purpose was to create *integrated regional frameworks* as the basis of 'An open international order for trade and economic development and rapid capital accumulation along capitalistic lines' (Harvey, 2003: 54). Deregulation, privatization, tariff-free access for US capital, and extraterritorial legal protection were fundamental to the approach. Linked to the dispossession of public assets and the opening up of new spaces for capital accumulation to occur is the dislocation and incremental disappearance of local cultures, lifestyles and languages, as the entry of foreign capital transforms the economic, cultural and demographic landscape.

Of course, it would be trite to claim that nothing should ever change or evolve. Indeed, much of the documented change that has occurred in language usages, in economic practices and in lifestyle choices is the result of forces of twentieth-century globalization and capital accumulation. These have led to interesting forms of sociocultural and sociolinguistic hybridization, from the fare available in a Beijing or Tokyo Starbucks to the superdiverse translanguaging of the street in translingual cities such as Hong Kong, London and San Francisco (Nederveen Pieterse, 2009; Blommaert, 2010; Otsuji & Pennycook, 2010, 2015; Li, 2018a, 2018b). Nevertheless, where global capital enters it cannot but impact upon the local ecology of language, culture and economy, often to devastating effect, leading in some cases to the outright annihilation of local languages and sociocultural traditions (Phillipson & Skutnabb-Kangas, 1996; Pennycook, 1998; Skutnabb-Kangas, 2000, 2012; Skutnabb-Kangas & Phillipson, 2010; Nkwetisama, 2017). Languages and cultural traditions unfortunately die out all the time. Some of this is inevitable, as a result of sociocultural change or unlooked for catastrophe [e.g. war, famine, natural disasters, etc.], but another part is due to the indiscriminate distortions of capitalism itself. When inward capital becomes centred in abundance upon a port or centre of trade, such as for example in Shanghai, Dar es Salaam or Djakarta, it has a centripetal effect upon the wider hinterlands around it, such that there is population displacement from outlying regions as people migrate to the trading centre in search of work. In Africa, for example, depopulation of the countryside and the emptying out of younger generations from local village communities has had a deleterious effect upon traditional languages, many of which are oral. Those who move to the cities accommodate themselves to city *lingua francas* such as Kiswahili and English and leave their home languages behind. Marriage and children with internal migrants from other parts of the country, often in combination with targeted government language policies, serve to exacerbate home language loss due to the absence of intergenerational transfer and so lead to what Phillipson refers to as *linguistic capital dispossession*.

> Individuals opt for the dominant language because it is felt that this linguistic capital will serve their personal or professional interests best. Individual agency and decision-making reflect a range of societal forces and ideologies, with education as a key site constraining individual freedom and choice. Linguistic imperialism involves a mix of push and pull factors, local and external pressures. When language shift is subtractive, and if this affects a group and not merely individuals, there are serious implications for other languages. If domains such as business, the home, or scholarship are 'lost', what has occurred is in fact linguistic capital dispossession.
>
> (Phillipson, 2017: 323)

Within the trading hubs of the core and the semi-periphery [but also in the core too] clientelism vis-à-vis global capital and the local employment of English as the favoured linguistic medium for engaging with it has been a marked feature of both the British and the US world-economies during the past four hundred years. The mechanism as always is endless capital accumulation and the never-ending search for profit as a fulfilment of the expansionary logic of capitalism – that is, as M-C-M' or M-M'. This process gathered momentum from its early trade beginnings with British capital in the 1600s, through the acquisitive colonialism of 'the long nineteenth century' between 1789 and 1914 (Wallerstein, 2011a: 275), and further under the tutelage of US capital thereafter, culminating in a shift to a US-determined mass financialization of the global economy after 1968, and which gathers increased momentum after 1991 (Arrighi, 2010; see also Chapters 4 and 5). The main difference between the British era of accumulation in the nineteenth century and the US era of accumulation in the twentieth century has been captured by Arrighi (ibid) as being distinguished by *extroversion* of economic activity on the part of Britain and by *autocentrism* of economic activity on the part of the United States. Extroversion refers to how 'the most important branches of British economic activity developed stronger links of complementarity with the economies of colonial and foreign countries than they did with one another' (ibid: 290). Autocentrism for its part refers to how for the US the integrated nature of its economy 'became the basis of "internalization" of the world market within the organizational domains of giant business corporations' (ibid) [and the global governance institutions of the US world economic system, such as the IMF and the World Bank]. In other words, from an economic perspective, the US made the world-economy and system in its image far more successfully than Britain ever managed to do, and this would account for the advanced structural power of US imperialism in economic and cultural production, in global credit and security institutions, in military reach, and in the global extent of its knowledge base as compared to that of Britain at the height of its power. Add to this the economic priorities of national governments, the capital aspirations of local class-based elites, and the cosmopolitan bilingualism of supra-national institutions of governance, international banks and TNCs, and it can be seen that English has arrived at a position of mostly unrivalled dominance and *edge* in the world-system. This is notwithstanding the competing claims of Mandarin and other global languages, such as Arabic, Spanish and French (see also Chapter 7).

I have argued that this is because English has been in the privileged position of being able to act as a free rider on global capital flows [$M^E\text{-}C^E\text{-}M'^E$; $M^E\text{-}M'^E$]. These flows were dominated first by Britain up to 1914 and then increasingly after that time by the United States, such that despite the US's present colossal foreign indebtedness, it remains the cornerstone of the world economic system with the US dollar as the preferred international currency of reserve. It is this which explains how it is that despite an unsteady stock market and its eye-watering $6.2 trillion foreign debt (Tooze, 2019: 6), the US dollar remains strong and is lauded by an ebullient Trump administration as evidence of the ongoing strength of the US economy and the correctness of his administration's macro-economic policies. In some ways, he may be right. On the other hand, this may also be a case of 'misrecognition' in the sense that Bourdieu (1977) gave it; that is, of the unconscious misattribution of power to an idea or concept for no other reason than the belief that the idea or concept is legitimately dominant. He called it 'misrecognized domination' (Bourdieu, ibid: 652) as there is no reason other than contingent structural power, and people's acceptance of it, that legitimates the dominant idea. Global English is also a case in point. Its dominance – in the format of a normative grammar – may also be said to be one of misrecognition since the privileging of this form of English over other forms, such as 'ELF' or other World Englishes, is principally based on the power of its relation to capital rather than on any inherent linguistic legitimacy it might seek to claim, such as being for example the tongue of the nations where English is spoken as a native language, or the intuitive referent for non-native speakers for learning the language – although these claims are also not so easily dismissed (see also Chapter 7).

In Bourdieu's words, 'When one language dominates the market, it becomes the norm against which the prices of the other modes of expression, and with them the values of the various competences, are defined' (ibid). It may be that standard English lacks any particular linguistic or even ethical legitimacy to be the preferred signified for global English, but thanks largely to its privileged relation to capital this form dominates nevertheless, and this is despite whatever moral arguments or linguistic agitations are presented against this. The link to capital would seem to be critical; what is missing is the history of this link. In the remaining chapters of this book, this is what I seek to provide.

Capital and normative English across the longue durée

This book contains eight chapters. In Chapter 1 I have presented an overview of the theoretical frameworks and perspectives which inform this book's stance on the global expansion of capital and its relationship to English, encompassing Marx's approach to capital and its circulation, classical theories of imperialism, world-systems theory, development theory, and theories of structural power in international political economy. It begins with the premise that the spread and continued reproduction of a normative standard model as the dominant signified for English in the world is dependent upon the global spread of capital and its endless accumulation. By this means, English has been able to act as a *free rider* upon capital and so also to become structurally dominant across four centuries of the capitalist *longue durée*.

Chapter 2 begins with a discussion of informal empire so as to establish the extent and the principle of a non-territorial imperialist empire existing alongside a formal territorial empire during the period of British hegemonic ascendancy. This chapter also engages in a discussion of the continuity of British imperialism across the *longue durée*. A central construct in this chapter is the empire historians Cain and Hopkins' notion of 'gentlemanly capitalism' as the overarching ideological and discursive concept guiding and legitimating British global capital expansion and imperial acquisition over a period of approximately two hundred and fifty years, from 1688 down to at least 1914. The chapter traces the origins of gentlemanly capitalism to a particular confluence of competing social, political and economic forces – landed, financial and industrial – which came together in the years after 1688 and in the outcomes of their struggles were responsible for determining later configurations of power within the elite echelons of the British class structure and its hierarchical body politic down to 1850, so impacting upon the kind of English that Britain exported – in other words, that it was a largely class-based normative standard.

Chapter 3 considers the political economy of global English from 1850 to the outbreak of World War I in 1914. This chapter continues the account of British capital expansion and the free riding of English upon it. The main theme is the extraordinary scale and reach of British capital expansion and colonial acquisition, which had inevitable consequences for the global dispersion of English. The discussion includes accounts of capital expansion and what is referred to as the *structuration* of English in diverse regions of the world, including Japan, Latin America, India, China and Africa. The chapter considers the port of Shanghai as an exemplar of this kind of structuration process which was widely replicated elsewhere. There is a specific focus on India as the 'hinge' of Britain's world-economy and also as a resource, in labour and in soldiery, for the vehicular projection of English across the world. The chapter then turns its attention to the expansion of English in Africa and also to railway imperialism and the global transportation of English by this means. The chapter concludes with a particular focus on the structuring of English in China as driven by railway development loans and the centrality of Britain to this process.

Chapter 4 is concerned with the political economy of global English from the end of the First World War in 1918 to the US-engineered systemic crises of the late 1970s. This is a period of transition from one hegemonic power to another, from a world-system dominated by Britain to one dominated by the United States. The chapter begins with an account of hegemonic transition between 1870 and 1918, when Britain enters into relative decline. The 1918–45 era is treated as the 'incubus period' of US capital expansion and of the development of a political economy of global English based upon US centrality in the world-system. The remaining sections of the chapter are dedicated to different phases of transition, from the US-led construction of the post-war 'Bretton Woods' governance system after 1944, through the early decades of the Cold War and US attempts to contain communism in East Asia, specifically through the hegemonic incorporation of Japan, South Korea and Taiwan in a strategic anti-communist alliance. The chapter also discusses how US-based capital networks were extended into Europe, Latin America and the Middle East after 1945. By the 1960s, the US was unequalled in its centrality to the capitalist world-system. This had an equivalent effect upon the global dominance and 'seignorage' of English, which the crises of the 1970s only further enhanced.

Chapter 5 brings the narrative up to more recent times with a discussion of 'capital-centric' English in the modern world-system. The chapter recounts how English was able to free ride on the US-led trans-institutional management of the global debt crises of the 1980s and 1990s through to the international financial contagion of 2007–8. US economic management, often driven by domestic interests, was often the trigger for these crisis events, from US manipulation of domestic interest rates through to ideologically driven market deregulation. International debt crises in Latin America and Asia were responsible for making English-mediated structural adjustment programmes the cornerstone of US-instigated policy management of global sovereign debt. In this way, debtor nations were drawn ever more closely into the nexus of neoliberalization and eternal debt peonage.

As a result of US 'dirty wars' in the 1980s and the collapse of the Soviet Union in 1991, US structural power was greatly enhanced, along with the position of English. China's turn to the 'open door' further strengthened this situation. The 2007–8 financial crisis and its resolution not only deepened the global prevalence of English, it also illustrated how in its relation to capital, English and its grammatically normative form had become a structural effect.

In Chapter 6, the account is brought up to the 2020s and the closure of the 'American century'. It presents a view of the prospects for global English at a time when the US hegemony in the world-system seems to be in decline, particularly in the face of the growing power of China. With the evidence of a prospective hegemonic transition mounting, this chapter asks what the outlook is for the US-led capitalist world-system and for a rising China as the system's potential hegemonic successor. In this light, it also considers the potential of Mandarin Chinese ^{C} to displace English ^{E} as the world's structural *lingua franca* [i.e. as M^C-C^C-M'^C; M^C-M'^C]. The chapter concludes with an overview of the key impediments to China's global hegemony.

Chapter 7 turns more directly to recent understandings and conceptualizations of English in the world and asks why in spite of the multi/plural turn to proliferated and superdiverse realizations of English, the global dominance of the normative standard persists. Under the collective heading of *superdiverse translingualism*, this chapter considers a range of different perspectives and concepts. These include language ownership and commodification and issues of resistance and phonocentrism in approaches to linguistic hybridism and multiplicity. Areas covered include superdiversity, translanguaging, translingual practice and trans-spatial assemblage. The World Englishes and ELF paradigms also form a part of this discussion. The aim is to show how in respect of capital and capitalism, hybridized and superdiverse realizations of English almost always find themselves in a secondary relation to the normative standard form, which is everywhere structurally privileged and desired.

Chapter 8 concludes the book. It contemplates what a terminal crisis of capitalism might mean for the present global hegemony of English in its normative standard form. It considers the current state of the capitalist world-system and capitalism's response to this. The chapter discusses the ineffectual addressing of global inequality and the destruction of the natural world and also examines how wealthy capitalist societies in the global North have sought to assimilate and neutralize anti-systemic opposition and dissent. The chapter presents a critique of the capitalist world-system and its leading global proponents as locked in a permanent state of ideological 'endism', according to which alternatives to capitalism cannot be countenanced. As the world-system hurtles towards seeming overwhelming internal contradiction and inevitable near-term collapse, this chapter asks where such a systemic failure would leave English and the global dominance of the normative standard form.

2 English and the political economy of informal empire, 1688–1850

The development of informal empire

Any attempt to make sense of the global spread of English has to contend with a range of competing interpretations of *empire*, or as Marxist as well as some liberal historians would prefer (Wallerstein, 2000 [1974]; Darwin, 2009), of empire as a *world-economy* having territorial and non-territorial components (see Chapter 1). Added to this is the importance of providing a diachronic account of such a world-economy, or 'empire'. That is, an account which traces its thread from its historical beginnings into the present day; and to do that, it is necessary to decide where that history begins. The trajectory which has been followed through Chapter 1 is that the global spread of English is deeply intertwined with the global spread of capitalism and, fundamental to this, with the creation of a hegemonic world-economy and the circulation of capital within it. The type of world-economy which I am concerned with in this book is that which corresponds to a capitalist world-system and, specifically, to a world-system whose linguistic foundations were, or have been, constituted in English [M^E-C^E-M'^E; M^E-M'^E]. During the past four hundred years [of the capitalist *longue durée*] there have been two notable world economies of this kind, the British world-economy, which from its beginnings in the 1600s lasted down to approximately 1914, and the US world-economy, or 'empire', which increasingly begins to make its presence felt from 1919 (see Chapters 4 and 5).

It might be argued that the US world-economy is not an empire, at least not in the popularly accepted sense of ruling over large territories and populations. Unlike the territorialized British empire, there is no red ink equivalent detailing the extent of US global territorial conquest and possession. The British empire, on the other hand, was a highly visible empire, involving the development of colonial administrations from Dublin to Madras to Hong Kong and the exercise of sovereign rights over large areas and populations. At its height, it covered 25 per cent of the earth's land surface and had suzerainty over four hundred and fifty million people. The US empire, for its part, while no less visible in its influence on the world, has been more notable for its lack of territorial acquisition, although both acquisitions and occupations have occurred, especially following major wars and conflicts, as well as through the Cold War, as may be witnessed by the vast number of US military bases which remain dotted around the world.[1] That the British and US empires are, or at least appear to be, different animals, is not in dispute (Strange, 1989: 171). But there is, nevertheless, a significant overlap between them, and this is the informal empire of mobile capital on which both were founded and in large part sustained. Standard histories, and this includes recent ones, have tended to opt for a largely fixed conception of the British imperial embrace, one which may be 'cut out' from history. Following from that, they have also opted for a largely 'cut-out' conception of the US one as well. This has led, for example, to the bracketing of the British empire as beginning around 1750, with Robert Clive's victory at the Battle of Plassey (1757) and the establishment of the East India Company (EIC) factory at Canton (1751), and being superseded, after many circuits, crises and anxieties, by a US system of global dominance after 1945. Added to this is that empire in the British case has been routinely and popularly conceived as a territorially formal construct, covering a fixed extent of the globe. Much less attention has been given to the informal aspects of Britain's empire, that is, to the global role played by British capital, particularly as commercial and financial capital, not just inside but also *outside* the boundaries of its formal domain – that is, in its *informal empire*. This denotes ports, hinterlands, territories and zones which lay outside Britain's formal possessions but which were from the beginnings of the seventeenth century directly or indirectly incorporated into British global networks of investment and trade; directly, by commercial treaty or force of might, indirectly, by informal agreement, mutual interest, or by the accident that they were en route to somewhere else. As Ferguson has pointed out:

> By 1914 the gross nominal value of Britain's stock of capital invested abroad was 3.8 billion, between two-fifths and a half of all foreign-owned assets. That was more than double French overseas investment and more than three times the German figure. No other major economy has ever held such a large proportion of its assets overseas. More British

---

[1] US territorial occupations during the past one hundred years or more have included the Philippines (1898–1945), Cuba (1899–1902), the Panama Canal Zone (1903–79) and Haiti (1915–34). After World War II, Japan and southern Korea were placed under US army military government administrations for a number of years. In recent times, the wars in Iraq and Afghanistan saw US-led military administrations installed following the defeats of Saddam Hussein's Ba'athist regime and the Taliban. Today, Puerto Rico, the US Virgin Islands, American Samoa, and a cluster of atolls and small islands worldwide continue to survive as US-administered territories and protected zones. There are also approximately 1000 US military bases located around the world exercising extraterritorial rights within their confines (www.globalresearch.ca/the-worldwide-network-of-us-military-bases/5564). This includes the notorious prison complex at Guantanamo Bay in Cuba.

capital was invested in the Americas than in Britain itself between 1865 and 1914.

(Ferguson, 2003)

It was not only in the Americas, but in Africa and Asia too. There are thus two empires to contend with, the formal territorial empire of atlas red ink and the more invisible, but no less palpable, empire of Britain's trade and investment around the world (see also Chapter 3).

The start and end dates of Britain's era of global suzerainty are also more fluid than many standard histories would suggest, so rather than beginning in the 1750s with the industrial revolution and the Battle of Plassey or after 1815 with the defeat of Napoleon, it is possible to trace its beginnings much earlier to the development of mobile capital as investment and trade, which heralded the birth of a capitalist world-economy, and then subsequently to England's mounting challenge to Holland, especially after 1651 and the promulgation of the Great Navigation Act in that year (see later). In Britain, the rise of capital as mobile in this sense followed the severe economic recession of the 1590s and developed in parallel with England's involvement in the transatlantic slave trade (1640–1807) and the centuries-long subjugation of Ireland as England's first overseas colony (1170–1801).[2] It was in the aftermath of the economic crisis that in December 1600 Elizabeth I decided to grant the English East India Company a Royal Charter 'for the increase of our navigation, and advancement of trade . . . by way of traffic and merchandize to the East Indies' (cited in Mukherji, 1918). While it was to be another one hundred and fifty-seven years until Clive's victory at Plassey and the consolidation of British rule in India, the beginnings of Britain's informal empire may be traced to this period. It is from the networks of Britain's informal empire and the flows of capital which sustained it [M^E-C^E-M'^E; M^E-M'^E] that the global spread of English from 1600 up to at least 1914 can most readily be explained: this is because it was through Britain's drive to trade that English became *parasitic* on the movement of capital and, due in large part to the hegemonic influence of the US, it remains so today.

The need for Tudor Britain to move more decisively beyond a feudal culture of economic self-sufficiency had been brought into sharp relief by the severity of the economic recessions of the 1560s and 1590s. In addition, the Elizabethans were eager to assert themselves as equal in might and capabilities to their European rivals the Spanish, the Portuguese and the Dutch (Puga, 2014).[3] Through the seventeenth century, EIC expeditions

---

2 The promulgation of the Great Navigation Act of 1651 coincided with the English 'Protector' Oliver Cromwell's brutal invasion of Ireland (1649–52), in which the south was laid to waste and tens of thousands of Irish Catholics killed (Kee, 1976; Shaw, 2011).
3 Portugal at this time was ruled by the Spanish Crown.

sought opportunities to establish trading outposts in economically strategic locations and so also to establish networks of trade. Factories were, for example, founded in Bantam (1602), Surat (1612), Hirado (1613), Siam (1613), Madras (1640), Bombay (1668) and Bengal (1668), as well as at a number of locations in the Persian Gulf and along the Red Sea coast. It is therefore the systematic movement from 1600 onward of capital outside Britain, and the establishment of trade networks in the East and also in the Americas, which denotes the beginnings of a British informal empire, as well as the beginnings of the expansion of English. It was the outward movement of capital that led to the eventual forcible colonization of India in 1757 and the process of British colonial acquisition thereafter (see also Chapter 1).

Coincidental with the evolution of mobile capital in the 1600s was the transition in Europe from feudalism to capitalism between approximately 1450 and 1600 (Marx, 1991 [1894]: 450–451; Wallerstein, 2000 [1974]: 93–94, 2011a: 67–68). Although Marx recognized capitalism as dating from the sixteenth century (see Chapter 1), he often tended to write of the period 1500–1750 as being principally pre-capitalist (Marx, 1976 [1867]: 928) and dominated by 'antediluvian' merchant capital (Marx, 1991 [1894]: 728). Set against this, or in support of it, depending on your view, Engels notes that there was 'trading capital long before there was any capitalist production itself and so long before any industrial profit rate was possible' (Engels, 1981 [1895]: 1045; see also Marx, 1976 [1867]: 876, 1991 [1894]: 442; Nichols, 2015: 20). The period thereafter, from 1750 to 1850, Marx viewed as quintessentially capitalist because it was, at least for him, dominated by industrial capital and the extraction of surplus value by means of 'unbonded' or free wage labour (see Chapter 1). Although Marx was often ambiguous on the point, following a world-systems perspective [while also accommodating the point of Engels] the periodicity of capitalism may be divided into one of agricultural capitalism (1600–1750) and industrial capitalism (1750–1850) (Wallerstein, 2000 [1974]: 84–85, 2011b: 5), and to do this on the basis of whether 'production for profit in a market was or was not occurring' (ibid: 2000 [1974]: 84). In Wallerstein's view, it was occurring, because peasants were being 'paid' for the crops which they produced, and therefore, indirectly, also being paid for their labour.[4] In his words,

> Capitalism thus means labor as a commodity to be sure. But in the era of agricultural capitalism, wage-labor is only one of the modes in which labor is recruited and recompensed in the labor-market. Slavery, coerced cash-crop production . . . share-cropping and tenancy are all alternative modes.
> (Wallerstein, 2000 [1974]: 85; see also Williams, 1994 [2004])

---

4 In relation to industrial capital, Marx observes that 'In the strict sense the farmer is just as much an industrial capitalist as the manufacturer' (Marx, 1976 [1867]: 914).

In these terms, it is not only 'when great masses of men are suddenly and forcibly torn from their means of subsistence, and hurled as free, unprotected and rightless proletarians on the labour-market' (Marx, 1976 [1867]: 876; see also Nichols, 2015: 20; Brenner, 1977: 54–56; Fine, 1978) that explains the nascence of capitalism, but also the orientation of capital to a world market in which products are produced, and *traded* for sale and profit, as occurred in Britain and in the wider world-economy after 1600. As Marx also seems to confirm, 'the sudden expansion of trade and the creation of a new world market had an overwhelming influence on the defeat of the old mode of production and the rise of the capitalist mode' (Marx, 1991 [1894]: 451). In this scenario then, it is the rise of a trade-based division of labour, of which free labour is an aspect, that heralds the transition to capitalism and a world-economy (Wallerstein, 1976: 277). The start of the industrial revolution in 1735 with the invention of Wyatt's 'Spinning Jenny' precedes the Battle of Plassey by twenty-two years. But by then a world market had already been established in which Britain, through its inroads in West and East Africa, the Persian Gulf, India and increasingly in China too, was a leading player. For Marx, it is the combination of manufacturing innovation, land expropriation and the growth in the world market which create the conditions proper for the capitalist mode of production. In this, 'The world market itself forms the basis of this mode of production' (Marx, 1991 [1894]: 451). It is also the world market which forms the basis for the movement of capital, and therefore, from the perspective of language, for the spread of English globally as well.

The development of Britain's informal empire lies at the heart of debates about the history of its formal empire and the extent of its reach and influence. It is only relatively recently that imperial historians have grappled with Britain's informal empire. For a long time, the principal frame of reference was the territorial empire – when it began, when it ended, its extent, and what occurred within its boundaries. The rise and decline of Britain as an imperial power was calculated and mapped according to the historian's theodolite and chain. In a seminal paper critiquing the preoccupation with territory, Gallagher and Robinson (1953) commented that 'The conventional interpretation of empire continues to rest upon the study of the formal empire alone, which is rather like judging the size and character of icebergs solely from the parts above the water-line' (p. 1). The main parameters of the debate regarding informal empire, in addition to being set out by Gallagher and Robinson in their paper, are also well documented in a second series of articles, as well as a book, by Cain and Hopkins (1980, 1986, 1987, 2013), who are seen by many as the natural heirs of Gallagher and Robinson, although their conclusions are rather different (see also Darwin, 2009). In the following pages, and moving into Chapter 3, I present an overview of the main arguments which these and some other authors present, as this will serve as a useful frame for the idea that for several hundred years it has been capital – as British or US – which has been the prime mover in the spread of English around the world. Taking this route is also useful for the fact that all the contributors to this debate deliberately distance themselves from classical Marxist explanations of imperialism and colonial acquisition, and yet their contributions add much additional weight to the idea that the crucial ingredient in this was the spread of capital.

The imperialism of free trade

Gallagher and Robinson's 1953 paper *The Imperialism of Free Trade* begins by setting out the ways in which their thesis of British imperialism differs from those which have gone before. In their account they draw attention to the year 1880 as being traditionally identified as the watershed moment in the history of the British empire, because the 'Scramble for Africa' and the 'spectacular extension of British rule' which this brings about dates from this time (Gallagher & Robinson, 1953: 2). They single out Hobson and Lenin on the left (see Chapter 1) and the imperial historians Moon (1926), Woolf (n.d.), Schuyler (1945) and Langer (1935) – among others within the liberal mainstream – as being united in viewing 'imperialism as the high stage of capitalism and the inevitable result of foreign investment' (ibid, 1953: 2). Imperialism according to these accounts therefore only properly begins after 1880 and represents 'a sharp deviation from the innocent and static liberalism of the middle of the century' (ibid). The thread which links these accounts together is their view of the development of free trade during the middle years of the nineteenth century. The period from 1840 to 1870 is usually identified as the height of the free trade era in Britain, and this period is said to have coincided with a distinct lack of enthusiasm for and indifference to empire, during which the empire did not expand, and where policy was resolutely 'anti-imperialist'; whereas the later post-1880 period is viewed as one of great enthusiasm and keenness for empire and much more resolutely imperialist. Gallagher and Robinson controversially reject the established view of an anti-imperialist/imperialist schism leading to a 'New Imperialism' in favour of a thesis of imperial continuity throughout the entire period.

> The trouble with [the New Imperialism] argument is that it leaves out too many of the facts which it claims to explain. Consider the results of a decade of indifference to empire. Between 1841 and 1851 Great Britain occupied or annexed New Zealand, the Gold Coast, Labuan, Natal, the Punjab, Sind and Hong Kong. In the next twenty years British control was asserted over Berar, Oudh, Lower Burma and Kowloon, over Lagos and the neighbourhood of Sierra Leone, over Basutoland, Griqualand and the Transvaal; and new colonies were established in Queensland and British Columbia.
>
> (Gallagher & Robinson, 1953: 2)

To Gallagher and Robinson, the key to understanding what was happening in the period is not to restrict attention to formal empire, and the expansion which occurred after 1880, but to look to Britain's interest in protecting its informal influence and paramountcy in diverse regions of the world throughout the nineteenth century. Seen in this light, the acquisition of territory during the free trade era from 1840 to 1870 was a calculated reflex in response to this interest. In the South African Boer Republics, for example, while there was no formal British control between 1852 and 1857, 'they were effectively dominated by informal paramountcy and by their dependence on British ports' (p. 3). When annexations did occur, as in Basutoland in 1868 and Griqualand West in 1871, it was in order to protect Britain's imperial influence over the region. Gallagher and Robinson extend this perspective to India, where 'the characteristics of so-called imperialist expansion at the end of the nineteenth century developed in India long before the date (1880) when Lenin believed the age of economic imperialism opened' (p. 4). This also applies to Hong Kong, Burma, Borneo and a range of other territories in this period, where annexations occurred and colonial administrations were installed during the height of the free trade era. Contrary to the classical leftist and liberal standard accounts, Gallagher and Robinson present a narrative in which continuity rather than schism is the significant characteristic of British imperial expansion in the course of the nineteenth century.

But this is only one half of the story, because of equal importance to the continuity thesis is the spread and influence of an informal empire within which imperial power, that is, forcible control or annexation, is only applied when 'new regions fail to provide satisfactory conditions for *commercial or strategic* integration' (p. 6, emphasis added), as for example happened in China, so leading to the First Opium War of 1839–42 and the subsequent annexation of Hong Kong. If, on the other hand, such regions were able to provide security of trade and investment, or to put this another way, if they were able to provide security for the movement of British capital and the generation of profit or could be relied upon to collaborate in the protection of British strategic interests, then they could be left alone. In these circumstances informal influence was sufficient. This leads Gallagher and Robinson to the conclusion that if there is anything distinctive about the mid-Victorian free trade era as compared to the later post-1880 era, it is that in the earlier period there was a willingness to limit the use of power 'to establishing security for trade' (p. 6). In a move which anticipates world-systems analysis by some years (see Chapter 1), Gallagher and Robinson argue for the treatment of British imperial expansion as a totality which includes both formal and informal dimensions.

> From this vantage point the many-sided expansion of British industrial society can be viewed as a whole of which both the formal and informal

empires are only parts. Both of them then appear as variable political functions of the extending pattern of overseas trade, investment, migration and culture. . . . A concept of informal empire which fails to bring out the underlying unity between it and the formal empire is sterile. Only within *the total framework of expansion* is nineteenth-century empire intelligible.

(Gallagher & Robinson, 1953: 6–7; emphasis added)

At the same time as Gallagher and Robinson critique the standard accounts for their neglect of the evidence of imperial continuity, they also concur with these and other accounts in their emphasis on 'The economic importance – even pre-eminence – of informal empire in this period' (p. 7). Where they differ is in the increased significance they wish give to political influences within the British government and the Foreign Office in steering economic concerns. For Gallagher and Robinson, the extent to which the British government was willing to exert Britain's imperial might was flexible and depended to a considerable degree on the perceived economic value of a territory or region to it, the willingness of local elites and rulers to collaborate, and the strength of the political systems which obtained there. Where the perceived economic benefits were high but local conditions were not propitious, imperial intervention was more likely than not.

Gallagher and Robinson's thesis placed a good deal of emphasis on the workings of the 'official mind', that is, the private calculations of the elite bureaucratic and political class centred on Downing Street and Whitehall[5] in determining whether imperial expansion occurred. In addition to wanting to include the informal empire in any account of British imperial expansion, they wished to see a closer connection made between the politics and economics of empire: 'it is the politics and the economics of the informal empire which we have to include in the account' (p. 7). This led them to claim, contrary to what had been standard expansionist policy during the free trade era, that the partition of Africa after 1880 was determined primarily by strategic calculations rather than economic ones, and that where Africa was concerned, it was the determination not to lose out to its European rivals that caused Britain to fall in with annexation and partition; economic considerations in these circumstances were almost an afterthought (Louis, 1976; see also Gallagher & Robinson, 1953; Robinson & Gallagher, 1961). This position led to several attacks disagreeing with their point of view (see Louis, ibid).

---

5 Whitehall is a euphemism for the major British civil service ministries which are located in an area known as Whitehall, near the British Houses of Parliament, in London. These include the Foreign Office, which oversees diplomatic and foreign affairs, as well as the Health, Education and Home Affairs ministries. Number 10 Downing Street is the official residence of the British prime minister and is also located in Whitehall.

Gallagher and Robinson were accused of being delusional to assume that evidence for the 'official mind' could be found in the official records, as the natural instinct of the political class of the day, and their incumbent administrators, would have been to be selective about what was left to posterity. In addition, they were accused of underestimating the role of local financial interests in deciding what course of action would be adopted. For example, the occupation of Egypt in 1882 – which was to last for another seventy years – was, from this perspective, forced upon the British government by a powerful lobby of the local business community, which was hugely alarmed by the economic and political disintegration of the formerly pliant Egyptian state and the rise of a nationalist Islamic movement in Cairo, which was much less inclined to tolerate the extraterritorial privileges which the over 100,000 strong [Anglophone-dominated] business community in Cairo had delegated to itself. The Suez Canal had been completed in 1869 and with this Egypt became Britain's strategic passage to the East. In the view of their critics, for Gallagher and Robinson to put so much emphasis on the workings of the 'official mind' as evidenced by official documents was to grossly underestimate the powerful factors which were everywhere in play locally on the ground: 'On their rules of evidence, no conviction could ever be secured against the business lobby' (Kiernan, 1964, cited in Louis, 1976: 12). In Gallagher and Robinson's defence, it seems odd that, despite the explicit emphasis which they place upon the relationship between informal empire and the economic edifice upon which it rested, their intervention should be remembered not primarily for their theory of imperial expansionist continuity but for the importance they give to the 'official mind' as being the originator of British policy in the nineteenth century. Their error, in hindsight, was probably to place too much emphasis on Africa, as well as to claim that the only authentic evidence lay in the official records – a point which historians of quite different intellectual alignments particularly objected to (see Louis, 1976). Thus for Marxists and Hobsonists, Gallagher and Robinson almost entirely neglect the exploitative motivations for imperial expansion, while for others of a more liberal persuasion, they are simply too preoccupied with the political machinations of the metropolitan mind and so lose sight of the activities of local economic interests and their agents in forcing interventions in the periphery.[6] The result has been to overshadow the not insubstantial economic dimensions of their account, particularly in the 1953 paper, which devotes much space to the discussion of British capital accumulation abroad. For Gallagher and Robinson, the crucial point was the development of British interests and capital investment in overseas regions, and not just within the formal empire: 'Whether they were

---

6 Nevertheless, a significant sub-theme in their African writings is the activities of these very agents in creating 'local crises' which necessitate intervention (see Louis, 1976: 7–8).

formally British or not, was a secondary consideration' (ibid). Anticipating world-systems analysis again, Gallagher and Robinson construct an argument for the spread of global capital in the nineteenth century through a policy of informal commercial *penetration*[7] of territories and nations, particularly in the Balkans, the East and West Indies, the Malay Peninsula, Latin America and China.

The effect of British investment was to encourage a relationship of clientelism with local agents and elites, and the structuring, with greater or lesser degrees of success, of a number of countries as 'satellite economies, which would provide raw materials and food for Great Britain, and also provide widening markets for its manufacture' (Gallagher & Robinson, 1953: 9; see also Frank, 1969a [1967]; Brewer, 1990; Phillipson, 1992; Wallerstein, 2000 [1974]). In Latin America, for example, a Brazilian politician of the era was moved to observe, 'When I enter the chamber [of Deputies] I am entirely under the influence of English liberalism, as if I were working under the orders of Gladstone.[8] . . . I am an English liberal . . . in the Brazilian Parliament' (cited in Graham, 1976: 213). Where informal influence fell short, Britain was prepared to intervene, for example on behalf of British investors in Guatemala and Colombia in the 1870s, and in Mexico and Honduras between 1910 and 1914 (Gallagher & Robinson, 1953: 10). At the forefront of these chains of influence, and manipulating them along their length, were the gentlemanly capitalists of the British government, the Foreign Office, the City of London, and the imperial frontier, who promoted British interests overseas, and who by creating local opportunities for capital accumulation lined their pockets at the same time. While self-enrichment may not always have been at the forefront of government and Foreign Office thinking, the unfolding of events, especially after 1815 and into the later century, suggested that the pecuniary interests of public office holders as well as of 'adventurer' private individuals certainly played their part, and that as capital penetrated the periphery so did the English language penetrate it as well [M^E-C^E-M'^E; M^E-M'^E]. To understand how this occurred and the effects which it had, it is necessary to step back in order to consider the historical periodicity and *intrusion* of capital once more, but now in the context of the ideological components that informed this, and which also informed and sustained the capital networks through which English was able to spread.

---

7 The term *penetration* is common to anglophone accounts of the economic interactions of industrialized and semi-industrialized countries with the rest of the world, especially in the nineteenth century. On the *phallogocentrism* of terms such as 'penetration' and 'intercourse', see Derrida (1975).
8 William Ewart Gladstone (1809–98) was British prime minister on four occasions between 1868 and 1894.

Gentlemanly capitalism

In the chronology of the debate about informal empire, the work of Cain and Hopkins (1980, 1986, 1987, 2013) follows that of Gallagher and Robinson (1953). But in Cain and Hopkins' account, the chronology starts much earlier, although not quite as early as in Marxist accounts of capitalism as a world-system (see Chapter 1). In their work, the history of empire is divided into two main periods: 1688–1850 and 1850–1945, with 1850 identified as a watershed year between the decline of an ascendancy based on landholding and the rise of one based on commerce and finance. The first period they subdivide into three sub-periods: 1688–1750, 1750–1815 and 1815–1850. In the first two sub-periods to 1815, it is agricultural capitalism and the landed interest which predominate. In the third sub-period, 1815–1850, the landed interest gradually concedes ground to industry but retains a superior cultural clout. Then, from 1850 to 1945, it is finance capital in the form of the City of London which becomes dominant.[9] Industrial manufactures remain important for a period after 1850, but for Cain and Hopkins, relative to City finance and commerce, they play a secondary role in the expansion and sustenance of empire to 1914 and beyond. Significant to this account is that Cain and Hopkins wish to place much less emphasis on manufacturing capital and the industrial revolution as the hinge on which an explanation of British imperialism in the nineteenth century rests: 'we reject the assumption that the industrial revolution provided Britain with an automatic route to economic supremacy and worldwide influence' (Cain & Hopkins, 1980: 465). They therefore take issue with both classical Marxist and non-Marxist accounts which in their view place too much emphasis on the industrial revolution.

The main elements of Cain and Hopkin's critique are summarized later. What is important about it is that even though they distance themselves from Gallagher and Robinson and from classical Marxist perspectives, what

---

9 This periodization may be compared to the 'periodization approach' of Howatt and Smith (2014) in respect of the modern history of ELT. They identify four periods of development: the classical period (1750–1880), the reform period (1880–1920), the scientific period (1920–1970) and the communicative period (1970–2000). In the classical period the 'core concern', as they put it, is *emulating the teaching of classical languages*; in the reform period it is *teaching the spoken language*; in the scientific period it is the *scientific basis for teaching*, and in the communicative period it is *aiming for 'real-life communication*. It is noticeable that the classical period begins with the twilight of the Dutch hegemony following the War of the Austrian Succession in 1748 and lasts until the European 'Scramble for Africa' in the 1880s. The reform period is also coincidental with the beginnings of British commercial decline in the 1870s and ends in 1920 at more or less the moment that the American rise to hegemony properly opens (see Chapter 4). In Howatt and Smith's periodization, it is also of note that at no point is it ever in question that each period – and the teaching methods pertaining to them – is premised upon the pursuit of an English that is referenced to native-speaker norms.

unfolds is a consistent adherence to the movement of capital as 'agricultural, commercial, and financial, as well as industrial' (Cain & Hopkins, 1986: 503, 2013: 34), through the different periods of capitalist enterprise which they delineate. The common second thread in all this is that, for Cain and Hopkins, Britain's empire develops and expands according to the interests of what is effectively an English-language-based class alliance between an antiquated English landed aristocracy, an established administrative and political English elite in the circles of government, and thrusting English financiers in the City of London. The organizing principle for explaining this alliance is the ideological concept of *gentlemanly capitalism*. With this concept their aim was to 'direct attention to the non-industrial forms of capitalism that, in our view, had been greatly underestimated by historians of modern Britain' (Cain & Hopkins, 2013: 7). In addition to distancing themselves from industrial accounts of capitalism, they also wished to adopt a 'non-ideological' usage of the term 'capitalism' itself, that is, one which did not automatically imply industrialization or the metaphysical logic of a theory of historical materialism (Cain & Hopkins, 1986: 503). Their usage of the term is instead rooted in a classically liberal, and now neoliberal, understanding of capitalism as 'the pursuit of private profit by rational means' (ibid: 503n). How this in fact makes their conception of capitalism non-ideological is less certain, since their definition is evidently ideological and in the absence of theory-free knowledge also necessarily partial (Bhaskar, 2008 [1975]; Haraway, 1988). However, for the purposes of this discussion, this is less important than the ideological and discursive notion of gentlemanly capitalism which they nevertheless articulate[10] and the account they give of capitalism through the different historical periods which they identify.

Gentlemanly capitalists represented an alliance of diverse but simultaneously overlapping class interests. They had their origins initially in the class preoccupations of the British landed aristocracy – the 'Old Corruption' (Cain & Hopkins, 2013: 648), which despite the move to a more market-based economy after 1700 still clung onto feudal notions of 'order, authority and status' and the land as 'an inalienable asset to be passed on intact, as far as possible, through the generations' (Cain & Hopkins, 1986: 504). Above all, they held a 'contempt for the everyday world of wealth creation and the profit motive as the chief goal of activity' (ibid) – they were *rentiers* with independent means, who did not need to work for a living. Their involvement in politics and other 'outdoor' activities were experienced as types of 'gentlemanly leisure' or as a gentlemanly means of 'carrying out one's duty'. Since money was no object, it was also of no real concern,

---

10 I regard ideology and discourse as more or less synonymous concepts. Marxists prefer ideology and poststructuralists prefer discourse. The distinction is an epistemological one based on attitudes to truth (see Foucault, 1980; Thompson, 1984; Pennycook, 2001; Holborow, 2015; O'Regan & Betzel, 2016; Georgiou, 2017).

and so all activities in the public domain were ideologically constituted as amateur pursuits: 'The "cult of the amateur" . . . had its origins in this "distinctive – because innate, hereditary and hence general – character of aristocratic power"' (Powis, 1984: 88–89, cited in Cain & Hopkins, ibid: 504). As the eighteenth century gave way to the nineteenth, this general character of aristocratic power became the aspired-to *habitus* of the moneyed new-capitalist plutocracy, in politics, in the judiciary, in the higher reaches of the public civil service, and in industry. But simply having money was not enough. The manufacturing industrialists of the nineteenth century liked to refer to themselves as 'gentlemen manufacturers' (Cain & Hopkins, 1986: 505), but they had not acquired sufficient cultural capital to count themselves amongst the gentlemanly capitalist elite (Bourdieu, 1984, 1986). They 'laboured' on accounts, business models, legal contracts and working hours, and this was a sufficient exclusion: 'full-time involvement in industry was incompatible with the gentlemanly ideal' (Cain & Hopkins, 1986: 505). Drawing on Weber's distinction between propertied and acquisitive or entrepreneurial wealth (Weber, 1978), Cain and Hopkins paint a picture of a social elite unencumbered by a vulgar reliance on work, and as a condition to which all the moneyed, and near-moneyed, classes aspired.

> Even the gentleman's gentleman, further down the hierarchy, gained prestige by reflecting the lustre of those he served. And it is worth stressing at this point that, throughout the period under review, British administrators and civil servants were drawn largely from the ranks of those whose economic ties were with landed, rentier or service-sector wealth, rather than with industry. Their social origin and education gave them an extraordinarily high degree of coherence which makes it possible to speak even today of 'family life in the Treasury or village life in Whitehall', where 'mutual trust is a pervasive bond' and where business takes place 'in the market place exchange of an agreed culture' albeit a culture remote from the world of industrial capitalism and often hostile to it.
> (Powis, 1984: 88–89, cited in Cain & Hopkins, 1986: 506)

Cain and Hopkins describe a Britain where the City – 'private and merchant banking, insurance, broking and acceptance' (Cain & Hopkins, ibid: 507) – is a centre of entrepreneurial activity and influence, and whose activities generate vast fortunes which are far greater than those attainable by means of industrial enterprise or 'ordinary' labour alone: 'The country house led to the counting house; the public school fed the service sector; the London club supported the City' (ibid: 509). As far as language was concerned, gentlemanly capitalists elevated the southern English grammar as their favoured marker of elite social identity and inclusion (cf. Stein, 1993; Wright, 2000; Milroy, 2000). Gentlemanly capitalists were in social, political and also linguistic terms a relatively closed club triangulated between the old landed aristocracy, the Houses of Parliament, Whitehall and the City, and extending their influence and qualified patronage to centres of finance and industry in the rest of Britain, as well as to the eager aspiring gentlemanly capitalists who operated out of them.[11] Having provided this backdrop, Cain and Hopkins divide the imperial era into two broad periods: 1688–1850, in which the landed interest dominated, and 1850–1945, in which financial and commercial interests dominated. In their words, 'these two phases of gentlemanly capitalism and the transition between them left an enduring mark on Britain's presence abroad' (ibid: 510). This is not so different to the more Marxist division given in Chapter 1 between an agrarian economy transitioning into an industrial economy (1600–1850), which is then followed by an era dominated by finance and commercial manufacturing thereafter (1850–1945). The main difference is the relative weights placed on the roles of industrial capital and industrialization, which Cain and Hopkins have been accused of downplaying. Like their predecessors, Cain and Hopkins present a view of empire as driven – at least in part – by a class alliance of elite groups located in the metropolitan core. They are just slightly differently configured alliances, and that is all. For Gallagher and Robinson, the official mind is an alliance of Westminster politicians in the government and their like-minded senior advisors in Whitehall. For Cain and Hopkins, this group is extended to include the old landed aristocracy and the City of London, with a good deal of overlap between them. Looked at from this perspective, Cain and Hopkins' criticism of Gallagher and Robinson for commenting that it was Britain's industrialization which was a principal cause of British expansion overseas seems selective and overdone. In recent years, Cain and Hopkins appear to have moderated their position, to acknowledge a much greater role for industrialization in explaining the British expansion overseas. Accused of a singular neglect of the part played by industrial forms of capitalism, they state that 'the process of industrialization is undoubtedly central to modern British history' (Cain & Hopkins, 2013: 35). But they still insist that financial and commercial services, and gentlemanly capitalism, played a far greater role in empire than is often acknowledged in standard economic histories, and it is this aspect of expansion [i.e. M-M′] which they wished to emphasize in their original studies. That accepted, they would nevertheless appear to be much closer to their predecessors than they would have us believe, and what they set out in

---

11 A less dispassionate – but probably more unerring – appraisal of the Victorian gentlemanly class is provided by Bruce Robinson in his study of the Victorian serial killer Jack the Ripper: 'I've spent rather a while enquiring into this "mystery", and incrementally I have learned to loathe much of what was the Victorian governing class. Wealth was a deity in Victorian England, and everything was subservient to the maintenance of it. Underpinned by their "right to rule", their cupidity and institutionalised hypocrisy, these defects constituted a potent amalgamation of the forces that conspired to turn this monster into a mystery' (Robinson, 2015: xii).

respect of the economic penetration of the non-European periphery is not so dissimilar to what Gallagher and Robinson present themselves, with the principal difference that Cain and Hopkins commence their narrative at an earlier date. Whether one follows an industrial or financial and commercial services perspective on the British global expansion, the phenomenon which is common to both is capital's spread, of which the shared effect has been the global dispersion of English [i.e. as M^E-C^E-M'^E and as M^E-M'^E].

The intrusion of capital, 1688–1815

A detailed rendering of Cain and Hopkins' studies of British imperial history is not possible here.[12] So, I plan to focus on the aspects of their narrative which lend weight to the thesis that mobile capital via the expansion of the British and later the US world-economies has been the underlying mechanism which accounts for the global spread of English around the world during the past four hundred years. In other words, it is the intrusion of capital into the British-configured capitalist world-economy which also explains the intrusion of English around the world. Cain and Hopkins (1986) begin their account of British expansion in 1688, although they could have started much earlier. In 1688, the North American eastern seaboard colonies were firmly in place, the West and East Indies were captive markets, the West African slave trade was at its height, Ireland was passing through the latter stages of a most savage English-orchestrated colonial plantation,[13] and the English East India Company was establishing its presence in the Persian Gulf, India and East Asia. They nevertheless begin their narrative in 1688 because, in their view, it is at this juncture that the peculiar mix of social, political and economic forces which were to shape British formal and informal expansion for the next two hundred and fifty years truly come together. The year 1688 was that of the 'Glorious Revolution', when the Catholic King James II of England was deposed by the Dutch Protestant William of Orange.[14] For Marx, 'The "glorious Revolution" brought into power, along with William of Orange, the landed and capitalist profit-grubbers. They inaugurated the new era by practising on a colossal scale thefts of state lands which had hitherto been managed more modestly' (Marx, 1976 [1867]: 884). The transfer of state lands to William's supporters created a new and powerful landed aristocracy which was loyal to him and which formed the basis of the landed interest in Britain [and Ireland] for the next two hundred years: 'The Crown lands thus fraudulently appropriated . . . form

---

12 See Cain and Hopkins (2013) for the definitive and most comprehensive account.
13 This was of Scots protestants and English loyalists on lands confiscated from Irish catholics (see Moody, 1974; Kee, 1976).
14 The final defeat of James occurred at the Battle of the Boyne, in Drogheda, Ireland, on July 12, 1690.

the basis of the present princely domains of the English oligarchy' (Marx, 1976 [1867]: 884). In the dominions closest to England, this was nowhere more keenly felt than in Ireland, where in an attempt to 'pacify' the Irish, English-instigated mass land clearances occurred ['The most catastrophic land confiscation and social upheaval in Irish history' (Moody, 1974: xlvi)] which over the next two centuries laid the basis for the near-annihilation of Irish and its replacement by English as the predominant language of the land (Hindley, 1990).[15] The period after 1690 also witnessed a revolution in finance, centred on London and founded on the creation of the Bank of England and the London Stock Exchange in 1694. Over the next one hundred years, the new landed aristocracy, the financiers in the City, and their investor clients in the south were quick in forming a mutual social bond: 'the new landed aristocracy was the natural ally of the new bankocracy, of newly-hatched high finance' (Marx, 1976 [1867]: 885). Corruption and embezzlement were rife: the indulgences of the landed aristocracy saw to it that estates and titles were bestowed on members of the new moneyed elite: 'Patronage and peculation were endemic to the system' (Cain & Hopkins, 2013: 648). Assisted by the flight of French bankers and old money to London as a result of the revolution in France, by the end of the 1790s, the City of London had emerged as the world's leading financial centre, with English as its principal language of exchange [M^E-M'^E].

In concert with the growth of the City, there was also an enormous expansion in international shipping and trade. The expansion in trade, financed by the City and its southern investors, also provided a stimulus to the movement of capital, which was in turn greatly facilitated by the Navigation Acts and the mercantilist [i.e. protectionist] ideas which dominated this era. The Acts were a series of protectionist shipping laws which had been in existence in England since the fourteenth century, and which between 1651 and 1849 were periodically revised in response to the international trading circumstances of the day. The Acts were designed to protect goods which were traded out of the English colonies, which then encompassed most of the eastern seaboard of North America, as well as out of ports in the West Indies, Latin America, Asia and Africa. They required, with a few exceptions, that exports destined for England or for any of its colonies be carried on English ships, and similarly that British goods destined for the colonies, or other parts of the world, were also carried on English ships (Mahan, 2010 [1890]). In the Great Navigation Act of 1651, these were defined as ships 'whereof the master and mariners are also for the most part of them of the people of this Commonwealth'. On this basis, a crew could be

---

15 The systematic brutalization of Ireland by England culminated in the Irish potato famine of 1845–9 in which at least a million died (Donnelly, 2002). The Irish language was in the process almost driven to extinction until the Gaelic League was founded in 1893 and embarked on a programme of revival (Hindley, 1990).

made up of individuals from non-English races and nations so long as more than 50 per cent were of English nationality. A revision of the Act in 1660 increased this to three quarters. That these were multilingual crews using English as a *lingua franca* is of interest, not only because this shows that such *lingua franca* contexts with English were common in this period, but also because of the role the Navigation Acts played in the dissemination of English via the trade in goods at the ports where they were landed, particularly in Africa, Latin America, and the West and East Indies. Here bilingual commercial 'factors' and agents would be engaged in mediating the trade for the English ships that came in, while the port itself would be a centre of multilingual exchange, in several languages, including English, as crews went in search of food, drink and sex (Zacek, 2010). From the perspective of the many-sided interconnections the Navigation Acts brought about, it was their implementation in the middle of the eighteenth century which supplied the legal and political infrastructure, enforced by British naval power (cf. Mahan, 2010 [1890]), that enabled the beginnings of an anglophone network of international trade and intercultural communicative exchange to be established. The Navigation Acts were in many ways the foundation of an informal empire made in English, because up to 1849, when they were abolished, they regulated the movement of British capital around the world, and so also the movement of English.

The rentier interest in the land in combination with the moneyed interest in the City made for a powerful alliance from which the manufacturing class was largely excluded. By the time of William's death in 1702, an intimate and lasting alliance based on mutual need and an outward appearance of class equity had been established between them. The landed interest relied on the City to manage the national debt, finance costly wars and underwrite the post-1688 revolutionary settlement, and so also to maintain the social hierarchy which the Revolution had established. The City interest relied on the rentiers to give them social legitimacy, as well as their spare cash, and access to the levers of political power. The manufacturing interest was not dormant – wool and cotton were established industries in the eighteenth century and made a significant contribution to export earnings and state revenues. But, according to Cain and Hopkins, 'The number of fortunes amassed by industrialists did not compare with those derived from land and from the financial and service sector, and industry's direct political influence remained limited long after the reform of 1832' (1986: 512).[16] Part of the problem was that the value of commodity exports remained fairly static through most of the eighteenth century, particularly to Europe, and this affected the political and social standing of the manufacturers in relation to

---

16 The reform of 1832 refers to the Reform Bill of that year which widened the franchise to include small landowners, tenant farmers and shopkeepers, as well as householders who paid rent of £10 a year.

the landed rentiers and the City financiers, who between them controlled agriculture, banking and shipping. Down to 1815, the principal interest of the old landed aristocracy was to maintain the self-sufficiency of agriculture, so as to exclude imports, while also expanding exports and export markets. In the words of Cain and Hopkins, 'The promotion of exports was . . . given high priority, for success in export markets expanded public revenue, increased private wealth, and generated employment – especially among the poor' (1980: 467). Exports were viewed as essential for the maintenance of social order, on the assumption that a labouring population that had the means to feed itself was much less likely to revolt.

Through the latter half of the eighteenth century the value of British manufacturing exports had been falling, but fortunes turned after 1780 with a dramatic rise in demand for cotton, particularly from the North American colonies and the West Indies, and the captive markets of Ireland, West Africa and the East Indies. Cain and Hopkins declare that 'For the first time non-European trade, and colonial trade in particular, had begun to play a major part in world demand for Britain's exports' (1980: 470). In India, the EIC vied with private British traders for local commercial advantage, but it was not until the 1820s that the EIC gained the upper hand. Nevertheless, with Clive's victory at Plassey, new opportunities for commercial plunder were opened up. These were brought to painful fruition by the end of the century through the ever-increasing export of Bengal opium to China, which would eventually lead to the First Opium War (1839–42) and the cession of the island of Hong Kong to the British. A number of extraterritorial 'treaty ports' were also designated along the coast, at Canton, Amoy, Foochow, Ningpo and Shanghai (see also Chapter 3).[17]

It is the rise of the Lancashire cotton industry after 1780 which is primarily responsible for the upsurge in British exports. The figures are impressive. Between 1780 and 1800, cotton exports rose by 5.1 per cent a year. By 1806, cotton accounted for 42 per cent of the value of total exports, and by 1807 at least two thirds of total cotton manufacturing output was being exported overseas (Cain & Hopkins, 1980: 472). For Cain and Hopkins, the competitive success of cotton in combination with the shock of the loss of the North American colonies in 1783 'began to alter the nature and location of the British presence abroad' (ibid: 471–472). Increased efforts were put into trade with what still remained of the old colonial empire in Canada, Australia, the Cape and the West Indies (Cain & Hopkins, 1986: 522; see also Williams, 1994 [1944]). But even though the North American colonies

---

17 After 1842, along the rest of the China coast, rather than outright annexations, the British settled instead for the opening of treaty ports to expand the opportunities for commerce and speculation. In these places international settlements were established in which principles of extraterritoriality were often claimed and enforced (see Mayers et al., 1977 [1867]; Crow, 1921; Greenberg, 1951; Nield, 2010; Bickers, 2010b; Kayaoglu, 2010; see also Chapter 3).

were lost, demand for British cotton was so high that North America still continued to be an export market for it. Nevertheless, the realization of their loss led the British to renewed efforts to establish alternative markets as well as centres for commercial investment. In this context, after 1800, attention turned more decisively to locations in Latin America, as well as to India and Asia. As Marx observes,

> The English East India Company, as is well known, received, apart from political control of India, the exclusive monopoly of the tea-trade, as well as of the Chinese trade in general, and of the transport of goods to and from Europe. But the coasting trade of India and between the islands, as well as the internal trade of India, were the monopoly of the higher officials of the Company. The monopolies of salt, opium, betel and other commodities, were inexhaustible mines of wealth.
>
> (Marx, 1976 [1867]: 917)

Capital export and the opening to free trade, 1815–1850

The defeat of Napoleon in 1815, and the end of the Second Hundred Years' War with France (1689/1714–1815),[18] opened up a new and unfamiliar social and economic terrain, for the landed interest in particular. Up to that time, Britain was still just about self-sufficient in agriculture. But in the decades that followed, export income failed to keep up with the employment needs of a rising population (Cain & Hopkins, 1980: 476), and agricultural production was no longer able to absorb and feed the excess pool of labour which resulted. This was exacerbated by the demobilization which followed Napoleon's defeat. The fears of the landed interest saw mercantilist policies applied with renewed vigour, but it made little difference to the value of exports, which continued to stagnate. It quickly became apparent, to those who made it their interest, that rapid industrialization was needed in order to absorb the rising population, and that it was necessary to increase manufacturing exports in order to pay for agricultural imports with which to feed the populace, as agricultural self-sufficiency could not be maintained. This posed a direct challenge to the landed interest, whose members found themselves obliged to confront an emergent reconfiguring of the elite social order, one that was led by manufacturing and the demand for free trade. The defeat of the French meant that, after 1815, the French navy was no longer an immanent economic threat, and this greatly reduced the immediate necessity

---

18 The first Hundred Years' War between England and France lasted from 1337 to 1453. The First and Second Hundred Years' Wars are described as such not because they were wars that lasted one hundred years, but because during both periods France and England were frequently in conflict with one another. The opening date of the Second Hundred Years' War is disputed as being either 1689 or 1714 (see Wallerstein, 2011b: 245–289).

for Britain to seek out new markets by force or annexation (Cain & Hopkins, 1986: 522). Even so, between 1815 and 1843, Britain, or the East India Company, acquired Gambia (1816), Singapore (1819), the Ultra Gangetic Territory [also known as the Straits Settlements: Malacca, Dinding, Penang, Singapore] (1825), Assam, Manipur and Arakan in Burma (1826), Fernando Po off the coast of West Africa (1827), West Australia (1829), South Australia (1835), Aden (1838) and Hong Kong (1842). In comparison with the rate and size of territorial acquisition during the previous three hundred years, this was still a relatively modest expansion. The need to increase manufacturing exports and the increased ability of the industrial and financial sectors to compete abroad without state aid had by the 1820s persuaded the government to take a step away from protectionist mercantilism towards free trade as a way of opening markets to new customers as well as reducing the costs to government and industry.

> The ultimate hope was that Britain's acceptance of free trade would persuade her competitors in Europe and the United States to shift factors back into agriculture by offering them the attractive bait of an open British market. Many business interests had convinced themselves that foreign protectionism was a response to Britain's own high tariffs and were strong advocates of unilateral free trade.
> (Cain & Hopkins, 1980: 477)

Despite the growing clamour in some quarters of government and in industry for free trade, it was another twenty years before the government of Sir Robert Peel (1841–6) split the Tory party and repealed the Corn Laws, in 1846. The laws had been the mercantilist cornerstone of the landed interest – and the largely landed Tory Party – because their purpose was to keep domestic grain prices high and foreign imports out – a policy and attitude that had appalling human consequences in Ireland when in 1845 the potato crop failed and famine was visited upon the land (Donnelly, 2002). Although the repeal bill was passed, a million Irish peasants died of starvation and at least a million more were driven to emigrate [with almost terminal consequences for the Irish language (Hindley, 1990)]. The tragedy of the Irish peasantry did not end the English landed interest's resistance to free trade, which persisted through the famine to the repeal of the Navigation Acts in 1849, the year the famine ended. For the advocates of free trade, it was not Ireland's catastrophe that motivated them. Rather, the abolition of trade restrictions was seen as a necessity for British manufacturing and was eventually accepted by the landed interest as the price to be paid in order to maintain its power and privilege. This had the effect of recalibrating the relationship of gentlemanly capitalism which had dominated up to then. As manufacturing became increasingly significant to the health of the economy, so manufacturers became more prominent in political life and were gradually welcomed into the gentlemanly club. In this way, by mid-century, a new tripartite class settlement had come into being in which the industrialists were also included.

From the 1840s, free trade principles along with British capital – and English – flowed outwards from Britain [M^E-C^E-M'^E; M^E-M'^E], and by a mixture of commercial treaty, careful diplomacy and manifest force, into multiple ports and hinterland markets in Africa, Asia and Latin America. Some of these belonged to the pre-1815 formal empire – for example Madras, Bombay, Ceylon, Sierra Leone, Grenada, Jamaica, St. Kitts, the Cape Colony etc., and others were informal domains which were outside of Britain's direct control – for example Cartagena, Buenos Aires, Valparaiso, Lima, Kobe, Nagasaki, Yokohama, Amoy, Shanghai, Foochow and Siam. Still others were taken by force – for example Hong Kong, Labuan, Natal, the Punjab and Sind. In some of the informal ports and territories, but not all, the British, often in collaboration with other Western powers, were able to establish extraterritorial municipalities, such as in Shanghai, Nagasaki and Yokohama, where English was commonly spoken (see Darwent, 1920; Crow, 1921; Hawks Pott, 1928; Mayers, Dennys & King, 1977 [1867]; Beasley, 1951). By 1842, the value of British exports being directed to the informal trade was more than four times larger than the exports which were going to the old colonial markets of the US, Canada and the West Indies (Cain & Hopkins, 1980: 478). Lord Palmerston, first as foreign secretary (1830–41, 1846–51) and then as prime minister (1855–8, 1859–65), was significant in pressing the free trade policy forward. Palmerston had been a committed free trader since the early 1800s and viewed force, when required, as a necessary means for advancing British interests. According to Cain and Hopkins (1986), the aim, by formal or informal means, was to create 'a cluster of satellite economies managed by foreign beneficiaries of English culture' (p. 523). This naturally included language as an inevitable accompaniment.

For Cain and Hopkins (ibid), it is metropolitan concerns which, after 1815, drive Britain towards free trade and so towards the expansion of informal empire. Unemployment was high, export revenues – especially from North America and Europe – were faltering, and agriculture, overburdened by a rotten mercantilism, was unable to feed a restless population. Through the first decades of the nineteenth century, social unrest was a considerable concern. Rioting routinely broke out, and by the early 1840s, high unemployment and social discontent was manifesting itself in radical political activism in the form of the Chartist movement.[19] Marx's synopsis of the suffering of cotton industry workers in the 1830s and 40s was a

---

19 The aims of the Chartists appeared extremely radical at the time: votes for all men; equal electoral districts; abolition of the requirement that Members of Parliament (MPs) be property owners; payment for MPs; annual general elections; and a secret ballot (see Marx, 1976 [1867]: 397).

circumstance of which Palmerston and the gentlemanly capitalists were all too keenly aware.

> 1830 glutted markets, great distress; 1831 to 1833 continued depression, the monopoly of the trade with India and China withdrawn from the East India Company; 1834, great increase of factories and machinery, shortness of hands. The new poor law furthers the migration of agricultural labourers into the factory districts. The country districts swept clear of children. White slave trade; 1835, great prosperity, simultaneous starvation of the hand-loom weavers; 1836, great prosperity; 1837 and 1838, depression and crisis; 1839, revival; 1840, great depression, riots, the military called out to intervene; 1841 and 1842, frightful suffering among the factory workers.
> (Marx, 1976 [1867]: 583)

But rather than intervene to alleviate the suffering, the official response was to put even greater emphasis on developing free trade and to enforce the 1834 Poor Law. In scenes oddly reminiscent of Britain in the twenty-first century, economic expansion and a blind commitment to austerity were deemed the only routes out of recession. Mercantilism was not working, and so free trade it had to be.

The greatest successes, even before the opening of the railways (see Chapter 3), were in Latin America, where commercial treaties were signed with several newly independent states. With independence in the 1810s and 1820s, Latin American states were eager to modernize in a European image and to become full members of the 'civilized' world. This was a sentiment which chimed fully with the ambitions of the British. The Foreign Secretary George Canning (1822–7) had set the tone in the 1820s, and it was fully shared in the 1830s by his successor, Palmerston, who declared that he wished to 'export abroad the same self-regulating system which was transforming British society' (cited in Cain & Hopkins, 1986: 523). Given this, it was fortunate, as well as no coincidence, that almost all the leaders of the wars of independence against Spanish and Portuguese rule, as well as all those who formed the first post-independence governments, were of European descent. They included Camilo Torres Tenorio in Colombia (1810), Bernardo O'Higgins in Chile (1810), Agustín de Iturbide in Mexico (1822), Dom Pedro in Brazil (1824), Simon Bolivar in Bolivia (1825) and José Gervasio Artigas in Uruguay (1830). In the hope of attracting capital investment as well as inward migration from Europe, these men, and the class-racial interests they represented, set about building investment-friendly state structures which were modelled along European lines. As they reformed formal administrative structures of the state, however, little serious consideration was given to reform of the quasi-feudal *hacienda* system on the land, where millions of *indigenos* laboured on tiny smallholdings on vast *latifundia*. These were enormous estates under the ownership of a single landowner, who was invariably of Spanish or Portuguese descent (Frank, 1969a [1967]; Loveman, 1988). On these estates indigenous peoples lived in a type of feudal bondage to their *hacendados*.

> As elsewhere in Spanish America, Spanish racism and social prejudices have generally reserved the highest social and political positions for those who claim purity of blood (*limpieza de sangre*), thereby creating caste-like stratifications that distinguished Spaniards from 'white' mestizos, 'Indian' mestizos, Indians, blacks, mullatoes, and *zambos* (offspring of Indian and black). From generation to generation stratification could become quite complex within the *castas* (racially mixed peoples), but customs and legal practices sought to ensure the 'integrity' of the ruling class, especially after the massive miscegenation of the sixteenth and seventeenth centuries.
>
> (Loveman, 1988: 38)

The closer one's connections to European heritage and tradition, therefore, the more assured was one's position in Latin American society. The colonization of Latin America by Europeans, and the settlement of the land, led to the institutionalization of class stratification along racial lines, with the 'Whiter' Latin Americans of European descent at the top. It was this group who occupied the positions of state power, whether in the military, the judiciary, the government, the clergy or the landed interest, and it was from this group that came the 'ideal pre-fabricated collaborators' for British capital in the nineteenth century (Robinson, 1976 [1972]: 134).

From the perspective of the British, Latin America with its imperfect but at least superficially European-style state structures, and its seemingly likeminded European leaders, was a far better prospect for capital investment than Africa or China. From about 1824, in line with Canning's and Palmerston's sentiments, Britain began making huge loans to a range of Latin American governments in return for trading concessions (Frank, 1969a [1967]). Anticipating the present-day operation of finance capital, the loans also had the additional effect of fuelling demand for British goods, and commodity exports to the region leaped ahead, from £2.9 million in 1821 to £6.4 million by 1825 (Luxemburg, 1951 [1913]: 422). Capital investment and development, however, was confined to the coastal provinces. Penetration of the interior proved more problematic, because as yet there were no railways to facilitate this. Despite the early difficulties which the British faced, for Cain and Hopkins (1980), 'expansion into Latin-American markets offers the most obvious example of an "informal" relationship based upon the collaboration of local elites freed from Spanish and Portuguese domination' (p. 479). This was particularly so in Brazil, where the British held 'a privileged position in Brazilian markets for thirty years after 1810' (ibid). Not all was plain sailing, however. Rising Latin American nationalism and calls for protectionism led Britain into a series of interventions, ultimately without profit, on the side of the liberal Colorado Party against the more protectionist National Party in Uruguay, by imposing a naval blockade on Buenos Aires during the Uruguayan Civil War of the 1840s. This was because the leader of the Argentine Confederation, Juan Manuel de Rosas, was supporting the National Party side. Despite these and other setbacks, British policy up to the 1850s, in Latin America and elsewhere, was determined by the Palmerstonian doctrine that 'it is the business of government to open and secure the roads for the merchant' (cited in Cain & Hopkins, 1980: 481). The colonization of Latin America had been undertaken by Spain and Portugal over several centuries, but by the middle of the nineteenth century it was Britain that emerged as the continent's most powerful commercial trading nation, with English becoming a frontier language in relation to the local Spanish and Portuguese, into which it had to be translated as the need arose. It was therefore at the nexus of capital investment in the major coastal cities and along the routes which capital then took that English as a language of commerce and finance penetrated Latin America [M^E-C^E-M'^E; M^E-M'^E].

In other parts of the world, free-trade came either at the point of a cannon, as in China, or through aggressive diplomacy, as in the North-West Frontier provinces in the 1830s, Turkey in 1838, and Egypt and Persia in 1841, where treaties promoting 'free trade and friendship' with Britain were signed (Cain & Hopkins, 1980: 480). The imperial account, up to the repeal of the Navigation Acts in 1849, shows an expanding network of capital movements between Britain and an informal empire which was based on free trade agreements, energetic diplomacy and economic favour. With the end of the mercantilist era, the Old Corruption of the traditional landed aristocracy was dealt a fatal blow, as the balance of social and political power shifted towards the free trade financiers in the City and a rising class of northern manufacturers. Despite this, the gentlemanly sensibility, and the uniquely British sense of entitlement and elite self-certainty which it fostered and sustained, lived on in an increasingly sedimented British class system whose modern outlines may be traced back to this era. Even though the power of the landed interest went into decline, as a cultural *habitus* and ideology it continued to exert a considerable influence upon the British psyche, such that it infected all strata of society, particularly those in finance and industry who had the wealth to buy into the gentlemanly ideal. But, for Cain and Hopkins, it is finance rather than industry which is the more significant, because in their account the main driver in the expansion in Britain's global influence after 1850 is the City of London.

> [T]he new economic and political structures which arose – and the imperialism which flowed from them were not dominated by industrial capitalism. From the middle of the nineteenth century the major area of growth was the service sector, and the most rapidly developing region was the south-east. The City was at the heart of both. London stood at

> the centre of a well-developed network of international services, and these were destined to expand rapidly as world trade increased in the second half of the nineteenth century. . . . After 1850, as one form of gentlemanly capitalism began to fail, another arose to take its place.
>
> (Cain & Hopkins, 1986: 525)

With English closely following in its wake, the gentlemanly capitalist ideal enabled the continuity of standard British English to be carried from the landed mercantilism of the seventeenth century into the modern capitalist era of manufacturing, commercial financial services and free trade [M^E-C^E-M'^E; M^E-M'^E] (cf. Howatt & Smith, 2014). The years after 1850 witness an astonishing expansion of British capital interests globally, particularly in Latin America, India, Africa and China. This is largely driven by the international communications revolution and the spectacular growth of the railways, which in addition to being largely British-engineered and built, were almost entirely financed through the City of London. The expansion of the railways, with British money and technical knowhow, worked as a conduit for the further dispersion of English, while also laying the commercial and linguistic foundations for the US world-economy which was to come. The expansion of British capital networks in the period from 1850 to 1914 and how these impacted upon the global spread of English is the subject of Chapter 3.

3 The political economy of global English, 1850–1914

The intrusion of capital post-1850

From the perspective of the mid-nineteenth century and the formal empire, Britain's sovereign influence stretched to India, West and East Africa, the Straits Settlements, Hong Kong, and the 'White' settlement colonies of Canada, Australia and the African Cape. From the perspective of Britain's traders and financiers and the informal empire, British influence also extended to Latin America, the Persian Gulf, the East Indies, and along much of the coast of China – together they made the *Pax Britannica*, or British world-economy. The growth in the invisible dimension of empire after 1850 was astounding and was centred on the City of London as 'the financial and commercial centre of world trade' (Cain & Hopkins, 1980: 481). Sterling became the currency cornerstone of the world financial system, as well as of world capital flows – through trade with Britain, which would be paid for in sterling and through loans to developing nations across the globe. In 1830–9 British foreign investments amounted to 0.9 per cent of gross national product and in 1831–5 the income derived from these loans averaged about £5 million a year. By 1876–80, returns were running at £56 million – a tenfold increase (ibid: 481). It is commonly argued that the beginnings of Britain's decline as an imperial power date to about this time as British manufacturing came under increased competition from a rapidly industrializing United States and Western Europe. Manufacturing may have started to feel the pressure of competition, but up to the 1870s it too maintained a remarkable rate of growth and increase in value. The ratio of exports to gross national product doubled between 1841 and 1870, but thereafter fell back (Cain & Hopkins, 2013: 151). As competition in manufactures increased, so Britain came to rely for its manufacturing exports on the markets of the formal empire. Here, exports of British products rose from 27.3 per cent of total revenues in 1846–50 to 35 per cent by 1909–13 (ibid: 153). Outside the land empire, in Latin America, Africa and East Asia, exports of British products remained reasonably healthy over the same period with steady increases in total volumes being recorded across the same period (ibid: 153). Despite this, after 1870, there was a marked decline in the value of net exports to foreign countries, which fell from £94.4 million in 1870 to a low of £19.3 million in 1902 (ibid: 156).

Where Britain lost ground in Europe, especially to Germany, it made up for this by its exports to 'semi-industrialized' countries – Australia, New Zealand, South Africa, India, Brazil, Argentina, Chile, Colombia, Mexico and Turkey, where it sold four times as much as Germany – $810 million as compared to $200 million (ibid: 157). In the words of Cain and Hopkins, 'this reflected a cosmopolitanism which no other trading nations of the time could match or even seriously challenge' (ibid: 157). Nevertheless, after 1870 a trade gap opened up in which the income generated from the export of manufactures failed to keep up with the costs of imports. That British industry was in relative decline after 1870 in comparison with its industrializing rivals in the United States and in Western Europe is the principal reason why this era is cited as the critical tipping point of British structural supremacy, with the 'Scramble for Africa' characterized, and often caricatured, as a last desperate throw of the British imperial dice. But Cain and Hopkins reject this view, because whatever trade gap that existed was more than made up for by the massive expansion in British 'invisible' exports in the form of capital flows and overseas investments, which marked the 1850–1914 period and which continued uninterruptedly after 1870, even as manufacturing revenues fell back. Significant in the expansion of the invisible trade were services in shipping, insurance and commerce, which 'developed so considerably that a large surplus was still left to finance a growing export of capital' (Lewis, 1949: 77, cited in Cain & Hopkins, 2013: 158). This was aided by improved communications through the steamship, the invention of the submarine cable, and the development of an intercontinental telegraphy system which was largely under British control (Headrick & Griset, 2001; Ferguson, 2003: 168–169; Hobsbawm, 1997: 76). By the 1880s there were over 95,000 miles of British cable circling the globe. Time distances were greatly reduced, as Marx observed: 'The main means of reducing the time of circulation is improved communications. And the last fifty years have brought about a revolution in this respect that is comparable only with the industrial revolution of the second half of the last century' (Marx, 1991 [1894]: 164). All the major continents were linked. A direct line ran, for example, from Montevideo to Shanghai, via Rio de Janeiro, London, Malta, Alexandria, Aden, Karachi, Bombay, Singapore, Manila and Hong Kong. Global communications were reduced from days to hours. The development of the submarine cable had by the 1870s laid the foundation for a globally networked international economy which was dominated by the City of London and by the circuits of English capital [$M^E\text{-}C^E\text{-}M'^E$; $M^E\text{-}M'^E$]. Here is Marx again:

> Thus, while capital must on one side strive to tear down every spatial barrier to intercourse, i.e. to exchange, and conquer the whole earth for its market, it strives on the other side to annihilate this space with time,

i.e. to reduce to a minimum the time spent in motion from one place to another. The more developed the capital, therefore, the more extensive the market over which it circulates, which forms the spatial orbit of its circulation, the more does it strive simultaneously for an even greater extension of the market and for greater annihilation of space by time.

(Marx, 1973: 539)

Complementing Marx's analysis, Cain and Hopkins note that between 1865 and 1914 approximately 60 per cent of British overseas investments were in countries and regions outside the formal empire, with the development of railways being the first preference of City investors: 'And, as the free trade regime established itself, Britain and the City of London grew in importance as banker, moneylender, insurer, shipper and wholesaler to the world at large' (Cain & Hopkins, 2013: 163). With regard to the geographical location of the invisible trade, Cain and Hopkins show that the main investments outside the formal empire were in Latin America and East Asia, as well the United States, especially in the railways (see later discussion). Alongside these developments British imperial acquisition proceeded apace. In the half century after 1850, Britain acquired sovereign rights over Kowloon (1860), Lagos (1861), British Honduras (1862), the Gold Coast (1867), Fiji (1874), Cyprus (1878), North Borneo (1881), Egypt (1882), Papua New Guinea (1884), the Maldives (1887), Brunei (1888), Sarawak (1888), Kuwait (1889), Trinidad (1889), the Hong Kong 'New Territories' (1898), Samoa (1899), and the 'free' Boer Republics (1902). Direct rule from London was also imposed on India following the Indian Mutiny of 1857–8. In the midst of these territorial aggrandizements, the 1880s witnessed the ill-named 'Scramble for Africa' and the continent's crude partition between the imperial powers of Germany, France, Italy, Spain, Portugal, Belgium and Britain.

Less visible than even the capital flows was the intrusion of English alongside them. This was mostly for the fact of English being so obtrusive as not to bear a great deal of comment. For the imperial diarists and scribes of the day, trade appears simply to have 'happened', and that was all that there was to be said about it. That it must have occurred in English, at some point or other, appears to have been less worthy of comment. Yet, 'intercourse' or 'exchange' – between people who were native-English speakers and others for whom it would have been a foreign language [M^E-C^E-M'^E; M^E-M'^E] – had to occur or capital could not be accumulated. In the port context, communicative exchanges took place across a range of social classes and occupations and involved residing diplomats of the foreign powers, ships' captains, factors, local agents, workers, servants, entertainers, street vendors, tea house proprietors, grog shop owners and sex workers, many becoming bilingually proficient in the process. Where a standard form was deemed over-complex for the purposes of conducting business, local interlocutors conversed in pidgins which, as in Canton, often had English as at least one of their roots.

For example, in Yokohama between 1859 and 1899 a pidgin developed which was almost unrecognizable as English even as it contained many English words and had close grammatical connections to Canton Pidgin (Inoue, 2006). But in 1897, in a population of 4000, of which half were Chinese and the other half European and American, over 1000 were speakers of English as a mother tongue, with the great majority of these being British. This had the consequence that the preferred *lingua franca* in the Yokohama settlement was English, followed by Dutch and French, followed by Canton English for communicating with the Chinese, followed by Yokohama Pidgin when all else failed. Even then, it was mostly Chinese intermediaries who were tasked with speaking it to the locals (Fujita, 1981). For official exchanges between the Yedo administration – the *Bakufu* – and foreigners, a mix of Dutch and English via Japanese translators was preferred (Beasley, 1951: 116–117). The expansion of British interests in Japan was accompanied in the 1850s and 60s by 'open door' agreements with Morocco and Siam, as well as 'frontier extensions' in the West African Gold Coast, British Colombia, South Africa and Fiji as Britain sought to consolidate its hegemony. Loans to Turkey and the British determination to make India a replacement market for cotton, following the rise in protectionist sentiments elsewhere, brought both into Britain's informal economic orbit. The zeal with which the British pursued new markets in combination with the frontier opportunism of locally based British officials led to the Second Opium War with China in 1856–60 (Epstein, 1956; Hurd, 1967). It also set the precedent for further foreign depredations of China to the end of the century.

According to Cain and Hopkins (1987), Britain's eager pursuit of new markets is not explained by a surfeit of capital in search of investment opportunities, but was due to the more mundane reason that free trade, and a protectionist Europe and United States, opened British manufacturing to unwelcome competition and falling profits. Whichever explanation is accepted, after 1870, capital expansion led to much greater British exertions in Burma, Malaya, West Africa and, with the opening of the Suez Canal in 1869, in East Africa as well. Financial expansion through loans was also a crucial aspect underpinning British influence in the 'White' settlement territories of Canada, Southern Africa, Australia and New Zealand – the 'Anglo-cluster' – where an anglicized as well as 'gentlemanly' cultural identity was shared (Carrington, 1968; Ashkanasy, Trevor-Roberts & Earnshaw, 2002; Cain & Hopkins, 2013), and in Latin America, where political institutions were established which aped those of modern Europe. In these circumstances, British financial influence exercised its global reach through a reliance on the coincidence of a shared anglophone, or in the case of Latin America, a shared European, identity. In both contexts nationalist pride was matched by an almost instinctive *nostalgia in absentia* for the cultural surety and 'civilized' traditions of an older Europe to which Hispanic Latin Americans believed they were attached. Britain as the foremost European power in the world took advantage of these sentiments to exercise an indulgent imperialistic paternalism, particularly in the 'White' settler nations, where up to at least 1945 the sense of a belonging to a common 'Britannic' civilization was strongly held and maintained (Darwin, 2009: 145). The large levels of loans both within and without the formal empire gave the British leverage over domestic economic policy when this did not accord – as the City of London saw it – with Britain's global economic role to maintain free trade and the free movement of capital. In Argentina, for example, the economic strategies which were adopted to deal with the financial crisis of the 1890s, which followed the local collapse of the British merchant bank Baring's, were deemed inflationary and protectionist. British threats to cut off lending persuaded the Argentinean authorities to revert to a policy of 'sound finance' and deep cuts in expenditure in order to appease British creditors. This was a common tactic. Where persuasion did not do the trick, as frequently occurred in China after 1850, in the Middle East in the 1860s and 70s, and in heavily indebted Egypt in 1882, then the option was often for an extension of control in order that capital investment could continue unimpeded and 'financial law and order' could be restored (Cain & Hopkins, 1980: 487); and where capital entered, English did too, in for example trade agreements, commercial contracts, political communiques and negotiations around these. With British capital as the dominant foreign capital in trade and investments, the instilment of English amongst clientelist groups in the capital-receiving regions naturally followed. As Canning had somewhat prophetically put it in 1824, 'Spanish America is free; and if we do not mismanage our affairs sadly, she is English' (cited in Gallagher & Robinson, 1953: 8).

The hinge of empire: India and the diffusion of English

The hinge on which Britain's empire swung was India. Here, East India Company factories and forts had been erected and steadily expanded from the early 1600s. Along the eastern and western seaboards huge Company 'presidencies' had been carved out centred on Madras (1639), Bengal (1664) and Calcutta (1696), trading in calico, chintz, silks, fine china and tea. As the Mughal empire collapsed in the 1700s so a British one gradually took its place. There was some stiff competition, mainly from the French, with whom from 1744 Britain was at war, and also from a number of Indian princes, who were allied to the French. But by the middle of the eighteenth century the well-funded and well-supplied Company and its armies were close to forging an unassailable position. The turning point came initially with a reverse. This was the rout of the Company garrison at Fort William in Calcutta in 1756 by the army of the Nawab of Bengal (Barber, 1965). This led to the advancement of Robert Clive, a military opportunist, privateer and unstable sociopath, who had distinguished himself in earlier fighting with the French, to take on the role of a Cromwell in India and bend the continent to Company rule. The denouement of Mughal India came with the defeat of the Nawab's army at the Battle of Plassey on June 23, 1757. Thereafter, decade by decade, the EIC consolidated its power, laying the foundations of what was to become the British Raj. British policy throughout this period was, for the most part, to allow the EIC to be given a free hand to govern its Indian possessions from its own revenues in return for a sizeable contribution to the British Exchequer.[1] It did so by a combination of strategic brutality and peculative exploitation. The incomes to be made from the Company's Indian investments were genuinely vast but were accompanied by severe deprivation on the land (Davey, 1975: 41). In the century after Plassey the insatiable pursuit of profit was responsible for appalling misgovernment on the part of the EIC and its officials. A culture of bribery, corruption and personal self-enrichment was encouraged, which became endemic in the Company's ranks. This was attended by an Orientalist indifference to conditions on the land, upon which the great mass of the Indian population laboured. Another consequence was an almost total lack of investment in India's economic infrastructure.

> During this period the management of the Company regarded the construction of a road, or a canal or expense on any such public work undertaking an unavoidable evil to be tackled only when there was no other alternative, and when the expense, from a military point of view could no longer be neglected.
>
> (Mustafa, 1964: 91)

As late as 1854, the soldier and British administrator Sir Henry Lawrence felt obliged to comment, 'our oldest Indian possessions have scarcely a road worthy of the name, not a railway, not a canal' (cited in Mustafa, ibid: 91). Rosa Luxemburg observed that unlike the Arabs, the Afghans and the Mongols, 'The British were the first conquerors of India who showed gross indifference to public utilities' (Luxemburg, 1951 [1913]: 375). In the absence of any coordinated management of the agrarian economy, severe famines were commonplace, leading to frequent rebellions which had to be forcibly suppressed. It was the knowledge that the EIC was not competently in control of the situation in India that was behind Lord Macaulay's notorious Minute of 1834 in which, faced with the incompetence of EIC rule, he laid bare the necessity 'to form a class who may be interpreters between us and the millions whom we govern; a class of persons, Indian

---

[1] There were some constraints applied from London. In 1813, the EIC's monopoly on the trade in the East was rescinded, and in 1833 the Company's India Charter was amended to make the association of government with direct profit making prohibited. However, the Company was given another twenty years to wind up its commercial arrangements 'with all convenient speed' (cited in Mustafa, 1964: 78). In 1853, the EIC Charter was again renewed, this time in perpetuity, until the Indian Mutiny of 1857–8 saw this withdrawn and direct rule from London summarily imposed.

in blood and colour, but English in taste, in opinions, in morals, and in intellect' (cited in Evans, 2002: 271). In 1835, under the aegis of the governor general, Lord Bentinck, a resolution was passed in Council for the 'promotion of European literatures and science among the natives of India' (cited in Roy, 1993: 42). According to Roy, 'This Minute made English the medium of instruction in government-subsidized schools and in effect made English the official language of British India' (ibid; see also Robinson Sirkin & Sirkin, 1971; Whitehead, 1995). It also added weight to moves to formalize an openly competitive, Indian-staffed, statutory civil service.[2] India's first English-medium universities were also established at this time in Bombay, Madras and Calcutta. Here candidates were educated not only for the civil administration, but also for the judiciary and the Indian parliament. It was on these bases that the British Raj, and in due course an independent India, were built. Although the formal embedding of English in India dates from this time, its initial imbrication dates much further back, to the 1600s. In the words of the late nineteenth-century Indian historian Sivnath Sastri, Macaulay 'sowed his seeds in prepared soil' (cited in Roy, ibid: 43). Company ambassador, Thomas Roe, on a visit to Surat in 1626, wrote of 'olive coloured Indian foot-boys, who can prettily prattle English' (ibid); and in 1673 the Company's surveyor general, James Rennall, put the number of interpreters at the disposal of the Company in Bengal at over a thousand (ibid). There also developed a growing commercial and legal class who were similarly oriented to English.

> *Banyans*, or brokers, who carried on business with the mercantile and banking houses, realized the advantage of learning English. With its victory at Palashi, the Company soon began to employ agents, or *gomasthas* who assisted them in a variety of ways: collecting revenues, keeping accounts, negotiating with Mughal courtiers and, in some cases, managing household affairs. Access to these new professions was largely restricted to the upper castes and sub-castes, who traditionally were the educated class, many of whom had barely eked out a living in the villages prior to being employed by the British.
>
> (Roy, 1993: 43)

By the 1700s, other factors included the recruitment of Indian ranks into the EIC standing army, as well as the unsanctioned proselytizing of English-speaking missionaries. The Company battalions required a chain

---

2 There had been from the very start of Company rule, in the presidencies over which it had established control, a civil administration staffed by Indians in 'uncovenanted' positions. The covenanted positions belonged to British EIC appointees. The Indians all formed part of what was known as the Bengal Native Civil Service (Llewellyn-Jones, 2007). A 'Statutory Indian Civil Service' was not established until 1879, but even then, the senior posts were nearly all held by British officials (Mustafa, 1964: 123).

of command, which incorporated both Indians and Europeans and which came from the top in English (Johnson, 2013: 280). The missionaries, for their part, acted illicitly and were considered a restraint on trade (James, 1997: 223–224). The centre of the EIC military establishment after 1757 was in Bengal, and it was here amongst the Indian ranks of the EIC army that English as a foreign language was first consolidated. On the godly side of the ledger, in Madras in the early 1700s, the Society for Promoting Christian Knowledge founded schools for the teaching of English, and by the end of the century further schools had been established at Tanjore, Ramanathapuram and Sivaganga (Roy, 1993: 42). The British politician, former chairman of the EIC, and newly converted evangelist Charles Grant had suggested in a tract in 1792, 'the communication of our knowledge shall be made by the medium of our own language' (p. 149).[3] He proposed further, 'By planting our language, our knowledge, our opinions, and our religion in our Asiatic territories . . . we shall probably have wedded the inhabitants of those territories to this country' (p. 220). By the terms of the 'Permanent Settlement' of 1793 the private ownership of land passed into law, so creating an entire legal bureaucracy to deal with matters of entitlement and dispute. As Roy notes, 'The bureaucracy, agency houses and law courts offered new job opportunities. For all of these, some knowledge of English was a necessary prerequisite' (1993: 43).

In spite of the instilment of English within the Indian institutional fabric, the diffusion of English as official policy had to wait another forty years. In the meantime, the EIC persisted in giving preference to economic rapine over measures for national development (Luxemburg, 1951 [1913]; Mustafa, 1964; Davey, 1975; Roy, 1993, 1994).

Despite the lack of any consistent or coherent administrative policy, by the mid-1850s the EIC was in control of the entire Indian continent from Punjab in the north to Madras in the south, and from Bengal in the east to Sind in the west. Wedged between these were vast quasi-autonomous 'Protected States' such as Rajputana, Mysore, Hyderabad and Berar. These were under the restive control of more than six hundred Hindu and Muslim princes. In the decades prior to the Mutiny in 1857, the EIC had been able to take advantage of the intense rivalry between the various princedoms to play one against the other and to impose order through a mixture of outright bribery, official patronage, and when necessary, military force. The Company's Indian standing armies – each presidency had its own – were the glue which bound the whole rotten system together. These were bolstered by twenty to thirty thousand British troops at a cost to the Company of more than £1 million a year (Darwin, 2009), but a vastly greater proportion of its number was made up of locally recruited Indian soldiers, or 'sepoys', of

---

3 Grant, C. (1792). *Observations on the State of Society among the Asiatic Subjects of Great Britain.* https://archive.org/details/observationsonst00gran (Accessed September 9, 2017).

which there were about 300,000. In the words of Lord Cromer, the Indian army was intended to be the basis of 'a system of administration in which native hands were to be directed by European heads' (cited in Mustafa, 1964: 85). But the European heads were greatly outnumbered by the local ones, and when the Mutiny broke in 1857 – 'the simple reflex action of a decapitated frog' (Mustafa, 1964: 68) – the British were taken by surprise. The advance of Company rule in India, and its steady annexation of huge tracts of territory in the north, south, east and west, in conjunction with the incompetence and barely concealed venality of its directors, military officials and local hangers on, as well as the unbidden activities of evangelizing missionaries, had caused widespread discontent and suspicion. Rumours were rife that the British design was to Christianize the entire continent. The act which provoked the revolt fell to the quintessentially English Colonel Edward Carmichael Smyth of the 3rd Bengal Light Cavalry, who, seeking to instil discipline in his Indian troops, gave the order to a parade of ninety sepoys at Meerut that they should load their rifles using new ammunition which it was widely, if mistakenly, rumoured was greased with a mixture of cow and pig fat, and therefore neatly offensive to the sensibilities of both Hindus and Muslims – the very faiths which made up the sepoy rank and file. The refusal of eighty-five of them to obey the order and their subsequent arraignment, conviction for insubordination, and the carefully orchestrated public humiliation which followed shortly after[4] was the spark which was to set the north of India ablaze for a year. The Mutiny and its suppression were accompanied by appalling atrocities on both sides – mass murder was employed as a deliberate act of policy.[5] Once the Mutiny was broken at Gwalior in May 1858, a British reign of terror followed, in which tens of thousands of Indians were summarily executed. But as Indians died, so did Company rule. By the Government of India Act in August of the same year, the East India Company was formally liquidated and direct rule from London imposed. As part of the new order of things, the British government directed that schooling through the medium of English should be actively encouraged as a 'necessary vehicle of "useful knowledge" [for] the modernization of a morally and economically bankrupt society' (Whitehead, 1995: 4).

4 The eighty-five were marched to a public parade ground where, one by one, they were stripped of their uniforms and placed in chains. The spectacle lasted the best part of a day.
5 The numbers of British civilians killed by mutineers, perhaps 1500 (Llewellyn-Jones, 2007), is dwarfed by the many thousands of Indians killed by the British, either as a result of military engagements during the Mutiny or in deliberate acts of retaliation and terror. At Meerut, Delhi, and in a few smaller British outposts in the first days of the Mutiny, indiscriminate massacres of Europeans occurred. In some areas, the rape and torture of European women also took place. The British response was ferocious: a scorched earth policy was adopted, entire villages were burnt to the ground, and anyone suspected of alliance with the Mutiny, regardless of age or sex, was executed (James, 1997: 250).

The saving of India for the British, if not for the EIC, was that the Mutiny was confined mainly to the northern provinces, and even as it was widespread, many sepoys – complemented by significant contingents of Sikhs and Gurkhas – remained loyal. It was around them, particularly the Punjabi Sikhs, that the post-Mutiny Indian army was rebuilt. But it became axiomatic from that time that no fewer than one half of the standing army in India should be made up of British troops (Darwin, 2009: 55). There were many causes of the Mutiny, but in addition to the gross incompetence and greed of the Company and the Christianizing of the missionaries, also lurking in the background was a resentment at enforced service overseas. Prior to 1857, Indian troops [including many with a knowledge of English] saw action in British theatres of war, including China (1839–42), Afghanistan (1838–42) and Burma (1852). This trend continued after 1858, with Indian regiments serving in China again (1860, 1900–1), Ethiopia (1867–8), Malaya (1875), Malta (1878), Egypt (1882), Sudan (1885–6, 1896), Burma again (1885); East Africa (1896, 1897, 1898), Somaliland (1890, 1903–4) and Tibet (1903) (Darwin, 2009: 183). The difference between the pre- and post-Mutiny Indian army was that recruitment to it moved decisively away from Bengal – the source of the discontent which ignited the Mutiny – towards Sikhs in the Punjab, and also towards Gurkhas in Nepal. The result was that after 1858, even in Bengal, Punjabis made up the great majority of army recruits. These changes were balanced by significantly increased numbers of British troops, such that in the three presidencies there would never again be such a disproportionately high reliance on native troops as before the Mutiny. To this end, after 1858, in the presidencies of Madras and Bombay the relative balance between Indian and British troops would be three to one, and in Bengal it would be two to one, with the majority the native troops being made up of Punjabis (Soherwordi, 2010: 12). The chain of command amongst all the Indian army regiments, including the Gurkhas, passed from British officers to British and Indian NCOs, and then to the great mass of native troops. English was utilized as the primary medium of communication between the English-speaking British officers and their native NCOs, with a mix of languages, including English, utilized thereafter. With the expansion of British strategic and economic interests globally between 1842 and 1914, tens of thousands of English-speaking Indians were deployed at many of the formal and informal bridgeheads of empire, and not only in military roles.

> Across the whole face of the 'British world', Indian manpower and commercial expertise helped open new regions to British influence and make colonial government financially viable. Indian labour made plantation agriculture possible in Malaya, Southeast Africa and the Pacific. It built the railway to Uganda. Indian peasants streamed into British Burma and made it the rice bowl of Southeast Asia. Indian retailers and merchants, with lower overheads than their European counterparts, built a

commercial infrastructure in places too exacting for the 'nation of shopkeepers'. In much of the tropical world east of Suez, British expansion was really an Anglo-Indian enterprise.

(Darwin, 2009: 183)

The outcome was a complex web of English-language connections spreading across the globe, facilitated by the commercial and military channels of a British territorial empire which was centred on India. But it wasn't only Indians who contributed to the expanding English-speaking diaspora of the post-1850s British imperium, although they were vitally important. Wherever British finance and commerce managed to gain a foothold, peoples from other nations invariably followed; these included merchants, bankers and financiers as a first tier, but below them there was a phalanx of lawyers, accountants, medics, clerks, compradors, linguists, middlemen, drivers, foremen, sailors, labourers, service workers and policemen. These groups were not confined to the formal colonies, such as Hong Kong, Egypt and Fiji, but were also to be found in the informal zones – in places such Tientsin and Shanghai, especially as the century progressed. They were an eclectic mix of religions and ethnicities, including Indian ones.

The social diffusion of English: Shanghai

Shanghai became a treaty port as a result of the 1842 Treaty of Nanking and, unlike Hong Kong, was occupied by the British as a *settlement*, not as a possession (Darwent, 1920: 180). A British zone was duly marked out on a prime location adjacent to the main port area, later known as the *Bund*, and this was followed by the more informal establishment of an 'American concession' immediately to the north. In 1863, the British and the American concessions merged to form the 'International Settlement', and thereafter cosmopolitan Shanghai rapidly grew (Bickers, 2010b).[6] Although they were in principle jointly administered, the newly established settlement was dominated by the British (Betta, 2000: 41). In 1849, the French had also had a settlement granted to them, under the same terms as the British, which was immediately to the south and was sandwiched between the British settlement and the old Chinese City. The International Settlement was the most important area for commercial purposes and was

---

6 The Chinese made no distinction between a 'concession' and a 'settlement', both being rendered in Chinese as 'zujie' 租界 (literally 'rented land'). As Bickers (2010b: 275n) points out, 'In practice the distinction helps highlight the difference between zones acquired by single foreign states (concessions), and those which were internationally administered (settlements)'. British concessions in the nineteenth century included Amoy, Chinkiang, Shameen (at Canton) and Tientsin. International settlements included Shanghai (after 1863), Foochow and Ningpo. (For an account of life in the treaty ports of China from the 1860s, see Crow, 1921; Greenberg, 1951; Nield, 2010; Bickers, 2010b).

governed by a British-dominated Shanghai Municipal Council, founded in 1854, which was elected by local non-Chinese commercial taxpayers. The Council made the International Settlement the focal point of cosmopolitan Shanghai until the Chinese Revolution of 1949. Its principal language of business was English. In the upper tiers of society, close to the British and the Americans, were the successful trading houses of Baghdadi, Parsee and Ismaili émigrés from India. And then through the settlement's wider working population there were Chinese, Japanese, Malays, Koreans, Annamese, Singalese, Persians, Turks, Javanese, Muslims, Sindhis, Hindus and Sikhs working in a range of mid- and lower-tier occupations: from clerks to shopkeepers, to bartenders, to club room entertainers – 'the service industries of treaty port life' (Bickers, 2000: 172). The Sikhs, for example, were particularly prominent in the municipal police. All these groups, if they wished to live[7] and work in the International Settlement, had to learn English. If not the standard form, even if only at a formulaic level, then a pidgin variety (Si, 2006, 2013). Amongst the émigré business elite – such as the Sassoon and Kadoorie families, who were Baghdadi Jews from Bombay – many over time became 'nativized' in English and their families bastions of Indian and Jewish émigré trade in the East. They were also, as Betta (2000) has reported, 'deeply committed Anglophiles, who staunchly supported the Crown' (p. 43). While English was common in the International Settlement, in the French-administered zone it was French that was not surprisingly spoken more widely. In the part of the International Settlement that had for a time been known as the American Settlement, a thriving Japanese quarter developed, and here Japanese was spoken (Crow, 1921: 104).[8]

This process of the social diffusion of English in places such as Shanghai was a pattern which was repeated in many locations where the British informally held sway, for example in China [the treaty port concessions], the Middle East [Egypt before 1882, the Persian Gulf], or sought to exert influence, such as Japan [Yokohama, Yedo, Kobe, Nagasaki];[9] and South America [Brazil, Chile, Argentina, Uruguay].[10] First, there was the introduction of British capital and the creation of onsite mercantile institutions

---

7 Chinese residents of Shanghai were not permitted to live in the International Settlement under a land regulation of 1845.
8 In later years after the occupation of Shanghai by the invading Japanese army in 1937, this area became formalized as a Japanese Settlement.
9 Even in the late 1870s, that is, more than twenty-five years after the US re-opened Japan to foreign commerce, it was Britain, rather than the US, which administered almost 90 per cent of the trade at the main Japanese ports (Storey, 1960: 122).
10 Legal privileges which were similar to that which applied in extraterritorial zones were often claimed and lobbied for in Latin America, but the principle of extraterritoriality was never applied in the way that it was in China, the Middle East and Japan. Extraterritoriality, as a Western concept, was only applied to non-Western states (Kayaoglu, 2010: 8).

[e.g. trading houses, godowns, banks,[11] municipal structures, etc.] for managing it. Concomitant with this was the physical staking out of tracts of land where core commercial activities might be concentrated, accompanied wherever possible by the creation, by treaty or accord, of a legal-political framework to secure them – ideally in the form of land rights, extraterritoriality [i.e. the extension of foreign privileges wherever a British person went] (Benton, 2002; Kayaoglu, 2010; Manchester, 1964; Bickers, 2010b),[12] and the removal of barriers to trade; finally, the development of a local service industry to meet the needs and diversions of those employed in the commercial operations of the settlement. The principle of extraterritoriality was widely applied by the British, as well as by the Americans and the French, in many parts of the world, including Japan, China, Siam, the Ottoman Empire, and in some parts of Latin America. In the treaty ports, 'Extraterritoriality came to mean more than a jurisdictional arrangement; it came to stand for a panoply of practices establishing and protecting foreigners' prerogatives in China' (Benton, ibid: 251). In Shanghai, connecting all of these nodal points together was the use of English structured at different levels of indexicality from pidgin English [e.g. with rickshaw pullers, servants and prostitutes] to more elaborate but still formulaic exchanges [e.g. with shopkeepers, higher-class servants and tailors] through to expert standard competence [e.g. in municipal and administrative bodies] in organizations like the Shanghai Municipal Council (SMC). The settlement superstructure was held together and reinforced by a rigid social hierarchy, at the very apex of which was a British expatriate elite made up of the merchants and financiers, managers and commercial assistants of the major British trading houses and their associated investment institutions. On a par with these would usually be a London-appointed British Consul with a small coterie of consular staff.

In the Shanghai International Settlement, after the British and to a lesser extent the Americans, the senior members of the Jewish Baghdadi trading businesses came next, and they were closely followed by the Parsees and the Ismailis. Through their massive investments in real estate, senior members of the most prestigious émigré firms were invited to sit on the SMC. Baghdadi members of the Council often claimed to be British through dint of their unswerving loyalty the Crown, their adoption of British customs and dress, and their use of English in preference to Judeo-Arabic. They also Anglicized their names. For example, Abdullah Sassoon, the elder son of the Sassoon trading house, adopted the name of (Sir) Albert, and many others like him

---

[11] The process of the development of financial infrastructure was copied from that employed in the formal empire. 'Most banks in Australia, the West Indies, and Canada, were founded with English capital, the dividends being paid in England' (Marx, 1991 [1894]: 725).
[12] Bickers (2010b) notes that the principle of extraterritoriality was often 'aggressively extended by firms to British owned property or goods' (p. 276).

followed suit (Betta, 2000: 48). Despite their presence on the SMC and their adoption of English manners and language, acceptance by the British expatriate establishment in Shanghai was still very hard won. Anti-Semitism and a generalized racialism amongst the community was rife, and membership of establishment venues such as the Shanghai Club, on the Bund, remained closed to them. The Baghdadis, and others like the Ismailis and the Parsees, were classed alongside Anglo-Indians and Eurasians as 'anomalous' peoples by the British elite (Betta, 2000: 49), and could at best only aspire to the status of 'marginal Westerners' in Shanghai (ibid: 38) – a racial experience which was repeated all along the China coast, but particularly in Shanghai and Hong Kong.

While the British may have endeavoured to maintain a studied social and racial aloofness, the English language which they used nevertheless percolated throughout the International Settlement and Shanghai more generally, via the commercial and administrative infrastructure of the International Settlement, via the emergence of bilingual street and shop signs (Si, 2006, 2013) and via local English-language newspapers like *The Celestial Empire*. In addition, a foreign-language institute, Guang Fangyan Guan 廣方言館 [School for the Diffusion of Languages], for the study of English and French was set up in Shanghai in 1864 (ibid). In time, a great many Chinese diplomats, translators and government officials graduated through its doors. The social diffusion of English in Shanghai and elsewhere was of necessity also driven from below, that is, from the service end of the economy [mainly as M^E-C^E-M'^E], in direct response to the needs of those who were situated above it, often very far above it. Most of the British expatriates in Shanghai refused to learn Chinese, viewing it as 'a demeaning compromise with indigenous society' (Bickers, 2000: 172). In these circumstances, most everyone who came into contact with the British had to learn English, or were imported in because they already spoke it. An example in microcosm was the Shanghai Municipal Police (SMP) which was made of a mix of 'Britons' [mostly from Scotland, Ireland and Wales], Sikhs, a few Japanese, and a large cohort of Chinese constables, who made up the majority of the thousand-strong force. The British members were greatly outnumbered by the Sikh and Chinese constables. As late as 1919 the British contingent only accounted for about 20 per cent of the total (ibid: 174). In replication of the practice in Britain's colonial possessions, the British held all the senior officer positions and also most of the ranks above constable. However, they relied on a small but significant number of English-speaking sergeants amongst the Sikhs [although many in the constable class undoubtedly knew a fair amount of English as well], the Chinese and the Japanese to convey and translate instructions and orders to their squads, which were divided along racial lines. Over the years, 'A career [in the SMP] attracted thousands of Sikh, Anglo-Saxon, and Chinese men' (Lee, 1995: 7, cited in Bickers, ibid: 171). Unlike the establishment elite in the British trading houses, the Britons who joined the Shanghai Municipal Police were mostly working-class men, a number of whom had been in the police in East Africa or Hong Kong (Bickers, ibid: 171). Still others were recruited directly from Britain and Ireland. A small number, especially in the later years of the Settlement, were the descendants of British Shanghai policemen and had themselves been born in Shanghai. Pay and social status for these men was low, but they had the advantage that they did speak English, a much-needed asset to the foreign community, as most of them 'refused to accept the services of Chinese detectives' (Bickers, ibid: 176). This was despite Darwent's observation that 'the one foreign language best known to the Chinese is English' (Darwent, 1920: 187).

A picture therefore emerges of a strictly hierarchized and chauvinistic Settlement society whose only genuine common bond was the English that it used to enable it to function across its internal social, economic and racial divides, whether this was the 'restricted' pidgin form of Canton 'jargon', a vernacular form spoken by its different ethnic groups [e.g. Indians, Chinese, Japanese], or the full-blown normative standard form [as likely spoken in the SMC] (see Chapter 1). Not dissimilar patterns of English diffusion were repeated elsewhere, in Hong Kong, Tientsin, Peking and Wei Hai Wei for example, as well as in West and East Africa, the Burma delta and the Middle East. In all these cases, local economic infrastructures for the sustenance of British capital were created and maintained, and in so doing social infrastructures invested with human capital were also invariably constituted in which English in a range of repertoires was able to take purchase and grow. In the formal and informal domains of Britain's empire, many races and nationalities participated in this, but in the world east of Suez and into the island territories of the Pacific, it was the Indian peoples that played a significant role. As Darwin suggests, 'Without their services, both territorial conquest and the task of building colonial economies able to bear the financial burden of imperial rule, would have been impossibly slow and expensive' (Darwin, 2009: 253–254). It can be added to this that without their services, as well as those of the myriad of other peoples who serviced British [and increasingly US] capital globally, the expansion of English could not have occurred either. The vast sums which were being dispensed around the world from the City of London, along with the movement of British products for trade, and the importation of raw materials for infrastructure projects, such as real estate development and railway building (see later), gave an enormous boost to the spread of English globally as it caught a ride on the octopus tentacles of capital.

At the level of the British world-economy, there was also the necessity of ensuring that states which had been the recipients of British loans continued to be able to service their debts. As Britain was also the principal financer, transporter and insurer of a large proportion of the manufactured goods being produced globally, free trade was essential for the purposes of ensuring that debtor nations could earn the foreign exchange with which to meet their obligations on their loans (Cain & Hopkins, ibid: 652). The

British government along with gentlemanly investors in the City were amongst the main creditors. Hence, so long as capital was able to flow and no unwelcome interruptions or 'blockages' in this process occurred, the inclination of British governments was to allow trade and finance to proceed without overt interference. As Palmerston put it, states and other centres of commerce in which the British had interests had to be 'well kept' and 'always accessible' (cited in Cain & Hopkins, 2013: 306). Where, on the other hand, there was a risk of interruption, either to the movement of tradable commodities or to the multilateral system of payments, or when it did not seem to actors 'on the spot' that sufficient opportunities for British capital accumulation were being exploited, the government would come under pressure to intervene. This is what occurred in Africa. It explains, for example, the British occupation of Egypt in 1882 (see Gallagher & Robinson, 1953; Robinson & Gallagher, 1976; Cain & Hopkins, 2013), as well as the formal extensions of British influence and control which occurred in the west and the east after the 1880s and down to the end of the century.

The expansion of English in Africa

In Africa, from the 1850s until the colonial partition of the 1880s, Britain attempted to maintain a policy of securing its interests as far as possible without resorting to outright annexation.[13] Despite this intention, by the end of the century, Britain had suzerainty over Egypt in the north, and large swathes of territory in the south, west and east. The overriding concern in each of these regions had been to ensure freedom of trade so that capital could move unhindered within and across the zones over which Britain already exercised its influence, either directly, as in Senegambia,[14] Sierra Leone[15] and the Cape Colony,[16] or indirectly, as through the more than fifty forts which Britain held along the Guinea coast, for example at Benin, Cape Coast Castle and Accra (DeCorse, 2016: 165). In its efforts to suppress the slave trade, Britain extended its influence in the region by occupying Lagos

---

13 There were exceptions. Sovereign control was imposed upon Griqualand West in 1871 and Walvis Bay in 1878. There were also anti-slavery wars with the Asanti in 1863 and 1874, and a punitive invasion of Abyssinia in 1867–8 to rescue missionaries and British diplomatic staff who were being held hostage. In addition, in the southern Cape, Britain fought a war with the Zulus in 1879 and with the Boers in 1880–1.
14 Senegambia denotes the regions known as Gambia and Senegal. Senegal almost completely surrounds Gambia. Britain had claimed the Gambia region to itself following the Treaty of Versailles in 1783. A large part of its attraction was the magnificent 1000 km inland waterway it afforded, which was navigable by ship for much of its length.
15 Freetown had been established by British evangelicals in 1787 as the base for a 'Province of Freedom' in Africa. The immediate hinterland was claimed thereafter, and the territory of Sierra Leone was incorporated as a British colony in 1808, with Freetown as its capital.
16 The Cape Colony had been occupied by the British in 1806 and permanently ceded in 1814.

in 1851.[17] The concern of successive British governments after 1850, and especially with the relative decline of manufacturing exports after 1870, was to maintain the City of London's position as the financial hub of the world-economy. It was a necessary function of this circumstance that British governments of the period came to play an active role in influencing and, when necessary, intervening in regions in order to better fashion the conditions under which trade and finance – and so the movement of capital – could prosper. The oft-unmentioned by-product of this movement, but no less important to it, was the introduction of English [M^E-C^E-M'^E; M^E-M'^E] along the routes which capital flowed – in the 'satellite' trading centres which became formally incorporated, such as Freetown and Hong Kong, as well as in those which did not, such as Shanghai and Buenos Aires. In Africa, outside the Cape and the coastal enclaves in the west, the other centres in which Britain had investments were Egypt and Zanzibar [within present day Tanzania]. By 1870, with its interests in the north and in the east, to complement those it already had in the south and the west, the parameters of Britain's concerns with Africa appeared to be set. Formal control was primarily centred on the Cape, which had become a colony in 1808, and select parts of the central west coast. Elsewhere, as in Egypt and Zanzibar, British influence was largely informal and locally confined. Yet over the next thirty years this profile was to change radically as Britain opted to intervene more forcibly: Lagos, which was initially occupied in 1851, became a colony in 1862. In 1877 sovereign rights were asserted over the Transvaal,[18] and Egypt was occupied in 1882, coinciding with the beginning of a protracted conflict in the Sudan (1881–99). In the west and the east, a slew of new geopolitical state entities often administered via chartered British private companies came into being [e.g. the Gold Coast, Lagos, the Niger Delta, British East Africa, Uganda, Zanzibar], as what had been informal or quasi-formal zones of British influence became formal zones of control. In the south, the Tswana region immediately north of the Cape was claimed as the Crown Colony of Bechuanaland in 1885 and fully incorporated into the Cape Colony in 1895. Under the imperialist impulses of the Cape prime minister, Cecil Rhodes (1890–6), and the British South Africa Company (BSAC),[19] British influence was also extended into neighbouring

---

17 Full annexation of Lagos followed in 1861 along with further development along the Niger coast (see Smith, 1974).
18 The attempted annexation was unsuccessful, and led to the First Boer War (1880–1). Transvaal, with the Orange Free State, remained an independent republic until the end of the Second Boer War (1899–1902).
19 The BSAC was a speculative trading company instigated by Cecil Rhodes in 1889 under a much-prized Royal Charter. This gave the Company the mission to expand British capitalism, to include railway lines and supporting infrastructures, beyond the borders of British Bechuanaland and the [still independent] Republic of the Transvaal, and into south-central Africa. The BSAC was given the same remit over the territories it brought under its control as the English East India Company had enjoyed in India.

Matabeleland and Mashonaland (1895), and Nyasaland (1891). This brought into existence a vast zone of British suzerainty which stretched from the Cape to the southern border of Tanzania.

The way in which British interests were configured prior to 1882 provides a major clue to how partition in the rest of Africa eventually unfolded, and therefore also to how English took purchase in different parts of the continent. The axis from north to south, from Egypt to the Cape Colony, represented the interests of British finance and service capital [e.g. banking, shipping, railways, business services]. The axis from west to east, from Senegambia to Zanzibar, represented the interests of British mercantile capital. This comprised manufacturing exports [e.g. cotton yarn and textiles, coal, iron, and steel] and speculative capital [e.g. mining, ivory, coastal transportation]. Along both axes, Britain found itself drawn into extensions of its influence as a result of events both on the ground and in relation to the functioning of its world-economy. On the ground, there were zealous Christian missions, rapacious private companies with powerful gentlemanly connections, vulnerable local polities and jostling European rivals to deal with. The result was a summary partition agreed by Britain, France, Germany, Belgium and Portugal in Berlin in 1884. This divided the western tropics into zones of foreign control, some with clearly defined borders, some without. Yet, in spite of the declared British position that there would be no forward policy in the west, the southern Niger basin was demarcated and declared a protectorate in 1885. Ten years later, the inland areas of the Asante Kingdom and the 'Northern Territories' were incorporated into the Gold Coast Colony, and the new borders confirmed by European treaty in 1898 and 1899. The change in British strategy came more because of the need to agree boundaries with surrounding foreign powers, in the interests of preserving free trade and access, than any overriding government desire to establish formally demarcated protectorates or colonies. Nevertheless, the incessant pestering of 'gentlemanly capitalist' privateers on the spot, as well as industrial exporters, shipping merchants and government 'Forward Party' petitioners, was difficult to ignore: Britain in the 1880s was in recession, and industrialists and other interested groups, in Britain and locally on the ground, pressed the government to secure British West African markets by means of more formal extensions of control (Louis, 1976: 23). The question after 1882 then became how to secure free trade and control in Africa without the necessity of formal occupation and assuming the burden and costs of administration and defence. Between 1882 and 1889, successive British governments responded to this challenge by the granting of Royal Charters to suitably grandiosely titled private companies 'authorizing them to administer and finance new regions under imperial license' (Cain & Hopkins, 1987: 13). These included the Royal Niger Company in the west, the Imperial British East Africa Company in the east, and the British South Africa Company in the south, all of which were deeply peculative concerns. The settlements reached at Berlin, and by accords such as the

Anglo-Portuguese Treaty of 1884, the Congo Arrangement of 1885 with Belgium, and the Anglo-German Agreement over East Africa in 1886, left Britain in control of what were, from the British perspective, the most valuable regions across the axis of the tropics. In West Africa these were the Niger delta and the Gold Coast. In the east it was the Zanzibar protectorate (1890) and what were to become the colonies of British East Africa and Uganda.

In comparison with West Africa, the development of East Africa was, if anything, even less enthusiastic. The City was reluctant to invest here at all. London money capital, seeking assured returns, was unwilling to take risks where there could be few guarantees, particularly in the absence of any imperial institutional oversight; and this was not visibly forthcoming. In these circumstances it was left to local speculative capital again to take up the slack. This came in the form of the British East Africa Association which had been set up by William Mackinnon (1823–93) in 1882. Mackinnon had been a senior partner in the Calcutta firm of Mackinnon Mackenzie, which had a long association with the India trade. With the opening of the Suez Canal in 1869 and with good gentlemanly connections in India and in London, Mackinnon had persuaded the British government to grant his firm a maritime subsidy to develop British commercial interests in the vicinity of the Persian Gulf and East Africa. Mackinnon wished to develop a British zone of influence which complemented that which was being developed in the west. It was at Zanzibar that Mackinnon initially attempted to begin his new business. He petitioned the sultan for a lease on a strip of the mainland opposite the capital as the headquarters for his company. He was turned down. As in West Africa, from the 1870s there had been those on the spot and in the British cabinet who lobbied for a more forward policy, again on the grounds of securing British zones of influence against foreign encroachment and because there were vast resources of untapped wealth to be discovered in the interior. According to Cain and Hopkins,

> more important still, by 1884 the Foreign Office was making quantitative assessments of East Africa's commercial potential, and had also persuaded itself that the indigenous population would welcome the establishment of good government – a sure sign that the Titans of officialdom were preparing to accept yet another burden.
>
> (ibid: 334)

In the end, events overtook Foreign Office deliberations, when, in 1885, Germany declared protectorates over a cluster of regions to the south which incorporated in them some of the principal trade routes to Zanzibar.

Prompted into action, the British government agreed [largely at the expense of the sultanate] to a partition of the region in which Britain was given control of the Zanzibar hinterland to the north [to become British East Africa, and later Kenya] and Germany was given control over the hinterlands to the south [to become German East Africa, and later Tanzania]. Free trade was preserved in both areas as part of the agreement. As had also occurred in the lower Niger region with the Royal Niger Company, Mackinnon's Association found itself well placed to take advantage of the changed political climate and was awarded a Royal Charter to administer the new protectorate, which included within it the island city of Zanzibar. The British East Africa Association was suitably retitled as the Imperial British East Africa Company (IBEAC) in 1887. Emboldened by its success, the IBEAC extended its reach well into the East African interior, and beyond the boundaries of the new eastern protectorate, into the territories which were [after 1890] to become Uganda. With the extension of its territory above Lake Victoria, the IBEAC found itself financially overstretched, and by the 1890s the Company was bordering on bankruptcy. Mackinnon petitioned the government for funds and threatened that the IBEAC would pull out of Uganda altogether if these were not forthcoming. After some hesitation in London, the Forward Party won out, and Uganda was incorporated into the British East African protectorate under the administration of Mackinnon's Company. The joining of Uganda to the British East Africa protectorate placed under British suzerainty an area of land which stretched uninterruptedly from the shores of Alexandria to the port of Mombasa. Uganda became a protectorate in its own right in 1894.

In the commercial centres which were either newly incorporated into the British sphere, such as at Zanzibar and Mombasa, or given greater formal recognition, as in Lagos and Accra, English was carried into the ports and the interior regions on the shoulders of capital – as both imports [e.g. cotton yarn and textiles, iron, metal products, steel; M^E-C^E-M'^E] and speculative investments [e.g. in mines, railway lines, and produce for export; M^E-M'^E]. This occurred, as elsewhere, through the contact of English-speaking traders and their retinues with local interpreters, middlemen, contractors, labourers and service employees of various kinds. In the Gulf of Guinea, for example, English-speaking Creoles, often from Sierra Leone, formed the backbone of the fledgling British bureaucracies and trading outposts which were established along the coast. A practical issue was that the Creoles were more resistant than their English overlords to the deadly sicknesses to which many of the Europeans succumbed (Clarence-Smith, 1994: 62). In addition to English employed in a normative standard form by British frontier capitalists, consular officials and missionaries, the history of African Englishes and African pidgins and creoles also have their origins here (cf. Huber, 1999; Bobda, 2010; Mufwene, 2014, 2015; McArthur, Lam-McArthur & Fontaine, 2018). English already percolated through the eastern interior, albeit on a modest scale, via the vast interior network of trading routes established by Indian traders in the earlier nineteenth century. Along these routes English was diffused – through the work of Christian missions and the dealings of anglophone speculating companies and adventurer explorers.

With the extension of British East Africa after 1890, these processes developed a greater intensity, as the southern frontier of Sudan became the northern frontier of Uganda. At the same time, and at huge expense to the British Exchequer [the £5 million cost run up by the IBEAC eventually had to be written off] (Darwin, 2009), Mackinnon's ambition for a rail link between Lake Victoria and Mombasa also came to fruition, with 32,000 labourers from British India being brought in to construct the line. The coming of the railways and multilateral agreements between powers to maintain free trade enabled capital and English to flow across borders and infiltrate the interior. From the perspective of the British world-economy, in addition to the priority of maintaining free trade, Britain had by 1900 achieved its objective of preserving to itself the most valuable parts of the African continent along its principal axes of interest: the finance axis from north to south, and the mercantile axis from west to east. In the process, as well as becoming centres for the diffusion of capital, the ports and hinterlands of British Africa also became centres for the diffusion of English and of Africa's underdevelopment (Rodney, 2012 [1972]). These processes were greatly augmented by the building of the railways.

Railway imperialism and the transportation of English

Majorly impacting on the development of country-internal as well as cross-border links in Africa, and within the other continents of the world-system, was the building of the railways. British capital, track and rolling stock were at the forefront of railway building in Latin America, India, Africa and Asia, where investments in railways took on boom proportions (see Davis, Wilburn & Robinson, 1991; Otte & Neilson, 2006; Lewis, 1983; Wright, 1974; Kerr, 1995). In Europe, Latin America, India, Siam, Burma, China and Japan, British companies and investors made a significant contribution, as did 'an unnamed army of British labourers, skilled masons, joiners, quarrymen, engine drivers, machinists, and fitters' (Woodruff, 1966: 228). The railway boom also encompassed North America and the English settler colonies of Australia, New Zealand, Canada and the Cape, as well as West and East Africa and Egypt. Although Rhodes' vision of a line running from the Cape to Cairo never materialized, it did lead to greater cross-border rail connections between the states of East Africa. In West Africa, the railway networks which were constructed, by the British and the French, for example in Senegal, the Gold Coast, the Niger protectorate, Dahomey and Togo, were all country-internal (Woodruff, 1966: 232).

In India, the railroad 'attracted the largest single unit of foreign investment of the nineteenth century' (Sethia, 1991: 103). Where in 1850 there had not been a foot of track, by 1900 there was over twenty-five thousand miles of it, which was more than for the whole of the rest of Asia put together (Woodruff, 1966: 233; Kerr, 1995: 186) – Marx's prediction that the British would draw 'a net of railroads over India' was fulfilled

(Marx, 1969 [1853]: 134). In addition to making for the more integrative, if uneven, development of the Indian economy, the rail networks also helped to make British rule more cohesive by drawing in the princely kingdoms and by generally improving internal communications. In Africa too, thanks to the activities of capitalist speculators such as Mackinnon and Rhodes, ambitious railroad schemes for the exploitation of the interior were pursued, even if some became costly white elephants – as in British East Africa, Uganda, and much of the south-central interior. But even when they did, the result was still the same: the creation of conduits for British capital to advance; and, on the back of capital, English [M^E-C^E-M'^E; M^E-M'^E]. In Burma and Malaya, the pattern of railway building followed a similar pattern to Africa –

> an almost complete dependence upon European skill, capital, and enterprise, an absence of national railway networks, and a concentration upon routes from the mines and plantations to the ports. Most of the lines were single-purpose railways, running from the hinterland to the main ports.
> (Woodruff, 1966: 234)

Outside the captive markets of the formal empire, Britain exercised its influence more indirectly. Prior to 1870 it did this through the weight of its manufacturing exports, and after that, through capital investments, usually in the form of government loans. In these zones, a key area of investment, amongst others, were the railroads. In Latin America, Britain was particularly active. In 1860, Cuba was able to claim five hundred miles of track – more than for the whole of the Latin American continent. By 1900, due largely to British capital investment, the continent had accumulated thirty-five thousand miles of track, with the greater part of it in Argentina, Mexico and Brazil, which were the main centres of British interest (Woodruff, 1966: 231, 253). British capital also held an advanced position in the railways of Chile, Peru, Colombia, Paraguay, Uruguay and Venezuela, and several of the lines were entirely British-managed or -owned (Darwin, 2009: 137; Herranz-Loncan, 2011). Asia matched Latin America in the extent of its investment in railway building, but the greatest part of this was centred upon India. Elsewhere, the numbers were less spectacular, but still significant. Between 1860 and 1900, Indonesia, Japan, Burma and China collectively laid nearly ten thousand miles of track: Japan [3920], Indonesia [2230], Burma [1350], China [1460] (Woodruff, 1966: 253), much of it made possible via loans raised in the City of London.

In addition to finance, British technological knowhow and expertise were also greatly sought after. In the diverse zones of British-led railway development, the construction of the railways involved the utilization of large quantities of British equipment, steel and railway technology, and with that, engineering skills and labour. British engineers, English-speaking navvies, in addition to local and foreign labourers, were employed on the lines. The British engineer D M Fox, who worked on the construction of the São Paulo Railway in the 1860s, noted that 'Englishmen were indispensable as foremen for plate-laying, &c., also as engine-drivers and fitters' (cited in Lamounier, 2000: 23). These specialist English-speaking workers were contracted to work alongside local as well as foreign labourers, often in a supervisory role: 'The English contractors boasted about their English, Irish, and Scots navvies, who were themselves quite conscious of their self-evident superiority' (Coleman, 1965: 177). The use of local and foreign labour also required the engagement of bilingual overseers whose job it was to convey the British engineers' instructions to the non-English-speaking workforce: the São Paulo Railway involved the employment of 'all nationalities and shades of colour' (Fox, 1870: 36, cited in Lamounier, 2000: 36). By comparison, much less imported labour was used in China. Chinese navvies built the railways but under the supervision of British engineers and select English-speaking overseers, both Chinese and British. The latter were brought in especially for the job (Coleman, 1965). Travelling along the lines in the reverse direction back towards the ports, the British engineers also needed to communicate with bilingual local agents who acted as representatives for commercial interests in the ports, for example at Buenos Aires, São Paulo and Shanghai. This included local clientelist groups [e.g. businessmen, bankers, lawyers, politicians, landowners, real estate developers, speculative capitalists, etc.], British consular officials, and local British representatives of the financiers in London [e.g. Barings in Argentina, the Hongkong and Shanghai Bank in China]. The result was a complex network of English-language connections which could be traced from the railway workings of the interior, via the commercial trading hubs on the coast, to the metropolitan core. As Ronald Robinson has noted, 'Steel rails had a capacity for transforming the societies through which they ran and for spreading imperial influence in their domestic affairs' (1991: 3). With Britain at the centre of the world-system and the principal investor, they also had the capacity for extending the reach of English. This was because the steel rails arrived with capital, and the capital arrived with English, thus giving a linguistic bias to the process of capital accumulation which the construction of the railways represented [M^E-C^E-M'^E; M^E-M'^E]. As British trade and investment increased with the subsequent use of the lines, so English was better able to fix its presence across ever-greater expanses of territory, assisted by the movement of British speculators, consular officials, labourers, missionaries and the local English-speaking service-support networks which they caused to be established. In Africa, India and China this involved the movement of English-speaking imperial troops alongside posted British contingents as well (Darwin, 2009).

Railway imperialism and the structuring of English in China

China's experience of railway building became the premise upon which the Chinese continent in the last quarter of the nineteenth century was divided into imperial spheres of influence, while simultaneously avoiding the fate of Africa and outright partition. China, as is well known, had been a focus of foreign depredation of its territory since the early 1840s. It had experienced two costly wars with the British: the First Opium War (1839–42), and the Second Opium War (1856–8, 1858–60), in addition to another with the French – the Tonkin War (1884–5). By the terms of the 'unequal treaties'[20] – most notably, the Treaty of Nanking (1842), the Treaty of Tientsin (1858) and the Convention of Peking (1860) – which followed defeats to the British, the Manchu government of the Qing regime (1644–1911) was obliged to open several treaty ports along the China coast to foreign trade, in addition to paying large indemnities to recompense the victors. The first ports after 1842 were at Canton, Amoy, Foochow, Ningpo and Shanghai. The island of Hong Kong was also at this time ceded to Britain in perpetuity, to be followed by the addition of the Kowloon peninsula in 1860. By the 1860 Convention of Peking several more treaty ports were established at locations such as Swatow, Tientsin, Chefoo, and at the harbours of Tanshui and Kaohsiung in Formosa (Taiwan). In addition to the ports, a number of inland locations were nominated as special centres of trade, notably at Nanking, Hankow and Kiukiang. In Peking, land was also set aside for a Legation Quarter for foreign ambassadors and their staff. In addition to these incursions, the Chinese government also had to contend with the predatory inclinations of the United States and France, and as the century progressed, with those of Germany, Italy, Russia and Japan. While, from a British perspective, the expansion and development of Hong Kong after 1860 was important in the context of railway building and the development of a wider commerce, it was the establishment of the treaty ports which was the more significant as these were to be the commercial hubs for the interior development of the railways.

At no time did the British contemplate the formal partition of China, although the Foreign Office was daily concerned about Russian and French manoeuvring on the northern and the southern frontiers, and the sabre-rattling of a modernizing Japan in the north-east. British interests, nevertheless, remained concentrated on the treaty ports and their development

---

20 The Treaty of Nanking (1842), the Treaty of Tientsin (1858), and the latter's ratification in the Convention of Peking (1860), are to this day, with some justification, referred to as the 'unequal treaties' in Chinese official and school texts. But the phrase is not confined only to treaties entered into with the British. Several others were signed over the years with the United States, France, Russia, Germany and Japan, on terms which were invariably unfavourable to China.

as entrepôts for orderly and profitable trade. As part of this strategy, the British committed themselves to maintaining the relative internal stability of China – so far as it did not affect British interests – and to support of the central government in Peking (Pelcovits, 1948: 363). The British vision of a flourishing entrepôt trade proved elusive, but this did not dampen hopes that with the development of the railways a change in fortunes might occur. Between 1875 and 1900, China accounted for about 12 per cent of Britain's total exports; most of this was in cotton and wool. The figure also includes iron and steel which accounted for about 2 per cent of the total (Woodruff, 1966, Table VII/3). In the absence of any marked upward shift in the trade figures, leading British firms in China [e.g. Jardine Matheson & Co] and other foreign trading houses began to move out of the staple import trades, including opium, and diversified into shipping, insurance, and banking, as well as 'an array of activities connected to property and utilities in the Treaty Ports' (Cain & Hopkins, 2013: 365). As they did so, they also gave a further boost to the licit and illicit percolation of English along the China coast [M^E-C^E-M'^E; M^E-M'^E]. Pelcovits notes that, according to a census taken in 1879, the total number of foreign residents in the treaty ports was 3814, of which 1953 were British, 420 were American and 384 were German. In addition, of the firms, 220 were British, 49 were German, 35 were American, with 9 French and 2 Danish. By 1885, the number of British firms in the treaty ports had increased to 299, with 2070 British nationals. Less promisingly, he notes that 'Even as late as 1897 there were fewer than 5000 British residents in the ports' (1948: 133). These numbers, while not large, excluded English-speaking groups such as travelling missionaries, members of the armed forces, merchant seamen, peripatetic diplomats, British workmen on temporary contracts, Sikh policemen, Americans, Australians, Canadians and merchants such as the Baghdadis and Parsees. Once the social infrastructures supporting these groups are also added in, the pool for the diffusion of English in China becomes a good deal larger than the official statistics on the numbers of British residents alone would suggest. It is impossible to arrive at a precise figure, but it may have been as much as twenty times the figure Pelcovits gives for British residents in the ports, and possibly much more (Dyer-Ball, 1903: 292–295).

The shift in business focus made financial speculation an end in itself, particularly through the provision of loans to the Chinese government, which were then funnelled into the building of the railways. The event which changed a gently assertive lending policy into an openly assertive one was the humiliation of China in the Sino-Japanese War of 1894–5. This led to the Treaty of Shimonoseki (1895). By the terms of the treaty, China agreed to the cession of Formosa (Taiwan) to Japan and was forced to recognize 'the full and complete independence and autonomy of Korea' (cited in Spence, 1990: 223). The treaty also required the payment of a large indemnity to the victorious Japanese of 200 million taels of silver,[21] with an additional 30 million to bring the Liaotung peninsula in Southern Manchuria – lost in the war – back under Chinese control (Pelcovits, 1948: 179).[22] This in turn necessitated much increased borrowing on the part of the Chinese government. As Cain and Hopkins point out, 'China now needed Britain's protection [in addition to its mediation] more than ever' (2013: 369; parenthesis added); the indemnity imposed by Japan would have to be financed in London and would need to be negotiated with the Chinese government principally in English [hence, M^E-M'^E]. The view quickly took hold amongst the rival powers that by means of 'indemnity loans' with certain conditions attached it might be possible to make good on the Western vision of opening up the vast Chinese interior to foreign commerce and investment. From this ensued the 'scramble' for railway concessions in which the Chinese government found itself under increasing pressure, backed up by the threat of force, to grant licenses and territorial bases to the competing powers for the purposes of building railways and extending imperial influence. The powers involved were primarily the Belgians, the British, the French, the Germans, the Russians and to a lesser extent the Americans. Within a very short period agreements had been reached with various foreign contractors, including British ones, for the construction of 6520 miles of railways in China by the end of 1898 (Davis, 1991: 159). The reality of the imperialist rivalry was that it was concentrated on the granting of concessions more than it was on the actual construction of the lines (Davis, 1991: 158), so that between 1880 and 1900 the total mileage of the railways in China only marginally increased from 1350 miles to 1460 miles. Thereafter expansion was much more rapid, reaching 6000 miles by 1913, and 7000 miles by 1920 (Woodruff, 1966: 235), nearly all of which was financed by loans taken out on terms highly beneficial to the concession holders and usually tied to the import of expensive railway construction materials from the nations concerned. Loans were notionally secured against the property and revenues involved in the railway enterprise, or against some portion of the tax income of the Chinese government, largely through customs duties (Davis, 1991: 160). It was convenient in this respect that the Chinese Imperial Maritime Customs Service (see later) had been under foreign [mainly British] control since 1854, with its most senior official, the inspector general, being a British appointee (Cain & Hopkins, 2013: 362; see also Morse, 1913: 366–371).

21 A tael is an ounce weight of pure silver.
22 Japan was persuaded to relinquish its claim to the Liaotung peninsula under pressure from the 'Dreibund' alliance of Germany, France and Russia. The strategically important naval base of Port Arthur, which was at the tip of the Liaotung peninsula, was subsequently leased to Russia in 1898.

While the paper assurances were welcomed by foreign investors, of much greater significance was the more or less universal belief that European governments would intervene to compel the Chinese government to meet its debt obligations in the event of any sign of a default (Davis, 1991). It was Britain that held the largest share of the railway loans, and approximately half of China's foreign debt by 1920 was made up of loans of this kind (ibid).[23]

Closely related to these and other developments – and indeed, facilitating them – was the development of English learning in China, especially after the 1860 Convention of Peking. The humiliation which defeat in the Opium Wars brought to China led to a reassessment of China's relationship with the West and necessitated on the part of the Manchu government and its official representatives a more developed accommodation with English beyond that hitherto afforded by Canton Pidgin. Treaties had to be negotiated [and renegotiated], concessions leased, commercial contracts drawn up, foreign loans agreed and everyday diplomacy undertaken; all of which required the acquisition of what Adamson has called 'Barbarian as a foreign language' (2002: 231). Britain, as the foremost foreign power in China, and after 1860 also in Peking, was at the forefront of these developments. It was no accident, for example, that Britain had arranged for the insertion into the Treaty of Tientsin in 1858 the stipulation that 'All official communications addressed by the Diplomatic and Consular Agents of Her Majesty the Queen to the Chinese Authorities shall, henceforth, be written in English' (Article 50). The same article further stated that communications

> will for the present be accompanied by a Chinese version, but, it is understood that, in the event of there being any difference of meaning between the English and Chinese text, the English Government will hold the sense as expressed in the English text to be the correct sense.

These stipulations made it essential that there were available to the authorities suitably trained Chinese who could read, write and speak the normative standard form of English in order that negotiations could occur and official documentation in English and in Chinese be drafted and agreed. It was also to this end that language institutions such as the Jingshi Tongwen Guan 京师同文馆 [Capital School for Combined Learning] was established in Peking in 1862, to be followed by the opening of the Guang Fangyan Guan 广方言馆 [School for the Diffusion of Languages] in Shanghai in 1864. Another relevant linguistic stipulation was contained in Article 51. This directed that the character for *barbarian* [*yi*, 夷] could no longer be used in Chinese official documents for referring to the British (Spence, 1990: 181).

---

23 Britain's position as China's principal railway creditor was only overtaken in the 1930s due to Japan's intensive railway construction in Manchuria (Davis, 1991: 160).

This neatly built on Article 11 of the 1842 Treaty of Nanking in which 'Instead of terminology such as "petition" and "beg", which foreigners had previously been forced to use, nonderogatory and nonsubordinate terms of address such as "communication", "statement", and "declaration" were to be used in future correspondence between Britain and China' (cited in Spence, 1990: 160). These measures made it a *de facto* necessity for there to be Chinese speakers who were proficient users of the forms of English which applied to such contexts.

The skills acquired by the interpreters and linguists trained in the Jingshi Tongwen Guan in Peking and the Guang Fangyan Guan in Shanghai, and other similar institutions in Canton, Foochow and elsewhere in China, were much needed in the years that followed. Negotiations with foreign powers over such issues as trade tariffs on imports, foreign juridical entitlements, policing of the treaty ports and much else were an almost daily concern for the Manchu authorities. The establishment in 1854 in Shanghai of the foreign-managed – but largely Chinese-staffed – Imperial Maritime Customs Service, which after 1863 was extended to cover the whole of China (Hawks Pott, 1928: 24), was to answer the issues arising from foreign trade and financially related concerns [M-C-M'; M-M'] initially arising in the treaty ports. The Inspectorate, although officially an institution of the Manchu government, was at its most senior levels under the management of suitably qualified representatives [such as ex-consular officials] of the foreign powers of Britain, France and the United States, with – for most of its pre-1949 existence – a British appointee holding the title of inspector general. From 1861 to 1911 this was the Northern Irishman and Sinophile Sir Robert Hart (1835–1911). Although Hart's employers were the Manchu government, his appointment, like that of his predecessor and his successor, had British consular approval. Unlike some of his other foreign colleagues, Hart was also an expert speaker and writer of Chinese. The British were strongly in favour of the foreign inspectorate principle. In the words of the last inspector general (1943–50), Lester Knox Little, an American,

> it seemed to be the one way to make the treaty system effective: foreign inspectors, *speaking English*, unafraid of British, American, or Chinese bullies or scallywags, impervious to threats and uninterested in bribes, could enforce the treaty tariff equally upon all comers.
> (Little, 1975: 6; emphasis added)

The extension of the authority of the Maritime Customs to the whole of China gave the foreign inspectorate an access to the Manchu government and the Qing that was only matched by the British diplomatic Legation in Peking. Hart's expertise in Chinese undoubtedly enhanced this perception, and he was at one point offered the position of British minister at Peking, only to turn it down (Fairbank, Bruner & Matheson, 1975). The advent of the Maritime Customs also gave the English language an institutional position within the Chinese administration which it had not had previously, and despite the expressed commitment in its articles to 'obtaining custom house officials with the necessary qualifications as to probity, vigilance, and knowledge of foreign languages, required for the close observance of treaty and custom house regulations' (Rule 1, cited in Morse, 1913: 367). This was because the Service relied at its more senior levels on an equal familiarity with English as with Chinese for the purposes of interpreting the most significant treaties – which were mostly in English – and for communicating with the different consular administrations in the ports, the most important of which were the British. Fleming (1959) reports, 'In 1899, the Imperial Maritime Customs employed 993 foreigners (of whom 503 were British) and 4611 Chinese' (p. 65). For this reason, the paperwork of the Maritime Customs was kept in both English and Chinese, and to a lesser extent in French and in German. It was also helpful that the inspector general himself was a native speaker of English. Together, these factors made the service an important conduit by which English and other languages were introduced into the Chinese body politic itself.

If the Maritime Customs was the left hand of non-statutory English-speaking influence in China after 1860, the Office for the Management of the Business of All Foreign Countries, or Tsungli Yamen 总理衙门, founded in 1861, was the right hand, because it was through this institution that the foreign affairs of China were conducted up to the time of the Boxer Rebellion (1898–1901). It was the Tsungli Yamen which took responsibility for negotiating the foreign treaties which came after the Convention of Peking, and it was the institution which signed the concessionary agreements for the building of the railways in the scramble which followed the defeat to Japan in 1895. The negotiation of the railway concessions necessitated on the Chinese side a phalanx of trained linguists in the several languages of the European powers, ably assisted by Inspector General Hart, for whom the Yamen officials were his and the Maritime Customs' direct superiors. In addition to these matters, the Tsungli Yamen was also responsible for dealing with issues of foreign protocol in paying homage to the emperor, missionary rights of passage through the interior of China, privileges of extraterritoriality in the treaty ports, the navigation of China's internal waterways, the control of opium sales, and management of the 'coolie' slave trade out of Macao (Spence, 1990: 204; Fairbank et al., 1975: 41n; Marx, 1951: 39). In almost every aspect of China's foreign relations after 1860, English was ever-present, even when agreements were negotiated with other foreign powers such as the Russians and the Germans. British domination of the Maritime Customs, and Hart's pivotal position between this organization and the Tsungli Yamen, meant that all agreements with foreign powers were as a matter of course translated into English as well as Chinese. This particularly applied to agreements over China's indemnity loans [M^E-M'^E], not least because after 1895 it was the Maritime Customs, by now almost as much an extension of the British Foreign Office as an administrative organ of the Chinese state, which managed both the concession agreements and the guarantees on the loans.

British policy in China after 1900 was one of visible intervention on behalf of British business to support and guarantee the loans which private capital made, and which would not have been forthcoming without it. Of particular note in this respect was the relationship which developed between the Foreign Office and the Hongkong and Shanghai Bank. The Bank became the pivot of British economic policy towards China as the British government utilized it to broker financial agreements with the other foreign powers and with the Manchu government so as to ensure 'responsible lending' and to pre-empt a financial crisis which might precipitate an agitation for partition. The lead financiers and senior officials of the Bank, like their foreign office counterparts, were mostly British and of a similar class disposition, in being largely drawn from the landed gentry and the professional classes. Despite its more cosmopolitan outlook at its inception in 1865, the Bank by the 1900s had become a bastion of British-inspired gentlemanly culture in the East (Cain & Hopkins, 2013: 374). This made it eminently suitable as the British political establishment's informal Bank in China and a useful complement to Britain's domination of the Maritime Customs and of the Legations in Peking. By these means Britain exercised a privileged supremacy in finance, commerce, diplomacy and language which other foreign powers in China could not match. Along with the activities of English-speaking missionaries, railway engineers, traders and service providers, it also gave a further dimension to the structural instilment of English in the Chinese state, as well as in centres of political authority and commercial enterprise. But it was the expansion of the railways, or more accurately, popular resentment of foreign indebtedness of which the railways were a symptom, which, initially after 1895 and then more pointedly after 1901, settled the question of the future of the dynasty.

At first, opposition was expressed as a general resentment of modernity and of foreign interference in Chinese ways of life. This is what had inspired the Boxer Rebellion. But as the indebtedness of the regime increased, anger spread from the peasantry to the Chinese gentry, who objected to such an essential object of modernity being in the sole possession of foreigners. They also saw in the willingness of the government to agree to vast foreign loans both political weakness and an over-centralization of power. It was here that Chinese proto-republicanism and opposition to the Qing had its origins (Davis, 1991: 161). China entered into a period of great unease, exacerbated by the venality of the foreign powers, who dogged the Manchu government to agree to more railway loans. To the provincial gentry and the Chinese populace at large the Manchu government appeared to be reconciled to total foreign ownership of China's railway system. Revolutionary nationalist cells allied to the Manchu opposition, the Tongmenghui 同盟会,[24] or Revolutionary Alliance, proliferated in various interior cities, their declared purpose 'to avenge the national disgrace' (cited in Spence, 1990: 263). The death of the Empress Cixi 慈禧 in 1908 and the succession of her three-year-old grandson, Puyi 溥仪, only heightened the sense of doom surrounding the Qing. Matters came to a head with the Manchu agreement to the Hukuang railway loan of 1911. This involved a consortium of Britain, France, Germany and the United States. Such was the sense of public outrage at the loan agreement that the Wuchang garrison mutinied on October 10. Further mutinies in Shansi and Hunan followed. At this point the rule of the Qing began to disintegrate, and on February 12, 1912, the Imperial Court announced the abdication of Puyi.

The foreign powers, realizing in advance that the Qing era was coming to an end, cast about for a successor who could unite China while maintaining commercial continuity. They threw their weight behind the army general Yuan Shih-kai 袁世凯, and on March 10, Yuan was invested as the provisional president of the new Republic of China. The elevation of Yuan occurred over the head of the nationalist Tongmenghui leader-in-exile, Sun Yat-sen 孙中山 (1866–1925), who, as the Qing regime collapsed, returned from over twenty years abroad to lead the revolution. On February 1, 1912, eleven days prior to the enforced abdication of Puyi, Sun had also been proclaimed provisional president of the Republic in Nanking. Sun, knowing that his Tongmenghui revolutionaries would be no match for Yuan's battle-drilled army, elected to stand aside in favour of Yuan on February 14, a move he later bitterly regretted. It is educative to note how far China's circle had turned, that having spent the previous two hundred years attempting to rid itself of the 'red-bearded barbarians', the first-declared provisional president of the Chinese Republic, Sun, should be a fluent speaker of English. But it was not Sun who was favoured by the foreign powers. This was because, in exchange for foreign support for his government, Yuan had agreed to adhere to the economic settlement which had been reached with the Qing, and he committed the new Republic to meeting China's debt obligations and to guaranteeing the concessionary arrangements which had been established in the various foreign 'spheres of influence'. This included respecting the terms of the treaty accords which had been signed with the Qing during the

---

24 The Tongmenghui was a nationalist revolutionary organization. The group had been founded by exiled Chinese in Tokyo in 1905, one of whom was Dr Sun Yat-sen. The Tongmenghui stood against what they saw as the backwardness and corruption of the Qing regime. In this respect, they were the precise opposite of the Boxers. They were also well organized. Their demands were encapsulated in the slogan 'Expel the Manchus, revive the Chinese nation, establish a Republic, distribute land equally among the people' [Quchu da lu, huifu Zhonghua, chuangli minguo, pingjun di quan 驱除鞑虏, 恢复中华, 创立民国, 平均地权].

seventy years which had elapsed since the Treaty of Nanking. The treaty port system would therefore continue as before, having only been rippled by the fall of the dynasty. In all respects, as far as Britain, British capital and English were concerned [M^E-C^E-M'^E; M^E-M'^E], it was to be business as usual: China's indebtedness and the maintenance of its ability to meet its debt obligations again emerged as the cornerstone of British policy in the East.

Invisible chains of English across the longue durée

The financing and building of the railways in different parts of the world, particularly in Latin America and Asia, extended Britain's economic reach and political influence globally. Importantly, it also facilitated the flow of English into zones which were well beyond the boundaries of the territories over which the British had formal or quasi-formal control, not only because the railways transported English along their tracks, but also because the export of British capital as finance and raw materials was responsible for their construction. As Robinson puts it, 'The railroad, up to 1914, was . . . a main generator of those insidious partnerships of imperial, financial, and commercial interests that go into the making of "informal" empire' (1991: 4). This has to be with the understanding that these partnerships were, in one way or another, always developed in the presence of English [M^E-C^E-M'^E; M^E-M'^E], thus making the English language itself a vital component in their development. In the historical narrative of the political economy of Britain's empire, both formal and informal, it is this dimension which is most often overlooked.

> The vast scale of British trade, the fleets of merchant shipping, the treasure chest of overseas investment and the resources it commanded were widely seen as the real embodiment of British world power. They supplied the economic energy to sustain the show of empire and pay for its defence. They formed the invisible chains that bound the visible empire of dependencies and settler states to their far off metropole.
> (Darwin, 2009: 141–142)

The involvement of English in the 'invisible chains' of imperial expansion is perhaps just too obvious as to have been rendered invisible by imperial economic historians like Darwin, Cain, Hopkins, Robinson and Gallagher. Yet, it is just this invisibleness which merits giving English more careful consideration in any historical account. Not only does it add a further dimension to our understanding of the dynamics involved in the global expansion of British power both before and after 1850, it also assists in explaining the spread of English in the semi-peripheral and peripheral regions of the capitalist world-economy. It also adds a new dimension to the account of what came later, once Britain's hegemony went into decline and was displaced by the hegemony of the United States. What changed was that after World War I 'Britain was no longer in a position to supply sufficient capital to fuel the international economy' (Cain & Hopkins, 2013: 654). Despite this running down, Britain, through the City of London and an admixture of military power and aggressive diplomacy, had spread its capital networks over the world. These carved their presence into the global terrain and made it possible for English to become the predominant global language of the whole of the twentieth century. When understood in this sense, the hyper-globalization of English which came after 1945 with the hegemony of the United States can be seen to have had its origins in the forward positions which the circulation of British capital had enabled across the *longue durée*. How the global language baton was passed from British capital to US capital after 1914 and the form that global US capital domination took is the subject of the next chapter.

4 The political economy of global English, 1918–1979

Handing over the baton: transition, 1870–1918

When considering the global spread of English through the nineteenth and twentieth centuries, it is evident that at some point Britain began to lose its position as the leading power in the capitalist world-system, to be succeeded, as fate would have it, by another English-speaking nation, the United States. Views differ as to when this transition actually occurred –for example, after 1870, 1918, 1930 or 1945; but what is not in doubt is that it is the coincidence of this shared relation, in combination with each nation's unrivalled economic and military power, which was responsible for guaranteeing the continuity of English as the most global, and the most vehicular, of all the world's languages (De Swann, 2001; Phillipson, 2008; Park & Wee, 2012; Lemberg, 2018). It has been a traditional standpoint in much imperial history, as well as in British history schoolbooks, that the last quarter of the nineteenth century is the significant point at which Britain's decline begins, and that the watershed moment is about 1870 with the dual challenges of industrializing Germany and the United States. From 1870, Britain's share of world trade began to witness a shrinkage. In 1860, Britain had accounted for 25 per cent of the total volume of world trade, France 11 per cent and the United States 9 per cent (Woodruff, 1966, Table VII/12: 313).[1] By 1913 it was 17 per cent, as against 13 per cent for Germany and 11 per cent for the United States. But despite the challenge from Germany and from the United States, 'neither was strong enough to displace Britain from its position as the leader of world trade, finance, and investment' (ibid: 275–276). As late as 1938, Britain's share of world trade [14 per cent] was still greater than the United States' [11 per cent] and of that of each of its main European rivals, Germany [9 per cent] and France [5 per cent]. In the case of Europe, this was because most of the European nations had, like France, concentrated the bulk of their trading interests on the European market. By

---

1 The statistical data is from Woodruff (1966). Page numbers are indicated where they are available, or the table number is given.

comparison, like its language, 'Britain's trade was dispersed over the whole world' (ibid: 276).

At the outbreak of World War I, Britain accounted for 44 per cent of the world's total foreign investments. This compared with just 7.8 per cent for the United States (ibid: 154). This level of disparity was repeated from continent to continent. In Latin America, for example, British investments were 42 per cent of the total, of which one-third was in Argentina, one-quarter in Brazil, and one quarter in Mexico. The rest was in Chile, Uruguay, Cuba and Peru. The United States came next with 19 per cent, and then France and Germany with 18 and 10 per cent respectively (ibid: 122, 154). Down to 1914, patterns of foreign investment in India, Asia and Africa were notable for how far Britain was ahead of all of its competitors, including the United States. In China, for example, Britain's share was 37 per cent, Russia's and Germany's was each 16 per cent, France's was 9 per cent, and the United States' was 3 per cent (pp. 128, 154). As Woodruff notes, 'This broad picture of capital formation and distribution in India and China holds good for Indonesia, Malaya, Siam, Indo-China, the Philippines, Burma, [and] Ceylon' (p. 129). In Japan too, around half of total foreign investment came from Britain, in war bonds for financing Japan's war with Russia (1904–5), and prior to that with China (1894–5), and for investments in public utilities such as the railways (Wall, 1964). On the eve of World War I, at $500 million, British investments in Japan were ten times the figure for the United States (Woodruff, 1966: 154). It is against this backdrop that Cain and Hopkins (2013) identify the 1850–1914 period as one in which British capital was both dominant and expanding, and in which '[British] capital flows funded economic development and "nation-building" across the world' (ibid: 651–652). In 1938, in Europe, Latin America, Asia, Oceania[2] and Africa, British foreign investment was still way ahead of US investment. The United States only came remotely close in Latin America [36.7 per cent to Britain's 43.4 per cent] (ibid: Table IV/4); elsewhere, the US was far behind. In Asia and Oceania, for example, the figures were 55 per cent (Britain) and 18.5 per cent (United States), and in Africa they were 53.1 per cent and 3.72 per cent respectively (ibid: Table IV/4). This difference was also reflected in the transition from normative British English to normative American English as the hegemonic standard language form of the world-system – it took until the mid-1960s for this transition more fully to occur. When it did happen, this was in large part due to the Cold War, the expanded global spread of US capital, and the proto-colonization by the United States of much of Latin America and non-communist East Asia (Rabe, 2012; Bevins, 2020).

The US world-economy that emerged was always going to be officially, and for the most part factually, an informal empire rather than a formal one (Gindin & Panitch, 2017). Even with America's rising global economic

2 Oceania is designated by New Zealand and Australia.

presence after 1870, the US government understood that to acquire a territorial empire to rival or displace that of the British was not only unrealistic but was to make an hypocrisy of the very existence of the United States and its official 'founding myth' (Panitch & Gindin, 2012: 38). In spite of this, in the years between the US defeat of Spain in 1898 and US entry into World War II in 1941, this hypocrisy was to be courted closely, and in some instances fully embraced. By 1918, for example, the United States had occupied, assimilated or extended protectorate status to the Philippines (1898), Hawaii (1898), Puerto Rico (1898), Guam (1898), Cuba (1898), (American) Samoa (1900), Wake Island (1899), the Panama Canal Zone (1903),[3] the Dominican Republic (1905), Nicaragua (1916), Haiti (1916) and the (US) Virgin Islands (1917) (Rosenberg, 1982: 47). Otherwise, in the areas it considered its spheres of influence, especially Latin America, US power was projected primarily through the establishment of US commercial advantage by means of financial indebtedness, support for semi-feudal *latifundist* autocracies, and when all else failed, the sharp shock of military intervention. The US occupation of the Philippines soon took on the character of colonial permanence, with Congress and the administration of William McKinley (1897–1901) viewing the Philippines as the United States' Hong Kong in the East (Rosenberg, 1982: 43). American English was subsequently vigorously promoted there (Lemberg, 2018: 563; May, 1980; Go, 2000; Tupas, 2003). Alongside these developments the US made efforts to share in the railway bonanza in China and to make good on the United States' strategic and commercial position alongside the British in Shanghai, and later at Peking (see Chapter 3). What quickly emerged was an overriding US commitment to an 'open door' for US products and US capital investment, even when this was not readily reciprocated by the US itself. In addition, a cornerstone of US commercial policy, which was to be carried through the entire twentieth century, was to seek the agreement of states to an English-language-scripted international rule of law governing the movement and investment of foreign capital, US capital in particular [as M-M' and as M-C-M']. The intended effect was to extend the principle of extraterritoriality to US capital investments and to US property overseas, so as to protect both from the threat of local confiscation.[4] In support of this principle, 'the US ended up supporting local dictators and landed bourgeoisies, thereby fossilizing social structures, blocking economic development, and creating the conditions for continued political instability and revolts' (Panitch & Gindin, 2012: 41). Where these measures were not sufficient, it also used force: '[B]etween

---

3 The US did not give up occupation of the Panama Canal Zone until 1979.
4 'Exported capital feels most comfortable ... when its own state in in complete control of the new territory' (Hilferding, 1981 [1910]: 322).

1869 and 1897 the US Navy, as small and under-equipped as it was, made no less than 5,980 ports of call to protect American commercial shipping in Argentina, Brazil, Chile, Nicaragua, Panama, Columbia, and elsewhere in Latin America' (Panitch & Gindin, 2012: 353n).

While preparations were being made for a new economic world order on one side of the Atlantic, on the other, the European Great Powers were preparing for a world war. No longer able to contain their rivalries, of which one part came down to market share and another down to the overweening arrogance of its elites, the European powers allowed themselves to be drawn into a war which in horror and death would surpass anything which had gone before – at least in Europe.[5] One aspect which made 1914–18 a 'global' war, apart from its extent and the vast number of casualties, was its internationalism, with soldiers from many parts of the world drafted in to fight or to act as labour on the supply lines (Hobsbawm, 1995: 23). In addition to large numbers of army recruits from the British 'White' settler colonies of Canada, Australia, New Zealand and South Africa, there were battalions of Indians, Africans and Chinese also drafted in, either as soldiers or as indentured labour. This had a diffusional effect on the uses of English and French, especially in the western theatre, as was noted at the time.

> An immediate effect of the presence of millions of English-speaking British and Americans in France and Belgium in the present war, will be the learning of French by English, and the learning of English by French and Belgians; to which sentiment will give a new impetus in making English the most favored foreign language in their schools after the war. English is already the language of commerce in every important port of the world. Even the Germans have seen the advantage of making English one of the most-studied languages, aside from their own, in their schools.
>
> (Eno, 1918: 69)

Britain and [from 1915] the US were at the head of the anti-German war effort, so making English the foremost language of the anti-German alliance, more so than French. This too left its linguistic mark on Europe [e.g. in the towns and villages that English-speaking troops passed through], and on the Indians, Chinese and Africans who participated, and who then either went home or dispersed themselves to other parts of the world where their English-language skills might come in use, such as in extraterritorial police constabularies, in the service industries at main centres of commerce, and on the building of the railways.

---

5 Approximately 17 million died in World War I, but upwards of 20–30 million died during the rebellion of the Taipings in 1850–64.

Networks of English and the rise of US capital, 1918–1945

The end of the war found Britain solvent but heavily indebted to the United States (Arrighi, 2010: 279). The most pressing issues for those nations that emerged as victors – Britain, the United States, France and Italy – were to place responsibility for the war on Germany and to exact retribution. This they did – particularly at the behest of France – in the form of swingeing reparations, a net reduction of Germany's land mass in Europe, and the confiscation of all its overseas territories in Africa and the Pacific. A number of these, such as Tanganyika, Kamerun and Togoland, or parts of them, later emerged as British protectorates (Hobsbawm, 1995; Wallerstein, 2000 [1973]; Cain & Hopkins, 2013; Darwin, 2009). In the aftermath of the war, despite being hugely indebted, Britain remained economically powerful owing to its continued dominance of world trade and sterling's ongoing function as the international reserve currency. But, for the first time, it was joined in this by the US dollar (Arrighi, 2010: 279). The strength of both sterling and the dollar was built on gold, of which the greater part of the world's reserves were stored in the vaults of the Bank of England and the relatively recently established US Federal Reserve, which had come into being following the US economic crash of 1907 (Panitch & Gindin, 2012: 42–43).

A chief concern on both the anglophone sides of the Atlantic was to re-establish the pre-war international monetary system, which from 1815 had been based on the gold standard,[6] the British pound, and increasingly after 1850 – when the first international communication cables were laid – English. The gold standard had been placed in indeterminate suspension in 1914 following Britain's entry into the war, which had led to a panicked run on sterling. Following the catastrophe of the war, the almost universal conviction emerged, backed by the newly established – and US-inspired – League of Nations, that only by re-establishing the pre-1914 system and its natural corollary free trade, 'this time on solid foundations', could future wars between the European powers be avoided and economic prosperity secured (Polanyi, 2001 [1944]: 23; Arrighi, 2010: 281). The US administration of Woodrow Wilson (1913–21) and of his successors to 1933, Harding, Coolidge and Hoover, viewed the restoration of the pre-war system as necessary to US interests on the basis that stable currencies would lead to stable trade and thereby secure the peace that was necessary for the United States to consolidate its rapidly expanding economic position in the world. It took time and a plethora of international conferences [in which English and French were usually the official languages], but in 1922, the Republican

---

6 The gold standard posited an equal value and convertibility between a particular denomination of currency and a particular weight of gold. In this way, a dominant currency could 'anchor' the international monetary system so as to create a relative stability of exchange rates between different currencies. In the nineteenth century, the currency which served as this anchor was the British pound sterling.

administration of Warren G Harding (1921–3), felt able to restore gold convertibility with the dollar, and in 1925 – more in hope than expectation – Britain followed suit with sterling (Skidelsky, 2003: 355–356). A shaky economic recovery in Europe was made all the more fragile by the economic consequences of the Russian Revolution of 1917[7] and the 'economic revenge' which the European victors had meted out upon Germany at Versailles in 1919 (Cain & Hopkins, 2013: 451). In the absence of liquidity in Europe, which was not forthcoming from the main holder of it – the United States – countries turned increasingly inwards. Tariff barriers, import quotas and capital controls followed, as the continental European nations struggled to stabilize their currencies. As Polanyi notes, 'While the intent was the freeing of trade, the effect was its strangulation' (2001 [1944]: 28).

Despite the difficulties elsewhere, the 1920s was a boom period for the US economy as it imposed high tariffs against imports from Europe and the rest of the world, while insisting on their lowering elsewhere. The Smoot-Hawley Bill of 1930 raised tariffs on foreign imports still higher, by an eye-watering 23 per cent. In spite of these measures, or because of them, productivity in the United States outstripped that of the debtor nations in Europe, and US capital exports, often in the form of loans to Latin America, expanded rapidly (Panitch & Gindin, 2012: 49). Congress-orchestrated protectionism and the strength of the US domestic and export economy made it difficult for the debtor nations in Europe and elsewhere to compete and also to service their debts. In lieu of debt repayments, the US built up a large portfolio of foreign assets, totalling some $8 billion by the end of the 1920s, 'with a rapidity . . . which . . . is unparalleled in the experience of any major creditor in modern times' (Dobb, 1963: 323, cited in Arrighi, 2010: 282). In anticipation of post-1945 IMF-backed structural adjustment programmes, US private 'financial advisors' were despatched to client states around the world to counsel [usually through English-speaking interpreters] on the conditionality requirements of US loans [hence M^E-M'^E], which included lowered tariffs for US exports, domestic budgetary management, and the extension of extraterritorial guarantees against the confiscation of US capital and property (cf. Hilferding, 1981 [1910]: 322). In the early twentieth century, this practice, which had been adopted for some of the US debtor nations in Latin America, was extended to include China, Columbia, Chile, Poland, Germany, South Africa, Ecuador, Bolivia, Turkey, the Dominican Republic, Peru and Iran (Panitch & Gindin, 2012: 51). US conditionality

---

7 The Russian Revolution of 1917 may have been a Russian affair, but the United States and Britain took the lead in making it an international one by militarily intervening on the side of the anti-Bolshevik [and therefore anti-socialist] 'White Army'. The US alone contributed 13,000 troops to the effort. Meanwhile, on the home front, its newspapers indulged in an orgy of propaganda concerning the threat that Bolshevik Russia posed to American civilization, setting a tone which was to continue almost uninterruptedly until the final collapse of the Soviet Union in 1991 (see Blum, 2014).

loans in the 1920s marked the beginnings of a uniquely American model for the economic structuring of the global economy. The loans, supported by the outward projection of US technical, corporate, military, religious, cultural and linguistic might, in addition to the requirement of adoption of the gold standard, contributed to the establishment of US global capital and communication networks [M^E-C^E-M'^E; M^E-M'^E] which after 1945 were principally structured through American English (Cain & Hopkins, 2013; Harvey, 2003; Lemberg, 2018; Panitch & Gindin, 2012; Phillipson, 2008, 2017; Rosenberg, 1982). These built upon the networks which had already been established in the pre-1914 era by the British [e.g. in East Asia, the Middle East and Latin America], or they forged them anew.

Hoping to take advantage of low borrowing rates in the surging US economy, US banks and private investors began calling in foreign loans, which created domestic liquidity problems for the rest of the world, leading to rapidly rising unemployment and recession in Europe, Latin America and East Asia. The Federal Reserve, in an attempt to reduce excessive domestic borrowing, then compounded the problems of its debtors by increasing US interest rates (Arrighi, 2010: 282). When in October 1929 reports started to come in of some domestic-based US banks having overstretched their loans, a wave of panic selling started which wiped out the New York exchange. In Europe and elsewhere, faced with capital flight on a colossal scale, affected nations were forced to introduce exchange controls in order to protect their currencies. The high US interest rates put enormous pressure on sterling and eventually forced Britain to devalue the pound by coming off gold in 1931. In the words of Arrighi, 'The suspension of the British pound in September 1931 led to the final destruction of the single web of world commercial and financial transactions on which the fortunes of the City of London were based' (2010: 282–283). With the abandonment of stable currencies, 'world capitalism retreated into the igloos of its nation-state economies and their associated empires' (Hobsbawm, 1991: 132, cited in Arrighi, ibid: 283).

With the abandonment of the British commitment to gold in 1931, the United States was determined not to follow suit with the dollar. This was despite heightened market speculation that a devaluation was imminent. The response of the Federal Reserve was to ratchet up interest rates in order to protect the dollar, but this only made the recession worse, both at home and abroad. Finally, in 1933, in a bid to end the market speculation and boost the domestic economy, the US government severed the parity of the dollar with gold, so allowing its value to fall, and for the rest of the decade the US turned inwards towards Congress-directed international isolation and Franklin D Roosevelt's New Deal. The retreat of capital globally, particularly of the US and British kind, and the return of protectionism and exchange-rate instability were undoubtedly contributory factors in the confluence of circumstances which led to World War II. The tensions which arose in Europe due to the contraction in global liquidity were exacerbated as well as exploited by the turn to Nazism in Germany, which was itself a product of the calculated vindictiveness of the economic and political settlement of 1919. In contrast, from the perspective of the global spread of English, US isolationism and the retreat of US capital after 1933 was not matched by the erasure of the anglophone linguistic networks which the dissemination of British and US capital had up to then made possible. This is because, as capital retreated, it left its imprint on the capitalist world-system in the communications networks it left behind. It was by means of these networks that English – as a 'network good' (Reksulak et al., 2004: 273) – had been able to flow [M^E-C^E-M'^E; M^E-M'^E]. English, in mostly British and American normative standard formats, had accompanied capital via trade, investment, treaties, communications technologies, extraterritorial arrangements and clientelism, as well as through institutional and sociocultural transfer, in the form of banks, business corporations, proselytizing religious groups, conscripted soldiers, ex-patriot communities and the service sectors which provided for them (Rosenberg, 1982; Bickers, 1998, 2010a). Although capital retreated with the severing of the pound's and then the dollar's links to gold, the networks through which capital had flowed remained and were strongly marked by the presence of English. As the post-1945 world unfolded, these networks would take on a renewed importance as the United States finally displaced Britain at the centre of the world-system. In respect of language, culture, capital accumulation and the projection of military power, the impact of the US on the world-system would be even more profound than that of Britain in the previous century. If the 1918–45 era was the incubus period for the rise of US capital and the political economy of global English 'American-style', the period after 1945 was to be the era of their opening into world domination.

English and the institutional structuring of the world-economy, post-1945

The Second World War witnessed the largest mobilization of land, sea and air forces in history, involving sixty-one participant countries and six hundred and ninety million service personnel, with theatres of war in Europe, Asia, Africa, the Middle East, and across the oceans of the Atlantic and the Pacific. Some 16.1 million Americans saw service in the war, with a further nine million recruits coming from the British Empire. This included five million from Britain itself and 2.5 million from India. At least another 1.5 million were provided by the 'White' settler dominions of Canada, Australia, New Zealand and South Africa.[8] There were also

---

[8] The statistics which are supplied in this section are taken from the following sites:
www.statisticbrain.com/world-war-ii-statistics/
www.bbc.co.uk/news/world-asia-india-33105898
www.nationalarchives.gov.uk/battles/dday/
www.wwiifoundation.org/students/wwii-facts-figures/ Accessed February 20, 2017.

sizeable English-proficient contingents from the Caribbean, from East and West Africa, as well as from neutral countries such as the Irish Republic. Smaller nations in the British Empire also supplied volunteers. While the great majority of nations that participated in the war against the Axis alliance of Germany, Italy and Japan were not English-speaking, British and US leadership in several key theatres, along with the numbers of US, British and Empire troops, and ancillary personnel involved [e.g. as nurses, drivers, mechanics, cooks, tailors], nevertheless made it a very English-speaking war (Bentley & Grebstein, 1956) and a simultaneously multilingual one as well. Poles, French, Indians and Czechs, for example, served alongside British pilots in the Royal Air Force, and the Fourteenth Army which liberated Burma in 1945 was made up of British, West African and Indian units under overall British authority. The Fourteenth Army was undoubtedly a highly multilingual force, but its command structure, as with the Shanghai Municipal Police, was entirely configured in English. US forces, although less inclined to operate with multinational combat divisions in the same way as the British did, were still very multilingual outfits because of the fact of the US largely being a nation of migrants.[9] All in all, the Second World War, by being directed and fought in the way that it was, and especially in the way that it ended, provided the ideological and military platform for US economic and linguistic domination after 1945. This was to be the era of the *Pax Americana* and of the deliberate manipulation of the world-economy in the interests of US capital and power.

What was required was a structuring of the world-economy to reflect the economic and strategic priorities of the US in the post-war era. This came initially in the form of the 1944 Bretton Woods Agreement, which promised a return to a stable currency order. The agreement also created the IMF and the International Bank for Reconstruction and Development (IBRD), later known as the World Bank. Under the agreement the gold standard returned, and currencies were fixed to the US dollar at $35 dollars to an ounce of gold. There were forty-four signatory nations to the Bretton Woods Agreement, but the principal architects were the Americans and the British, in that order. Signatories to the agreement were given reassurances that it was

---

9 It was also a nation which included African Americans who were descended from slaves, and Native Americans whose ancestry predated Columbus. In 1945, 1.2 million African Americans were serving in the war, but in segregated units.* As many as 44,000 Native Americans also served in the war. Navajo speakers were used as front-line radio operators in the Asia-Pacific theatre because their languages were considered to be indecipherable to the Japanese.† Chocktaw speakers had been employed in the First World War and had confounded German intelligence.

* www.nationalww2museum.org/assets/pdfs/african-americans-in-world.pdf Accessed February 16, 2017.

† http://armedforcesmuseum.com/the-role-of-native-americans-during-world-war-ii/ Accessed February 16, 2017.

in their interests to follow US policy preferences, that is, the decisions of the Federal Reserve, in order to optimize stability. It is worth mentioning too that the document that was finally drawn up amid 'the great variety of unintelligible tongues'[10] was written in English, before being translated into other languages (Schuler & Rosenberg, 2013; Cooper, 2014). For the British economist John Maynard Keynes (1883–1946), it was the culmination of a life's work, or was presented as such. But in the words of his biographer, Robert Skidelsky,

> Keynes gave the Bretton Woods Agreement its distinction, not its substance. The Agreement reflected the views of the American, not the British, Treasury. . . . The Agreement was shaped not by Keynes's *General Theory*, but by the US desire for an updated gold standard as a means of liberalising trade. If there was an underlying ideology, it was [the US Secretary of the Treasury] Morganthau's determination to concentrate economic power in Washington.
>
> (Skidelsky, 2003: 767)

Bretton Woods marked a tectonic shift in the world-system away from Britain [and normative British English] and towards the United States [and normative American English], which both Keynes and the British recognized but were in no position to resist. It also fundamentally changed the dynamics of money capital in the world-system from one based largely on private bankers and financiers to international organizations which were primarily concerned with the welfare and security of the capitalist world-system (Arrighi, 2010: 287). The shift in global fiduciary power from international private banking in the City of London to the IMF and the World Bank had the effect of placing the US Federal Reserve at the centre of the world monetary system, working in concert with the central banks of nations which were allied to the US, such as Britain and Japan, and the European Bank of International Settlements in Basel. Adding the finishing touches to this new global centrality, the IMF and the World Bank were constructed according to systems of administration and governance which were modelled on US institutional and linguistic practices (Gardner, 1956; Harvey, 2003; Arrighi, 2012). They also had American directors. Although the pretence was maintained of a strict separation between the financial role of the new institutions in the world-economy and the political implications arising from that role, few were under any illusions regarding which nation would exercise the greatest influence over them. In a memo of the International Trade Policy Division of the US State Department in October 1945, it was stated, 'If we tickle the palms of foreigners with a few billions [they will] conduct their international economic affairs according to the pattern we advocate'

---

10 John Maynard Keynes, cited in Panitch and Gindin (2012: 80).

(cited in Rosenberg, 1982: 194). The pattern that was advocated, and which the IMF and the World Bank were in effect charged with following, was one of low or negligible tariffs on the movement of US [and other nations'] goods and capital within a stable international currency framework tied to a renewed gold standard that was based primarily on the dollar and managed though the medium of English [M^E-C^E-M'^E; M^E-M'^E].

What the war had demonstrated to ordinary people and governments was what could be achieved through carefully orchestrated state intervention in the economy and collective popular endeavour. In the advanced capitalist countries of Western Europe, and also in the communist East, this sentiment carried through strongly into the post-war era and was given economic credibility by Keynes' *General Theory of Employment* (1936), in which Keynes had argued that the principal cause of the Great Depression was a scarcity of liquidity in the affected economies [rather than workers pricing themselves too highly, as the classical economists would have it],[11] and that in such circumstances it ought to be the role of governments to take 'an ever greater responsibility for directly organising investment' (Keynes, 1936: 164) and to do this by means of the fiscal stimulation of aggregate demand, in order to produce, as an overarching goal of economic policy, the conditions of full employment. For Keynes, keeping people in employment through a 'socialisation of investment' (ibid: 378) would generate effective demand, which would in turn support employment that would create further demand, in a virtuous circle. It was by managing demand, not wages, that full employment could therefore be achieved and, according to Keynes, with an acceptable cost in terms of inflation (Skidelsky, 2003: 536).[12] Roosevelt's New Deal in the 1930s, as a response to the Depression, had been just such an exercise in Keynesian demand management, and it was this which Keynes now advocated for Europe, with the assistance of the Marshall Plan. In East Asia, the national-economic solution for Japan, South Korea and Taiwan, bankrolled by the US and based on direct government subsidy, was to some extent textbook Keynes,[13] and enabled these nations to become in the space

---

11 The classical liberal perspective could not explain the Great Depression, as the event did not correspond to the prognostications of classical liberal theory in which such a generalized crisis was denied (Harvey, 2010: 67; Skidelsky, 2003: 530).
12 'A moderate [increase] in effective demand, coming on a situation on which there is widespread unemployment, *may spend itself very little in raising prices* and mainly in increasing employment' (Keynes, cited in Skidelsky, 2003: 536, emphasis added).
13 That said, the idea that Keynes advocated nationalized industries and 'hands-on' government planning is wide of the mark. Rather, Keynes was a bourgeois paternalist, as well as an instinctive elitist in the gentlemanly capitalist tradition, who did not readily subscribe to the notion of a democracy of the people. In the words of his biographer Robert Skidelsky, 'He was no pluralist. . . . He wanted to devolve and decentralise only down to the level of Top People' (2003: 365).

of a generation advanced capitalist economies themselves, complete with their own internal contradictions, social inequalities, economic crises and policy positions on the necessity of English. Another effect in the West was that due to the full-employment policies, 'the "Marxian" mechanism [of the predicted increased immiseration of the worker] had substantially been blocked' (Pivetti, 2015: 151; parenthesis added). This was because 'Rises in wages . . . were not allowed to be answered by rises in unemployment; hence they *lasted*, thereby sustaining consumption growth' (ibid). In short, the economic boom of the post-war era, especially in Western Europe, was based on an acceptance that capital could no longer remain indifferent to mass unemployment, huge disparities in wealth and widespread poverty, because these were the things which made the whole system vulnerable to Soviet-inspired communism (ibid). Therefore, a new social contract had to be developed, which in the short run was detrimental to returns on capital, particularly in Western Europe.

The indebtedness of the European nations at the end of the war and the need to rebuild their broken economies and infrastructures gave them little option but to accede gratefully to the terms of the Bretton Woods Agreement and to the loans which its architecture made possible. The US loan strategy for Europe, known as the Marshall Plan, was matched by a Truman Doctrine for Greece and Turkey and what was known as Point Four for the developing nations. Each of these arrangements were also negotiated and then given documentary reality using English as the primary language. In 1947, the US also underwrote as chief signatory the General Agreement on Tariffs and Trade (GATT) and pressed for other nations to sign up to it (Rosenberg, 1982: 193). The overall ideology of the era, as far as political economy was concerned, was the promotion by the US of a liberal-developmentalist approach to economic advancement (see Chapter 1), which was particularly directed at Latin America but was official US policy for most of the rest of the world as well. The international regulatory and institutional frameworks which were established, in combination with their underlying liberal-developmentalist discourses of openness, low tariffs and free trade, were responsible for the final dismantling of the nineteenth-century British-directed system of capital accumulation and its re-centralization on the US (Arrighi, 2010: 304; Wallerstein, 2000 [1988]: 356–357; Harvey, 2003: 54–55).

Cold War and the structuring of English in East Asia

In the immediate aftermath of the war, the economic uncertainty which existed across Europe and the world had made the US a safe haven for foreign capital and so given it unparalleled reserves of liquidity. It was upon these reserves that the various administration plans for rebuilding Europe and rejuvenating the world-economy were based. The government saw that without economic growth in Europe and elsewhere, US consumers would not be able to buy the foreign products which their war-enhanced incomes enabled them to buy, and neither would consumers in the rest of the world be able to purchase US goods. If not addressed, it was feared that the imbalance in global liquidity could lead to over-production bottlenecks in the US and mass layoffs. But even though this was apparent, private capital [as is the norm] was reluctant to lend overseas without cast-iron guarantees. Roosevelt also had to negotiate the extreme reluctance of Congress to relinquish control of the vast reserves of liquidity which the US had built up. With Roosevelt's death in 1945 and his replacement by Harry S Truman, the impasse was broken by what Arrighi refers to as 'the "invention" of the Cold War' (2010: 304): 'The genius of Truman and of his advisors was to attribute the outcome of systemic circumstances which no particular agency had created or controlled to the allegedly subversive dispositions of the other military superpower, the USSR' (ibid). The US regularly demonstrated throughout the Cold War that it was not averse to supporting brutal dictatorships and the financing of rebel armies and coup d'états if it suited its strategic economic and geopolitical interests (Rabe, 2012; Blum, 2014; Bevins, 2020). The Cold War viewed in these terms was a game of capital flows, in which the accumulation of violence and oppression were treated as collaterally acceptable so long as capital was also able to accumulate and the violence, when it occurred, was confined to countries and zones ideally well beyond the borders of the US. States within the orbit of the US world-economy, which were willing to abide by its rules and to participate in its US-dominated international institutions, such as South Korea [after 1953] and Chile [after 1973], would receive preferential treatment. They would also in this context turn out to be the most amenable to English – e.g. by making it an important language in the school curriculum and often a requirement for university entrance as well (Matear, 2008; Kim, 2011; Paik, 2018). States electing to place themselves outside the US world-economy, such as Cuba [after 1959] and Vietnam [after 1975], and which were antagonistically inclined towards its institutions or choosing not participate in them at all [e.g. IMF, World Bank, GATT] would be isolated and punished. They were also likely to be the most resistant to English, with Russian and Chinese being popular alternatives.

With the surrender of Japan in 1945, following the dropping of US-built atomic devices on the cities of Hiroshima and Nagasaki, the balance of geopolitical and linguistic power in East Asia was permanently transformed. For the first time in more than fifty years of Japanese incursion into its territory, China was on the side of the victors in a war with Japan but now found itself mired in a civil war of its own. In the Treaty of Shimonoseki in 1895, China had been forced to recognize the formal independence of the tributary state of Korea and the cession of Taiwan to Japan. The treaty gave Japan effective suzerainty over Korea and was a preliminary to the country's formal annexation in 1911. The atomic annihilation of Japan's will to fight in 1945 suddenly opened a vacuum which the allied powers, led by the US, eagerly sought to fill. Japan and the southern part of Korea up to the 38th parallel were occupied by allied troops under US command and US army military governments installed. North of the parallel, Korea was occupied by the forces of the Soviet Union. In both zones, the liberating powers sought to impose compliant Korean regimes while outwardly expressing the desire to see Korea united as one country. In Burma, Malaya, Singapore and Hong Kong, the pre-war British colonial administrations which had been deposed by Japan were restored. In China, the defeat brought to an end to years of Japanese aggression and enabled Chinese forces to recover Manchuria, which had been invaded and annexed by Japan in 1931. China had been at war with Japan continuously since 1937[14] – a fact made possible by a truce between the nationalist Kuomintang under Chiang Kai-shek 蔣介石 (1887–1975) and the Communists under Mao Zedong 毛泽东 (1893–1976), whose armies united in the common cause of expelling the Japanese from China. Once both the USSR and the US entered the war a few months apart in 1941, the Chiang Kai-shek government, wishing to align itself with the likely victors, followed suit and formally declared war on Japan.[15] But until final victory came in 1945, the duplicitous Chiang secretly kept a line of communication open with the Japanese, in the event that Japan should emerge victorious instead (Epstein, 1956: 109–111). The sudden termination of Japanese resolve, in addition to ending the war, also had the calculated consequence that the Soviet Union would have no say in the post-war settlement in Japan and therefore no say in its linguistic settlement either. The US also took the opportunity presented by the defeat to send large numbers of troops to Manchuria to facilitate a Japanese surrender to the Kuomintang. Truman and his Secretary of State Dean Acheson's fear was that Japan's defeat would give Mao's Communists the upper hand in China, and so they threw their weight behind Chiang [and his charismatic American-sounding English-speaking wife, Song Mei-ling 宋美龄],[16] mainly in the form of US strategic supplies and training for the nationalist armies, in a move that was to set a precedent for later US practice during the Cold War. A Sino-American Trade Treaty which guaranteed tariff-free access for US capital and goods was also quickly agreed with the Nationalists. Strikes over the Nationalist government's economic policies, and public opposition to US interference, were brutally suppressed by the Chiang regime. But this did little to quell the huge swell of popular support which was building

---

14 At the time of writing, the Chinese government has officially revised the date at which war between China and Japan commenced to 1931 and the annexation of Manchuria.
15 Until 1941, although China and Japan were at war, no formal declaration of war had been made.
16 She spoke English with a southern Georgia American accent picked up from her schooldays in the US.

behind the Communists in the interior, who demonstrated in every village they 'liberated' their commitment to land reform, the eradication of power abuses,[17] and a new deal for the Chinese people. As the civil war dragged on into 1948, Kuomintang resistance began to disintegrate. Morale was low, and a general unwillingness to fight against fellow Chinese spread through Nationalist ranks, especially when its soldiers learned of the land reforms which Mao's advancing forces implemented as they advanced. Many Kuomintang fighters and units chose to switch allegiance rather than fight the liberators of their home towns and villages. The retreat of the Nationalists became a rout through 1949, with what was left of the Kuomintang armies, its leadership and its support base fleeing to Taiwan. With the mainland emptied of resistance, on October 1, 1949, the People's Republic of China was declared.

This was not the outcome which Truman and Acheson had hoped for, but the fact of it was to have a profound effect on the kind of East Asia which was to emerge, not only in respect of the political and economic alignments which later materialized between a communist mainland China and a US-dominated Philippines, Taiwan, South Korea and Japan, but also in respect of English as the newly preferred principal foreign language of post-war non-communist East Asia. The Philippines was a US colony until 1946 when it was given its independence. But it remained closely aligned with the US, which had a number of military bases there. Taiwan, under Chiang Kai-shek, was also strongly pro-US, and both Japan and South Korea were under US occupation. The 1949 Revolution fundamentally changed the geopolitics of the Asia-Pacific region, but the timing of it was also significant because it coincided with the rise of McCarthyism in the US and, from an anti-communist perspective, the almost convenient outbreak of the Korean War one year later. The Chinese Revolution came as a gift to the narcissist-demagogue-cum-Senator Joseph R McCarthy (1908–57), whose House Un-American Activities Committee made it the pretext for a witch hunt of supposed communist infiltrators in the US government and wider establishment who were deemed responsible for allowing – and plotting to allow – the 'loss of China' to occur (Ambrose, 1993; Blum, 2014). The linguistic, cultural and economic 'Americanization' of East Asia in the years following 1949, in addition to being a reaction to events on the ground, was in large measure also a reflex of domestic McCarthyism and 'the great fear' of communism which this provoked. The emerging Cold War policy positions of the Truman administration (1945–53) allied with 'Red Scare' McCarthyism at home made the US and its brand of capitalism appear – to US citizens and sympathetic international observers – the natural ideological alternative

---

17 In this period China, in addition to suffering from foreign depredations of its territory, was also plagued by endemic official corruption and warlordism in the provinces.

to Marxist-Leninist and Maoist communism. It also willingly positioned the US as the global power whose responsibility it was to protect the 'free world' [i.e. free to accumulate capital] from the 'Soviet-orchestrated' menace. From this premise, the logic proceeded that if communism was to be 'contained', it was essential that the US nurture and protect its new-found allies in the East, and elsewhere, so as they might act as a bulwark against the encroaching communist tide. It was inevitable that along with this came US English as the language of allied strategic coordination in East Asia.

The US strategy owed much to the thinking of the academic and then US Ambassador to Moscow George Kennan, who argued in an anonymous paper published in *Foreign Policy* in April 1947 that 'the mean element of any United States policy toward the Soviet Union must be that of a long-term, patient but firm and vigilant containment of Russian expansive tendencies' (Kennan, 1947: 6). These tendencies, in addition to referencing developments in Europe, were understood to include China and the growing communist threats in Vietnam and Korea. They also included potential threats in Latin America and the Caribbean. The Kennan paper provided the intellectual basis for what in April 1950 became the National Security Council policy paper, number 68; also known as NSC 68.[18] This document set out for the first time the formal US position towards the perceived Soviet threat and the options which the US had for dealing with it. Following Kennan, NSC 68 declared that the fundamental design of the Soviet Union was 'the complete subversion or forcible destruction of the machinery of government and structure of society in the countries of the non-Soviet world and their replacement by an apparatus and structure subservient to and controlled from the Kremlin' (NSC 68: 3). The document advanced four possible courses of action. These were (a) a continuation of current policies, (b) a return to 1920's isolation, (c) war with the USSR, and (d) 'A more rapid building up of the political, economic, and military strength of the free world' (ibid: 30). Option (d) was settled upon as the preferred course of action. NSC 68 placed particular emphasis on the communist threat in Europe and Asia, noting 'an increasing nervousness in Western Europe and the rest of the free world [and] ominous signs of further deterioration in the Far East' (ibid: 34). As a response it advocated substantial increases in economic and military aid to the affected regions. Like Kennan's 1947 paper, NSC 68 presented the idea that the USSR was set upon world domination as an incontrovertible fact. This was despite the overwhelming evidence that the USSR had been so economically devastated by the Second World War that it could

---

18 *NSC 68: United States Objectives and Programs for National Security. A Report to the President Pursuant to the President's Directive of January 31, 1950* (April 14, 1950) www.citizensource.com/History/20thCen/NSC68.PDF Accessed April 6, 2017.

not afford expansion on such terms even if it desired it. Ideologues in the US State Department, of which there were to be a long line after Kennan and the authors of NSC 68, also conveniently ignored the ideological limitations of Soviet-style communism, which with its longstanding adherence to the Stalinist principle of 'socialism in one country' – first coined in the 1920s – undercut the USSR's own pretensions to global conquest and world domination, even as it provided piecemeal financial support to socialist movements in foreign states and kept Eastern Europe in oppressive thraldom. The consequence was that the State Department treated the USSR as being behind all challenges to the US-inspired post-1945 world order, regardless of whether in fact it was or not, and this coloured US foreign policy thinking for the next forty- five years. From the perspective of 1950, the Chinese Revolution and the Korean War were all part of a grandiose Soviet plot to take over the world, in which East Asia was a new front line in urgent need of defence.

Communist containment and English incorporation

Given the perceived threat, Japan, South Korea and Taiwan were singled out for especial US attention. Up until that time, the US plan had been that Japan, Okinawa[19] and the Philippines would be a sufficient 'chain of defense' (cited in Ambrose, 1993: 115). The Korean War (1950–3), following hard upon the Chinese Revolution, markedly changed this perspective and allowed Truman and his Secretary of State Acheson to pursue a much more forward policy in Asia, which incorporated not only Japan, but also South Korea and Taiwan. Military aid was also extended to the Philippines, where the government was facing local opposition from the Huks, and to France in Vietnam in its struggle to maintain its hold on French Indo-China. Adding strength to the new line of defence was America's ally, Britain, whose forces had reoccupied Hong Kong following the Japanese surrender. In Japan and South Korea, US army military governments had been installed after 1945 to prepare the way for a return to civilian rule. The outbreak of the Korean War, however, saw Truman make a binding US commitment to the non-communist integrity of South Korea and Japan and to the protection of Formosa (Taiwan) from communist attack, declaring that any settlement of the status of Formosa 'must await the restoration of security in the Pacific, a peace settlement with Japan, or consideration by the United Nations' (cited in Ambrose, 1993: 117). In both Japan and South Korea, the end result of US policy was the creation of US-compliant one-party states – complete with several US military bases – beneath a thin democratic veneer.

---

19 Okinawa did not return to full Japanese sovereignty until 1972 and still retains a large US military facility.

In Japan, the administrative architecture of the pre-war state had been left intact but with its militarist dimensions stripped out, and a new US-drafted – and English-scripted – constitution imposed. Of particular significance was Article 9. By this article, Japan renounced war as a sovereign right and committed itself never to maintain any kind of land, sea or air forces which had 'war potential'.[20] A peace accord was formally signed in 1951, in which Japan renounced all claims to its former occupied territories and colonies and saw its borders return to where they had been in the mid-1850s.[21] The peace treaty came into force in 1952, and this marked the formal ending of the US occupation outside the strategic retention of US military bases across the Japanese archipelago, particularly within the Ryukyu and Ogasawara island chains (Storey, 1960: 257–258).

In Korea, Soviet and US policy within the different occupied zones made the prospect of unification increasingly remote. Both occupiers set about installing ideologically compliant regimes in which the interests of the Korean people as a whole were a secondary concern. North Korea was made subject to the narcissist rule of the quasi-Stalinist Kim Il-sung (1912–94). In South Korea, the fully Americanized and deeply conservative Korean nationalist Dr Syngman Rhee (1875–1965) was brought back from decades of exile in the US to lead a puppet government in the south. His principal qualifications were that he was ethnically Korean, reliably anti-communist and could speak English fluently. This was enough for the US army military government in Korea (USAMGIK), which handed power over to Rhee with the declaration of First Republic of Korea on August 15, 1948 (Kim, 2011: 195). As in Japan, the architecture of the pre-war government administration was retained, even to the extent of keeping some Japanese colonial officials in post during the transition (Blum, 2014: 50). The claims to leadership of the local Korean People's Republic Party (KPR), which had more broad-based support amongst ordinary Koreans, were swept aside by the US authorities in favour of Rhee. For the USAMGIK and the supreme commander of the applied powers, the increasingly otherworldly General Douglas MacArthur (1880–1964), it was much easier to deal directly with the linguistically and culturally familiar Rhee than

---

20 The full text reads, 'Aspiring sincerely to an international peace based on justice and order, the Japanese people forever renounce war as a sovereign right of the nation and the threat or use of force as means of settling international disputes. In order to accomplish the aim of the preceding paragraph, land, sea, and air forces, as well as other war potential, will never be maintained. The right of belligerency of the state will not be recognized' http://japan.kantei.go.jp/constitution_and_government_of_japan/constitution_e.html Accessed April 12, 2017.
21 For an excellent account of the political situation in Japan after 1945, see Potter (n.d.). Evolution of Japan's Postwar Foreign Policy. Available online at https://office.nanzan-u.ac.jp/cie/gaiyo/kiyo/pdf_09/kenkyu_03.pdf Accessed April 12, 2017.

with the diverse Korean-speaking leaders and groupings of the left-leaning KPR. After several advances and reversals on both sides, and much loss of life, the Korean War ended in stalemate exactly where it had begun, at the 38th Parallel (Blum, 2014). In its aftermath, it quickly became apparent, even to the US, that Rhee's approach to government would be populist, corrupt and authoritarian. As the new regime evolved it was accompanied by the routine repression and torture of opponents, the rigging of elections, and the rewriting when it suited him of the South Korean constitution. Rhee remained in office until 1960 before fleeing to Hawaii on a US transport plane. His legacy, like that of his counterparts in Japan, the Philippines, and to a lesser extent Taiwan, was to facilitate the strategic Americanization of South Korean society, primarily through reform of the education system, which adopted the US model, and through the promotion of American cultural products – e.g. film, music and sport – and the teaching of American English in schools. He also permitted the establishment of several US military bases across the country, thus adding a security dimension to the linguistic and cultural Americanization processes which were occurring elsewhere.

In Taiwan, in comparison with Rhee, the US conversion to the non-English-speaking Chiang Kai-shek was much less enthusiastic and might not have happened at all but for the Korean War. The US government viewed with ambivalence the regime which Chiang allowed to be installed following the defeat of Japan in 1945, when he appointed the inept and corrupt General Chen Yi as Taiwan's governor. Chen instituted a two-year reign of terror that involved the imprisonment, torture and murder of tens of thousands of Formosans as well as the systematic plunder of the local economy by Kuomintang government officials and troops. Chen was eventually removed at the behest of the US in 1947.[22] US views of Chiang and his competence to lead China were little better than the ones which they had come to hold about Chen. Chiang too was corrupt and inept, and prone to barbarity. His only redeeming feature in the eyes of the US government was his wife, the American-educated and fluent English-speaking Song Mei-ling 宋美龄, or Madame Chiang (1897–2003), who throughout the 1940s had acted as the main conduit for US dealings with her husband. But her extraordinary venality – she redirected much US-raised China aid into her own private accounts – in combination with Chiang's political incompetence in the conduct of the civil war put them out of favour with Truman just as Mao's Communists were gaining the upper hand. With the Chinese Revolution in October 1949, fatalism overtook Truman for a time as his administration contemplated the imminent invasion of

---

22 He was later executed as a traitor in June 1950 under the orders of Chiang (Manthorpe, 2005: 194).

The economy of global English, 1918–1979 121

Taiwan. Despite private misgivings, Truman publicly announced that the US was withdrawing its support for Chiang and for the Kuomintang on Taiwan, in the expectation that he would soon be dealing with Mao. But rampant anti-communism at home, and vociferous Republican accusations about the 'loss of China', put Truman under increasing pressure to placate his critics and to bring clarity to US policy in the East. It was in this circumstance that Truman instituted the review which became NSC 68. Within two months of its delivery to Truman in April 1950, war broke out on the Korean peninsula. The effect was a complete reappraisal of the position of Taiwan and of Chiang's hold on the island. Taiwan, under the iron grip of Chiang's Kuomintang, now found itself promoted to the front line in the US battle against Soviet-orchestrated communism and US-directed capital accumulation in East Asia. US aid poured into Taiwan at the rate of $100 million a year (Manthorpe, 2005: 203), and Chiang allowed himself to fantasize about relaunching an invasion of the mainland which would oust Mao and restore the Chinese Republic for the Nationalists. The fantasy never materialized, but it continued to be promoted to the point of tedium by Chiang for several years as Taiwan under the Kuomintang became a US client state in the mould of Japan and South Korea, but also like them, with its own distinctive fusion of East and West. The restructuring of education in each of these nations according to a US model, as well as the (re)introduction of English as a formal language of study in schools and in universities, also dates from this time (Braibanti, 1949; Kubota, 1998; Mogi-Hein, 1999; Kanno, 2008; Seargeant, 2009; Kim, 2011; Chang, 2016; Lemberg, 2018). As the journalist, Ernest K Lindley, writing in the mid-1950s, reported:

> In nearly all of Free Asia, English is the second language where it is not the first. It was the official language of the Bandung conference.[23] It is the only language in which most Asian countries can communicate with each other. In many, including Indonesia,[24] the study of English is now compulsory, beginning in junior high school. One specific result of this prevalence of English as the second language is that most Free Asian students who go abroad to study – as thousands want to do – prefer English speaking countries. Many of these young people will rise rapidly to positions of influence – in most Asian countries trained men and

---

23 The Bandung Conference which took place in April 1955 included twenty-nine Asian and African nations, a number of which had recently become independent, such as India and Pakistan. The aim of the conference was to promote economic cooperation between developing nations and to oppose colonialism.
24 According to Lemberg (2018), 'The Ford Foundation dispensed nearly two million dollars on English teaching-teaching initiatives [in Indonesia] between 1951 and 1956' (p. 24).

women are in very short supply. It would be shortsighted of us not to provide more opportunities for them to study in the United States.

(Cited in Bentley & Grebstein, 1956: 399)[25]

In Japan and South Korea, US client status also had significant cultural effects through the influences of American music and popular culture, and in the 1950s and 60s a thriving jazz scene grew up in the larger cities with home-grown singers and bands offering their own often-hybridized takes on popular US standards – Chiemi Eri and the Tokyo-Cuban Boys' cover of Rosemary Clooney's 'Come On-a My House' is a good example of the genre. With American music and English also came US fashions and hairstyles and the increased Westernization of dress, as more and more people eschewed traditional garments and opted for Western modes of attire and appearance. In addition, 'the English language gained the privileged position as the language of the new occupier' (Kim, 2011: 199; see also Hoshiyama, 1978; Kitao, Kitao, Nozawa & Yamamoto, 1985). The same applied to Taiwan, although the US occupation there was confined to US-appointed government advisors and covert CIA operatives who counselled the Chiang regime. Nevertheless, the overall effect was the same, because it made English, in particular in its American form, the new first foreign language on the educational curriculum of each of these states, so setting the linguistic seal on their incorporation into the world-economy of the United States (Clough, 1991; Price, 2014; Kim, 2011; Song, 2011; Kanno, 2008; Shibata, 2008).

The incorporation of strategic economic buffer zones in East Asia into the US world-economy heralded a huge increase in global capital flows, much of which came from the US in the form of military expenditures to fund the security needs of the Cold War, the US wars in Korea and Vietnam, and government-backed loans and grants to support the development of compliant states. These expenditures were underwritten by the US Federal Reserve, by now acting assertively as the world's central bank. With the greatly increased capital flows, world trade and production witnessed a correspondingly massive expansion. In the twenty-year period from the end of the Korean War in 1953 to the Paris Peace Accords of 1973, which ended the Vietnam War, manufacturing output quadrupled and the trade in manufactured products increased more than tenfold (Hobsbawm, 1995: 261). According to one commentator, the 1950s and 60s marked 'the most sustained and profitable period of economic growth in the history of world capitalism' (cited in Arrighi, 2010: 307). Hobsbawm (1995) describes it as

---

25 Lindley went on to note, 'I think every American will realize how valuable this second language factor is to the spread of American ideas and ideals. But just to emphasize its potential importance, let's imagine the situation were reversed. Think what a staggering blow it would be if the second language of Free Asia were Russian' (cited in Bentley & Grebstein, 1956: 399).

the 'Golden Age of the Anglo-Americans' (p. 258) in which all previous economic records were surpassed. Classical liberal economics was everywhere in retreat as it was largely held responsible – both intellectually and in the popular imaginary – for bringing about the Great Depression, which was then almost immediately followed by the horrors of the Second World War.

US post-war capital networks: Europe, Latin America and the Middle East

Just as the onset of the Cold War was responsible for further establishing English in the East, that is, beyond that already established by the British (see Chapters 2 and 3), the US desire to rebuild Western Europe and to make it an open market for US capital accumulation had similar consequences in the West. The main difference was that the education and political systems of Western Europe, with the significant exception of Germany (Shibata, 2008), returned more or less to what they had been prior to 1939 and were not reformulated according to a US schema. Nevertheless, the Marshall Plan alongside the restructuring of the world-system through Bretton Woods had a profound influence upon Europe and upon the wider world-system of the US world-economy, both in what they did economically and in the fact that they did so utilizing English as their primary medium of implementation (Schuler & Rosenberg, 2013; Cooper, 2014). Complementing the new economic and institutional architecture of the US system, there also occurred a large-scale transfer to Europe of 'forms of production and accumulation which had been developed in the US' (Panitch & Gindin, 2012: 100). This also included the transfer of 'American technology and related productive and managerial systems' (p. 101). It also therefore inevitably included English as a 'structuration effect' on how this process occurred; for example, shipping manifests had to be drawn up, English-speaking experts exported, operations manuals translated, and new systems and protocols introduced, all of which involved English, mostly in its standard form.

Elsewhere in the world, for example in Latin America, US policymakers and the US business lobby encouraged domestic policies that created an economic and legal environment favourable to foreign capital investment and secure from local expropriation. US policy throughout the 1950s and 60s promoted import substitution industrialization (ISI) in Latin America as a means to this end. Under ISI, nations would first import machinery and equipment in order to produce domestically the goods that they would otherwise import. In Latin America, a good deal of this machinery and equipment naturally came from the United States, and unlike the arrangements made for East Asia, this had to be paid for in US dollars. The only way to earn these dollars was through the export of labour-intensive domestic goods and agricultural products, but the US market proved itself difficult for the Latin American nations to penetrate (Panitch & Gindin, 2012: 103). In addition, with US state funds committed to Europe and East Asia, the US government looked to private capital to provide the primary investment initiative. This, as usual, was not readily forthcoming (Arrighi, 2010: 288–289).[26] The consequence was that in Latin America and much of the developing world in the 1950s and 60s 'the dynamic of reconstruction, development and integration into a liberalizing global capitalism [that had worked so well in Europe and Asia] largely failed to arise' (ibid: 105). Nevertheless, the principle of attempting to create the conditions for capital accumulation and FDI to take place in Latin America were still a sufficient basis for the increased purchase of English to occur [as M^E-C^E-M'^E and as M^E-M'^E], particularly amongst the clientelist networks for US capital which already existed. The leftist Argentine president, Arturo Frondizi (1958–62), described their members as 'those who are tied to foreign capital by economic ties (directors, bureaucratic personnel, lawyers, newspapers that receive advertisements, etc.) and those who, without having economic relations, end up being dominated by the political and ideological climate created by foreign capital' (cited in Frank, 1969a [1967]: 53). The difference was that linguistic integration into the US world-economy was slower in Latin America than in Europe and in some parts of Asia because of the reduced capital flows which were involved – so necessitating less policy planning for English – and the slower pace with which they moved from being wholly agrarian economies to being more industrial ones (Hobsbawm, 1995: 261). On the capital flow side of the ledger, Europe had the Marshall Plan and Bretton Woods as probably the two most successful structural adjustment programmes in history (Panitch & Gindin, 2012: 89). The East Asian client states, although not signatories of Bretton Woods, were also tied into its post-war architecture and benefitted from US procurements for the Cold War and non-repayable grants for state-financed industrialization. Latin America, Africa and the Middle East were similarly tied into the Bretton Woods institutional architecture – but they lacked the same level of financing for their economic development ambitions. As a result, it was mainly the clientelist elites in these societies who were the most readily integrated into the US system and language, while local economies and living standards continued to stagnate – or remained ideologically feudalist, as in much of Latin America and the Middle East. Another aspect of this process was that in the 1960s economic nationalism became increasingly popular in the Third World, especially amongst states which had gained their independence from British colonial rule or took the Soviet Union as their inspiration.[27] This made them resistant to the extraterritorial business norms which had developed, and which the US insisted upon, regarding

---

26 Although the scale of US investment in Latin America did not approach that in Europe and the 'Bamboo Curtain' states of East Asia, according to Frank (1969a [1967]), 'By 1950, 300 American corporations accounted for more than 90 percent of direct investment holdings in Latin America' (p. 299).
27 During the 1950s, the USSR matched or exceeded the growth rates of the major capitalist countries. It was not until the mid-1960s that it began to lose ground (Hobsbawm, 1995: 259).

internationally enforceable legal safeguards and guarantees for international capital investments and foreign-owned property. The key issue for these states was whether, in the fullness of time, they turned towards or away from the *Pax Americana*. Some, such as India, Indonesia and Egypt, for a period experimented with turning away (Lemberg, 2018). Others, such the 'Asian Tiger' economies of Malaysia and Singapore, were more compliant and welcomed US FDI and the legal-political and linguistic frameworks which accompanied it. Still others, such as China, Cuba and later Vietnam, opted out altogether. Vietnam is an interesting case, because due to the US war effort in the south, there had been a programme of massive investment in English, such that by the late 1960s, one US observer reported, 'English has replaced French as the language of wider communication in Vietnam' (cited in Lemberg, ibid: 27). In the Middle East, especially the Persian Gulf, the US focus at the end of the war was oil and the relationship the US had with the ruling elites of the region for ensuring its uninterrupted flow. Rather than seeking simply to secure cheap oil supplies and to create forward positions for US oil companies, both of which were important, the US had an overriding interest in ensuring that oil flows from the Persian Gulf were 'available to fuel international trade and economy as part of its global superpower responsibilities' (Myers Jaffe, 2004, cited in Panitch & Gindin, 2012: 103).[28]

US superpower responsibility for the world capitalist system was made possible, even inevitable, by the combination of the Bretton Woods international system with the Cold War policy positions of NSC 68. Through its influence over the Bretton Woods institutions of the IMF and the World Bank, and the central place of the Federal Reserve in providing capital liquidity for the global economy [by printing US dollars], the US in the 1950s and 60s derived a position of unrivalled authority over the world-economy – and over the designation of English as its dominant language – which was even greater than that of Britain at the height of its empire between 1873 and 1914. By the late 1960s the world-economy had become a transnational system in which capital accumulation by means of finance and the internationalization of business was occurring on a money scale [in the trillions] which had not been seen before. In addition, although borders became ever more permeable, the US was the only nation that managed to stand aloof from the economic strictures this implied. This is because it was a US world-economy, at the heart of which was the US government and the Federal Reserve, and this gave the US an advantage which other states did not have (Wallerstein, 2000 [1988]; Arrighi, 2010; Panitch & Gindin, 2012; Dunn,

---

[28] In Iran, with the aim of protecting British and US oil interests there, MI6 and the CIA conspired in the overthrow of the democratically elected government of the secular democrat Mohammed Mosaddegh in 1953 and his replacement by Shah Mohammed Reza Pahlavi (1919–80). The dictatorship did a good deal for the dissemination of English in Iran, but its unremitting brutality and incompetence led to its forceful overthrow in the Islamic Revolution of 1979.

2014). The vast flow of dollars also gave the system a potential instability as the volumes involved could not in practice be redeemed for gold, and this is what eventually brought the system down. But for the best part of thirty years, up to 1971, it worked well enough in ensuring global economic stability (Gilpin, 2001: 236).

US linguistic seignorage and the transnationalization of English, 1968–1979

The move to a transnational and predominantly financialized global economy [M-M'] – and so also to the global *transnationalization* of standard English [as M^E-C^E-M'^E and M^E-M'^E] – occurs between 1968 and 1973, during which time, according to Arrighi (2010), there was 'a massive withdrawal of money capital from trade and production' (p. 307) and a redirection of it into the currency accounts of 'offshore' investment centres, which the increased flows of dollars had brought into being. 'Offshore' accounts were to be found in the currency markets of the City of London and other major exchanges, which were tied into an abundance of financial mini-states that had sprung up [e.g. Monaco, San Marino, Liechtenstein, Andorra, Bermuda, Gibraltar, Hong Kong, Singapore, the Virgin Islands]. These offered low or negligible rates of taxation and minimal regulatory surveillance of financial investments. Once considered 'economic jokes' and 'not real states at all' (Hobsbawm, 1995: 281), the offshore centres made themselves economically viable by offering financial services, usually in the medium of standard English [M^E-M'^E], directly to the global economy. Through their activities they also facilitated the transnationalization of business domiciles and capital, as multinational corporations (MNCs) and capitalist entrepreneurs took advantage of the light-touch tax and regulatory regimes on offer to re-register their business domiciles and re-invest their capital. Most of this capital was denominated in US dollars, and in the international exchanges of the City of London, Tokyo and New York it was primarily traded in English.

Currency speculation was nothing new; it had been going on for centuries. But after 1968 there was a noticeable 'upward jump' in what was called the Eurodollar or Eurocurrency market (Arrighi, 2010: 308). This market traded in US dollars which were deposited in non-US banks and, in being 'offshore' [even if traded in New York], were not subject to US regulatory oversight. In the words of Hobsbawm, Eurodollars became 'a negotiable financial instrument' (1995: 278). Such were the volumes of dollars flowing through the global financial system – thanks largely to US overseas expenditures – that this enabled an explosion of uncontrolled lending and speculation in 'un-repatriated' dollars, that is, outside US regulatory control, but also still redeemable for gold at $35 per ounce (Gilpin, 2001: 237). Because governments did not have control over the massive liquidity flows involved, their only recourse was to manipulate the values of their currencies 'in order to attract or repel liquidity in offshore markets to counter shortages or surfeits in their domestic economies' (Arrighi, 2010: 308). But this option was closed off to them by the fixed exchange rate system of Bretton Woods, which was not proving flexible enough for many nations, and this put the system under enormous strain. At the same time the US, inebriated on the dollar's centrality to the world monetary system, engaged in reckless policymaking in respect of its expenditures, both domestically and overseas. Dollar centrality gave the US certain advantages in the world-system which were not available to other nations – what economists refer to as 'seignorage' (Gilpin, 2001: 246–247; Panitch & Gindin, 2012: 145; Dunn, 2014: 158). This gave the US the right to pay its own debts in dollars and to give itself debt flexibility – in effect the ability to default on debt – through the devaluation of its own currency. The billions of non-repatriated dollars functioned as a huge interest-free loan to the United States (Gilpin, ibid: 257), because the Federal Reserve could simply print more dollars as and when it needed to and go deeply into debt without having to fear the consequences. In the words of one commentator, the United States was 'able to tap the resources of the rest of the world virtually without restriction, simply by issuing its own currency' (Parboni, 1981: 47, cited in Arrighi, 2010: 319). In addition, being denominated in dollars, the debt would over time be 'naturally' inflated away. It also had the advantage for the US of not incurring costs on currency transactions. It was seignorage that enabled the US to fund its involvement in the Vietnam War in addition to its wider crusade against communism as part of NSC 68. The downside was that the continued printing of dollars caused US domestic inflation to begin to run too high. It was one thing to inflate the debt away, but if inflationary pressures became too strong and the balance of payments deficit too large, the US domestic economy and living standards would suffer. Added to this was sustained market speculation against the dollar, which currency traders sensed was fixed at an unsustainable rate. In order to relieve the economic pressure domestically and to get the currency markets off its back, the Nixon administration (1969–73) made the decision in August 1971 to devalue the dollar, and to do this by severing the dollar's link with gold. The price of Nixon's move was the collapse of the Bretton Wood's system of fixed exchange rates and the shifting of the international monetary system back onto a flexible exchange rate regime. Despite its devaluation, huge demand for the dollar ensured its continued role as the international reserve currency (Gilpin, 2001: 236; Arrighi, 2010: 318).

This also enabled the US to retain all the benefits of seignorage. Amongst these benefits was *linguistic seignorage*, thanks to the position of standard English as the preferred *lingua franca* of global finance and trade [M^E-C^E-M'^E; M^E-M'^E] and within the US world-economy as the foreign language of preference in education systems and language classrooms around the world (Braine, 2005). For a time in the 1970s, postcolonial nationalism in Africa and in the Indian sub-continent made nations in these regions less amenable to accommodating English and Western-capitalist economic orthodoxies, but this was short-lived. By the 1980s, those countries that were not totally devastated by war, famine or brutal dictatorships had abandoned their resistance to English and persuaded themselves of the efficacy of open markets, English linguistic seignorage and FDI, even in the nations of the African Francophonie, where French increasingly found itself challenged by English (Thérien, 1993; Ouedraogo, 2000; Mazrui, 2004; Albaugh, 2009; Mufwene, 2008, 2011; Vigouroux, 2013). In the 1950s, 60s and 70s, dictatorship, rather than an impediment to English, had often acted as its stimulus, as in South Korea, Iran and Chile, where it was formally set into these nation's educational systems and became the foreign language of choice of the elite, as well as of the aspiring classes below them (Borjian, 2013; Goodrich, 2020; J-K Park, 2009; J S-Y Park, 2010; Song, 2011; Jenks, 2017; McKay, 2002; Matear, 2008). In India, the plan following independence had been for English to be phased out during a post-independence transitional period and replaced by Hindi as the official language. As the time of transition approached, severe rioting against Hindi broke out in the non-Hindi-speaking south, and this persuaded the Indian government to retain English on an equal footing with Hindi and also to recognize the official legitimacy of India's regional languages as well.[29] In the 1960s and 70s similar conclusions were reached in other postcolonial nations of the former British Empire, such as Nigeria, Ghana, Tanzania, Kenya, Pakistan, Sri Lanka and Bangladesh (Osa, 1986; Bamgbose, 1991; Ouedraogo, 2000; Mazrui, 2004; Ochieng, 2015; Adamson, 2020; Michieka, 2005; Rahman, 2015; Fernando, 2012; Jayaweera, 2019; Chowdhury & Kabir, 2014; Seargeant, Erling, Solly, Chowdhury & Rahman, 2017; Islam & Hashim, 2019). In many of these states, once the new postcolonial hierarchies had become established, and experiments with economic and linguistic nationalism had been indulged, English often re-emerged to (re)claim an official, or quasi-official, role for itself in government, the economy and education. As Fishman (1998–9) commented, 'Almost every colony that won its independence from England (sic) either kept English as an official language or at least recognized its utility' (p. 27). Fishman reproduces a quasi-Orientalist perspective here (Said, 1978). But in addition to the apparent economic utility of English – which is questionable on a number of levels (Ricento, 2015b; Simpson, 2020) – a further significant issue was the wilful acquiescence of the newly emergent postcolonial elites to the hegemonic control of English standards and norms, regardless of what national governments and ministries of education might say about the importance of local languages in public. A significant catalyst for English in the postcolonial world were

---

29 The Official Languages (Amendment) Act (1967) provided for English to become an 'associate' official language alongside Hindi. The act also recognized eighteen regional languages as having the right to function as the official languages of individual states.

parents, particularly well-off parents, who saw in English opportunities for the social and economic betterment of their children. In Tanzania in the 1980s, for example, where Kiswahili became the dominant postcolonial *lingua franca*, wealthier families sent their children to neighbouring Kenya and Uganda to be educated in English-medium schools (Ochieng, 2015: 27). Such was the high demand for English in Tanzania that during the economic liberalization of the 1990s there was an explosion in English-medium education in the country, to become 'the most needed language by the elite class in Tanzania' (ibid: 27). Added to this was the very high demand amongst members of the educated classes in the postcolonial world as a whole for English proficiency for graduate and professional training overseas, which were deemed essential by local governments for national development purposes, and which were, not unexpectedly, also welcomed for the economic opportunities they opened up to members of local ethnic and class-based elites, many of whom were also in government.

Assisting the re-emergence and global entrenchment of English following the collapse of Bretton Woods was the 'dollarization' of national currencies, particularly in the developing world. Dollarization processes were, and still are, a corollary of US dollar centrality and seignorage (Gilpin, 2001: 258–259). It refers to the 'pegging' of a nation's currency to the US dollar, either by aligning the value of the local currency with the dollar, or in some cases by adopting the dollar outright as the national currency. The economic rationale is to provide exchange rate certainty and monetary stability to combat inflation. The political rationale is that it assists stability where legal and institutional structures are weak, as is the case in Cambodia, for example (Menon, 2008: 3). Ideologically, it also reassures local elites and the populace at large in the knowledge that what money they have is denominated in the most valued global currency of account. Dollarization became popular in the mid-1970s and has accelerated ever since. Many countries formally and informally peg to the US dollar [e.g. Hong Kong, China, Jordan, Bolivia, Angola, Fiji], and several others use the dollar as currency, or in tandem with a local currency [e.g. British Virgin Islands, Panama, Zimbabwe, Cambodia, Bolivia]. As the Global Policy Forum has noted,

> Much trade is now dollar-based, countries prefer to hold their central bank reserves in US dollars, and private companies as well as wealthy citizens often hold dollars or dollar-denominated assets. The United States derives great economic and political power from this dollar hegemony.[30]

---

30 www.globalpolicy.org/economic-expansion/dollarization-8-21.html Accessed August 6, 2017.

An almost inevitable side effect of dollarization is that it also gained hegemony for US and related normative standard forms of English [as both M^E-C^E-M'^E and M^E-M'^E], as what counted as money capital and what counted as linguistic capital became merged in public perceptions (cf. McKay, 2002; Chowdhury & Phan, 2014; Piller & Cho, 2014; Phan, 2017).

The decade of the 1970s was a turbulent one for the world-economy, punctuated as it was by a series of severe economic shocks, as well as a few US-inspired ones, of which the collapse of the Bretton Woods arrangement in 1971 was the first of these. Despite these problems, the US would by the end of the decade emerge even stronger than it had been at the beginning. The principal reason was a massive expansion in the global circulation of US dollars and, as part of this, an explosion in FDI. A further reason, also related to the expansion in FDI, was the global spread of US-based MNCs. Each of these was accompanied by the externalization of US economic principles and practices (Panitch & Gindin, 2012: 119), amongst which, and linguistically structuring the whole system, was the use of normative standard English as the favoured *lingua franca* of international financial and commercial exchange. The increase in the volumes of US dollars in circulation has, in part, been accounted for previously. Dollar centrality in the world-system and dollarization were two causes; a third cause was the massive increase in financial flows related to FDI. These were mainly funnelled through New York, Tokyo and London and were also denominated in US dollars. A side effect of the increased FDI was a change in the language policies of many recipient nations towards English as a key language on the curriculum. Inward FDI has been shown to correlate strongly with changes in language policy on the part of the recipient nation (Kim, Liu, Tuxhorn, Brown & Leblang, 2014; see also LeClerc, 2011). In the words of Kim et al. (ibid), 'FDI-receiving states teaching a foreign/second language that matches the FDI-sending state's official languages receive more FDI from the sender-state than receiver-states that do not teach matching foreign/second languages' (p. 3). In the 1970s, and in subsequent decades thereafter, the global balance in FDI was heavily weighted towards the United States, mainly in the form of investments by US-originating MNCs.

A distinguishing feature of the world-economy in the 1970s which differentiated it from the previous decades was the transfer of control over world liquidity from public to private hands (Arrighi, 2010: 318), that is from government-led accumulation to accumulation that was generated by the financial markets. In the immediate decades following World War II, US economic expansion was primarily led by US government investment in Europe and East Asia, and to a lesser extent in Latin America (see earlier), in which the US practised a type of 'global military Keynesianism' based on economic and military might (Wallerstein, 2000 [1992]: 399; Arrighi, 2010: 315). By the 1970s, however, the main players in overseas international investment had moved from the government offices of Capitol Hill to the private banks of Wall Street and the City of London (Walter, 1991: 182, cited in Arrighi, ibid: 318). Their clients were institutional private investors, national governments and MNCs. The dollar numbers were impressive. Arrighi estimates:

> Overall, between 1970 and 1978 the *accumulated* value of US foreign direct investment more than doubled (from $78 billion to $168 billion), while that of non-US (mostly European) foreign direct investment more than trebled (from $72 billion to $232 billion) raising the non-US share of the total from 48 to 58 per cent.
> (Arrighi, 2010: 314)

While the US overall share of FDI fell back in relation to previous decades, thanks to the dollar, the world-economy was by the end of the 1970s indelibly on an American footing and almost entirely financialized [M-M']: 'international financial flows dwarfed trade flows by a ratio of about 25:1' (Gilpin, 2001: 240). In place of Bretton Woods, in 1976 the leading global powers convened the committee of the G7 in an attempt at the loose coordination of global monetary policy and to combat crises. The G7 was made up of finance ministers and central bankers from the world's seven most advanced capitalist economies. It was dominated by the US. Canada and Britain were also sitting members. In the words of Baker (2006: 11, 27), the G7 was in essence 'a vehicle for providing support and endorsement for US-generated initiatives and ideas' (cited in Panitch & Gindin, 2012: 135). The principal official language of the G7 was English. According to Paul Volcker, who was chairman of the Federal Reserve from 1979 to 1987, in such an environment 'senior officials with responsibility for their governments' policies would frankly review economic and political developments within their countries, consider the implications for international markets, explain their own policies, and even hint at future policy plans' (ibid: 124). They would do so mostly by means of English, even when instantaneous translation was available, as many of the non-anglophone bankers and politicians attending could speak and understand English well. As Kim et al. (2014) have suggested, 'Proficiency in a shared language is a basic necessity for political actors across countries to interact smoothly, even in the presence of interpreters' (p. 13).

The other notable feature of the world-economy in this period was the rise of the multinational [aka transnational] corporation (MNC or TNC). The modern US model of the MNC has its origins in the expansionary dollar-denominated capital flows of the 1970s. US business corporations, facing stiff competition from their European counterparts worldwide, sought to transnationalize their operations in order to protect their global market positions by exporting ever-increasing amounts of capital overseas. In the words of Arrighi (2010), 'the transnational expansion of US corporate capital was both a critical means and a highly significant outcome of the US government's pursuit of world power' (p. 315). He continues with a summary from Gilpin:

> In conjunction with the international position of the dollar and with nuclear supremacy, the multinational corporation became one of the cornerstones of American hegemony. These three elements of American power interacted and reinforced one another . . . American political and military supremacy arising out of World War II was a necessary precondition for the predominant position of American multinational corporations in the world economy. But the reciprocal of this is also true: corporate expansionism in turn became a support of America's international political and military position.
> (Gilpin, 1975: 140, cited in Arrighi, 2010: 315–316)

The internationalization of MNCs in the 1970s inaugurated the transition to a truly transnational global economy, one which was based on a new international division of labour, offshore finance and the hegemony of standard English (Hobsbawm, 1995; Gilpin, 2001; Wallerstein, 2000 [1974]; Phillipson, 1992, 2008; Marschan-Piekkari, Welch & Welch, 1999; Piller & Cho, 2014). But as these processes proceeded apace, periodic crises dogged the system.

1974 oil crisis and debt structuring in the capitalist world-economy

In the aftermath of the collapse of Bretton Woods, there followed the OPEC oil price rises of 1973–4. Following an initial doubling of the oil price at the end of 1973 in response to the by-now-depreciated US dollar, there was a further threefold increase in the price of oil in 1974 (Arrighi, 2010: 315). On this occasion, it was OPEC's political desire to punish the United States for its support of Israel in the 1973 Yom Kippur War which was the main catalyst for the increase. In addition to having a major deleterious effect on world inflation, which took a marked jump upwards, a notable net result was a further massive increase in the global circulation of US dollars, in the form of what became known as 'petrodollars'. These were the dollars in which oil was bought and sold, and the OPEC nations of the Middle East were the main holders of them. The circulation of billions of petrodollars in tandem with Eurodollars and US domestic-issue dollars created a dollar glut, along with accompanying capital bottlenecks, in the world financial system.[31] The necessity of recycling these dollars safely and efficiently, so as

---

31 As Marx was at pains to point out in *Capital Volume II*, 'The circuit of capital proceeds normally only as long as its various phases pass into each other without delay' (Marx, 1978 [1884]: 133; see also Harvey, 2013: 257, 331).

to avert a *crisis of circulation* – where 'credit suddenly dries up, payments congeal, [and] the reproduction process is paralysed' (Marx, 1991 [1894]: 620) – caused the US-led international banking system to encourage a frenzy of lending to any nation deemed to be remotely creditworthy. Major beneficiaries of this lending were several Latin American states, including Mexico, Brazil, Argentina and Peru, and even some select socialist states in Eastern Europe, most notably Poland and Hungary (Hobsbawm, 1995: 474). The newly indebted nations, particularly those in Latin America, welcomed the funds as a boon which enabled their governments to put off structural reform to address social inequality while also stimulating their economies. The loans also drew Latin America much more closely into the nexus of the US capitalist world-system, alongside Western Europe and East Asia. Although designed to punish the US, the 1974 oil crisis had indirect benefits for the US as well, because unlike its main economic rivals in Europe and Asia, all of whom [with the exception of Britain and Norway] were net oil importers, the US was a major oil producer and largely self-sufficient. The hike in oil prices therefore made the non-oil producing OECD (Organization of Economic Cooperation and Development) countries less competitive.[32]

The saturation of the world-economy in US dollars as a response to the 1974 crisis, in addition to enhancing US structural power (Strange, 1989; May, 1996; Harvey, 2003; Helleiner, 2006; see also Chapter 1), further entrenched the hegemony of English in the world-system [mainly as M^E-M'^E]. As overseas governments eagerly took the dollar loans on offer in the hope that it would aid their economic development; many also instituted language education policies which were meant to aid this process (cf. Ricento, 2015a; Barakos & Unger, 2016; Tollefson & Pérez-Milans, 2018). What the recipient nations did not know was that in the 1980s the loans they had taken out would come back to haunt them in the form of the Latin American debt crisis and English-mediated structural adjustment programmes (see Chapter 5).

The massive expansion in the global circulation of US dollars in the 1970s led to an acceleration in financial crises affecting the world-economy through the 1980s and 90s as debtor nations found themselves in repayment difficulties. Where crises arose, an indirect effect was to increase the structural power of English by creating the necessity for international responses which required US strategic leadership in addition to international institutional coordination often through the US Treasury, the IMF and the World Bank to resolve. The linguistic institutionalization of English as a structural facet

---

32 Wallerstein (2000 [1992]) goes so far as to suggest that the 1974 oil price hike was a deliberate US strategy, carried out 'under the leadership of the US's chief agents in the affair (Saudi Arabia and the Shah of Iran)' (p. 398). The aim being to hurt its oil-reliant competitors and arrest the relative decline in US economic advantage since the 1960s.

of the modern world-system rose to a new level with the Latin American and Asian financial crises of the 1980s and 90s, along with the geopolitical shocks which followed the fall of the Berlin Wall and the collapse of the Soviet Union across the same period. How these events enhanced the global position of English is the subject of the next chapter.

5 Capital-centric English and the modern world-system, 1979–2008

Capitalist crisis management and the structuration of English

Even without the 1974 oil crisis, ever since the commencement of the Cold War, the United States had presided over an era of 'loose money' during which US interest rates were kept low. This made it possible for the US to facilitate global and domestic borrowing, subsidize allies, fight communism and stimulate the world-economy. With the additional massive dollar flows that the oil crisis created, major inflationary pressures built up in the US and worldwide which proved increasingly difficult to control. By 1978, such were the volumes of dollars in circulation that the US was faced with the dilemma of allowing the loose money era to continue with the risk [as the US government saw it] of US financial ruin (Arrighi, 2010: 324), or it could bring order to the system by asserting control. The decision was reached that capitalist rationality would have to prevail: that the era of loose money would end and that 'sound money' would – at least for a time – take its place (ibid). The man who would deliver this message was the new head of the Federal Reserve, Paul Volcker, who in the last years of the Carter administration (1977–81) and then with greater ferocity and determination under the administration of President Reagan (1981–9), increased US interest rates to '"painfully high" levels – the substance of the so called Volcker shock – as would prove that beating inflation trumped all other policy goals' (Panitch & Gindin, 2012: 163). If confidence was to be restored, holding onto dollars – rather than splurging them about – had to become attractive again, and the only way to do this, as Volcker saw it, was to increase interest rates, thus giving reasons for investors to want dollars and to hold onto them. The rise in interest rates had the overall effect of restricting the world money supply, as more dollars were taken out of circulation, while also simultaneously imposing a regime of austerity on the US economy and on the economies of international debtor nations such as Mexico and Brazil. The severe contraction saw unemployment in the US double to around 10 per cent in late 1982, but it had the desired effect of halting the domestic inflationary spiral; US inflation fell back to just over 3 per cent, and it remained at that level until the end of the century (ibid: 168). But as in the past, the symptom of capital accumulation which low interest rates allowed became a cause of the global deepening of English, particularly when the system was thrown into crisis and then had to be rescued.

In Latin America, the US interest rate increases represented a financial catastrophe, as Mexico, Brazil, Venezuela and several other Latin American nations threatened to default – or did default – on the interest payments on their debts, much of which had been incurred through the aggressive recycling of petrodollars after 1974. Incredibly, Volcker had not foreseen this consequence of the rate increase for the Latin American debtor nations, or he was simply too focused on arresting the decline in the value of the dollar and reducing US domestic inflation to care too much about this at the time. But, as a result of Volcker's policy, net interest payments on Latin American debt 'skyrocketed from 33 to 59 percent of total export income between 1979 and 1981' (ibid: 214), thus triggering the Latin American debt crisis, which required concerted US-led coordination and the remainder of 1980s to bring under control. The debt crisis had significant consequences for the promotion of global English, particularly of the US standard variety as various English-proficient international agencies, such as the IMF and the World Bank, were brought into play in dealing with the crisis. Day-to-day management of the crisis was also devolved to the Federal Reserve. At the level of international negotiation, responsibility for the crisis was most noticeably located in the persons of US Secretary of State to the Treasury James Baker (1985–8) and his successor in the role, Nicholas Brady (1988–93), who gave their names to the successive international rescue plans which were targeted at it. These involved complex IMF-backed loan restructuring initiatives [aka the Baker and Brady Plans], as well as demands for strict adherence to English-scripted structural adjustment programmes (SAPs). These were imposed as conditions by international creditors and financial agencies if debt relief and rescheduling were to be forthcoming (Harvey, 2003: 181). SAPs invariably involved privatization and shrinkage of the public sector, the reduction of state spending, and the opening up of the local economy to FDI. In the words of Soederberg, 'SAPs locked Latin American, Asian and African economies into an open world market economy, guaranteeing freedom of entry and exit for mobile capital across the globe' (2002: 180). In addition, they brought about 'the neoliberalization of each recipient state' (Panitch & Gindin, 2012: 216). Internal social relations of production and exchange were in this way reorganized so as to favour the further penetration of external capitals (Harvey, 2003: 67, 151, 181). Being formulated largely through the Fed, the US Treasury, the IMF and the World Bank, SAPs were articulated and given meaningful existence by being discussed and then documented primarily through the medium of English, as well as being interpreted and translated into other languages, including Spanish and Portuguese. English, however, always took the lead. Panitch and Gindin's account of the Mexican debt restructuring negotiation is salutary, even though English is never mentioned.

> The Fed 'spoon-fed' Mexican banks until the presidential election, after which negotiations with the new De La Madrid government yielded the structural-adjustment agreement with the IMF that became the model for the rest of Latin America and beyond. This included the 'thousands and thousands of high-priced negotiating hours in the 1980s,' in which the most senior officials of the Fed and Treasury, as well as the IMF and World Bank, met with finance officials from other states who 'by virtue of experience, tenure, and training [were] almost uniquely able to deal with each other on the basis of close understanding and frankness,' as Volcker puts it. It also included the many parallel meetings that took place with the chairmen of the dozen or so largest banks in the world, trying to convince them of their 'common interest' in resolving the crisis – given that if Mexico, Brazil, Venezuela, and Argentina failed to meet their payment schedules, commercial banks faced possible loan defaults totaling more than $175 billion.
> (Panitch & Gindin, 2012: 215)

Interpreting and translation into and out of English would have been one of those high prices. Another would have been the production of the key documentation in specific official languages, particularly English. Yet another would have been the salaries and travel expenses of the high-ranking officials of the various agencies involved – the Fed, the Treasury, the IMF, the World Bank – as well as of the local finance officials with whom they were negotiating. Most revealing though is Volcker's reference to how by virtue of their shared backgrounds they were 'almost uniquely able to deal with one another on the basis of close understanding and frankness'. It seems likely that part of the reason for this is that many of the non-anglophone representatives of the groups present could easily communicate with Volcker and his colleagues from the Fed and the US Treasury because – by dint of being members of the 'transnational bourgeoisie' (Soederberg, 2002: 178) – they were proficient speakers of English. Many had spent part of their education in elite centres of learning in the US or Britain, such as Harvard, Cambridge or Oxford, as continues to be the case today (Block, 2012b, 2017a; Harvey, 2003; Hannerz, 1990; Ives, 2010; Myers-Scotton, 1993; Phillipson, 1992; Sonntag, 2009; Vandrick, 1995, 2011, 2014).

Of course, the matter they had come together to discuss – structural adjustment of the economies of the debtor nations – did little to address the long-standing economic and social inequalities which had historically affected the Latin American continent, very often serving instead to calcify further the extreme disparities in wealth and opportunity which already existed within its nation-states, even as it created new elites and new divisions of labour. With the increased tying of national prosperity to SAPs, the elites and middle classes of Latin American societies became eager to consolidate and defend their economic position and social status and that of their children. This had an inevitable impact on the demand for English, which became ever more associated with personal advancement and the acquisition of capital in all its Bourdieusian forms (Bourdieu, 1977), in addition to its Marxist forms as well (Harvey, 2004). National governments responded accordingly by advocating education policies which made the learning of English an important [if not compulsory] subject on the curriculum (cf. Friedrich, 2000; Niño-Murcia, 2003; Velez-Rendon, 2003; Friedrich & Berns, 2003; Matear, 2008; Porto, 2014, Lopes Cardozo, 2012; Lehman, 2016; López-Gopar, 2016; Sayer, 2018). The private educational sector was very often one step ahead: offering English and English-medium instruction to the wealthier classes who were able to afford it (Sowden, 2012: 93–94).

The debt crisis to which Latin America gave its name threatened the solvency of the entire world financial system but was not confined only to Latin American states, and by the end of 1982, nearly forty nations had become drawn into its net. In addition to countries in Latin America [e.g. Argentina, Bolivia, Brazil, Chile, Costa Rica, Ecuador, Mexico, Nicaragua, Panama, Peru, Uruguay, Venezuela], the crisis enveloped countries in the Caribbean [e.g. Guyana, Honduras, Jamaica], several countries in Africa [e.g. Equatorial Guinea, the Ivory Coast, Liberia, Madagascar, Malawi, Nigeria, Somalia, Sudan, Uganda, Zaire], as well as reaching out to Asia and ensnaring the Philippines (Sachs, 1986: 397n). Resolution of the debt crisis came when the debtor nations succumbed to SAPs which left them at the mercy of the global markets:

> They could no longer rely on their relationships with foreign and domestic banking syndicates, and could now only attract capital if they submitted fully to the impersonal global financial markets. It was this submission which made the US Treasury's Brady Plan successful.
> (Panitch & Gindin, 2012: 216)[1]

Arrighi, with surgical precision, picks up the narrative:

> As if by magic, the wheel had turned. From then on, it would no longer be First World bankers begging Third World states to borrow their overabundant capital; it would be Third World states begging the First World governments and bankers to grant them the credit needed to stay afloat in an increasingly integrated, competitive, and shrinking world market.
> (Arrighi, 2010: 334)

---

1 For a summary of what the Brady Plan did, see *The Brady Plan* www.emta.org/template.aspx?id=35 Accessed August 13, 2017.

If the financialization of the US world-economy was not already the pivot for the unrivalled ideological dominance of English in the later twentieth century, it is perhaps in the US-orchestrated international response to the Latin American debt crisis, and its social and economic consequences for the nations concerned, that this pivot may be identified. The crisis required the massive institutional mobilization of the IMF, the World Bank and the G7, in tandem with creditors in the financial markets, and a broad swathe of national governments, in an unprecedented act of crisis management which was led by the US Treasury. It involved the assertion on a global scale of English as the premier language of international negotiation – and of its documentation – in order for a resolution to be reached (see also Chapter 6). The resolution had profound consequences for the economies concerned and for the manner in which they approached their relationship with the world-system. In most every case, this involved the promotion of English as a national priority for engagement with a *given* US-dominated globalized world. The ELT industries of the US and other 'inner-circle' English-speaking nations duly took advantage by free riding and aggressively promoting native-speaker models to them.

In the 1980s, the structural power of the US in the global economy was complemented and reinforced by the conduct of a series of 'dirty wars' against perceived system threats – communist and otherwise – in the developing South, particularly in Latin America and Africa (Harvey, 2003; Livingstone, 2009; Rabe, 2012; Blum, 2014). The US had a long history of such interventions, including China (1948–9), Iran (1950–3), Guatemala (1953–4), Vietnam (1950–73), Indonesia (1965–6), Angola (1975–80), and the infamous CIA-backed overthrow and murder of the democratically elected socialist president of Chile, Salvador Allende, in September 1973 (Loveman, 1988; Haslam, 2005; Guardiola-Rivera, 2013). The Reagan administration of 1981–9, awash with neoliberal and anti-communist ideologism following the Volcker shock, maintained this precedent with clandestine and often chaotic meddling in the countries and regions it considered as representing or harbouring threats to US capitalist power and interests. In the 1980s, this included covert operations in the Seychelles, Morocco and Libya (Blum, 2014). In addition, the US countenanced the direct military invasion of Grenada in 1983 and bankrolled the right-wing rebel 'Contra' armies in their clandestine terror war against the socialist Sandinista government of Nicaragua between 1981 and 1990. In spite of the Sandinistas' democratic popular mandate, Reagan described them as 'a cruel clique of committed Communists at war with God and man' (cited in Livingstone, 2009: 76). The US government also simultaneously engaged in a hugely expensive arms race which significantly contributed – against expectation – to the economic and political collapse of the Soviet Union in 1991. The cost to the Soviets of trying to keep pace with the US eventually became unsustainable, and this reality was then overtaken by the fall of the Berlin Wall in 1989 and the swift political and economic defection away from the

Soviet orbit of the USSR's vassal states in Eastern Europe. A number of these states were already drawn into the US world-economy as a result of the petrodollar loans which they had accepted from the financial markets in the aftermath of the 1974 oil crisis. These included Poland, Yugoslavia and Hungary (Panitch & Gindin, 2012: 217). In Russia, the realization that Soviet-style planning was no longer able to rely on a single-minded commitment to the Stalinist model of 'socialism in one country' to deliver economic progress had led in 1985 to the promotion of the relatively youthful Mikhail Gorbachev to the presidency (1985–91) and to a period of economic reform (*Perestroika*) and ideological thawing (*Glasnost*). But the process soon spiralled out of control, with the result that 'those who gained from the "market" were preeminently well-placed members of the former *nomenklatura*, speculators, and gangsters' (Cox, 1992: 26 cited in Panitch & Gindin, 2012: 218). The total collapse of the regime swiftly followed, leaving the US in 1991 as the sole global superpower and the apparent 'victor' in the ideological battle between US capitalism and Soviet communism which had commenced some forty-six years earlier.

The strengthening of the structural power of the US in the decade preceding the collapse of the Soviet Union was also assisted by the decision of the People's Republic of China in late 1978 to abandon the catastrophic economic and ideological legacy of Mao [while simultaneously repackaging this in a more ideologically palatable form], and to inaugurate an 'open door' policy which allowed for FDI and the development of capitalist enterprise and private accumulation, while keeping the levers of political power firmly in the hands of the party (see also Chapter 6). The policy was presented, with no hint of irony, as one of building 'socialism with Chinese characteristics' by the Chinese premier, Deng Xiaoping 邓小平 (1904–97), whose brainchild it was (Spence, 1990). Where the Russian Communist Party failed abysmally to manage the transition to a more open economy while holding onto political and ideological power, the Chinese Communist Party (CCP) was spectacularly successful, but only because it was able to rely on state coercion and the unflinching loyalty of the People's Liberation Army and the party apparatus to silence dissent. This enabled the transition to be gradual as well as tightly controlled. The recourse to state coercion was neither available nor politically tolerable in the disintegrating Russia of Gorbachev. In contrast to the gradualist approach of China, the transition to capitalism in Russia and its ex-satellite states took the form of a stampede (Panitch & Gindin, 2012: 218). The opening up of the countries of Eastern Europe, including Russia, to FDI and market capitalism would also open them up to English [M^E-C^E-M'^E; M^E-M'^E], particularly as the Russian language was in many East European states rapidly demoted from being a compulsory language on the school curriculum and supplanted by English, which had 'acquired the symbolic value of rescue from a communist regime' (Ustinova, 2005: 240; see also Fishman, 1998–9: 36). As far as the global projection of US power during the era of the Cold War was concerned, such an outcome could not have been better scripted.

Despite US advances, not everything went its way. The Iranian Revolution of 1979, following close upon US defeat in Vietnam a few years earlier, was a humiliating reversal in what was believed to be a regime secured to US interests, and with its leader Shah Mohammed Reza Pahlavi one of its closest anti-communist and English-language friendly allies (cf. Borjian, 2013; Blum, 2014; Goodrich, 2020). In addition to the loss of Iran, the US also lost control of Iraq, which under Saddam Hussein quickly took on the character of a 'rogue state' by instigating the Iran-Iraq War of 1980-8, and then attempting to annex oil-rich Kuwait, leading to the first Gulf War of 1990-1. Despite these disturbances, the US world-economy proved highly resilient, so that the US emerged from the 1980s in a position of increased strength. This was bolstered still further by the Soviet Union's collapse, leaving the US as the sole superpower in the world – a seismic event which Fukuyama (1992), aping Hegel,[2] prematurely characterized as the 'end of history' (p. xi). It was not the end of history, but due to US structuration of global capital accumulation in the decades after Bretton Woods (see Chapter 4), it was perhaps the end of the historical process by which English had become hardwired into the mainframe of the world-system [as M^E-C^E-M'^E and M^E-M'^E] and its foremost language of choice (Reksulak et al., 2004; Piller & Takahashi, 2006; Seargeant & Erling, 2011; Chowdhury & Phan, 2014; Ricento, 2015b; Phan, 2017).

Standard English as the capital-centric lingua franca of the capitalist world-system

The history of the US-led capitalist world-economy since the fall of the Soviet Union has been nothing if not tumultuous. Financialized systemic crises became more frequent, and the risks of destabilization and global breakdown that much greater. Shocks to the system and to its architecture became the main indices of structural crisis because the buoyancy or otherwise of global trade had come to be dictated by preternaturally fickle capital markets in conjunction with the strategic policy manipulations of the US Federal Reserve. In this environment gloom in the capital markets easily translated into gloom in the world-economy, and panic sentiments amongst market traders could quickly proliferate to become a contagion. Instantaneous financial panic became possible because of the huge expansion in commercial banking and credit operations in the 1970s and 80s along with the

---

[2] Hegelian thought posits the idea that once human beings acquire a state of full consciousness, the end of history will occur and people will be truly free (see Hegel, 1956 [1837]). Fukuyama was provocatively suggesting that, with the apparent 'victory' of capitalism over communism in 1991, that time had come.

seemingly inexorable rise of plastic money and complex derivatives. This was driven forward on the back of the information technology revolution, which automated much of the everyday financial trading while also making colossal trades available at the click of a mouse. Futures markets were created where 'hedged' fictitious capital (M-M') could be traded according to imagined future scenarios. These provided expansive virtual spaces for accumulation to occur (Harvey, 2010: 259). In the words of Marx, it is banking and credit which are 'the most powerful means for driving capitalist production beyond its own barriers' (1981 [1894]: 742).

From the 1980s and into the 1990s, what Harvey refers to as a 'fetish belief' increasingly took hold, one which was centred on credit and 'the virtues of growth' (2010: 259). Wrapped in the ideological trappings of neoliberalism (Hayek, 1944; Friedman, 1962; see also Peck, 2010; Stedman-Jones, 2012), the pursuit of growth became the dominant objective of the economies and governments of the capitalist world-system. Growth had become so important that it became the sole measure of the economic health of the world-economy and the nations within it. As Peter Taylor put it at the time, 'In a very real sense capitalism *is* economic growth, *it cannot stop*' (1996: 231). In addition to being ruthlessly pursued by governments domestically through the application of neoliberalist policies, it was also ruthlessly pursued internationally through the requirements attached to international financing and the free movement of capital. Nations that found themselves in financing difficulty, as many did, were subjected to IMF-sponsored SAPs to bring them back into line or, as happened with Russia in 1998 and Argentina in 2001–2, were abandoned to their own devices. In the world-economy at large the growth fairy was out of the bottle, and along with capital-centric English it appeared to consume all.

Fuelling the endless pursuit of growth was the endless pursuit of debt (Graeber, 2011). This emerged in the 1990s in the form of an ever-growing mass indebtedness of working individuals and families, of national governments and economies, and of the manipulators of capital themselves [i.e. manufacturers, corporate service providers, property speculators, financiers, local clientelist elites, middle-persons, etc.]. 'Debt for growth's sake' became the most fetishized of unspoken fetish capitalist universals. Accompanying and further fuelling the endless pursuit of debt was the seemingly endless reproduction of standard English – the symbiont free rider upon capital – since it was primarily through this medium that all international financial crises were managed and contained (see previously). In 1994, when Mexico entered into a second full-blown currency crisis, again initiated by the interest rate policy of the Fed, it was yet again through the medium of English in countless US-coordinated international rescheduling meetings that a wider financial contagion was averted. A $40 billion rescue package was put together between the US Treasury, the IMF, the World Bank and the Bank of International Settlements (BIS) to convince the markets that Mexico would not default (Panitch & Gindin, 2012: 252). It was the biggest ever bailout of a sovereign nation since the post-war Marshall Plan. But the price was the acceptance by Mexico of eternal debt peonage and further foreign capital penetration of its economy.

Writing in 2005, Harvey recorded that since 1980 'over fifty Marshall Plans (over $4.6 trillion) have been sent by the peoples in the Periphery to their creditors in the Center' (Harvey, 2005: 162). In these circumstances, the deep structural inequalities of Mexican society were unlikely to be remedied or altered in any meaningful way, and this included those that were based upon proficiency in standard English and other in-country linguistic distinctions, such as that which existed between Spanish and Mexico's many indigenous languages (López-Gopar, 2016). Mexican elites and their offspring would continue to have their private access to 'native-like' [or even entirely native] standard English, while the rest in state municipal schools made of English what they might, or made nothing of it at all. This was a pattern which was widely replicated across the whole of the Latin American continent and with an ever-growing intensity that was driven by US geopolitical obsessiveness with the region (Rabe, 2012; Blum, 2014). It was the acquiescence of the Mexican government to US neoliberal exigencies in the 1980s and early 1990s that led directly to the neo-Marxist Zapatista uprising in Chiapas on 1 January 1994 (Montessori, 2009). The continued neoliberalization of the Mexican economy and its opening up to foreign capital had been demanded by the US and by Canada as a condition of entry into the North American Free Trade Agreement (NAFTA), which was promulgated on the same day as the Chiapas revolt. The principal medium for the spoken and documentary negotiation of NAFTA was English, although the final agreement was also produced in French and Spanish (see also Chapter 6). The immediate downside of NAFTA was that it made Mexico even more sensitive, if that were possible, to US-instigated interest rate movements, as the currency crisis which followed in December 1994 revealed when pesos were fire-sold for dollars as capital fled the country.

There were seventy-two financial crises among low- and middle-income countries in the 1990s (Panitch & Gindin, 2012: 250), and each of these was managed by English-proficient international teams under the auspices of what Wade and Veneroso (1998) have referred to as the 'Wall Street-Treasury-IMF Complex'. The formal policy response was to ensure, whatever arrangements were made, that the debtor nations affected made continued binding commitments to restructure their economies along neoliberal lines in exchange for debt rescheduling and continued access to the international capital markets, thus pushing them still further into the eternal cycle of debt. As an inevitable accompaniment, elite groupings within the debtor nations became still more attached to the cultural and linguistic trappings of US-engineered processes of global capital accumulation (Nederveen Pieterse, 2009), and this inevitably included English in a normative standard form. This general pattern was repeated with the Asian financial crisis of 1997–8 and was also followed for the Argentinean crisis of 2001–2. In both these crises, IMF international teams directed by the US Treasury were closely involved in designing bailout and rescheduling packages which were put in place in negotiation with senior treasury officials and finance ministers of the affected nations, with English being a dominant spoken and documentary *lingua franca*. The Asian crisis led to a resolution which was satisfactory to its creditors, if not necessarily to the mass of the peoples of the nations that were affected. But the Argentinean crisis led to the decimation of the economy and widespread social unrest.

The Asian crisis was caused by an excess of unregulated private sector borrowing which went sour when it became apparent that the loans were grossly overextended. Capital flows into Asia had jumped from $40 billion in 1995 to $110 billion in 1996 (Panitch & Gindin, 2012: 254). The extent of the borrowing led to a full-scale liquidity crisis for Thailand, where the crisis broke, which soon spread to South Korea and Indonesia. The US Treasury, which had wished for Japan to carry the liquidity burden, decided to intervene once it became clear that without its support a contagion could not be averted. This had become the default market expectation for international crisis management and therefore the only way to prevent capital flight. South Korea presented a particular challenge as it was a capitalist mainstream economy. As the price of its intervention, the US Treasury in combination with the IMF demanded a doubling in the ceiling limit on foreign investments in South Korea from 26 per cent to 50 per cent (Panitch & Gindin, 2012: 257). They also demanded the emasculation of the local labour unions, which were viewed – both by the markets and by the newly elected Korean government itself – as overly militant and an impediment to neoliberal structural reform. A government-sanctioned programme of severe austerity was imposed which in addition to crushing the unions [by causing mass redundancies] had the side consequence of creating such an atmosphere of fear and insecurity that many Koreans found themselves driven to 'a collective neurosis of English fever' (Kim, 2002, cited in J-K Park, 2009: 50), particularly for American English. Since 1998 this has seen middle-class Koreans invest billions of Korean won in English-language learning inside and outside of Korea (J-K Park, 2009; J S-Y Park, 2010; Song, 2011; Block, 2012b). Korea is perhaps an extreme case, but not dissimilar waves of 'English fever', especially amongst the upper and middle classes in East Asia [e.g. Taiwan, Thailand, Indonesia], also date from this time (Chen, 2006; Lin, H-Y, 2012; Bennui & Hashim, 2014; Trakulkasemsuk, 2018; Hickey, 2018; Rini, 2014; Zein, 2019). The rush to normative English following the Asian crisis was also echoed in China's efforts to assert itself more forcefully within the global arena, particularly after its accession to the World Trade Organization (WTO, formerly the GATT) in 2001 and then in the run-up to hosting the Beijing Olympics in 2008 (Lo Bianco, Orton & Gao, 2009; L. Pan, 2015; Simpson, 2017; Gao, 2018). Vietnam too caught the English wave as it attempted to copy the

China growth model by positioning itself as a capitalist investment hub in Asia (Nguyen, 2017; Battelle, 2018; Karlin, 2019).

At the heart of the 1997 Asian crisis was an excess of financial deregulation in the economies that were initially affected – Thailand, South Korea and Indonesia. This allowed the private banking sectors in these countries to develop overseas debt exposures which were unsustainable. In the year prior to the crisis, the US Treasury with the full backing of Wall Street had persuaded the IMF to change its articles to '*require* member governments to remove capital controls and adopt full capital account convertibility' (Wade & Veneroso, 1998: 19). The Wall Street-Treasury-IMF Complex then sought to extend this policy to the WTO, in a move that was widely resisted, particularly in Asia, until the Asian crisis broke. With the crisis, the objections were overcome and more than seventy countries signed up to a WTO financial services accord for which the official primary documentation, as well as the accord itself, was drawn up in 'authentic' (*sic*) US English, in addition to Spanish and French. The resolution of the Asian crisis witnessed the imposition of neoliberalizing SAPs which involved the input of English-proficient, or native-fluent, 'outside experts' on the implementation of structural reform. Many of these agents were seconded from leading US investment banks such as Goldman Sachs, Merrill Lynch, JP Morgan, Lehman Bros and Morgan Stanley (Panitch & Gindin, 2012: 261). The structural reform process for recipients of IMF emergency assistance was in this way always mediated by English in a standard form. When the Asian crisis spread to Russia in 1998, the Russian parliament refused the IMF's terms and Russia was left to go it alone. But even in the process of negotiating its refusal, Russia's government representatives drew on their long experience of Soviet Cold War dialogues with the US to be able to present the Duma's refusal in a language which the US Treasury and the IMF would understand. An additional outcome of the Asian crisis was the further strengthening of US centrality in the functioning of the international financial system. The successful overcoming by the US of opposition to increased ceilings on the free movement of capital and FDI had an indelible effect because it marked the point at which the world-economy became so financialized that all crises would require US intervention if they were to be contained. The creation of the G20 alongside the G7 also dates from this time and was symptomatic not only of the US desire to integrate weaker states into supporting the financialized economic model which it favoured, but also in a language sense of how normative standard English had become the dominant language of capital [M^E-C^E-M'^E; M^E-M'^E] and of capitalist crisis management. The G20 came to take on a greater importance as the number of economic crises increased. Not only did it provide cover for US direction of the world-economy by bringing more nations into the strategic coordination process, it also became a means for the US to widen financial responsibility for containing the crises that occurred, especially following the crash of 2007–8 (Panitch & Gindin, ibid: 302).

A banking crisis in Brazil in 1999 and then in Turkey in 2001 was followed by the Argentinean peso crisis of 2001–2. The Brazilian and Turkish crises led to significant currency devaluations for the nations concerned, whiles the crises themselves were managed by the IMF through by now customary English-mediated SAPs. Like the Brazilian and the Turkish governments, the Argentine government initially agreed to submit itself to an IMF-sponsored SAP. But by August 2001, the US Treasury had come to the view that 'pulling the plug on Argentina could not result in serious financial consequences internationally' (Blustein, 2005, cited in Panitch & Gindin, ibid: 303). This view was also shared by the G7, whose senior member was also the US Treasury. Under G7 instruction, the IMF duly abandoned Argentina in late 2001 citing a lack of commitment to structural reform. The withdrawal of the IMF forced Argentina into an immediate default on its $93 billion external debt. The social dislocation and economic pain which this caused for Argentina over the next several years was immense and led to extreme political instability and a major intensification of poverty in what was already a deeply inegalitarian society. That a more general financial contagion did not follow the Argentinean default has been put down to the Fed's coincidental decision to cut interest rates in 2001, for fear of domestic deflation, and to keep rates low for the next five years. This enabled Argentina to claw its way back to relative stability – principally by rejecting external creditors' demands for structural reform (ibid: 304) – and then as it recovered to renegotiate its debt with its creditors and with the IMF. Access to the capital markets was also restored, but at the cost of a 25 per cent contraction in the Argentinean economy and Argentina's reinsertion into the eternal cycle of capital-induced debt. This was bad enough, but as in Mexico in 1994, it also calcified and further deepened the gross inequalities of Argentinean society, with a near tripling of the number of people living below the poverty line. In its own peculiar way, the Argentinean crisis also reinforced the dominance of normative American Standard English as the most-favoured language of international resort, since it was this form, or that which was associated with the imperial British, which the wealthy elites of Buenos Aires continued to send their children to learn. Even in the immediate aftermath of the worst of the crisis, when the opportunity to reflect might have suggested an alternative view, Friedrich (2003) found amongst university MBA students, 'These Argentines do not readily acknowledge other varieties of English other than American and British' (p. 178). More recent studies such as by that Porto (2014) do not suggest that a great deal has changed, even as she is critical of the linguistic imperialism view of Phillipson (1992). While there may be a greater consciousness of language variation in ELT in Argentina and more widely, this does not readily translate into a preference in language policy, in the activities of elites or in wider global-capitalist practice for anything other than 'nativized' norms. The reason for this is capital, which in every corner of the capitalist world-system presents us with English in an overwhelmingly normative standard form.

Harvey observed not long after the 1998 Asian crisis had passed,

> The effect [of the bailout] was to project US economic power outwards (in alliance with others wherever possible), to force open markets, particularly for capital and financial flows . . . and impose other neoliberal practices . . . upon much of the rest of the world.
>
> (2003: 70)

The projection of US power was also in its own way the systematic projection outwards of normative standard English, because by freeing capital to allow its 'easy entry and exit everywhere' (Wade & Veneroso, 1998: 20), so were nations and their national representatives drawn still further into the economic structural framework of the US world-economy and into its linguistic structural framework as well, with English in its by now mainly American standard form serving as the primary language of international resort, both in restructuring negotiations and in their documentation. This was despite there always being other available languages to draw on, since very many of the participants in these negotiations were highly proficient capital-networked translinguals themselves. Their presence at these meetings was, and still is, a structural 'outgrowth' of a capitalist world-economy which has been dominated by the United States since 1919, and before that by Britain (see Chapters 2 and 3). That normative standard English has the status of being a capital-networked *lingua franca* has the consequence that whenever the structural linguistic outgrowths – that is, agreements, contracts, legal protocols, treaties, communiques, terms of reference etc. – of the Wall Street-Treasury-IMF Complex and its state-based international interlocutors are placed on record – that is, *written down* – they are done so in an English in its normative standard form. This equally applies to the English-language communiques and diplomatic political statements of national governments around the world (see also Chapter 7).[3]

Within the realms of international diplomacy, politics and finance, the written [and very often spoken] omnipresence of normative standard English has played a determinant linguistic role in the dynamics of global capitalism and in the language policy priorities of national governments within the modern world-system. Not only does the free flow of capital 'ratchet up the power and legitimacy of the owners and managers of capital in the world at large' (Wade & Veneroso, ibid: 20), it also ratchets up the power and legitimacy of English in its standard form. The palpable obviousness of US power globally and of there being a formalized, if always idealized,

---

3 Witness for example the political statements in English of the Hong Kong Chief Executive, Carrie Lam, during the 2019–20 political crisis in the territory, as well as the statements officially translated into English that were issued by China about the crisis through official diplomatic channels and news agencies.

normative English which is associated with that power has not surprisingly made it a form which is in great popular demand amongst the largely class-based national and international elites from whose members many of the employees of the IMF, World Bank, OECD, UN, WTO and BIS etc. are drawn, and whose task it is to serve as the administrators and managers of the US-dominated capitalist world-system. Casting the net wider, these groups are also to be found in national governments, in the diplomatic corps, in finance ministries and central banks, in international trading networks [e.g. EU, ASEAN, MERCOSUR, NAFTA], in private international banking, in the capital markets, in multinational corporations, in export-oriented private businesses, in international news media and in global academia. They are the bedrock of elite capital and class-based elite education the world over (Block, 2014; Tupas, 2015, 2019; Zein, 2019). In these circumstances, it comes as no real surprise that the language policies of national governments and the entire output of the global ELT industry are geared towards the promotion of these forms, since the weight of capital behind them, both economic and cultural, in addition to the desire for it, is historically overwhelming. As Harvey puts it, 'the power centre can only operate in the way that it does because the rest of the world is networked and hooked into (and effectively "hooked on") a structured framework of interlocking financial and governmental (and supranational) institutions' (2003: 72). It is in this guise that the modern world-system of the twenty-first century is also networked and hooked on *capital-centric English*. This is a normative standard English which derives its dominance in the present day from the hegemonic power of US capital in the modern world-system and by free riding upon it [M^E-C^E-M'^E; M^E-M'^E]. Prior to this, it was primarily derived from the hegemonic dominance of the capital networks of the City of London (see Chapters 2 and 3).

Sub-prime, the derivatives revolution and capital-centric English

The monetary liquefaction and spatial expansion of global finance which technological innovation and the trade in derivatives made possible also made the world-economy a much more volatile place. Systemic crisis became a more regular occurrence, often due to the domestic and international economic interests of the US leading to policy decisions which impacted adversely, and often with savagery, on other parts of the world, as well as its own citizens. Up until 2007 the crises that occurred had been regional and mostly located in semi-peripheral economies outside the capitalist core, such as in Argentina, Indonesia, Russia, the Philippines and Thailand, or in states that were on the cusp of the core, such as South Korea and Singapore. This was to change when the multi-trillion-dollar trade in mortgage-backed derivatives exploded in the market's face. The difference here was that the epicentre of the crisis was the United States and that responsibility for it lay squarely with the unregulated proliferation in the US of a derivatives market whose foundations were the mortgage debts of officially uncreditworthy, or 'sub-prime', US borrowers. These borrowers came from the most vulnerable and least financially secure sections of US society, mainly the working class and the poor, especially African Americans and ethnic minorities in this latter category. What seemed to be – at first sight – a localized liquidity problem on the margins of the US economy quickly became a global financial conflagration when the sub-prime borrowers – who had been ruthlessly targeted by predatory US-based mortgage brokers and banks – began defaulting on their debts. As the crisis unravelled in 2007–8 the mortgage-backed derivatives, which up to then had made huge returns, were revealed to be a gigantic Ponzi scheme.[4] Warren Buffett would later describe them as 'financial weapons of mass destruction, carrying dangers that . . . are potentially lethal'.[5] Through a complex series of financial trades, the default risk attached to sub-prime debt was passed from one market investor to the next, with the investor at each price-enhanced level of the trade being responsible for insuring the leveraged loss of the investor one level below them. To add to the complexity, the risky sub-prime debts were innovatively parcelled up inside what appeared to be superficially sound debt portfolios, or credit default swaps (CDSs), which had – through a wilful act of amnesiac denial – been given a 'triple A' rating by US credit agencies. Like Marx's commodity, the debt portfolios only revealed their fetish appearance to investors who, blinded by the profits on hand, were less than interested in the reality of the social relations which lay behind them. The investors higher up the investment chain included many of the world's leading financial institutions and a large number of major domestic banks in different parts of the world, including Europe, the US and Asia. Mesmerized by the returns on derivatives, the markets and its individual traders, complicit with the US Treasury and government, allowed a collective amnesia to descend regarding the precise origins of the mortgage debts which made up the derivatives portfolios and which had been aggressively foisted onto sub-prime borrowers through the sharp practices of an almost entirely deregulated US mortgage market.

In the markets, the sole purpose of the individuals who were responsible for making the derivatives trades was simply to make the trade. What happened to the CDS afterwards was of little or no concern; it was the problem and responsibility of the next leveraged purchaser higher up in the chain, and with whom the ultimate risk now lay. When the sub-prime crisis broke, the derivatives-based debt portfolios were shown to be built on thin air, and like a house of cards they duly collapsed as holders tried to offload them

---

4 Named after Charles Ponzi (1882–1949), who created the first one in Boston in 1919, a Ponzi scheme is a pyramid investment vehicle which promises guaranteed – and often very large – returns based on a 'virtuous' cycle of investment. But once any investor defaults, or there is an unforeseen external shock, the virtuous cycle is 'broken' and the entire scheme collapses.

5 www.berkshirehathaway.com/letters/2002pdf.pdf Accessed August 11, 2017.

to avoid being saddled with the by now gigantically over-leveraged CDSs. By mid-2008, for example, 'the market for credit default swaps exceeded the entire world economic output by $50 trillion' (Zucchi, 2019). At their source the derivatives portfolios relied critically upon sub-prime borrowers in the US maintaining their mortgage repayment commitments. Once they did not, as ominously began happening on a noticeably increased scale, first in Cleveland and Detroit in 2006 and then in working class districts of Florida, California and Nevada in mid-2007 [the Fed ended the low interest rate regime it had been favouring since 2001 to adopt a higher interest rate regime], it led to a market contagion which spread to engulf the entire financial system: 'It was because US finance had become so integral to the functioning of twenty-first century global capitalism that the ultimate impact of this crisis throughout the international economy was so profound' (Panitch & Gindin, 2012: 311). Holders of derivatives-based debt portfolios when the crisis hit – mostly domestic banks in the US, Europe and Asia and large global financial institutions like Lehman Bros, JP Morgan and Goldman Sachs – were left with enormous liabilities on the toxic derivatives portfolios which they held, and which they did not have the financial resources to meet. Despite the telegraphed warning signs from as early as 1998 that the derivatives market was out of control, the US government and Treasury, mostly under the watch of the Republican Bush administration (2001–9), chose to ignore them and were caught cold when the market self-destructed. A bewildered George W Bush watched supinely from the White House [as did neoliberal governments the world over] as Lehman Bros went bust under an avalanche of derivatives-based sub-prime debt on September 15, 2008. Overnight a global financial sclerosis broke out as markets froze and inter-bank lending dried up. Since no one knew who was holding the bad debt or how much, and the US Treasury and government were so obviously sitting on their hands, nobody would take the risk of lending and finding themselves exposed. The rest, as they say, is history.

Once the true extent of the financial sector's exposure became more fully revealed, the markets and the banks were massively bailed out by huge injections of taxpayers' money in an internationally coordinated – and English-mediated – multi-trillion-dollar Keynesian intervention by national governments and central banks across the world (Panitch & Gindin, 2012: 320). This was carried out in the face of much public anger in the economies affected, while a massive systematic whitewashing of ideological neoliberalism's responsibility for and complicity in the crisis immediately got underway. In the eyes of the leading capitalist economies of the core, since there was no question of dismantling capitalism or admitting that the promises of neoliberalism concerning endless growth and shared prosperity for all were in reality a fetish illusion, it was overgenerous public spending that was somehow singled out for attention, and for blame. In this narrative it was not so much a reform of capitalism that was required as an increased need for governments to exercise even greater financial probity by reducing public spending and by the further shifting of assets in the public domain into the more 'economically efficient' private domain, while also making a show of introducing some regulatory controls and safeguards to ward against unfortunate market aberrations. In this way, in an astonishing act of self-denial, the considered solution to a crisis wrought by neoliberalism was sought and legitimated in the further application of neoliberalism. It was to be business as usual. The neoliberal response to the market failure was realized in the form of an austerity model that was savagely applied in Europe, Asia and Latin America, and which plunged the world-economy into recession over the next several years. The US was not immune, although it was spared the worst of the global downturn by the dollar's continued centrality and seignorage within the world-system.[6] Nevertheless, foreclosures spread and the traditional rust belt industries of the industrial United States – particularly automobiles, steel and coal – suffered greatly. A largely White, blue collar American working class, in regions such as Detroit, Pennsylvania, West Virginia and Illinois, watched as the factories, manufacturing plants and mines which gave them employment were shut down in the face of stiff overseas competition and in the absence of any government support. As a consequence, many of those in the towns and cities that were most affected became willing consumers of populist neoliberal explanations for the recession and also of the simplistic protectionist 'post-truth' antidotes which were offered up by right-wing demagogues like Donald Trump (Block, 2019).

Less well-remembered was that it had been George W Bush who when in office had undoubtedly initiated the downturn by implementing the most neoliberal economic policy agenda since Reagan in the 1980s and compounded the error by blindly pursuing a policy of ideological market deregulation that inexorably led to the 2007–8 financial crash. Yet this was fairly much forgotten as soon as Barack Obama took office for the Democrats in 2009. The Obama administration (2009–17) found itself almost entirely hamstrung by the scale of the financial crisis which it had inherited from Bush, as well as overwhelmed by the severe economic recession which this brought forth; in addition, his administration also inherited several US-promulgated global war zones created as a result of 'knee-jerk' US foreign policy decisions following the 9/11 attacks in 2001.[7] His room for manoeuvre being extremely restricted, Obama [who was himself no instinctive Keynesian] discovered that he could do little more than carry through

---

6 In 2020 foreign investors held approximately $6.2 trillion in US public debt. The largest holders of this debt were Japan at $1.15 trillion and China at $1.07 trillion. www.statista.com/statistics/246420/major-foreign-holders-of-us-treasury-debt/ Accessed April 25, 2020.
7 One consequence of the Bush administration's foreign policy initiatives after 9/11 was that the war zones they created also became sites for the production and reproduction of normative standard English, alongside other realizations, as the English of the US occupiers and its allies became the official international language of occupation while also intermingling with the languages of the peoples who came under allied control.

the market bailout package that had already been agreed under Bush, while also continuing to commit his administration to the principles of open markets and US leadership of the world-economy under the *Pax Americana* (see Chapter 4). Ideologically, Obama was also severely hamstrung by the Republican dominance of Congress throughout the period of his presidency, which made it extremely difficult for him to do anything more than make piecemeal interventions at the margins of US political and economic life [with the possible precarious exception of Obamacare], as much as he publicly attempted to pursue a more intellectually informed agenda on both the domestic and international fronts. Obama's inability to protect US industry from the economic ravages of the bailout and the ensuing recession enabled Trump to lead a racially charged, anti-Washington and pro-protectionist presidential campaign in which Obama and free-trade Democratic liberalism were blamed for the fallout from the financial crisis and for the subsequent economic slump. The strategy paid off and Trump duly repelled the [exceedingly poorly managed] White House bid of the Democratic nominee Hilary Clinton to emerge as president in 2016.

The complicity of the markets and of the neoliberal ideology which railroaded them to disaster was after 2009 mostly papered over or ignored. What had occurred was also so staggeringly complex that there was little public stamina for the detail, and this made it easier for neoliberal apologists to obfuscate about responsibility for the crisis while also absolving the market of any intrinsic wrongdoing, since there was 'obviously' no other choice to the market, or so it seemed. Something had evidently gone terribly wrong, but few beyond a relatively small coterie of left- and centre-left economists, politicians, political activists and academics wished to spend time following a trail which might lead to the justifiable conclusion that what was really necessary was the dismantling of financialized capitalism itself. For the champions of ideological neoliberalism on the other hand, market failure was and is an anathema, since all crises are the result of the ineffective liberalization of economies and the constraints which are placed upon capital and its accumulation. This leads to market distortions which prevent markets from doing their job of naturally reaching equilibrium (Duménil & Lévy, 2011; Stedman-Jones, 2012; Mirowski, 2014; Harvey, 2014). The Keynesian correction which straightforwardly showed this claim to be false and which saved the market from itself was treated as 'an ongoing or permanent state of exception' which could conveniently be ignored (Davies, 2013, cited in Mirowski, 2014: 85). The neoliberal calculation following the crisis was, as it always had been, to commit people freely to the rational irrationality of the market to such an extent that to turn back and take another course would not be a conceivable option. As Marx puts it, they found themselves 'compelled to submit to the dictates of capital' (1976 [1867]: 532). Hence, so long as a majority of the public were convinced that an outright capitalist collapse would be a personal and familial catastrophe – e.g. in terms of income, life savings, home ownership, credit repayments, university fee annuities, pension funds and so on – as much as it would be a societal one, it would not be in their rational interests to opt for an alternative, that is, one which might be more interventionist and socially inclusive and which would place limits on the unbound freedom of capital to accumulate and crash.

Bhaskar refers to this conundrum as a TINA compromise formation: A TINA ('there is no alternative') formation is basically 'the suppression by the false of the truth on which it depends and which sustains it' (Bhaskar, 2002: 219, cited in Hartwig, 2011: 247). Here, the falsity that is neoliberal capitalism is sustained by the freedom of humans to choose rationally between better or worse outcomes. Human beings, imagining no way out, are in this manner freely contracted into the maintenance of their own oppression. It has been a singular aim of the neoliberal project that fear of market failure should become part of the neoliberal subject's conscious subjectivity (Foucault, 2008 [1979]). In a similar manner, the pluralized hybridism of Englishes and of documented English realizations in the world tends to fall away once capital is invoked in relation to them; which is to say that human beings are free to express themselves in English as they will, but when and where capital is present or at stake, their freedom to choose most usually directs them to the normative standard form (see later). This assumes of course that this form is within their repertoires to be able produce it, or that they at least have this aspiration. For example, international multi- and plurilingual workers[8] in the modern world-system – e.g. economists, politicians, lawyers, accountants, market traders, information technologists, veterinarians, doctors, NGO activists, international academics, diplomats, development workers etc. – as well as the institutions that they work for, are critically agential in this respect. Their existence as ambassadors and reproducers of the normative form is undoubtedly significantly responsible for the perceived social and economic value that is widely attached to it, and for its ongoing global persistence.

Language as a dialectical practical consciousness and the financial crisis of 2007–8

Drawing upon the base-superstructure perspective of Marx (see Chapter 1), the 2007–8 financial crisis was a dialectical event in that it was not only economic and material, it was also semiotic and ideological. Language [along with other semiotic modes] acted as a *practical consciousness* for the crisis and for its wider realization (Williams, 1977: 29; see also Chapter 1). The dialectical element is important here, for language is not a simple reflection of reality. As was argued in Chapter 1, language, like Foucault's power

---

8 I think of multilingual and plurilingual as synonymous terms. The latter has, however, become increasingly current for describing speakers of two or more languages.

(1980), produces and shapes reality, while also continuously being shaped by it. But in people's daily activity, the conventional structures which govern language and those which govern reality are for the most part unconsciously selected and reproduced, in addition to being already made. As Bhaskar (1998) has argued, just as people do not consciously marry in order to sustain the nuclear family or the capitalist world-economy, neither do elite plurilinguals consciously select normative standard English in order to shore up the global dominance of inner-circle forms or elitist inter-class distinctions.[9] But this structural effect 'is nevertheless the unintended consequence (and inexorable result) of, as it is also a necessary condition for, their activity' (Bhaskar, ibid: 35). That is not to say such choices are never consciously made, since it is evident that the pursuit of the normative standard in global ELT is often consciously driven at the personal and industry levels by economic, cultural and class considerations, as much as it is by fetishized [i.e. fantastical or misrecognized] individual concerns with linguistic authenticity and correctness (Blommaert, 2010; Cavanaugh & Shankur, 2014; Lacoste, Leimgruber & Breyer, 2014).

These circumstances are as Bhaskar says a 'necessary condition' because society pre-exists us: 'social forms are a necessary condition for any intentional act, that their pre-existence establishes their autonomy as possible objects of scientific investigation' (Bhaskar, 1998: 25). In opposition to the notion that human action determines social formations or that social formations determine human action, we have instead the conception that social formations are something that people do not construct themselves but whose existence is nevertheless a consequence of their activity (ibid: 1998: 34; see also Marx, 1978 [1852]: 595). Human beings do not construct social formations themselves because such formations do not spontaneously arise from the activity of people – 'people do not create society [because] all activity presupposes the prior existence of social forms' (Bhaskar, 1998: 36, 34). Desiring social change – such as desiring for example that users of English should globally desist from deferring to native-speaker norms (Widdowson, 1994: 382; Jenkins, 2006: 171) – is therefore not in itself a sufficient basis for social change to occur (see also Chapter 7). When changes in social forms or structures do occur, 'the explanation will not normally lie in the desire of agents to change them that way' (Bhaskar, ibid: 35). The actions of human beings, and that includes practical and conscious acts of language, are all incidences of praxis within a socially reproductive and dialectical relation of process: 'When praxis is seen under the aspect of process, human choice becomes a functional necessity' (Bhaskar, ibid: 34). Choice becomes a necessity because the social forms which exist, and which also pre-exist us, must be viewed as enabling and not only as constraining or restricting,

---

9 Although a concern with maintaining one's elite position and that of one's family can be a conscious motivation of members of elite groups.

although they are that as well. As Foucault often said in respect of power, 'Power is exercised through networks, and individuals do not simply circulate in those networks; they are in a position to both submit to and exercise this power. They are never the inert or consenting targets of power' (2003: 29). Similarly, for Bhaskar, we are enabled to act within the social forms which precede and envelop us and which reproductively rely upon us. But not in any one-dimensional or deterministic way. Bhaskar suitably draws an analogy from language:

> [W]e can allow that speech is governed by the rules of grammar without supposing . . . that these rules exist independently of usage (reification) or that they determine what we say. The rules of grammar, like natural structures, impose limits on the speech acts we can perform, but they do not determine our performances. This conception thus preserves the status of human agency, while doing away with the myth of creation (logical or historical), which depends upon the possibility of an individualist reduction. And in so doing it allows us to see that necessity in social life operates in the last instance via the intentional activity of agents.
>
> (Bhaskar, 1998: 36)

The modernist illusion of there being an immutable and timeless canon of normative rules existing separately from actual language use,[10] whether spoken or written, is the common resort of the language prescriptivist, who revels in the tortures of language stasis and stifling linguistic conformity – of language imagined as a unified and enclosed system of abstract code (Otsuji & Pennycook, 2010; Dufva, Suni, Aro & Salo, 2011; Park & Wee, 2012; Blommaert, 2016). Nevertheless, the constraint which abstract grammatical conventions provide is both sociolinguistically sustained and simultaneously undermined by the human capacity for agency and creativity (Hymes, 1974). Human beings can choose to abide or not to abide by socially given constraints, but in Bhaskar's meaning they do so in accordance with their comprehension of the 'processual real' and how they have been socialized into this. Where their socialization calls for the reproduction of the normative form, they will reproduce it [if they can]. That is, they will consciously adapt their language practice to the processes which govern the standard's realization (Bernstein, 1971; Bourdieu, 1991; Otsuji & Pennycook, 2010; De Costa, Park & Wee, 2016, 2019), as is common in English-medium international academia for example. But where this constraint is absent or less manifest, they can choose to do otherwise and opt for alternative realizations and varietal forms (Mauranen, 2015; Canagarajah, 2018).

---

10 NB This is a distinctly un-Chomskyan notion and should not be confused with what Chomsky has to say about universal grammar.

In such circumstances, actual practices and beliefs about practices rarely coincide (Blommaert, 2016).

For Bhaskar's dialectic, as it was for Marx's, 'it is the task of the different social sciences to lay out the structural conditions for various forms of conscious human action' (Bhaskar, 1998: 36); that is, to ask what the material processes are that must be in place to make particular social acts possible; for example, for acts of state terror to occur, for there to be mass migrations of people from the global South to the global North, or for there to be environmental destruction of the planet. Following this line of reasoning, if we ask what economic and historical processes need to be in place for normative standard English to be the default signified for international communication, we find that these processes are represented by the endless accumulation of capital within a capitalist world-system in which the dominant hegemonic powers for nearly four hundred years have been anglophone nations. This processual reality has enabled the development of a dialectical practical consciousness whose unintended consequence [but evidently also at times intended (Phillipson, 2008, 2018; Lemberg, 2018)] has been the endless reproduction and free riding of normative standard English (Gramsci, 1975: 2343; Ives, 2010: 528: Park & Wee, 2012: 109) as the fetishized universal for global English production and use [M^E-C^E-M'^E; M^E-M'^E], and against which all deviations are implicitly compared (see Chapter 7).

In this light, the derivatives revolution, which was conceived in Wall Street in the 1970s and which issued from the US to colonize the world's financial system in the years down to the 2007–8 crash, can be seen to have crucially relied upon the concerted collaboration of international capital investment networks for which normative standard English [by means of its proximity to US capital] was the consequent default language of resort. It was employed at a concrete level for the negotiation and documentation of trades within the world-economy and at a more abstract level as a *transactional lingua franca* (see Chapter 1) for the facilitation of the M^E-M'^E capital circuit. In addition, for the 2007–8 global financial crisis to become the full-blown crisis it became, it required a shared language through which the crisis, and the panic that created it, could be mediated and spread (see also Chapter 1). Lastly, it also necessitated a language through which the international bailouts that followed, mainly under the oversight of the G20, could be negotiated and disbursed. The structural frameworks of the global capital markets and the institutions of global financial governance, such as the IMF, World Bank, the Fed, G7 and G20, thus provided the necessary conditions for normative standard English to be called upon by means of the conscious linguistic practices of the plurilingual and monolingual users of English who worked in and through them. Bringing in the G20 was a deliberate attempt to widen responsibility for the management and resolution of the crisis beyond the G7 and was principally pushed forward as a strategy by the UK government acting with US support. This created the coincidence that the lead governments in the international response to the crisis were successive hegemons of the world-system in addition to being native purveyors of English standard norms. This certainly facilitated communication between the US and the UK, but it also represented a further affirmation, if any were needed, of the supremacy of normative English in the management, administration and reproduction of the capitalist world-economy. This supremacy is now being contested by the developing structural power of China and of Mandarin Chinese as a rival global language to English. Whether China is to succeed the United States as the next global hegemon, and as part of that, whether English is likely to be displaced by Mandarin as the dominant language in the world-system, is the subject of the next chapter.

6 The decline of the US world-hegemony

US hegemonic decline and the rise of China

The United States has been the leading power of the capitalist world-system for over one hundred years, and the dollar has been the international reserve currency for all of that time within an international monetary and trading system which the US took the lead in designing, and which by the 1980s had placed it in a position of enormous structural power in the world-system. The only clear rival to the US was the Soviet Union, but its rivalry was mainly geopolitical and military, because economically the USSR was already a spent force, and outside of clientelist states, Russian was not a rival to English. In the 1990s, with the collapse of the Soviet Union, the United States believed that it no longer had a rival, that the world it had inherited was a unipolar one, and that the US was at its summit. But a relative fading of the US hegemony had already set in. In retrospect, it was initially telegraphed by Nixon's unilateral decision to take the US off the gold standard in 1971 and by the economic crises which then followed through the 1970s and 1980s (see Chapters 4 and 5). Nevertheless, such was the extent of US structural power and seignorage, enhanced further by the demise of the USSR, that its gradually weakening economic position was obscured by the lack of a credible challenger, and also by its singular foreign policy aggressiveness in its governance of the international monetary system (see Chapters 4 and 5). In East Asia, it was Japan that in the 1970s and 80s had been considered the main global contender for mounting a serious economic challenge to the dominance of the US. But by the 1990s, Japan had slipped into a protracted period of economic stagnation from which it has never properly recovered (Akram, 2019). In Europe, the only credible candidate was the EU, but like much of East Asia, this owed its strategic security to the US and was far from being a unified or coherent political challenger, even as it was in some areas – and mainly in the form of Germany – a mighty economic one. As a beneficiary of the postwar international trading system, it was also not in the interests of the EU or its member states to destabilize or disrupt a global trading system which had since 1945 seemed to serve Europe so well. Given these circumstances, the US in the 1990s tended to view itself as the unrivalled leader of a largely integrated international political and trading order to which states that desired engagement in it were required to conform. There were a few significant outliers, such as North Korea, Cuba, Vietnam, and in those days China too. They were also not members of the WTO [until 1995 known as the GATT]. Despite this, they and other non-WTO members were still obliged to trade on a world market and within a world-economy that was configured along US lines and dominated by the dollar and English [M^E-C^E-M'^E; M^E-M'^E].

Such was the new-found sense of US power that China's accession to the WTO in 2001 was taken as a sign that Beijing was readying itself for a market-led transformation of its internal economy, which would make FDI and access to China's enormous domestic market much easier. In successive White Houses in the 1990s and 2000s, the belief was widely held that the increased marketization and opening up of China would also inevitably lead to democratization and reform. This was because US senior foreign policy advisors as well as many liberal international relations theorists held to the view that China's burgeoning middle classes and its increasingly wealthy 'new capitalist' elites would in time refuse to accept one-party rule and that their demands for greater political freedom and representation would in due course become irresistible, as had historically occurred in the West (see Chapter 2). In addition, with its accession to the WTO, China appeared to have opted for the path to socialized cooperative compliance with 'the rules and norms of the contemporary international order' (Dian, 2016: 127; see also, Zoellick, 2005; Johnstone, 2007). Structural realists, on the other hand, rather than seeing the development of capitalist enterprise as a possible new democratic opening, drew attention to the Chinese state's pathological obsession with state control and the historically institutionalized unequal partnership that had always existed between the state and commercial interests in China since the time of the imperial dynasties (Milanovic, 2020). In the international arena, China was viewed by some commentators not as a socialized co-operator, but as a significant source of regional instability and threat: 'A wealthy China would not be a status quo power but an aggressive state determined to achieve regional hegemony' (Mearsheimer, 2001, cited in Dian, 2016: 125; see also Mearsheimer, 2006; Goldstein, 2007; Friedberg, 2011).

The culmination of China's acceptance into the international capitalist order was symbolically commemorated by Beijing's success in winning the bid to host the 2008 Olympics. The period between 2001 and 2008 also saw an even greater surge in the popularity of English-language learning in China (Adamson, 2004; Orton, 2009; L. Pan, 2015; Gao, 2018), and the preparations for the games themselves saw a transformation of China's linguistic landscape as regional authorities set about the 're-assemblage' of public signage to include both Chinese and English text (Fong, 2009; Pan, 2010). A noticeable example at the time was the bilingual reinvention of mass transport systems in cities such as Beijing, Guangzhou and Shanghai so that they came to resemble those of Hong Kong and Singapore, where such practices had long been the norm. In language policy too, while making English the central foreign language on the school curriculum and also for university entrance, the Chinese Ministry of Education also consistently distanced itself from associating English with any particular cultural model, characteristically preferring to emphasize its instrumental utility for international business, presentation of the Chinese way of life to others, and the patriotic cultivation of 'national spirit', while also ambivalently advocating in language education and pedagogy a functional conformity to normative forms (Pan, 2011; Z. Pan, 2015; Gao, 2018; Feng & Adamson, 2019).

China's structural power

China's rise has been nothing short of meteoric. In 1978–9, when the 'open door' policy was initiated, China's share of global GDP was 1.8 per cent (Lin, 2011). By 2017, it had grown to 15.24 per cent,[1] with average growth rates of 10 per cent per annum between 1990 and 2010. Its annual GDP in 2019 was $14.1 trillion, which was more than Japan, the UK, Germany and India combined, and second only to the United States with $21.4 trillion.[2] It has also since 2010 outstripped the US as the largest annual contributor to world growth.[3] Prior to the onset of the COVID-19 pandemic, it had been estimated that by 2030 China would have overtaken the US as the world's largest economy. As yet, it is not clear whether this can still be achieved, although the indications would appear that it remains likely. China is also the largest holder of foreign exchange reserves in the world, with holdings to the value of $3.06 trillion in March 2020,[4] the vast majority of which is held in US dollars (Ito & McCauley, 2019). This is for an economy that was once dismissed outright as a Maoist 'basket case' (Wallerstein, Collins, Mann, Derlugian & Calhoun, 2013; Tooze, 2019), and even after the opening up in 1978–9 was not taken seriously as a global rival to the US until some years into the 2000s. Even then, more attention was still being given to Japan and Europe than to China. In some respects, the rise of China literally 'crept up' on the United States. For Fareed Zakaria, the singular error of the US after the collapse of the USSR was 'to stop paying attention' (Zakaria, 2019: 14). According to this narrative, the US had become

---

1 www.investopedia.com/insights/worlds-top-economies/#2-china Accessed April 14, 2020.
2 www.imf.org/external/pubs/ft/weo/2019/02/weodata/index.aspx Accessed April 14, 2020.
3 www.cnbc.com/2019/09/24/how-much-chinas-economy-has-grown-over-the-last-70-years.html Accessed April 14, 2020.
4 www.ceicdata.com/en/indicator/china/foreign-exchange-reserves Accessed April 14, 2020.

weary of its hegemonic role and had already psychologically determined to disengage:

> By the mid-1990s, it had lost all interest in the world. . . . Even amid the foreign economic crises that hit during the Clinton administration, U.S. policymakers had to scramble and improvise, knowing that Congress would appropriate no funds to rescue Mexico or Thailand or Indonesia. They offered advice, most of it designed to require little assistance from Washington, but their attitude was one of a distant well-wisher, not an engaged superpower.
>
> (Zakaria, 2019: 14)

When George W Bush became US president by a whisker over Al Gore in 2000, much of the rest of the world was taken aback that the most powerful nation on earth could elect for its president someone so intellectually wooden and wholly lacking in charisma as Bush. Bush lived up to his billing and had a disastrous presidency, both as a ruinously ultra-orthodox neoliberal on the domestic front and as a 'knee-jerk' right-wing hawk in the international arena. The administration's response to the 9/11 attacks massively destabilized the Middle East, and its ideology-led deregulation of corporate finance and banking led directly to the economic crash of 2007–8 (see Chapter 5). Bush and his closest advisors seemed for a time to be paralyzed by the fallout and meekly looked on as the world's financial system began to collapse. In the end, it took the collective intervention of the G20 at the behest of the British prime minister, Gordon Brown, to shake the US administration out of its shell-shocked torpor.

In the first decade of the new century while Bush committed the US and its allies to an all-out war on Islamist extremism and bailing out the global financial system, China followed the adage of Deng Xiaoping 邓小平: 'Hide your strength, bide your time' (cited in Zakaria, 2020: 60). The US became so deeply embroiled in the regional geopolitics of the Middle East and in coming to terms with the aftermath of the global financial crash that it seemed as if China had become the second largest economy in the world almost unnoticed. This was not truly the case, because China had been noticed, but there were few in Washington who thought that such an overtly authoritarian model of capitalism could be sustained into the long run, and that China would sooner or later succumb to the 'middle-income trap' of a being a developing country that is permanently unable to catch up with the rich nations of the global capitalist elite (Woo, 2012; Tooze, 2019; Zakaria, 2020). In 1913, for example, Argentina had been the fastest growing nation of the preceding forty-three years, and it was assumed at the time that Argentina would soon advance to become one of the richest nations in the world, as had other settlement territories such as Australia and the United States. But it did not happen that way as Argentina foundered in economic mismanagement, social inequality and political authoritarianism. Many observers believed that China would go the same way unless it committed itself to political democratization, deep market reform [i.e. far beyond what it was already doing], and as Woo puts it, to 'the global perspective that is required of a world leader who will work for the protection of the global environmental commons, the global trading system, and global security' (Woo, 2012: 332).

This also mattered a good deal for English, because at a global level, it meant that China was still doing much of its international politics and its external business on terms dictated by the world-economy of the United States, and that included using normative standard English as the *lingua franca* of choice for its diplomacy, its international commerce and finance, and the ideological promotion of its particular brand of authoritarian political capitalism (Milanovic, 2020). China's approach to capitalism, or what Deng Xiaoping dubbed 'socialism with Chinese characteristics', was most notable for its consistent centralized state authoritarianism, even as it liberalized its economy, and for the evident development successes which this engendered. After the 2008 crash it soon became clear that the international geo-economic battleground, as well as that of ideological contestation, would for the future be between competing visions of capitalism: the neoliberal quasi-meritocratic model represented by the United States and the state-led authoritarian model represented by China. This competition took on added vigour and poignancy with the election of Xi Jinping 习近平 as leader of the Chinese Communist Party (CCP) and president of China in 2012. Under his personal rallying leitmotif of 'Chinese Dream' 中国梦, Xi oversaw the most brutal and oppressive centralization of power in China since the era of Mao (McGregor, 2019). Under the guise of a far-reaching anti-corruption drive, the Party apparatus was ruthlessly purged of potential rivals and opponents, and in ethnic minority regions such as Xinjiang and Tibet political dissent was severely curtailed by means of intrusive surveillance measures, compulsory work-based political training in 'Xi Jinping thought' 习近平思想, and the mass internment of suspected minority activists in gigantic purpose-built re-education camps. After the economic trauma and political chaos of the later Mao era, the rehabilitated Deng Xiaoping had provided that the new constitution of 1982 should limit the presidency to a maximum of two five-year terms. The article stating this was adhered to until 2018, when Xi arranged for the National People's Congress to abolish the two-term limit so making it possible for him to remain president in perpetuity. It was as if China and the CCP had witnessed the twenty-first century resurrection of Mao. A critical dimension of the political-economic regime that has been instituted by Xi is the strict paramountcy of the Party in all spheres, including that of private enterprise – which accounts for more than 60 per cent of China's GDP – and unwavering support for the state sector, even when unprofitable (McGregor, ibid). For Xi, there is a balance to be struck between the private sector and the state, and that balance necessitates that China's private sector unquestioningly supports and is firmly in the service of the state and the CCP. Xi has made many enemies in the process amongst the wealthy classes and party officials caught up in his corruption purge, within the Party's side-lined technocratic elite, amongst private companies whose profits the CCP has sequestered, and overseas amongst Asia's regional powers, who see Xi's China as a growing menace and destabilizing force.

Internationally, in 2013 Xi launched the $1 trillion dollar 'Belt and Road Initiative' (BRI), through which China has offered huge development loans to prospective partners in Asia, Africa and Europe for the building of major infrastructure projects, for example in Myanmar, Kenya and Italy, while also signing cooperation agreements with several countries in Latin America (Myers, 2018).[5] The BRI and its financial scale – three times the size of the post-war Marshall Plan for Europe (Cui, 2018) – serves to extend China's global influence and 'soft power' (Nye, 2004) and at the same time provides an export outlet for China's much put upon state-run heavy industry sector. In the way it is constituted, the BRI represents an ideological challenge to the West's way of doing development (Milanovic, 2020), which has for the most part been directed at creating favourable institutional, legal and linguistic frameworks within developing countries that will allow for and facilitate the free flow of capital and guarantee it against local appropriation. Whereas the West has concentrated on structural reform and capital flows, China's focus in the BRI is on giant physical infrastructure projects such as harbours, railways, airports, roads and dams (ibid). Taking a leaf out of China's experience of Western imperialism (see Chapters 2 and 3), China has placed high demands on partners to give China what are in effect extraterritorial concessions at key BRI infrastructure hubs, which become formalized by treaty when debt repayments cannot be maintained. The giant port of Hambantota in Sri Lanka was for example acquired by China on a ninety-nine year lease in 2019, and it looks a possibility that the port of Mombasa in Kenya may go the same way. China is now the single largest foreign financier and builder of infrastructure in Africa. Forty African states, along with the African Union, have also signed memoranda of understanding with China for the development of infrastructure projects.[6] In the struggle over global structural power, the BRI is a majorly ambitious project, one which demonstrates Xi's determination to project China's power and influence overseas and increase its global economic reach. Of great linguistic significance, too, is that at the vital BRI junctures of negotiation, financing and agreement the language that is most used between China and

---

5 See also https://uk.reuters.com/article/us-bri-latam/belt-and-road-initiative-to-boost-chinese-lending-in-latam-idUKKBN1ZR2GG Accessed April 17, 2020.
6 https://economictimes.indiatimes.com/industry/transportation/shipping-/-transport/kenya-risks-losing-port-to-china-casting-shadow-over-indias-outreach-in-eastern-africa/articleshow/72136046.cms?from=mdr Accessed April 16, 2020.

its BRI partners is not Chinese, but English. The 2019 BRI memorandum of understanding between Italy and China is indicative of this. It states, 'Signed in Rome on March, 2019, in two originals, each in the Italian, English and Chinese languages, *all texts being equally authentic*. In case of divergence of interpretation, *the text in English will prevail*' (emphasis added).[7] As of the end of 2019, China had signed 197 cooperation documents on the Belt and Road development with 137 countries in Asia, Africa, Europe, Latin America, and the South Pacific region and 30 international organizations.[8] The vast majority of these had an agreed English text in addition to a version in Chinese and, where it was deemed necessary, in the national official language of the partner signatory. In all cases, the English text is written in the normative standard form.

Hegemonic transition in a world-system

From a world-systems perspective, the rise of China as a challenger to a declining United States appears to mark the beginning of a new cyclical transition phase from one global hegemon to another, and maybe even from one global language to another (see later discussion). Up to now there have been three hegemonic powers in the world-system: the Dutch United Provinces, Britain, and the United States. Wallerstein (2011b) treats this process of transition as four moments in time. The first moment begins immediately after the position of the hegemon is no longer uncontested. This moment marks the commencement of the slow decline of the hegemon's power. For the United Provinces this decline begins in the 1660s, for the United Kingdom it begins in the 1840s, and for the United States it begins in the 1970s (Wallerstein, 2000 [1983]: 256, 2011b: xxiii). The second moment marks a relative balance of power as different rivals contest the hegemonic succession: 'the two contenders for hegemony struggle to secure geopolitical and world-economic advantage' (ibid: xxiii). After the uncontested period of the Dutch hegemony (1648–1660s), the two rival powers were France and Britain. After the uncontested period of the British hegemony (1815–48), the two powers were Germany and the United States. And since the 1970s, the rivals to US hegemony have been first the USSR and then the regional hubs of Asia and the European Union (EU). In the third moment, 'the struggle becomes so acute that order breaks down and there is a "thirty years' war" between the contenders for hegemony' (Wallerstein, 2011b: xxiii). In the fourth moment, 'one of the contenders wins definitively and is therefore

---

7 www.governo.it/sites/governo.it/files/Memorandum_Italia-Cina_EN.pdf Accessed April 15, 2020. See also www.beltroad-initiative.com/documents/ Accessed April 16, 2020.
8 www.xinhuanet.com/english/2018-09/07/c_137452482.htm and www.beltandroad.news/2019/11/16/china-had-signed-197-cooperation-documents-on-belt-road-construction/ Accessed April 16, 2020.

able to establish a true hegemony' (ibid); that is, until such as time as it too begins to decline, and then the cycle is repeated.

In the present era, the world-system seems to be passing from the second moment into the third, which properly begins in the mid-2010s, with the difference that due to the 2007–8 financial crash and the ten years of severe economic austerity which followed, the EU, Japan and South Korea all definitively fell out of contention to succeed the United States. With the largest foreign currency reserves in the world, and since 1990 the highest continuous rates of growth, it is China that has emerged as the main contender to displace the United States as the world's hegemonic power, which if history does indeed repeat itself, it will do between 2030 and 2050 (Wallerstein, 2011d: xvii). Due to the COVID-19 pandemic and Donald Trump's self-defeating response to it, it might possibly occur even earlier. The start of the third moment begins in the window between the 2007–8 financial crisis, in which China's rivals in Europe and Asia are eliminated, and the election of Donald Trump in 2016. The election of Trump, rather than being a new departure for the United States, can also be viewed as a more decisive resumption of the US turn to disengagement which had been gathering pace in the mid-1990s and which led to the election of George W Bush. The rude awakening of 9/11, the catastrophic US-promulgated wars which followed, and the US-originating global financial crisis of 2007–8 served to convince an ideologically intemperate, hyper-religio-nationalist and hard-line neoliberal Republican faction in Congress and in the country at large that the United States' best interests lay with itself and not with its leadership of the international order.

The presidency of Barack Obama, as much as it marked a collective sigh of relief for world governments in comparison with that of his predecessor, was met amongst Republicans and the extreme right in the United States with a level of popular loathing and detestation that had not been seen before, even at the lowest points of the Nixon and Reagan presidencies. The vilification of Obama as the first Black president of the United States by an out-of-control right-wing media corps with only the most tenuous purchase on reality, or no purchase at all, and with the open connivance of 'Tea Party' Republicans, plumbed new depths in the history of racist politics in the United States. Obama was subjected to the equivalent of a political lynching by a pitilessly vindictive Republican-controlled Congress and its allies, who could not come to terms with Obama's election. Through the sustained propaganda and misinformation campaign that the Republicans unleashed, which far exceeded anything McCarthy or Nixon had ever achieved, they managed to convince large swathes of the US White working class that their economic woes were inflicted by 'cheating' foreign competitors and illegal immigrants rather than by neoliberal economic mismanagement, corporate corruption and reckless Republican-sanctioned financial deregulation (see Chapter 5). Thanks also to longstanding Republican gerrymandering of the US electoral system, this was enough to enable the election of Donald

Trump as the 45th US president on a minority of the popular vote. The tenor for what was to come was set by his inauguration address:

> We've made other countries rich while the wealth, strength and confidence of our country has disappeared over the horizon. One by one, the factories shuttered and left our shores, with not even a thought about the millions and millions upon American workers that were left behind. The wealth of our middle class has been ripped from their homes and then redistributed all across the world. But that is the past and now we are looking only to the future. We assembled here today are issuing a new decree to be heard in every city, in every foreign capital, and in every hall of power: From this day forward, a new vision will govern our land. From this day forward, it's going to be only America first, America first.[9]

In many ways nothing and everything had changed. Since at least 1919, in its international relations, the US had always put itself first. From its absentee direction of the League of Nations after World War I, to the Bretton Woods post-1945 configuration of the governance structures of the world-economy, through to the 'dirty war' geo-politics of the Cold War and IMF-backed structural adjustment programmes which it pushed so hard (see Chapter 5), the United States had always prioritized its interests and shaped the world-economy to its advantage (see previous chapters). There was nothing new in this. What was new was that for the first time the United States had become acutely aware of its relative decline as it witnessed the assertive emergence of China and of Xi Jinping.

The optimism that China would cooperatively socialize itself to the US-dominated world order while also reforming both its domestic market and its political system more or less evaporated in the few years after the 2008 crash as it became increasingly obvious that Beijing had no intention of acceding to the fully fledged market reform that overseas governments and investors hoped for, or of liberalizing its political system. Instead, China would pursue a uniquely authoritarian model of political capitalism, which was in stark contrast to the neoliberal market capitalism of the US or the slightly more restrained social capitalism of the EU. It would also be by some degrees a good deal more authoritarian and 'vertical' than the relatively 'diagonal' capitalisms of Singapore, Hong Kong, South Korea and Japan, where the Western notion of the 'rule of law' was explicitly embedded and more or less consistently applied. By contrast, China's political model of capitalism manifested itself in manipulative economic behaviours and laws that were compulsory for some and optional for those with the right connections. China's appalling treatment of its ethnic minority populations,

---

9 https://ig.ft.com/sites/trump-inauguration-annotations/ Accessed April 17, 2020.

particularly the Tibetans and the Uighurs, was also an uncomfortable reality, but fears of provoking economic retaliation muted many governments' response.[10] Of greater immediate concern than human rights, particularly to the US, but also Europe too, was China's economic and military behaviour. On its home market, for example, as well as handing out generous subsidies to its inefficient state-owned enterprises (Pei, 2020), China has been accused of engaging in discriminatory economic practices, such as mandating that overseas companies that wish access to its market form joint ventures with Chinese firms and compulsorily transfer their technologies. This has been accompanied by widespread intellectual property 'theft' as local companies have illicitly duplicated the transferred technologies, while the government has simultaneously utilized the insights gained to enhance China's own technological capacities. The government also regularly diverts the profits of listed private companies in which it has a share to support state-approved initiatives, such as building up the Chinese navy.[11] For the US, these are all uncooperative 'market-distorting practices' (Colby & Mitchell, 2020: 120) which do not make for 'open' capital-friendly economies of the kind the US – usually at its insistence – is accustomed to doing business with. This is despite the fact that amongst the BRICS[12] nations China is consistently rated as having the most open and competitive economy (Zakaria, 2020: 57). But, for the US, the forced joint ventures, the technology transfers, and the state subsidies all add up to an unfair advantage.

Alarm has also been caused by China's aggressive military expansion in Asia, which is viewed by the US and China's regional neighbours to be far in excess of its defence needs [as is also the case for the US, the UK, France and Russia] (Zakaria, ibid: 62).[13] In addition, China has also heightened tensions with Vietnam, the Philippines, Taiwan, Malaysia and Brunei by staking claim to 80 per cent of the South China Sea, along with all of the islands and the natural resources within it. China argues that it has 'historic rights' to the area and does not recognize the United Nations Convention on the Law of the Sea, to which the other interested nations adhere, as being applicable. It is also engaged in an overt programme of militarization of artificially constructed islets in the contested area, and from time to time closes off sea spaces within it for naval exercises.[14] Other points of tension are the Taiwan Strait, the East China Sea and the Korean Peninsula, where China has been asserting its territorial rights over islands and reefs which are also claimed by its neighbours. But the South China Sea is probably the one area where the US can no longer claim military supremacy (Westad,

10 www.ft.com/content/51a1bf9a-2015-11ea-92da-f0c92e957a96 Accessed April 19, 2020.
11 www.ft.com/content/84aa7b66-6ba9-4fce-adc7-431036a0d5c0 Accessed April 18, 2020.
12 The BRICS nations are Brazil, Russia, India, China and South Africa.
13 The size of China's armed forces, for example, has grown at comparatively the same pace as its economy over the last thirty years.
14 www.ft.com/content/1ab003c8-5790-11e9-91f9-b6515a54c5b1 Accessed April 18, 2020.

2019), while its military position in East Asia as a whole is also under some duress. Managing the security dimensions of China's military build-up in East Asia requires considerable diplomacy between the US and its allies in the region, between the US and China, and between the affected protagonists themselves. At summit meetings involving China, these exchanges usually occur with English being used alongside others as a principal official language, except in the case of Taiwan, where Mandarin is an official national language. But even here, English will be widely present in the translation services provided for observers and for all the official documentation that is produced. For example, an agreed version in English exists of the official documentation arising from the Eighth Japan-China-Republic of Korea Trilateral Summit in December 2019, in addition to versions in the official languages of the main summit participants. A full archive of the English-language documentation for all of these summits is available on the Ministry of Foreign Affairs of Japan website.[15]

US economic nationalism and the challenge of China

The perceived relative economic and military weakening of the US vis-à-vis China led the United States in 2018 into a trade war underpinned by an almost pathological determination on the part of the Trump administration to 'reset' the balance of the world-economy more firmly in the interests of the United States. This was despite the fact of that balance having been uninterruptedly well in its favour since at least 1919 (see Chapter 4). For Trump and his more extreme hyper-realist foreign policy advisors such as Mike Pompeo, China had to be 'kept in its proper place' (Pompeo cited in Zakaria, 2020: 62). Protectionist tariffs were duly imposed on almost half of China's exports to the US ($550 billion),[16] leading to retaliatory tariffs in kind from China ($185 billion).[17] At the time of writing, the trade war continues, although an uneasy truce of sorts was agreed between Trump and Xi in January 2020.[18]

The years since the onset of the 'open door' policy in 1978–9 have led to a good deal of entanglement between the economies of China and the US, so much so that, in the view of Westad, 'Attempting to disentangle the United States' economy from China's through political means, such as travel

---

15 www.mofa.go.jp/region/asia-paci/jck/summit.html Accessed April 19, 2020.
16 www.ft.com/content/b5a08862-b3f8-11e8-bbc3-ccd7de085ffe Accessed April 21, 2020.
17 www.china-briefing.com/news/the-us-china-trade-war-a-timeline/ Accessed April 24, 2020.
18 At the time of this book going into production, Trump was defeated in the US presidential election of November 2020 by the Democratic candidate, and former Obama vice-president, Joe Biden. It is hoped that the inauguration of Biden as the 46th president of the United States will lead to a more multilateral and less economically nationalist approach in US foreign policy from the start of 2021, although it seems likely that the trade war with China will continue.

restrictions, technology bans, and trade barriers, will not work' (2019: 91); that is, unless a war between China and the US were to cancel all trade. Nevertheless, Trump's manoeuvres do not seem designed simply to establish a new trade accord with China. Rather, in spite of the extreme irrealism involved, his administration is seeking a conscious 'decoupling' of the US economy from China, in order to deny China access to its vast market and its sophisticated technology (Pei, 2020: 85). If that proves impossible, then 'nothing less than the immediate and complete transformation of the Chinese economy' (Bown & Irwin, 2019: 133) is the aim. In an eerie echo of early nineteenth-century Orientalist attitudes, China is viewed as a society where 'every change is excluded' (Hegel, 1956 [1837]: 116), so change has to be forced from outside (Wallerstein, 2000 [1989]: 279). The calculation amongst the ideologues around Trump is that China, like the USSR before it, either will eventually collapse in the face of sustained US pressure or will submit itself to trading on US terms, especially within its own market.[19] For Xi, neither decoupling nor reform of China's market are acceptable. Firstly, because it is China's brand of authoritarian political capitalism which guarantees the absolute power of the CCP and, therefore, also the power of Xi himself. Secondly, because the legitimacy of the authoritarian capitalist model relies on the necessity of sufficient sustained economic growth so as to be able to 'buy off' the consent of the mass of the population to the Party's totalitarian rule, while also keeping China's prospering middle classes and its new capitalist elites quiescent (Milanovic, 2020). The 'distorted' nature of China's domestic market, the 'Belt and Road Initiative', and China's showcase nationalist and militarist global belligerences are all of a one in keeping the Party's rule absolute, while also serving the purpose of projecting China as a major global power in its own right, as well as in its own backyard.

In search of global financial structural power to augment its growing economic and military power, in 2015 China established the Asian Infrastructure Investment Bank (AIIB) as a rival to the US-sponsored World Bank and Asian-Development Bank, for the purposes of providing loans for the BRI. China is also a founding member of the BRICS New Development Bank (NDB) and the central participant in the annual Japan-China-Republic of Korea Trilateral Summit. The AIIB has 102 approved members worldwide, including the UK, Australia, Canada, Ireland, New Zealand, Hong Kong, India and Singapore.[20] The US is not a member. As the AIIB and NDB

---

19 Anything the US can do to hasten China's collapse is what motivates the current [at the time of writing] unwillingness of Trump to compromise. A similar strategy is being rolled out against Iran, no matter how unrealistic that may be or ultimately costly to global peace.
20 South Africa is listed as a 'Prospective Founding Member'. See www.aiib.org/en/about-aiib/governance/members-of-bank/index.html Accessed April 18, 2020.

websites demonstrate,[21] the principal working language of both institutions is English, and the memorandum of understanding which exists between them is also written in English.[22] The current president of the AIIB, Jin Liqun, who is a native of China, is a fluent speaker of English; as is the current president of the NDB, K V Kamath, who is from India. English is also one of the primary documentary languages of the annual Japan-China-Republic of Korea Trilateral Summit, which has been meeting since 2011.[23] It seems that even in respect of the development of its structural power, regionally and globally, China is entirely comfortable with using English as a standard *lingua franca* [i.e. as based upon $M^E\text{-}C^E\text{-}M'^E$; $M^E\text{-}M'^E$] for its global infrastructure networks, for the regional summits in which it is a key player, and for the multilateral institutions it has had a leading role in creating. Whether this is about to change in the near future with a switch to Mandarin Chinese [i.e. as $M^C\text{-}C^C\text{-}M'^C$; $M^C\text{-}M'^C$] is a matter of speculation, but much will depend upon China's ability to displace the global structural power of the United States in its entirety, and as part of that, supplanting the governance institutions of the US world-economy with governance institutions of its own. Much will also depend going forward on the fortunes of the US dollar relative to the Chinese renminbi (RMB), or yuan, and whether the dollar is able to maintain its seignorage as the international reserve currency in the global monetary system.

Currently, the greatest threat to US structural power in the world, and in the longer term to the global dominance of English, is the United States itself.[24] Due to Donald Trump's fulsome embrace of economic nationalism, the US appears to be in open retreat and disengagement on multiple fronts. In this process, it has also caused great consternation and alarm amongst its traditional allies and trading partners in the Americas, Europe and Asia. Despite the self-inflicted economic damage that cutting itself off was likely to do, the US under Trump seems determined to destroy the international trading system that came out of Bretton Woods and to recast it in such a way that the US is no longer economically or militarily responsible for its global coordination and security. At the same time the US has set itself the incommensurable goal of ensuring that whatever trading arrangements

21 For AIIB see www.aiib.org/en/index.html. For NDB see www.ndb.int Accessed April 19, 2020.
22 www.aiib.org/en/news-events/news/2017/_download/20170502101038900.pdf Accessed April 19, 2020.
23 www.mofa.go.jp/region/asia-paci/jck/summit.html Accessed April 19, 2020.
24 The COVID-19 pandemic is also likely to play a part depending on how the US responds to it; that is, to what extent it is one which is focused solely on the US or more globally coordinated between the major continents and powers of the world. A local, self-interested response is likely to be more economically damaging to the US and to everyone else in the longer run than one which is more globally coordinated through institutions and international groupings such as the WHO and G20.

survive the system's collapse are firmly skewed in its favour by threatening to withdraw access to its market if nations who desire to trade with the US do not comply with its demands. This is the attitude it presents to the whole of Asia, to Europe and to the rest of the world, which in the Trump world view has for too long taken advantage of the US by 'free riding' on US largesse in global trade and in international security, particularly in Europe, the Middle East and Asia, while also conveniently overlooking the grossly uneven advantages which these arrangements have historically conferred upon the US (see Chapter 4). It was this conviction that led Trump to withdraw the US from the Trans-Pacific-Partnership (TPP) in 2017. This was a proposed trade agreement between Australia, Brunei, Canada, Chile, Japan, Malaysia, Mexico, New Zealand, Peru, Singapore, Vietnam and the United States. But with the withdrawal of the US, the TPP was never ratified. Following the US withdrawal, the other partners went ahead with a separate trade agreement between themselves. This new agreement was ratified in English.

US destabilization of the international trading system

Until 2020 and the outbreak of coronavirus, the most pressing concern for the world-economy was the Trump administration's apparent unrepressed willingness to wreck the global trading and governance system which had evolved out of Bretton Woods after 1944 and which the US had taken the lead in constructing (see Chapter 4). Such is Trump's disdain for the international trading system that he has [at the time of writing] also threatened to pull the US out of the WTO, an organization which the United States created in order to cement its uncontested hegemony after 1945. Now he says, 'I don't know why we're in it. The WTO is designed by the rest of the world to screw the United States' (*The Guardian*, August 31, 2018).[25] He has followed this up by blocking judicial appointments to the WTO so that it cannot perform one of its primary functions, which is to adjudicate [in normative standard English] on trade disputes between members (Bown & Irwin, 2019).[26] Upon his election, Trump also demanded a renegotiation of the North American Free Trade Agreement (NAFTA) with Mexico and Canada, and of the US-Korea Free Trade Agreement. NAFTA was reworked after much wrangling as the United States-Mexico-Canada Agreement (USMCA) in 2019, so neatly excluding the words 'free trade'. A new

---

25 www.theguardian.com/us-news/2018/aug/30/trump-world-trade-organization-tariffs-stock-market Accessed April 18, 2020.
26 In response to the US action, in May 2020, a 19-member temporary global trade dispute system – the Multi-Party Interim Appeal Arbitration Arrangement (MPIA) – was convened. This included China, the EU, Canada, Mexico, Australia, New Zealand, Singapore and Hong Kong, as well as several other countries in Europe, Latin America and Asia. In a significant move, the US, Britain, Japan and India chose not to participate.

version of the US-Korea Free Trade Agreement, known as KORUS, was also signed off in the same year. Adding to the free trade funeral pyre, Trump has demanded similar bilateral reworkings of trade with Japan and Germany as the price of continued access to the US market for their automobile industries.[27]

Compounding the US-instigated global destabilization, Trump also singlehandedly wrecked the foreign policy centrepiece of the Obama administration by withdrawing the US from the internationally backed Iran deal on nuclear proliferation. He then imposed hugely vindictive sanctions on Iran as a punishment for the 'hostage crisis' humiliation of the US in 1979–80. The sanctions have greatly exacerbated regional tensions and added fuel to ideological extremism amongst key protagonists in the Middle East, including Saudi Arabia and Israel. From this purview, the Trump presidency and its conscious abdication of global leadership has been without question hugely damaging for US hegemony and for global capitalism itself, since it strikes at the heart of the global system by which the US is itself sustained. With the explosion of the COVID-19 pandemic in the United States in April 2020, the US government's international standing decreased still further as Trump sought to deflect blame to the WHO and China for the abysmally slow response of his administration to the crisis. However, the policy blunders and self-inflicted catastrophes of the Trump presidency have as yet made little or no difference to the hegemonic position of English in the world, because in spite of Trump, US structural power remains a considerable force across all the parameters which Susan Strange identified thirty years ago: namely, production, finance, security, and knowledge (see Chapters 1, 4 and 5). As yet, only the first and the third parameters have been in any way stressed, and not even mainly by China, but in neither of these parameters does China yet have global superiority relative to the United States. It is in production where China is making the most advances and also presenting the greatest challenge.[28] Were it not for the impact of the COVID-19 pandemic in 2020 which caused Chinese GDP growth to go into negative figures for the first time since 1976, China was predicted to be on course to have the largest economy in the world by 2030 (Zakaria, 2020). Thanks to the long-term damage Trump has done to the US economy as a result of the actions he has taken, it may still do so, but there remains some way to go in each of the other three areas of structural power if China is to displace the United States as the global hegemon (Tooze, 2019).

In production, the annual GDP of the US at $21.44 trillion continues to exceed that of China ($14.4 trillion) by a considerable margin.[29] The

---

27 It remains to be seen whether the Biden administration will follow suit.
28 www.cia.gov/library/publications/the-world-factbook/fields/216.html#CH Accessed April 21, 2020.
29 www.investopedia.com/insights/worlds-top-economies/#2-china Accessed April 21, 2020.

Federal Reserve, the World Bank and the IMF also remain the cornerstones of the international financial system, with the US dollar as the preferred international currency of reserve, as was strikingly demonstrated by the stampede into dollars when the COVID-19 pandemic hit Europe in the early months of 2020.[30] As a broker put it at the time, 'People are craving the most secure asset they can find, and that is the dollar. People are hoarding dollars. Banks are hoarding dollars' (*Financial Times*, March 19, 2020).[31] In Asia, although the RMB has become a more important currency and is increasingly used for regional trade (Dian, 2016), from an international reserve perspective the RMB is still in its infancy in comparison with the US dollar and shows no signs of closing the gap.[32] It is estimated that 75 per cent of global loans and 90 per cent of all global financial transactions occur in dollars, even when no US partner is involved in the transaction (Sharma, 2020: 73). The dollar also continues to serve as an anchor against which up to 60 per cent of countries in the world peg their currencies, including China (ibid). It may be that in the next thirty years [which is the time it took for the US first to overtake UK GDP per capita and then, in the 1920s, for the dollar to surpass the pound sterling as the international reserve currency] the RMB will find itself in a more favourable position. But that depends on many imponderables, such as the ability or not of the US government to pull back from the outright destruction of the international trading system it created and, as its growth slows further, from the temptation to interfere politically in the Fed's management of the dollar and the global monetary system.[33]

It also depends on China's willingness to commit sufficiently to economic reform measures and currency liberalization to win what Susan Strange called the 'trust of credit' with those who might be persuaded to hold the RMB instead (cited in Dian, ibid: 138). But, given Xi's concern to maintain the absolute power of the CCP and the tensions this produces in the choice between centralized authoritarian state power and a quasi-democratized market liberalism, this does not seem likely. It also leaves the RMB firmly in an inferior position vis-à-vis the dollar. While this is so, the possibility that in comparison with global English Mandarin will exert anything more than a soft power influence regionally or globally seems unlikely. Further, although China has markedly built up its military capacity, particularly in Asia and especially in the South China Sea, it is currently ranked third in the world behind the United States and Russia for military power. The US defence budget of $750 billion for 2020 is also more than three times that of China's.[34] In addition, of the nations ranked in the top 25 for military power,

---

30 www.ft.com/content/3ee752c6-684e-11ea-800d-da70cff6e4d3 Accessed April 20, 2020.
31 www.ft.com/content/dca1873a-69bf-11ea-800d-da70cff6e4d3 Accessed April 20, 2020.
32 www.scmp.com/economy/china-economy/article/3098118/chinas-wish-end-us-dollar-dominance-unlikely-come-true-no Accessed August 20, 2020.
33 www.ft.com/content/cdb3edb4-fbc2-11e9-a354-36acbbb0d9b6 Accessed April 21, 2020.
34 www.globalfirepower.com/countries-listing.asp Accessed April 21, 2020.

several are allies of the United States [e.g. Germany, UK, South Korea, Japan, France] so that China finds itself globally outflanked by nations which are more favourably inclined towards the US. Not that this would be a point of issue in an all-out war, since mutual annihilation on all sides is a certainty; more that, as a $1.78 trillion dollar industry in which the US and its allies are some of the biggest players,[35] English is also the main *lingua franca* for the business contracts of the global arms trade [M^E-C^E-M'^E].

Impediments to the Chinese global hegemony

There are several additional factors which are working against China being the hegemonic successor to the United States, and so also delimiting the possibility of Mandarin Chinese ^{C} challenging and eventually replacing English ^{E} as the dominant global language in the world-system [i.e. as M^C-C^C-M'^C; M^C-M'^C]. First amongst these is the willingness of China itself to use normative standard English as the principal language for its international relations, for example for its Belt and Road diplomacy and related BRI agreements, and for the international organizations it has played a leading role in creating, such as the AIIB and the NDB. China is also a member nation of the US-dominated international trading and financial system through its membership of the WTO, the World Bank and the IMF, in addition to the full range of UN system organizations and agencies. According to a paper originally published in 2001, as of the start of the century, China was a member of over 50 intergovernmental organizations and more than 1000 international non-governmental organizations (Kent, 2013 [2001]: 133).[36] The number is even more now (Shambaugh, 2016a). The great majority of the organizations and networks which China engages in at an international level, whether as an outcome of its own initiatives, such as the BRI, the AIIB and the NDB, or resulting from systems and networks established prior to the 'open door', such as the World Bank and the IMF, overwhelmingly employ normative standard English as a principal working language for

---

35 https://data.worldbank.org/indicator/MS.MIL.XPND.CD?end=2018&start=1960&view= chart Accessed April 21, 2020.
36 The US Central Intelligence Agency (CIA) in its *World Factbook* gives this acronymic list for intergovernmental organizations to which China belongs: ADB, AfDB (nonregional member), APEC, Arctic Council (observer), ARF, ASEAN (dialogue partner), BIS, BRICS, CDB, CICA, EAS, FAO, FATF, G-20, G-24 (observer), G-5, G-77, IADB, IAEA, IBRD, ICAO, ICC (national committees), ICRM, IDA, IFAD, IFC, IFRCS, IHO, ILO, IMF, IMO, IMSO, Interpol, IOC, IOM (observer), IPU, ISO, ITSO, ITU, LAIA (observer), MIGA, MINURSO, MINUSMA, MONUSCO, NAM (observer), NSG, OAS (observer), OPCW, Pacific Alliance (observer), PCA, PIF (partner), SAARC (observer), SCO, SICA (observer), UN, UNAMID, UNCTAD, UNESCO, UNFICYP, UNHCR, UNIDO, UNIFIL, UNMIL, UNMISS, UNOCI, UN Security Council (permanent), UNTSO, UNWTO, UPU, WCO, WHO, WIPO, WMO, WTO, ZC. www.cia.gov/library/publications/resources/the-world-factbook/fields/317.html#CH Accessed April 21, 2020.

their governance and administration. This does not seem to present China and its representatives with any particular issue or difficulty and may well suit its international purposes as being a convenient vehicle for the projection of its structural power into the immediate, medium and longer term, since it is solely as a 'truncated repertoire' (cf. Blommaert, 2010; Canagarajah, 2018) for strategic international relations' purposes that it is employed (see Chapter 7).

This also fits well with the narrow instrumentalism of China's domestic language policy in respect of how English should be taught and learned (Pan, 2011; Z. Pan, 2015; Simpson, 2017; Gao, 2018; Feng & Adamson, 2019) and also with its imperialist experience at the hands of foreign powers, particularly during the 'unequal treaties' era between 1842 and 1949, when in China's perception it allowed foreign nations too much intimacy (Teng & Fairbank, 1954). All the more reason to use English, a language in which many Chinese people have proven themselves expert, as a means of keeping competitor nations at a distance and under control. Moreover, with over 300 million learners of English, and with English-language proficiency well established in Chinese higher education and academic research, China also appears to be accepting – despite the internal political ambivalences this presents (Gao, 2018) – of the widespread dominance of English in the global knowledge structure, where all the major [and the not so major] research journals are published in English. Next to these global realities, it seems that whatever hybrid, spatial, translingual, superdiverse, regional, commodified or multi-*lingua franca* usages of English exist in the world (see Chapter 7), they are secondary to normative standard English in its especial link to capital [M^E-C^E-M'^E; M^E-M'^E]. This connection has also withstood the year-on-year increase in China's outward direct investment since the global financial crash. Over $1 trillion in Chinese capital has flowed overseas since then, with $89.1 billion being invested in 2018.[37] Most of this capital is denominated in US dollars rather than RMB, but even if it were not, it would still flow through the same global capital markets where most of the brokers are high-performing cosmopolitans with a good-or-better command of English [hence, M^E-M'^E]. If anything has changed linguistically over the last twenty years, it is in respect of Mandarin's soft-power presence as a means of promoting Chinese cultural values and ideals abroad. Since 2004, through its Hanban Headquarters, which is a subsidiary of the Chinese Ministry of Education, China has established more than 500 Confucius Institutes worldwide and vigorously promoted the teaching of Mandarin in education systems across all the major continents of the world. Through the promotional and coordinating work of the Confucius Institutes some

---

37 www.ey.com/Publication/vwLUAssets/ey-china-overseas-investment-report-issue-8-en-new/$File/ey-china-overseas-investment-report-issue-8-en.pdf. Also, www.visualcapitalist.com/chinese-investment-overseas/ Accessed April 21, 2020.

2 million school-age pupils have been exposed to the learning of Mandarin and another 13 million have engaged in over forty-one thousand Hanban-funded cultural activities (Hubbert, 2019: 5). But while these numbers are impressive in themselves, in comparison with the take-up and use of English in the world, particularly as a language for the governance and administration of the world-economy and of multilateral inter-state relations and treaties, Mandarin still has some way to go. For reasons which I come to below, it seems doubtful that Mandarin will ever properly arrive.

Although Trump and Xi wield power in very different ways, both are in at least one respect identical: they are both compulsive egomaniacs. With the precipitate Trump, his egomania is always on show. With the technocrat Xi, it is the reverse; his egomania is quietly concealed. What we are encouraged to see instead is the carefully crafted image of Xi the unflappable leader, even as he rules with an iron fist. Were Trump to be re-elected in 2020,[38] Xi's personal global stock in the propaganda war between the US and China is likely to rise, particularly if Trump's behaviour were to remain unpredictable. Yet even if Xi managed to win some public image successes over Trump the person, or Trump fell to electoral defeat [as has occurred], many obstacles and problems lie in the path of China challenging and displacing the structural power of the United States, and as a corollary of this, the dominant position of English in world. China's greatest problem domestically, and also the greatest challenge for the CCP, is to maintain China's dramatic rate of growth, because it is primarily through this that the CCP derives its legitimacy (Shambaugh, 2016a; Milanovic, 2020). As Marx says, 'a constant *expansion of the market* becomes a necessity for capitalist production' (Marx, 1976 [1867]: 967). But China's rate of growth is slowing. It was slowing anyway, before COVID-19 struck at the start of 2020 and sent it 6.8 per cent into the negative. This was due partly to very high levels of public and corporate debt, the exhaustion of available bank credit to support uneconomic state industries, and the challenges presented by an ageing population (Pei, 2020; Sharma, 2020). Total debt in China is close to 310 per cent of GDP (*Financial Times*, March 12, 2020).[39] In the US by comparison it is 250 per cent of GDP (Sharma, 2020). But the US is not a developing country, and China is. China's military build-up in East Asia, the Belt and Road Initiative and other overseas projects designed to enhance China's standing in the world have also proved extremely costly, which raises the prospect of China becoming economically and geopolitically overstretched. If growth slows too much, there is also the possibility of political unrest, not only amongst its over-mortgaged middle classes, but also in its politically

---

38 Which he was not due to his defeat at the hands of the Democratic presidential candidate Joe Biden. Despite Trump's downfall, the hegemonic outlook for China on the world stage remains much the same.
39 www.ft.com/content/17943d46-62fa-11ea-b3f3-fe4680ea68b5 Accessed April 23, 2020.

sensitive autonomous regions where economic amelioration and ethnic resentment of Beijing are finely balanced. A glimpse of what political opposition to Xi and to the centralized the rule of the CCP might look like was provided by the mass demonstrations in Hong Kong during 2019–20. Xi's greatest fear is of similar disturbances spreading to other parts of China. Were that to happen, it seems certain that given a choice between political and economic reform and outright state repression, Xi's China would opt for state repression, as the passing of the Hong Kong security law in 2020 showed. The only thing that keeps Xi from sending in the People's Liberation Army in Hong Kong is the huge economic damage to China and to its favoured public image such an aggressive crackdown would cause: partly because of the size of Hong Kong's economy, but also because, unlike in Xinjiang or Tibet, it would also happen in full media view, such is Hong Kong's connectivity to international news networks. It seems that just as Trump [when in office] set himself the incommensurable goal of wrecking the established international trading system while guaranteeing US access to other nation's markets, so Xi has set himself the incommensurable goal of combining state totalitarianism with the economic empowerment and widespread education of those who have no political power. This is also why Xi and the CCP go to such great lengths to emphasize Chinese patriotic nationalism as a further means of containing potential political opposition. But at some point, China will have to face the capitalist economic reality that what inexorably goes up must eventually come down (Marx, 1976 [1867]; Wallerstein, 2011d; Wallerstein et al., 2013; Sharma, 2020). Since 1976, Chinese capitalism has known nothing other than expansion; it has never experienced a recession, or economic stagnation, and it is still an open question how an authoritarian political capitalism as vertical as China's would fare in such a situation, as there are no precedents to draw upon.

The other areas where China shows hegemonic unpreparedness is in relation to Woo's point about taking leadership in 'the global environmental commons, the global trading system, and global security' (Woo, 2012: 332). China is by volume the world's greatest polluter, but it is not willing to sacrifice economic growth for significant carbon emissions.[40] By becoming more energy efficient, however, it has received international praise for hitting its carbon reduction targets, and in the world at large shows public leadership and initiative on climate change which is almost entirely absent in the US. But this needs to be set aside the conviction of Xi that any substantial carbon reduction must follow the arrival of China to first world global power status, and not precede it. Moreover, China is not the largest polluter per capita; that is the United States. So, for China, it is the nations which have already achieved first world status that should make the more significant

---

40 https://medium.com/wedonthavetime/is-chinas-carbon-intensity-reduction-a-cause-for-celebration-5a1e8b96ced Accessed April 24, 2020.

reductions. This also overlooks the global environmental impact of the BRI, which is not included in China's pollution statistics and which make the reductions achieved by China less impactful than they may seem. But even without these figures, the reductions being achieved by China, while welcome and in some areas extremely impressive, are nowhere near enough to avert a climate catastrophe by the end of the century.[41] So while it is possible to conclude that China is indeed showing leadership on the environment, particularly in comparison with the United States, its leadership still falls short of what would be required to make a global difference.

On trade, China's economy and its economic model is considered protectionist, obstructionist and highly nationalistic. It is largely because of these factors that its currency lacks the 'trust of credit'. Its external economic partnerships, particularly through the BRI – in a twenty-first century reproduction of colonial accumulation by dispossession (see Chapter 1) – are quasi-imperialist by being built upon debt forgiveness in exchange for extraterritorial rights. As an authoritarian economic model, it also lacks popular global appeal in comparison with the liberal 'free-for-all' cultural-ideological model which is associated with the United States. Its primary advocates are also to be found in state governments where power is highly centralized, corruption and prebendalism are often rife, and principles of civic responsibility and human rights are often abused. Examples include Myanmar, Vietnam, Azerbaijan, Russia, Algeria and Rwanda (Milanovic, 2020). On global security, its track record has been largely one of a passive observer with little interest in coordinated political problem solving. Current examples of Chinese non-commitment include Iran, Syria, Yemen, North Korea and Ukraine. Rather, China prefers to make suitable gestures from a diplomatic distance and to encourage nations to settle the differences which beset them by peaceful means. In the words of David Shambaugh, 'Chinese diplomacy remains remarkably risk-averse and guided by narrow national interests' (2016b: 28; see also Nye, 2016). These interests seem to be principally oriented to putting on the best possible show for the public at home in order to demonstrate China's renewed global importance and great-power status in the world. It also does this in a manner which to international observers often seems far too obviously wrapped in pretence to be taken seriously.

Against this, China has won praise for its involvement in UN peacekeeping missions, anti-piracy operations, overseas development assistance, disaster relief, combatting international crime, and dealing with public health pandemics (Shambaugh, 2016b: 28). But in most of these areas China is still more of a partner with others than a global leader. During the COVID-19 crisis, China won plaudits and condemnation in equal measure: on the one hand for seeming to act with decisiveness and a resolute unity of purpose,

---

41 https://climateactiontracker.org/countries/china/fair-share/ Accessed April 24, 2020.

on the other for attempting to stifle news of the initial outbreak, and once admitted, engaging in sustained and deliberate under-reporting of the true rate of deaths so as to present itself in the best possible light, particularly in comparison with the US and Europe. As the US sank into the mire of coronavirus in April 2020, Xi reached out to Trump to settle the trade war and to work collaboratively together to deal with the pandemic and global climate change, all of which made China and Xi look good, but the likelihood of any of these initiatives being acted upon by Trump was close to nil. As growth contracts, it is likely that Xi and the CCP will pay still more attention to China's global image in order to ramp up nationalist sentiment at home as a means of deflecting attention away from shortcomings in the economy. Even in the areas where China has evident strengths, such as in military expansion, the net effects are not promising because China has no allies, except perhaps North Korea: 'Not a single other nation looks to Beijing for its security and protection – thus demonstrating a distinct lack of strategic influence as a major power' (Shambaugh, 2016b: 29). Moreover, one of the unlooked-for consequences has been of encouraging and reinvigorating counter alliances and security arrangements against China, particularly in Asia, while also reinforcing the use of English as the *lingua franca* of US-led transnational security cooperation and exchange.

Even when all of the aforementioned is discounted, one of the greatest impediments to China's global power is its extreme secretiveness and hyper-sensitivity regarding its internal affairs, from its treatment of its ethnic minority populations, to its reactions to the demonstrations in Hong Kong, to the true figure of its economic growth or to the incredibly low death count that it claims over COVID-19. The result is that the markets and many governments do not trust China (*Foreign Affairs*, April 15, 2020).[42] This may, at some level, be a grotesque Sinophobia. There are, after all, a great many nations and peoples in the world that also have good historical reason not to trust the United States. It was also none other than Noam Chomsky who described the US as 'a leading terrorist state' (Chomsky, 2001) [for which he is not far wrong]. But with global capital, it is perceptions of the possibility of accumulation that count, whether accurate or not. In the words of Ruchir Sharma, 'Global elites may not trust the current US president, but they trust US institutions, which is why the United States emerged from the 2010s as a financial empire without rivals' (Sharma, 2020: 74). The effects of Bourdieusian capitals notwithstanding, this is also why normative standard English remains the favoured global repertoire of the capitalist world-system. This also means that if there is a threat to the dominance of English, it is not going to come from China and Mandarin. It is much more likely to come from the direction of the US itself as it oversees and even

---

42 www.foreignaffairs.com/articles/united-states/2020-04-15/pandemic-wont-make-china-worlds-leader# Accessed April 24, 2020.

hastens the collapse of its hegemony and of the capitalist world-system it superintends. The apparently unassailable nature of global English has to be set against diverse perspectives in the academy which understand English [and *Englishes*] as – inter alia – superdiverse, commoditized, fluid, flexible, hybridized, spatial, decolonized, dehisced, emancipated, translanguaged and translingual; in addition to being 'micro-physical' sites of resistance against the capitalist hegemony of standardized norms. In the next chapter, I turn to a discussion of these perspectives in the context of the argument of this book and ask why, despite these contributions, the dominance of the normative form persists.

7 Superdiverse translingualism, commodification and trans-spatial resistances

The multi/plural turn and the persistence of the normative form

The bringing down of the Berlin Wall in 1989, followed by the collapse of the Soviet Union in 1991, which were documented in Chapter 5, were seismic geopolitical events that had a major impact upon US governance of the world-system. While these events changed the world's geopolitics in a fundamental way, they also majorly impacted upon the nature of Western intellectual enquiry, particularly in the social sciences, as postmodern and poststructuralist modes of thinking, with their emphasis on the hybrid, the fluid and the fractal in constructions of the modern world became more popular (Jameson, 1984; Haraway, 1988; Lather, 1993; Lyotard, 1986 [1979]; Bauman, 2000; Hartwig, 2011). It is also around this juncture that the 'social turn' occurs, and the study of discourse becomes a much more prominent reference point in qualitative social scientific research (Dreyfus & Rabinow, 1982; Weedon, 1987; Gee, 1991; Fairclough, 1992; Coupland & Jaworski, 1999). In linguistics – at least in its applied linguistic and socio-linguistic forms, it also appeared to mark a turning away from the social study of 'languages' conceived as discrete and enclosed entities as language scholars in different fields oriented themselves increasingly to the study of linguistic hybridization and pluralization in diverse communicative sites and cross-cultural contexts (Lave & Wenger, 1991; Rampton, 1995; Baynham, 1995; Dixon, 1997; Cook, 2000; Lin, Wang, Akamatsu & Riazi, 2002). Issues of multiplicity, hybridity, diversity, flexibility, fluidity, complexity and performativity in English, often in combination with other languages, came increasingly to the fore (Makoni & Pennycook, 2005; Harris, 2006; Morgan, 2007; Vertovec, 2007; Pennycook, 2007, 2009, 2010a, 2017, 2020; Jørgensen, 2008; Kumaravadivelu, 2008; Otsuji & Pennycook, 2010, 2015; Li & Zhu, 2013; Canagarajah, 2013, 2018; Blommaert, 2013, 2015; García & Li, 2014; Arnaut & Spotti, 2014; Budach & de Saint-Georges, 2017; Li, 2018a, 2018b; Kramsch, 2018; McNamara, 2011, 2019). In addition, the perspectives which arose were often categorized as belonging to 'late modern' or 'late capitalist' processes of globalization (Chouliaraki & Fairclough,

1999; Rampton, 2006; Fairclough, 2006; Saxena & Omoniyi, 2010; Blommaert, 2010; Duchêne & Heller, 2012; Boutet, 2012; Pérez-Milans, 2015; Heller & McElhinny, 2017; Heyd & Schneider, 2019) while also simultaneously drawing upon or being influenced by the turn to the postmodern that had dominated the later decades of the twentieth century through the work of theorists such as Derrida, Foucault, Laclau, Baudrillard and Deleuze. In the short space of twenty years the old modernist orthodoxies – particularly in philosophy and in the social sciences – appeared to have been overthrown to be replaced by bourgeois capitalist triumphalism, individualist neoliberalism and a 'presentist' ludic postmodernism (Hartwig, 2011; Block, 2012a; Bhaskar, 2016). It seemed an odd mix.

Of course, the postmodern did not begin in the late twentieth century so much as 'mushroom' well beyond where it had been in the 1970s [and previously] when it was largely confined to continental philosophy and the margins of literary criticism (de Man, 1979). The 'social turn' which occurred in the social sciences and the humanities realized itself in applied linguistics as a multi/plural or dynamic turn (Kubota, 2016: 475) which gave rise in the early twenty-first century to the overlapping fields of superdiversity, translanguaging, and translingual practice (*passim*), or what I am referring to collectively as *superdiverse translingualism*.[1] The multi/plural turn also brought with it a proliferation of related prefixes for describing the linguistic diversity that was being observed, such as trans-, poly-, metro-, super- and pluri- (Pennycook, 2017: 269). In closer or lesser empirical alignment with these fields have been the competing *World Englishes* (WE) and *English as a Lingua Franca* (ELF) paradigms, each of which in their own way make claims regarding the legitimacy of the diverse realizations of English in the world, often involving the detailed documentation of 'original' as well as 'local' lexico-grammatical formulations produced by speakers [and communities of speakers] for whom English is not a first language (Firth, 1996; Widdowson, 1997; Bhatt, 1995, 2001; Seidlhofer, 2001, 2007, 2012b; Jenkins, 2006, 2017; Higgins, 2009; Mauranen & Ranta, 2009; Murata & Jenkins, 2009; Kirkpatrick, 2010b; Jenkins et al., 2011; Mauranen, 2012; Cogo & Dewey, 2012; Smith, 2016; Canagarajah, 2006, 2013, 2018; Li, 2018b). The immediate issue to be addressed is not whether the shift to superdiverse translingualism and related themes is a worthwhile object of study, or where superdiverse translingualism exists to determine whether it is indeed a feature of late capitalism; myself and others have already engaged with these questions (Blommaert, 2010; Park & Wee, 2012; Sowden, 2012; O'Regan, 2014, 2021; Pavlenko, 2017; Rösler, 2017; Viebrok, 2017; Grin, 2018; Ives, 2019; Simpson & O'Regan, 2018, 2020). Rather, it is how [and

---

1 This is to distinguish it from Canagarajah's neologized preference for the term 'translingual practice' to encompass superdiversity, translanguaging and other related nomenclatures (Canagarajah, 2013, 2018; see also Grin, 2018).

why] in the midst of evident superdiverse translingual practices and hybridized postcolonial varieties the dominant global hegemony of English in its standard form persists.

Kubota captures the ongoing problem of global English well when she states that 'The dominance of English and standard varieties of English is intact both globally and within English-speaking countries, marginalizing and disadvantaging non-English-speaking or nonnative-English-speaking populations' (Kubota, 2016: 489). This includes in inter- and intra-national English-speaking politics [e.g. in the UK, USA, Australia, Ireland etc.], in the institutions of international political economy [the Wall Street-Treasury-IMF Complex], in circles of elite cosmopolitanism (Hannerz, 2006; Ives, 2010; Vandrick, 2014; Garrido, 2017; Preece, 2019; Sato, 2019), in so-called high culture (Bourdieu, 1984; Ostrower, 1998; Michael, 2017), in state-level English-language policies (De Costa, 2010; Price, 2014; Gao, 2018; Kang, 2020), and in international English-medium academia and higher education (Z. Pan, 2015; Phan, 2015, 2017; McKinley, 2019; McKinley & Rose, 2019), particularly where the chosen English medium is *written*, or is speech presented in a 'written-like' form; that is, following a 'normative grammar' as opposed to a 'spontaneous' or 'immanent' grammar (Gramsci, 1975: 2343; Ives, 1998: 40, 2010: 528, 2019: 69).

At a recent international conference,[2] the respected World Englishes scholar S N Sridhar presented a plenary lecture in which he argued that inner-circle Englishes were outmoded and no longer relevant referents for English in the world (Sridhar, 2019). He further stated that the core/periphery model of Englishes and of the global economy which had dominated theoretical thinking for so long was unsound, because 'History teaches us that the center does not remain the center' (ibid) but is always shifting – for example, today, economically to Asia, and for English sociolinguistically, to diverse regions across the world. It is evident in actual language use, for example, that the periphery, in the words of Sridhar, has 'invaded the core' and that pluricentricity is the new orthodoxy in the sociolinguistics of English (ibid). This argument, as he noted, is not new; World Englishes scholars have been saying this since at least the 1980s. His point was well made, as was the plenary itself, which although unscripted was nevertheless delivered in a recognizably normative standard form. This should not really be surprising since the use of the normative form is not unusual at English-medium international academic conferences when expert international scholars present. But given Sridhar's forthright dismissal of inner-circle models and of the core/periphery dichotomy, the overwhelming immanence in his lecture of such a conforming normativity was strikingly apparent. Also apparent was his neglect of any consideration of US

---

2 The 24th Conference of the International Association for World Englishes (IAWE), University of Limerick, Ireland, June 20–22, 2019.

structural power in relation to the global dominance of the normative form, and in which Sridhar – a postcolonial scholar who is tenured in the United States – is also inevitably implicated (cf. Kubota, 2016: 490, for a similar argument).

While it would be not a little absurd to expect well-trained plurilingual international scholars who have acquired an expert competence in the normative form to employ anything else in their academic work[3] or in international conference presentations, very little attention seems to be paid by detractors of this form, either as native speakers or as expert users, to their own roles in its reproduction and dissemination.[4] If we explore why this is so, the trail always seems to lead back to capital, both in the economic form which preoccupied Marx and in the symbolic form which preoccupied Bourdieu.[5] Indeed, to understand the continued global dominance of this form in international contexts such as the one just described, it is evident that economic and symbolic capitals are closely intertwined, and have been for a long time (Fraser, 1995). International scholars are employees of universities, whose personal economic livelihoods [as waged workers] in addition to the [symbolic] success of their careers, and that of their universities, depend upon their teaching and supervision activity, the 'winning' of competitive research grants, their cumulative research outputs, and the [symbolic] growth in their international profiles. For international scholars writing for publication and presenting at academic conferences in English, success in the economic marketplace of academic waged labour also depends to a great extent on success in the linguistic marketplace of standard English (Bourdieu, 1977, 1984, 1991). The predominance of standard English is in these circumstances determined or, to borrow Althusser's phrase, 'overdetermined' (1996 [1965]: 101) by monetized and symbolic capital in a cumulative relation, as well as in dialectical combination with issues of race, gender, education and social class (Wallerstein, 2000 [1975]; Fraser, 1995; Block, 2014, 2018a; Jordan, 2015; Tupas, 2019; Simpson & O'Regan, 2021).[6] This dominance magically persists despite the obvious transgressions of – and apparent resistances to – standard English which localized superdiverse translingual practices present (García & Li, 2014;

---

3 Some have, on the other hand, deliberately flouted these norms, if only for illustrative purposes (Parakrama, 2012).
4 Henry Widdowson's tirade against 'The custodians of standard English' (Widdowson, 1994: 379) in his lecture on the ownership of English at the 27th Annual TESOL Convention is an archetype of this kind of performative contradiction.
5 This is not to ignore the entirely reasonable use of such a repertoire in international English-medium contexts for reasons of personal familiarity, sociolinguistic convention and considerations for one's audience. Nor is it to suggest that international scholars ought not to use this form if using it is what they wish to do.
6 All of which are themselves shot through with the conditions of capital.

Creese, Blackledge & Hu, 2018; Pennycook, 2010a, 2010b, 2017, 2020; Li, 2018b; Canagarajah, 2018; Sridhar & Sridhar, 2018; Canagarajah & Dovchin, 2019; Highet, 2021). Beliefs about how language *ought* to be used here win out over alternative translingual possibilities for how language *could* be used and very often *is* used when the stakes are socially different and/or not so high (Mauranen, 2015). This is because capital presents itself, in Marx's phraseology, as 'the real foundation' to which certain forms of language have historically attached themselves 'as definite expressions of social consciousness' (Marx, 1976 [1859]: 3). To put this another way, it is a question of indexical scale. As Blommaert recounts:

> [S]cales need to be understood as 'levels' or 'dimensions' . . . at which particular forms of normativity, patterns of language use and expectations thereof are organized. . . . The point of departure is really quite simple: indexicality, even though largely operating at the implicit level of linguistic/semiotic structuring, is not unstructured, but *ordered*. It is ordered in two ways, and these forms of indexical order account for 'normativity' in semiosis. The first kind of order is what Silverstein . . . called 'indexical order' the fact that indexical meanings occur in patterns offering perceptions of similarity and stability that can be perceived as 'types' of semiotic practice with predictable (presupposable/ entailing) directions. . . . This is where we meet another kind of order to indexicalities, one that operates on a higher plane of social structuring: an order in the general systems of meaningful semiosis valid in groups at any given time. This kind of ordering results in what I call orders of indexicality – a term obviously inspired by Foucault's 'order of discourse'.
>
> (Blommaert, 2010: 37–38)

The scale at which [economic] capital operates in relation to language gives standard language forms an enhanced and 'misrecognized' (Bourdieu, 1977: 652) social indexicality which in the absence of capital they would not otherwise possess, and so it would not matter so much whether these forms were employed (see also Chapter 1). It will be the perceived proximity to economic capital, and consequent upon this to social value, which will determine whether the normative form is employed, assuming that it is in the speaker's repertoire and personal interest to be able to produce such a capital-centric form. This does not preclude the possibility that it might not be in their interest to do so at all, as social and economic value may also be placed on non-standard forms in everyday local business and trading contexts in international cities and elsewhere (Otsuji & Pennycook, 2015; Higgins, 2015; Pennycook, 2017, 2020; Creese et al., 2018), as well as in globally popular forms of music culture, such as hip hop and rap (Alim, 2006; Pennycook, 2007; Domingo, 2014).

The ownership of English

The argument regarding capital and linguistic capital-centrism also puts into a somewhat different light scholarly preoccupations concerning the 'ownership' or better still 'non-ownership' of English, which have been routinely employed as a means of pointing up the moral injustice and seeming irrealism of the normative hegemony, and in what amounts to the same thing, of the apparently self-evident '(in)appropriateness of native-speaker standard English' (Jenkins, 2006: 171) as the pedagogic model for the learning of English in the world. The positions against the normative hegemony bring into coincidental alignment a diverse range of perspectives from linguistic imperialism, postcolonial studies, superdiverse translingualism, World Englishes and ELF. On the issue of the ownership or non-ownership of English, however, it has tended to be WE and ELF scholars who have specifically emphasized this concept (Kachru, 1985, 1990; Widdowson, 1994; Seidlhofer & Jenkins, 2003; Jenkins, 2006, 2011; Saraceni, 2009; Sonntag, 2009; Tsuda, 2010; Seidlhofer, 2012a; Bolton, 2013; Tupas & Rubdy, 2015; Sadeghpour, 2019; but see also for comparison Rampton, 1990; Norton, 1997; Phan, 2015; Li, 2016, 2018b; Mori & Sanuth, 2017; Canagarajah, 2018). The term at first sight appears to be a metaphor for what is taken to be the 'false' ideological presupposition that having or 'possessing' native-speaker competence in English confers unlimited authority to adjudicate over what may be counted as the acceptable forms which the language may take. As Jenkins puts it:

> The difficulty for many native English speakers, both academics and non-academics, as far as the globalisation of English is concerned, seems to be that they still regard themselves in some sense as 'owners' and 'custodians' of the language. For many, thus, the internationalisation of English simply means the distribution of national British and/or North American English varieties around the globe. Such native English speakers have yet to appreciate Widdowson's point that '[t]he very fact that English is an international language means that no nation can have custody over it. To grant such custody is necessarily to arrest its development and so undermine its international status' (1994: 385).
>
> (Jenkins, 2011: 933)

Of note here is that it is not the concept of the property right itself which is disputed but that, due to the internationalization of English, so called native speakers of that language may *no longer* legitimately claim such a right in relation to it. In Widdowson's words, 'It is not a possession which they lease out to others, while still retaining the freehold. *Other people actually own it*' (1994: 385; emphasis added). What this suggests then is that there was indeed a historical time – albeit ill-defined – prior to the internationalization of English when such a right could be legitimately claimed but that this is no longer reasonable, since so many people in the world now have English in their repertoires and use it in ways which do not conform with native-speaker norms. For Widdowson, and it seems also for Jenkins and others, these users of English are now 'owners' too and are legitimately entitled to exercise their property rights over it. The very concept of the 'ownership' of language, rather than being refuted as it probably should be, is instead here reaffirmed and universalized (see later discussion).

A further implication which follows is that native speakers of languages which are not as internationalized or as 'hyper-central' as English *do* retain this property right in a way that native speakers of English do not. Arguments of this kind regarding linguistic ownership or non-ownership are not for example applied to Farsi, Catalan or Kannada, such that speakers of these languages can allowably be presumed to 'own' them. Not so, it seems, with English. But to say that 'English is my language' is not automatically in the same semantic category as 'Fido is my dog', or ought not to be. Yet in the argument about the ownership of English, there appears to have been a levelling or 'muddying' of the semantic distinction between English as a property or *trait* of a speaker, in the sense of it being a part of their socialized nature [e.g. as a native speaker], and English as property in the legal sense of the ownership of objectified and alienable 'things' (Simpson & O'Regan, 2021). In this discussion it has tended to be the latter conception which has taken precedence over the former in order to make it possible to extend the right of linguistic property ownership to all speakers of English wherever they may be. In Widdowson's words, 'communities or secondary cultures which are defined by shared professional concerns *should be granted rights of ownership* and allowed to fashion the language to meet their needs' (1994: 383; emphasis added).[7] That non-native speakers of English are unjustly being denied these rights is, for Widdowson at least, due to an unspecified group of native speakers representing the inner-circle nations [i.e. presumably, governments, educational and cultural institutions, native-speaker educators, etc.] who have appointed themselves upholders of the normative standard form: 'So when the custodians of standard English complain about the ungrammatical language of the populace, they are in effect indicating that the perpetrators are outsiders, nonmembers of the community' (p. 381). This for Widdowson, and for others who have followed this position, is patently unjust, because unlike most languages 'English is an international language' (p. 385) and so is the rightful property of everyone (see also Rubdy, 2015: 52).

This position echoes what Nancy Fraser has referred to as a politics of recognition in liberal welfare capitalism, in which 'claims [to recognition] often take the form of calling attention to, if not performatively creating, the putative specificity of some group, and then of affirming the value of

---

7 We might also note here, granted these rights by whose authority?

that specificity' (Fraser, 1995: 74; see also Block, 2018b). This is the type of specificity which scholars promoting the legitimacy of non-standard and 'non-native' realizations of English have widely documented. With regard to performance, thanks largely to the data available concerning ELF, World Englishes and superdiverse translingualism, there is abundant evidence of linguistic non-standardness and translingual hybridization in English(es) going on (*passim*). But performance also has a negating side, which is the regrettable lack of self-awareness of many scholars working in these fields of their own performative complicity in the reproduction and dominant distribution of the 'rejected' standard form. Yet, while many may well be aware of this, most remain unreflecting and continue in fetishistic fashion to (re)produce it anyway (Žižek, 2012: 315; Simpson & O'Regan, 2021). While it may be true that 'standard English is not fixed by exo-normative fiat from outside: not fixed, therefore, by native speakers' (Widdowson, 1994: 386), this begs the question as to what it is fixed by, which beyond the workings of unnamed and secretive 'custodians' is left mysteriously unaddressed in a lot of this kind of argumentation: 'And yet there is no doubt that native speakers of English are deferred to in our profession' (ibid). Given the lengths to which applied linguists like Widdowson, Jenkins, Seidlhofer and others have gone to act as exemplars of the misrecognized model, it seems remarkable that there should be any wonder in this. But even the recognition of this complicity does not really explain anything. The real issue is why the complicity exists at all. But also, more importantly, why despite such protestations, well-meaning as they may be, outside of applied linguistics nothing much really seems to change in the unequal global socioeconomic reality of English-language production, use and exchange (Blommaert, 2010; Tupas, 2015; Rubdy, 2015; Ives, 2015; Jaspers, 2018; Block, 2018b; Highet, 2021).

It is easy to acknowledge, for example, that academic publishing in English has become a billion-dollar industry, as has the international competition between academics to win external funding. Many hours of an academic's time are dedicated to these twin activities: publications have to be written and peer reviewed, and lengthy applications for funding have to be composed and evaluated, often with little prospect of success. The widely unquestioned medium for writing these publications and grant proposals is standard English. It continues to be very difficult to get published or funded in international English-medium academia if one's English does not conform to the expectations of the global linguistic gatekeepers – e.g. journal reviewers, editors, grant evaluation panels etc. – who filter what does and does not get published and what does not and does not get funded. That is, for a journal reviewer or grant panel, it may be easier or more instinctive to discount something that does not conform to a normative grammar than to accept it. This is because of the overwhelming misrecognized expectation of conformity to standard norms (Bourdieu, 1977: 652) to which all international scholars regardless of their language backgrounds are subjected. But calling for recognition of the misrecognition has been shown to make no difference (Block, 2018b). Worse still, many of those calling for such recognition are in their work exemplary producers of the misrecognized form. This is the part that seems much less easy to acknowledge, because they too are located in their daily activity in long-established capital networks in which standard English is the capital-centric norm. So, in their 'silent compulsion' to capital (Marx, 1976/1867: 899), from which there is no exit, they make an effort to redeem themselves by acting as champions in standard English of non-standard English forms. The perceived capital-centricity of the normative form is the principal reason why plurilingual transnationals in elite international networks [e.g. IMF, World Bank, WTO, OECD, G7, G20, EU, Council of Europe, the world's capital markets, diplomatic missions] in addition to other agents [e.g. the global ELT industry, local clientelist elites, national governments, ministries of education, NGOs, international academicians etc.] consistently produce and reproduce the misrecognized form.

There is also an unfortunate 'folding-back' which occurs, because when plurilingual non-native speakers of English in these networks do reproduce the misrecognized form, they reproduce it in what still looks to be a grammatically normative 'native-speaker' form, as almost any official document produced in English by the IMF, or by any number of international organizations or corporations, will attest.[8] Simultaneous with this is the reproduction of the US-dominated institutional structures and networks of the capitalist world-economy (see Chapters 4 and 5). The more these structures and networks are reproduced, the more the impression is given of a globalized standard that is tied to inner-circle norms, and the greater the understandable perplexity of many scholars that 'although English has become a global language, native-speaking English varieties from North America, the United Kingdom, Australia, and New Zealand are still often regarded as the desired standards for international education' (Phan, 2015: 224). The non-native English-speaking plurilingual agents of globalized standard English – and the native-speaking supporters of their right to transgress – are in this way seemingly caught in an endless circularity in which the English they produce in international [as well as national] contexts of use appears grammatically indistinguishable from that of the inner-circle normative form.

Language commodification

This still leaves us with the concept of the ownership of language itself and whether it is truly feasible to speak of 'owning' language [or languages], that

---

8 This is notwithstanding the burgeoning literature on, for example, Euro-Englishes and Asian-Englishes. However, these seem to be almost entirely directed at features of speech (see Modiano, Seidlhofer & Jenkins, 2001; Forche, 2012; Crystal, 2017; Modiano, 2017; Kirkpatrick, 2010b; Wee, Pakir & Lim, 2010).

is, as a personal property that is alienable. Certainly, from what we have seen of ELF and WE approaches, there are those who appear to think it is, while also suggesting for English that the days of its native-speaker 'ownership' are past. From a rather different direction, much has been written in recent years about the commodification of language as this has occurred under the conditions of 'late capitalism', and often as part of this, about the commodification of English itself (Cameron, 2000, 2012; Heller, 2003, 2010; Da Silva, McLaughlin & Richards, 2007; Rassool, 2007; Alsagoff, 2008; Singh & Han, 2008; Tan & Rubdy, 2008; Tupas, 2008; Duchêne & Heller, 2012; Park & Wee, 2012; Flubacher & Del Percio, 2017; Del Percio et al., 2017; Muth & Del Percio, 2018; Codó, 2018). Duchêne and Heller (2012), for example, note that 'during the 1990s and into the twenty-first century, we are witnessing the widespread emergence of discursive elements that treat language and culture primarily in economic terms' (p. 3). Park and Wee (2012) are more explicit, stating that 'When we speak of the commodification of language, we are speaking of the conditions under which language comes to be valued and sought for the economic profit it can bring through exchange in the market' (p. 125). In a similar vein, Del Percio et al. (2017) 'define language as a resource that, under certain political-economic conditions, can be exchanged for other symbolic or material resources' (p. 1), and Da Silva et al. (2007) have asserted that 'language, as a commodity, is no longer an inherent quality of certain individuals or something that individuals own, but something that is separate and external to their personhood' (p. 185).

Despite the evident continuities of capitalism as an exploitative world-system (see all previous chapters), the idea that we are in a new era, which some call 'late capitalism' or occasionally the 'new economy' (Del Percio & Duchêne, 2012; Heller & Duchêne, 2016; Heller, Pujolar & Duchêne, 2014), is an understandable one. Since the 1980s, technological advances, particularly in areas such as global communications and information technology, have been significant, resulting in a massive intensification of information flows, as well a speeding up of the activities of the working day. This has occurred as individuals in their capacities as waged workers and as social beings have taken on ever greater amounts of information processing in their daily working lives and as part of their socially networked subjectivities (Fuchs, 2014, 2015). This has been coupled with a marked ideological shift in perspective concerning the economic management of capitalism. This had its beginnings in the shift to the greater financialization of the world-economy in the late 1960s and the sharp move away in the 1970s from a redistributive Keynesian model of capital accumulation to the savagely rapine neoliberal model of 'dispossessive' accumulation to which we are subject today (Harvey, 2004, 2010; Peck, 2010; Panitch & Gindin, 2012; Stedman-Jones, 2012; Mirowski, 2014; see also Chapters 1, 4, 5 and 6).

The intellectual shift towards a largely fantastical pre-1930s model of economic liberalism[9] brought with it changes in working practices alongside changes in economic policy, not only within the advanced capitalist economies of the core, but also within the world-economy as a whole as public assets were aggressively privatized, regulatory controls on foreign capital investments pared back, and secure employment increasingly precaritized. A particular focus of many researchers of language commodification has been the concomitant global expansion in service industries within this neoliberal frame, in which English is widely employed by 'non-native' plurilingual workers in sectors such as tourism, aviation, phone sex and banking. Amongst these developments, the international call centre is often referenced as an archetype of the neoliberal business model of the new economy and of the way that language itself has been commodified (Graddol, 2006; Duchêne, 2009; Rahman, 2009; Heller, 2010; Pujolar, 2018). Much of the initial impetus for this understanding can be traced to the neoliberal conception of human capital theory (Becker, 1993 [1964]) and the emphasis this places on the acquisition of competitive skills in an economic marketplace.[10] This was to become the inspiration for Foucault's account of the neoliberal *homo economicus*, who is 'an entrepreneur of himself, being for himself his own capital, being for himself his own producer, being for himself the source of [his] earnings' (Foucault, 2008 [1979]: 226). In an influential critique by Urciuoli (2008), she refers to this notion as the 'worker-self-as-skills-bundle'. She explains that, in this notion, 'not only is the worker's labor power a commodity but the worker's very person is also defined by the summation of commodifiable bits' (p. 211). From her survey of Internet sites in which skills-related services were being marketed, Urciuoli noticed the skill of English, amongst several others, as being one of those commodifiable bits. This then appears to be language being commodified under 'a skills-discourse enregisterment' (ibid: 215), and 'acting like' or 'becoming' a commodity in the discursive sense that many researchers in linguistic anthropology and in applied linguistics have indicated. We might also suggest a continuity with Marx due to the 'tendency [of capitalism] to transform all possible production into commodity production' (Marx, 1978 [1884]: 190).

---

9 As we have seen, Keynesianism in its various formulations maintained its hegemony in Britain and the US until the late 1970s, when liberalism, now in the guise of neoliberalism, reasserted itself. What is less well known is that the liberalism that was being promoted by Hayek, Friedman and others was not really a rejuvenation, or even a renewal, of liberalism in the classical mould of Smith or Ricardo. This was a different kind of liberalism altogether. See Mirowski (2014) for a useful summary and critique.
10 Although Becker is certainly an economic liberal, his notion of human capital in relation to human beings is not quite as reductively neoliberal as is often suggested (see Gazzola et al., 2020: 136). It is also evident, however, that what Becker calls human capital would not qualify as capital in Marx's terms.

But this is in fact a false trail because the exchangeable commodity in Marx only has value, and therefore only is a commodity, in that it is the product of the capacity, or 'power', of the worker to labour (Nicolaus, 1973: 46–47; see also the discussion in Chapter 1). It is the labour time embodied in the commodity *in exchange* which gives the commodity its value: 'As exchange values, all commodities are merely definite quantities of *congealed labour time*' (Marx, 1976 [1867]: 130). To bring this distinction into sharper relief, you may purchase a chair, the separate parts of which have over a period of time been shaped from blocks of raw lumber by a worker in a carpentry works. These pieces of wood are then laboured upon by that worker for a further period of time in order that they may be fashioned into a chair. The labour time expended on the chair, averaged out and unitized for like chairs, is the real value of the chair. Marx refers to this averaging out of time as 'socially necessary labour-time' (Marx, 1976 [1867]: 94, 129).[11]

> Socially necessary labour-time is the labour-time required to produce any use value under the conditions of production normal for a given society and with the average degree of skill and intensity prevalent in that society. . . . What exclusively determines the magnitude of the value of any article is therefore the amount of labour socially necessary, or the labour time socially necessary for its production.
>
> (Marx, 1976 [1867]: 129)

The chair is a commodity in Marx's terms since the owner of the carpentry works has entered into a relationship with the worker that can be captured by the M-C-M' capital circuit: money (M) has been advanced [to the worker in wages] for the production of a commodity (C) which is then sold on at an increment (M') which the owner of the carpentry works collects (see Chapter 1). This is made possible because the wages paid to the worker are less than the real value of the worker's time, which is the price at which the chair is sold. If we apply the same logic to the call centre worker's production of English, we can see that it is not the worker's English which has been bought – although this is clearly a relevant concern for both the caller and the employer – but the worker's labour time as based upon an average estimation of call duration which has been more or less arbitrarily determined by the call centre owner [but minimally at a rate that will allow workers to supply themselves with the necessities they need to reproduce themselves, such as food, clothing and shelter]. This is the 'socially necessary labour-time' which the call centre owner expects it to take *on average* for the call worker to deal with client calls, which is then unitized and charged to the

---

11 The notion of there being an average 'socially necessary' period of time which can be unitized is for Marx crucial for determining the value of labour. Otherwise, inefficient workers would be paid more than efficient ones.

caller by the minute, and for which the call centre worker receives a lesser part of that unitized value in wages. It is therefore the worker's labour during the call, and in effect the call itself, which is the commodity, not the worker's English, although this is indeed an aspect of the call centre worker's labour-capacity. But it is not alienable. If it really were possible to make language into a commodity in Marx's sense, that is, make it alienable, then it would be possible to purchase, say from a language teacher or a call centre worker, a certain quantity of language a word or a sentence at a time, and to come into 'ownership' of that language so as to be able to 'take it away' with us. But it is evidently not the language that is being purchased in this manner, but the teacher's or the call centre worker's *capacity to labour*. That is to say, it is the lesson or the call which is being purchased and accumulated; these are the commodities, not the language itself.

Yet, while it is the case that the language commodity is often placed in a discursive frame so that it seems like a commodity 'that can be exchanged in the market' (Park & Wee, 2012: 124), this kind of discursive or metaphorical framing opacifies what it is that is actually being purchased while also conflating quite different conceptions of what a commodity is or can be. Marx also recognized this:

> Things which in and for themselves are not commodities, things such as conscience, honour etc., can be offered for sale by their holders, and thus acquire the form of commodities through their price. Hence a thing can, formally speaking, have a price without having a value. The expression of price is in this case imaginary.
> (Marx, 1976 [1867]: 197)

In these examples, honour and conscience can *appear* to be commodities but contain no 'real' value, as no labour time has been expended in order to produce them (Holborow, 2015; Gray, 2016; Block, 2014, 2018c; Simpson & O'Regan, 2018). The price that is put on these human traits is 'imaginary', as Marx suggests, because their price – whatever that may be – cannot be based on a calculation of the socially necessary labour-time embodied within them. Rather, their price is more a calculus of human desire (Piller & Takahashi, 2006; Blommaert, 2009; Park & Wee, 2012; Chowdhury & Phan, 2014; Cavanaugh & Shankar, 2014; Phan, 2017) than of any intrinsic commodity identity or 'value' which they possess. As Will Simpson and I have argued, language and languages also fall into this category, so that while they have acquired 'the form of commodities', in the absence of an embodied labour relation, they are not commodities or products in any 'real' or economically measurable sense (Simpson & O'Regan, 2018; see also McGill, 2013; Grin, 2018, for similar arguments). To position language as a commodity as many have done (Gal, 1989; Irvine, 1989; Heller et al., 2014; Heller & Duchêne, 2016; Del Percio, Flubacher & Duchêne, 2017) may be understood as a type of discursive framing, which while illuminating in its own way of certain aspects of 'the material (*sic*) conditions of language and social life' (Muth & Del Percio, 2018: 129) can also be rather misleading, because it does not tell us enough about how, in respect of language, relations of exploitation under the material conditions of the capitalist production and consumption of commodities actually proceed and what the 'real' mechanisms are which lie beneath them. It is, as Wittgenstein says, to 'treat only of the network, and not what the network describes' (cited in Bhaskar, 2008 [1975]: 36).

From this perspective, the idea of one's language as an alienable product which is separate from oneself is problematic, because language is inalienable. Hence, rather than owning language and selling it as we will, we have instead created for ourselves a substitute or 'stand-in' for the language skills that we have and which it is possible to alienate away. Before we can avail ourselves of this stand-in, we first need to make the conception of language itself alienable (Simpson & O'Regan, 2021). This alienable conception consists in language as an idealized construct or abstract entity which can be *learned*. That is to say, one can move from having no knowledge of it to having some or even considerable knowledge of it. It is this idea, this idealization, that makes the very idea of learning 'a language' possible. Marx would probably say that it was a fetishized form, since it belongs to the modernist notion discussed earlier of language imagined as a unified and enclosed system of abstract code, which most applied linguists would agree does not really exist (Otsuji & Pennycook, 2010; Dufva et al., 2011; Park & Wee, 2012, 2013; García & Li, 2014; Blommaert, 2016; Canagarajah, 2018; Holliday & MacDonald, 2020). It is therefore a fetish conception. A second fetish conception is that the only means of marketing one's skill in this area is by a second alienation. That is, by gaining or having English-language accreditation – e.g. IELTS, TOEFL, TOEIC etc. – or documented ethno-legal status [e.g. as an acknowledged native speaker] – in order to 'verify' that you have this skill. In this way, the appearance of the credential literally *becomes* one's language skill, because others' acknowledgement of the alienable credential *stands in for* the inalienable skill (Simpson & O'Regan, 2021; Park, 2021). Here, knowledge of one's apparent credential is mistaken, that is, fetishized, for the thing which it is about. Bhaskar (2008 [1975]), from the direction of critical realism, refers to this as the epistemic fallacy: 'that statements about being can be reduced to or analysed in terms of statements about knowledge: i.e. that ontological questions can always be transposed into epistemological terms' (p. 36) (see also Fairclough, 2003, 2010; Pennycook, 2007). This kind of ontological reductionism seems misdirected if our interest is to understand the inner workings of the commodity form – as a product of labour [e.g. as lessons, materials, scholarly works, call slots, tutorials, cabin service, etc.] – in relation to how language is utilized in relation to that; but on a quotidian basis it allows us to make our language skills alienable and to an extent 'saleable' in a linguistic market. As Will Simpson and I have noted elsewhere:

> Whether or not one accepts such credentialed tokens of language as unproblematically representative of what language really is, or should be, the ownership and exchange of such tokens on the labour market *works in practice as if it really does*, independent of one's beliefs about language, education or the market.
> (Simpson & O'Regan, 2021: 17)

But as with the language of the call centre, it is not language itself which is exchanged, but rather the promissory note, or credential [e.g. language qualification, passport, birth certificate, curriculum vitae etc.], which stands in for it. Even then, this is still not a commodity exchange, as nothing has been produced: this is the linguistic market of Bourdieu, not the economic market of Marx. In this linguistic market an imaginary price is placed on the credential by means of the wage which it – along with other claimed skills which have been presented by the putative language worker – enables access to. We might say that the credential as an apparent certification of competence assists the bearer, along with their other 'skills', to pass to a particular threshold wage bar, without which they would not be employed at all. Commodity exchange by means of the exploitation of the worker's labour capacity [of which their linguistic capacities or 'skills' are a composite part] has yet properly to begin (Simpson & O'Regan, 2021). Moreover, once it does begin, the control of workers over the structural conditions of their exploitation is in fact negligible, and so focusing on what service workers do with their language, or for example widening that to 'the ways individuals and actors express control over their own communicative conduct as well as over the languages, behaviors and bodies of others' (Muth & Del Percio, 2018: 129), does not seem to lead to much more than the close ethnographic description of micro-practices or 'micro-physical techniques' (Del Percio, 2018: 241), albeit a 'thick' one.[12] This in turn raises the issue of resistance and how in the interests of social change this may be effected.

Resistance and superdiverse translingualism

Advocates of superdiverse translingualism – as represented by the fields of translanguaging, superdiversity, translingual practice, metrolingualism, assemblage etc., and in which for the purposes of this discussion I am also

---

12 As my colleague John Gray once commented regarding the seeming lack of a radical programme in Foucault, 'It is a rather like making a brick and not throwing it' (personal communication).

including World Englishes and ELF[13] – have often in a similar manner suggested that it is the act of normative transgression which, in addition to being a micro-physical act of resistance itself, is the key to wider systemic resistance and change. Canagarajah and Dovchin (2019), for example, in discussing the politics of translingualism, refer to 'the ordinariness of everyday resistance. That is, when people engage in linguistic resistance in everyday life' (p. 128). This becomes the basis for the development of 'communicative practices for radical change' (p. 142). This also echoes the position of García and Li (2014), for whom 'Translanguaging . . . refers to languaging actions that enact a political process of social and subjectivity transformation which resist the asymmetries of power that language and other meaning-making codes, associated with one or another nationalist ideology, produce' (p. 43). Pennycook from a translanguaging and 'assemblages' perspective (Deleuze & Guattari, 1988) offers a more nuanced conception of resistance in the notion of *distributed language* which 'challenges the idea of languages as internalised systems or individual competence, and argues instead for an understanding of language as embodied, embedded and distributed across people, places and time' (Pennycook, 2017: 276; see also Pennycook, 2020). This also chimes with Canagarajah's emphasis on the meaning of *trans* as suggesting 'more mobile, expansive, situated, and holistic practices' (Canagarajah, 2018: 32). Like Pennycook, Canagarajah also moves to a conception of language and of semiotics which is based upon assemblages and upon translingual practice as a spatial repertoire; one which goes 'beyond abstract, homogenous, and closed structures' (p. 33) to encompass 'sign forms beyond verbal resources' (p. 34). This may sound like multimodality (Kress, 2010), but Canagarajah rejects this connection.

> The notion of assemblage helps to consider how diverse semiotic resources play a collaborative role as a spatial repertoire . . . when language is not predefined as the sole, superior, or separate medium of consideration. Assemblage corrects the orientation to non-verbal resources in scholars addressing 'multimodality'. From the perspective of assemblage, semiotic resources are not organized into separate modes. To think so is to fall into structuralist thinking. According to assemblage, all modalities, including language, work together and shape each other in communication.
>
> (Canagarajah, 2018: 39)

It is worth dwelling in a little more detail upon Canagarajah's argument, since it is illustrative of a widespread anti-structuralism in connected applied language fields, particularly towards language understood as an enclosed

---

13 Both of these fields are committed to a view of English and variations thereof which, like the other perspectives mentioned, is hybridized, pluricentric and translingual (*passim*).

unitary structure, or entity. It is with Saussurean structuralism which Canagarajah and others working within a poststructuralist frame primarily take issue, because in Canagarajah's words, 'These constructs territorialized and essentialized language, providing ownership to certain groups of speakers and/or their lands' (ibid: 32). The turn to poststructuralism, which is evident in trans accounts such as Canagarajah's, is also to be found in approaches which come under the banners of superdiversity, metrolingualism and language commodification (cf. Blommaert, 2016; Pennycook, 2010a, 2010b; Otsuji & Pennycook, 2015; Del Percio et al., 2017). Translanguaging, World Englishes and ELF approaches, for their part, seem much less theoretically developed in this sense but still share with these other approaches a similar anti-structuralism in regard to the boundedness of language (cf. García & Li, 2014; Smith, 2016; Sridhar & Sridhar, 2018; Jenkins et al., 2011; Jenkins, 2017). Canagarajah's purpose is to 'articulate how a poststructuralist paradigm might help us theorize and practice translingualism according to a spatial orientation that embeds communication in space and time, considering all resources as working together as an assemblage in shaping meaning' (Canagarajah, 2018: 31). His eschewal of language as 'a self-defining and enclosed structure' allows him to expand upon his theme of spatial repertoires and the need to give an accounting of semiosis in the round, or of what Silverstein (1985: 220) terms the 'total linguistic fact' (cited in Canagarajah, 2018: 34). To illustrate this, Canagarajah recruited a group of research participants, all of whom were 'international Science, Technology, Engineering, and Mathematics (STEM) scholars in a Midwestern American university' (ibid: 34). They comprised one South Korean participant, one Turkish participant, and twenty-four Chinese participants. There were also four one-hour video recordings of two Chinese math teaching assistants to analyze. The interactions between the STEM scholars were, Canagarajah informs us, studied through video observation, discourse-based interviews, photographic documentation and textual analysis of multiple drafts of published articles and other written genres. From analyzing his data closely, Canagarajah comes to some noteworthy conclusions.

He notices, for example, that many mentioned that 'they were fluent in their academic and professional communication' but struggled with more casual encounters. The South Korean scholar in his study, Jihun, is one who has this issue, but Canagarajah notes that 'his writing for disciplinary purposes was very advanced,' and his initial drafts were also 'grammatically well formed' (p. 35). Canagarajah identifies this capacity to use particular words and grammars for specific activities as 'truncated multilingualism' (Blommaert, 2010: 23) since it is an expertise that is confined to select language activities while being absent or less well developed for others.

> Jihun mentioned that his professional activity involved shuttling between Korean and English constantly. He mentally planned his research articles in Korean and wrote them in English. He discussed

> some English academic publications and experimental findings with a Korean colleague in Korea, and wrote about them in English. Even if the final draft of Jihun's published article is in 'standard written English', he has shuttled between Korean and English in various interactions and stages of the writing process in shaping this final product.
>
> (Canagarajah, 2018: 36)

For Canagarajah, what this suggests is that 'labeled language structures do not necessarily constrain one's situated professional activity' (ibid). Instead, they are used in combination in order to produce the final product. This is important for Canagarajah and is a trait which other participants in his study also share; for example, by writing initial drafts of their academic papers in Chinese before translating them into English. In addition, other participants utilized a mix of languages for notetaking, 'though the source was in English' (ibid). This leads Canagarajah to state that 'language works with an assemblage of semiotic resources, artifacts, and environmental affordances in specific settings to facilitate communicative success' (ibid). This is what he and others, such as Pennycook and Otsuji (2015: 83), mean by 'spatial repertoires'. But Canagarajah extends this meaning to include 'all possible semioticized resources . . . assembled *in situ*, and in collaboration with others' (2018: 37). Despite this, Canagarajah does not deny the existence of labelled languages such as Korean and English: 'At a limited scale of consideration, certain words index certain places and communities, and develop identities as distinctly labeled or territorialized languages' (ibid). But, for Canagarajah, such constraints tend to be overcome *in practice* as translingual scholars carry out their daily activities, and it is this that constitutes their resistance.

> The translingual practice of the international scholars suggests that they appreciate the value of language diversity and *subtly act against dominant policies and discourses*. Even though the lack of diverse languages in the publications in high stakes contexts suggests international scholars satisfying dominant norms, we must not forget that the earlier drafts, notes, and revision interactions involve translingual resources, suggesting their value in generating the finished products. Though such translingual practices occur in safe and protected sites, away from surveillance or high stakes interactions, *we must not underestimate their transformative potential to diversifying the workplace or pluralizing high stake activities in the long term.*
>
> (Canagarajah, 2018: 48; emphasis added)

Canagarajah acknowledges that in the final analysis there is still a notable absence of translingualism in the finished products for publication. These are, in his words, 'high stakes contexts' where international scholars are 'satisfying dominant norms'. Resistance is instead embodied in the employment of translingual resources in the *process* of generating the finished products, and here lies 'their transformative potential to diversifying the workplace or pluralizing high stake activities in the long term' (p. 48). Canagarajah seems to concede that in spite of the translingual activities in which international scholars engage, they are still compelled to produce finished products [i.e. academic papers as exchangeable commodities] which conform to dominant norms in relation to such matters as the use of standard English and the discourse expectations of the academic genre that they are working in (Heng Hartse & Kubota, 2014). Transformation is also configured as no more than a potential, albeit one which should not be underestimated, and which occurs through the more or less contingent activity of everyday translingualism, and what is more, 'in safe and protected sites, away from surveillance or high stakes interactions' (Canagarajah, 2018: 48).

Unfortunately, in framing his argument this way, Canagarajah not only succeeds in making translingual practice appear politically etiolated – since it is primarily concerned with calls to recognition rather than with acts of redistribution (Fraser, 1995; Harvey, 2014; Block, 2018b) – but also *dependent upon* the fact of dominant norms, which in translingualism and related fields are simultaneously eschewed. These norms, in a philosophical sense, constitute the *implicit ontology* for translingual practice (Bhaskar, 2008 [1975]: 40), since the 'trans' nature of translingualism in academic written scholarship and other language practices implicitly relies upon the notion of an 'other' that must be transgressed (cf. Ferri, 2018), but which for the purpose of translingualism and its interests is marginalized and suppressed. Canagarajah himself explicitly points to this other as being 'territorialized and essentialized language' (p. 32) and elsewhere as 'labeled or territorialized languages' (p. 36). This other that must be transgressed is the source of his anti-structuralism. In this sense, the perspective of translingual practice, or of superdiverse translingualism, seemingly repeats the error of becoming too much entangled in the network at the expense of dealing with the overarching 'structure' which is being transgressed, and which in spite of this activity retains its dominance (Block, 2013; Heng Hartse & Kubota, 2014). Canagarajah lays the explanation for this dominance mainly at the door of language ideologies, 'which subtly enter through the unproblematized "context"' (2018: 32) that is assumed by enclosed and supposedly 'value free' language structures.

Elsewhere, Canagarajah and Dovchin (2019) present a more expansive view of these issues in their study of the translingual practices of teenage social media users in Mongolia and Japan, referred to earlier, in which they also address the accusation of complicity in the inculcation of individualist neoliberal subjectivities which has been levelled at some approaches to superdiverse translingualism (Flores, 2013; O'Regan, 2014, 2015; Kubota, 2015, 2016; see also Blommaert, 2016). They note that their young participants' transgressive practices, like those of Canagarajah's translingual international scholars in the US, were 'hidden forms of resistance' and that they left dominant language forms in 'the public and visible social spaces unchallenged' (Canagarajah & Dovchin, 2019: 142). Their response is to call for critical awareness among non-scholars of 'the transgressive nature of their practices' that they might 'critically analyse dominant language ideologies, and develop their communicative practices for radical change' (Canagarajah & Dovchin, 2019: 142). While there is no doubt that language ideologies play a contributory role in the dominance of normative forms (Gal & Irvine, 1995; Phillipson, 2008; Georgiou, 2017), this is to ignore political economy and the structural link to capital (Block, 2017a, 2018b; O'Regan, 2021). Instead, approaches in superdiverse translingualism, and in language commodification too, have thrown themselves upon a preoccupation with individuated micro-resistances and the politics of recognition without dealing with 'the underlying generative framework' (Fraser, 1995: 82) or 'the generative complexes at work' (Bhaskar, 2008 [1975]: 48) which are responsible for the (re)production of particular kinds of social activity. In the political economy of global English and the dominance of the normative form, these are the generative complexes of capital itself, principally in economic capital's circulating form [M-C-M'; M-M'], and which has served as a scaffold for the historical account of global English structuration in this book [i.e. as M^E-C^E-M'^E; M^E-M'^E].

Phonocentrism in superdiverse translingualism

Approaches in superdiverse translingualism, in which in addition to World Englishes and ELF I will now for ease of reference also include studies of language commodification, make a persuasive case for closer attention to be given to the radical indeterminism and linguistic pluralism of human communication and individualist agency in the dynamic hum of lived space and time (Jacquemet, 2005; Pennycook, 2010a, 2010b, 2017, 2020; McLellan, 2010; Heller & Duchêne, 2012; Cogo & Dewey, 2012; Arnaut & Spotti, 2014; Schneider, 2014; Otsuji & Pennycook, 2015; Li, 2018a; Canagarajah, 2018; Creese et al., 2018; Sridhar & Sridhar, 2018; Kramsch, 2018). In the words of Blommaert, 'We see thus *registers* in actions, not Languages . . . and such registers operate chronotopically, in the sense we see them being put to use in highly specific timespace configurations, with specific identity-and-meaning effects in each specific chronotope' (2016: 7). In such a perspective emphasis is placed upon the *dehiscing* of 'language-as-entity': the scattering [and shattering] of the discrete linguistic code, and the development of 'mobile, expansive, situated and holistic practices' (Canagarajah, 2018: 32), in which ' "the vast spillage of things" . . . are given equal weight to other actors and become "part of hybrid assemblages: concretions, settings and flows" ' (Thrift, 2007: 9 cited in Pennycook, 2017: 277). In the field of World Englishes, and from the direction of Schneider's influential dynamic model (Schneider, 2003, 2007, 2014), much attention is likewise given to 'innovative uses and sociolinguistic settings in which English is involved in expressions of cultural and linguistic hybridity (and contact)' (ibid, 2014: 24). In the sister field of ELF, the orientation is currently to 'transcultural communication among multilingual English speakers, who . . . make use of their full linguistic repertoires as appropriate in the context of any specific interaction' (Jenkins, 2017: 7). And we find something not dissimilar from the language commodification perspective, where the focus is not so much the kinds of linguistic and semiotic practices which are engaged in and 'meshed', although these are also an important consideration, as that the contexts which are studied are very often distinguished – as in these other approaches – by the fact that they involve actors and agents who are involved in 'practices' involving or implying *speech*.

For example, in the words of Heller, 'The commodification of language confronts monolingualism with multilingualism, standardization with variability, and prestige with authenticity in a market where linguistic resources have gained salience and value' (2010: 107). That is to say, they have gained salience and value as 'saleable' caches of *spoken language*, for example in call centres, care-giving, tour-guiding, language teaching, domestic service and performance art, which are amongst the examples which Heller gives (ibid). Similarly, for Heller and Duchêne, in language commodification the terms 'pride' and 'profit' are the structuring mechanisms 'used to justify the importance of linguistic varieties and to convince people to *speak them*, learn them, support them, *or pay to hear them spoken*' (2012: 4; emphasis added). The orientation to speech is also marked in what is referred to as 'policing for commodification'. In a recent special issue with that title, Muth and Del Percio explain that the aim is to examine 'the regulatory processes that are at work when languages and speakers are recast as and turned into commodities' (2018: 130). Alongside, or as part of this, they identify such processes as largely existing 'within an economic logic of investing into *speakers whose communicative resources represent an added value*' (ibid: 132; emphasis added). Similarly, Park and Wee draw attention to how in the past language was considered to be entwined with 'one's social identity and therefore not something subject to exchange' (2012: 125). Again, we see here the implication of language as performance – as Saussurean *parole*. Commodification changes this relationship so as to make language alienable from the person and 'an economic resource to be cultivated for material profit' (ibid). We have already seen how this apparent alienableness is in reality a sleight of hand: rather than language being alienated away, it is something else which stands in for language that is alienated away, albeit at a fictitious price (see earlier). The emphasis which is placed on language and its apparent alienableness, in addition to the focus on how language is performed – for example in call centres, interviews with migrant job seekers, and television news programmes – seems undoubtedly a consequence of the framing of language commodification in terms of symbolic capital and the linguistic market of Bourdieu (1977, 1984, 1986, 1991), for whom the proper object of a sociology of language, as for Saussure, is an unapologetic *phonocentrism* and privileging of speech.

> [A] sociological critique subjects the concepts of linguistics to a threefold displacement. In place of *grammaticalness* it puts the notion of *acceptability*, or, to put it another way, in place of "the" language (*langue*), the notion of the *legitimate* language. In place of relations of communication (or symbolic interaction) it puts *relations of symbolic power*, and so replaces the question of the *meaning* of speech with the question of the *value* and *power* of speech. Lastly, in place of specifically linguistic competence, it puts *symbolic capital*, which is inseparable from the speaker's position in the social structure.
> (Bourdieu, 1977: 646)

The language commodification literature consequently follows Bourdieu in being concerned principally with *spokenness* and with the practices, policies and indexicalities around spokenness (Sonntag, 2009; Heller & Duchêne, 2012, 2016; Boutet, 2012; Davuluy, 2012; Lorente, 2012; Park & Wee, 2012; Del Percio et al., 2017; Schedel, 2018; Van Hoof, 2018; Del Percio, 2018; Pujolar, 2018). In the words of Heller and Duchêne, for example, 'We draw on Bourdieu (1982) to argue that language can be understood as a social practice that consists of circulating communicative resources' (2016: 139).[14] In this and related perspectives, the position is taken that 'language in late capitalism is being transformed' (Cavanaugh, 2018: 265), and that it is being transformed primarily through the discursive valorization of language as speech. Here, in the realm of spokenness and linguistic phonocentrism, 'the bounded system cedes ground to the idea of language as a set of circulating, complex communicative resources' (Heller & Duchêne, 2012: 4). Where exceptions exist, and they do exist, they often move in the orbit of the documenting of artefacts in the linguistic landscape, such as iconic landmarks, literary heritage sites and bilingual signage (Del Percio & Duchêne, 2012; Pujolar & Jones, 2012; Brennan, 2018), but often also in combination with a concern for how policies and practices concerning language as speech are articulated with them.

The phonocentrism of the language commodification perspective, which it shares with superdiverse translingualism [in which I am still retaining World Englishes and ELF],[15] recalls Derrida's critique of Western philosophy, or 'metaphysics', and its historical privileging of speech over writing (Derrida, 1976). According to Derrida, writing has been denigrated in the long history of Western philosophy because it merely

---

14 But unlike Bourdieu they tend to neglect structure (see Block, 2013).
15 On linguistic phonocentrism in ELF, see Sowden (2012): '[I]t only really takes account of the spoken language; when formal writing is involved, it has little to offer' (p. 95).

stands in for speech, which since Aristotle has been taken to be the site of essence, oneness and truth. Believing in the primacy of the spoken sign, J J Rousseau for example declared that 'writing is nothing but the representation of speech' (cited in Derrida, 1976: 27). Saussure's structuralist method, and that of 'all semiological structuralism' (Spivak, 1976: lxviii), including that of Husserl, Jakobson, Lacan and Lévi-Strauss, is likewise marked by a preoccupation with speech, which is underpinned by Saussure's insistence that in linguistics, 'The linguistic object is not defined by the combination of the written word and the spoken word: *the spoken form alone constitutes the object*' (cited in Derrida, 1976: 31). Saussure's sign is phonic, not graphic, because writing is artifice, whereas speech is natural, and that is why it is necessary to exclude writing from linguistic consideration:

> First, the graphic form [*image*] of words strikes us as being something permanent and stable, better suited than sound to constitute the unity of language throughout time. Though it creates a purely fictitious unity, the superficial bond of writing is much easier to grasp than the natural bond, the only true bond, the bond of sound.
>
> (Saussure, cited in Derrida, 1976: 35–36)

That this should matter so much is derived from the philosophical assumption that 'the voice . . . has a relationship of essential and immediate proximity to the mind' (Derrida, ibid: 11) and is somehow also closer to human essence and the modernist desire for 'a "central" presence at beginning and end' (Spivak, 1976: lxviii):

> The notion of the sign always implies within itself the distinction between signifier and signified, even if, as Saussure argues, they are distinguished simply as the two faces of one and the same leaf. This notion remains therefore within the heritage of that logocentrism which is also a phonocentrism: absolute proximity of voice and being, of voice and the meaning of being, of voice and the ideality of meaning.
>
> (Derrida, 1976: 11–12)

This inclination towards speech as a *metaphysics of presence* [i.e. a yearning for a centre, completion, oneness, pure being][16] has been mapped to the phenomenology of Husserl (Derrida, 1973), and, as we have seen, continues

---

16 Why is the phoneme the most 'ideal' of signs? Where does this complicity between sound and ideality, or rather, between voice and ideality come from? . . . When I speak, it belongs to the phenomenological essence of this operation that I hear myself [je m'entende] *at the same time* that I speak. The signifier animated by my breath and by the meaning intention . . . is in absolute proximity to me.

(Derrida, 1973: 77)

all the way through to the sociology of language of Bourdieu, which has in turn been so influential upon anthropological approaches to 'late modern' language practices (*passim*). The structuralist spillage of phonocentrism into areas such as language commodification, superdiversity, translingual practice and trans-spatial assemblage seems somewhat out of joint given the often overt anti-structuralism of these approaches. Yet it is also present in translanguaging, World Englishes and ELF perspectives, which are less known for taking up explicit socio-theoretical stances (O'Regan, 2014, 2015; Li, 2018a) but which also place a similar emphasis on the dynamic enmeshment of diverse spoken linguistic practices, especially when individuals engage in what appear to be acts of transgression and resistance against the implicit ontology of normative standard forms (Schneider, 2014; Canagarajah, 2018).

In this respect, the privileging of speech over writing in Western philosophy is shared with the aforementioned approaches so that the innate phonocentrism which structuralism implies is somehow secreted within them and is revealed by the priority which is given to spoken utterances and exchanges as representing the more authentic voice of multilinguals by being closest to their innermost 'real-time' feelings and dispositions (Heller, 2010; Kelly-Holmes, 2016). That these individualist voices are also trampled upon and coerced into 'finessed' formulations in call centres, academic presentations, job-seeker interviews and language classrooms, often by processes of power and exploitation, seems only to intensify the drive to phonocentrism as the principal means of identifying in the acts of the speakers themselves a radical politics of resistance to such domination, while also extending 'the commodification of language in ways that make it available for work it has not had to do before' (Heller & Duchêne, 2016: 140). While it is good that linguists and anthropologists wish to find paths to resistance in speech, it is with *writing* that the hegemony of English in the world rests. Speech plays its part as well, but very often – contrary to the dynamic emphasis in superdiverse translingualism – as both a reflection and a reinforcement of an idealized normative written form, so adding

---

Canagarajah (2018), while criticizing applied linguistics for focusing on language as its unit of analysis, invokes the metaphysics of presence as being about 'prioritizing the [linguistic] influences that are locally visible . . . in a monolithic and passive notion of "context"' (p. 46). This is not precisely what Derrida means by a metaphysics of presence. It is not so much the foregrounding of language *per se* that is at issue [i.e. to the exclusion of other spatio-semiotic elements as Canagarajah suggests], but the conception and *sentiment* that it is voice which is closest in proximity to mind, that being can be read in terms of knowledge about being, and that signs can be fully present to themselves. It is perhaps the sentiment of human immediacy and essence which attaches itself to phonocentrism that comes closest to capturing the dilemma of linguistic anthropology and applied linguistics in relation to the fetishism of speech.

to this form's seeming permanence and stability and making it appear 'better suited than sound to constitute the unity of language throughout time' (Saussure, cited in Derrida, 1976: 35). In opposition to Rousseau, it seems that in the present era it is not so much that writing is the representation of speech but rather the reverse; it is speech that is the representation of writing. This is in the sense that in global English the speech of capital is that of the normative written form, and it is this form which dominates the world-system in all its structural facets.

The normative form as a social relation of capital and capitalism

To find examples is not difficult. Multilingual users of this kind of English are common in international corporate conglomerates, transnational governance institutions, global banking, the transnational university sector, and the higher echelons of international diplomacy. It is these persons and groups of persons who are very often responsible for producing the greater part of the English-medium documentary literature of their organizations and fields and who are also to be found as these organizations' public spokespersons, speechwriters, professors and CEOs. At bottom, a 'native-like' competence in written English is a prerequisite, very often honed by means of a suitable linguistic apprenticeship in a postgraduate programme of study in the English medium and, as a desirable addition, work experience in relevant institutional contexts where the use of written and spoken standard English is the norm. In the circumstance of the 2020 COVID-19 pandemic, it was strikingly apparent just how much of the global information feed in English was delivered in the normative standard form, by high-ranking European Central Bank officials such as Christine La Garde,[17] who is French, and by senior global health experts such as Tedros Adhanom Ghebreyesus, the Ethiopian director of the World Health Organization (WHO). That this may be a 'truncated multilingualism' (Blommaert, Collins & Slembrouck, 2005; Blommaert, 2010; Kubota, 2016; Canagarajah, 2018), which is functional for their users only in the prestige institutional contexts in which they work, is perhaps the significant point, since spoken and written language of an indexicality that is much less normative, or even translingual, is of no particular consequence for capital or for these kinds of multilingual producers of the normative standard form. For them, like the respondents in the university-based study of Canagarajah (2018; see earlier), this may well be their principal repertoire in English, and that is all that really matters. It matters personally, because their jobs and the jobs of those like them depend upon having this kind of demonstrable competence

---

17 Formerly, La Garde was president of the IMF.

in the normative form, and it matters structurally since the documentary production of the global governance institutions of the world-economy, along with its corporate, financial and knowledge sectors, are historically steeped in this form.

This kind of taken-for-grantedness is inevitably ideological and, as such, is an example of misrecognition (Bourdieu, 1977). But it is a misrecognition which exists not simply because of the symbolic value of English in the linguistic market – that is too discursive and unilinear – but because of the connection of normative standard English with a capitalist world-system across the *longue durée*. This should not be misinterpreted as indicating a somewhat crude Marxian determinism as some scholars have suggested (Gal, 2016; Del Percio et al., 2017; Heller & McElhinny, 2017). It is more an attempt to draw attention to the *dialectical* relationship of capital in its dominant accumulating form to the indexicalities of language. That is to say, it is not so much that ideological misrecognition is mostly or even entirely responsible for the prevalence of indexical normativity in global English. Rather, it is that English as an ideological [or discursive] *practical consciousness* (Williams, 1977; see earlier) is *dialectically structured* by its instilment – alongside other factors such as race, class and gender – in the material historical dominance of British and US capital in a capitalist world-system. In other words, there are elements in processes of capital accumulation that have become habitually internalized in the social relations of capitalism, which in turn play their part in reproducing the practice of accumulation. As we saw in Chapter 1, the original accumulation of capital was framed by Marx as an act of dispossession or 'theft' so as to expropriate into private hands what had been 'common social wealth' (Nichol, 2015: 21). Having started down this path, accumulation became a 'silent compulsion' (Marx, 1976 [1867]: 899), to be endlessly and expansively pursued through the centuries 'lest the motor of accumulation die down' (Arendt, 1968: 28). We recognize this today as the remorseless neoliberal conatus for economic growth at any price, including that of the planet and all of its inhabitants.[18] This has consequences for human social relations and what are considered to be the most important or favourable social relations [including linguistic social relations] for capital and its accumulation. Weber's protestant work ethic, Schumpeter's theory of creative destruction, Foucault's *homo economicus* and Becker's human capital theory, for example, are each interpretations of the human relationship with accumulation and, in the final analysis, of

---

18 It was this compulsion which was at the heart of the Trump administration's extreme sociopathological reluctance to enforce a nationwide 'lockdown' as the COVID-19 crisis enveloped the United States in early 2020: 'Kill the curve, not the economy!' he and right-wing TV demagogues railed, as deaths from the virus daily mounted.

accumulation's relationship with nature and all its species (Pennycook, 2018). In the words of Nichol:

> What follows from this is that dispossession comes to name a distinct logic of capitalist development grounded in the appropriation and monopolization of the productive powers of the natural world in a manner that orders (but does not directly determine) social pathologies related to dislocation, class [race, gender and language] stratification and/or exploitation, while simultaneously converting the planet into a homogeneous and universal means of production.
>
> (Nichol, 2015: 27; square parenthesis added)

The global spread of English and then, emerging from this, the global spread of English in its normative form is a dialectical function of capital and its accumulation as this has occurred under the auspices of the world-economies of Britain and the United States. From the early seventeenth century and on into the centuries that followed, the senior overseers of capital's spread have also been the centurion representatives of the normative form, from the factors of the English East India Company, all the way through to the gentlemanly capitalist functionaries of the Bank of England, the National African Company, the Chinese Maritime Customs, the League of Nations, the post-1918 gold standard, the Shanghai Municipal Council, Bretton Woods, the Marshall Plan, multi- and transnational corporations, the World Bank, G7, G20, IMF, Dow Jones, FTSE, Davos, and so on. Capital as an ontological mechanism brings forth normative standard English as its epistemological other [M^E-C^E-M'^E; M^E-M'^E], and normative standard English in turn brings forth accumulation, or at least so it is believed; and that, it seems, is enough for this form of English to have an unrivalled 'abstract objectivism' and hegemonic 'edge' in the capitalist world-economy (Vološinov, 1973: 48; Wallerstein, 2000 [1983]: 257). Whether it is true that English competence really accelerates economic development is less clear (Ricento, 2015b, 2018), although there is evidence to suggest that a government's decision to promote English as part of its national language policy will [for fetish reasons] lead to that country attracting greater FDI (Kim et al., 2014; LeClerc, 2011; see also Chapter 4). In addition, language economists have argued that, under certain conditions, being bilingual and having English in one's repertoire appears to attract an economic reward (Grin, 2001; Gazzola, Grin & Vaillancourt, 2020). This though is not the same as claiming that English is exchangeable in a commodity form, only that bilingualism with English seems to bestow an economic advantage, where monolingualism without it, or even with it, does not (Gazzola et al., ibid). Against this history, and on the back of US-dominated capital and US structural power, normative standard English remains the principal *lingua franca* of the capitalist world-economy. But it is dominant in a world-economy which since the turn of the century has been going through a mounting intensity of systemic shocks, most recently through the COVID-19 pandemic, but also more generally through the rising challenge of China and the relative decline of the United States (see Chapter 6). But even beyond that, there is the sustainability of capitalism itself as its crisis momentum intensifies. If the global hegemony of English is not about to be displaced by a superpower transition from the US to China, then perhaps it is with the demise of capitalism itself that this will occur. This is the subject of the next and final chapter.

8 The demise of capitalism and the end of the hegemony of English

Capitalist crisis and the normative hegemony

This book began with the rise of capitalism, so it seems right to conclude with its predicted demise and what this might mean for English. This is not, however, English in the misleading sense of English as a foreign language, or of Englishes of the inner-circle, or even as the English of native speakers, but as an English which exists in a normative standard form that is linked to capital in a capitalist world-system. This 'capital-centric' form of the language is realized in societies and in the world-system as a *normative grammar*; that is, as 'a governing stratum [*ceto*] whose function is recognized and followed' (Gramsci, 1975: 2343, cited in Ives, 1998: 40). For Bourdieu (1977), as we have seen, this is more accurately a misrecognition, since there is no ethical or innate basis underlying the selection of this construct as the dominant form. With this in mind, we may note that for reasons of the particular history of the world-system and the hegemonic roles of Britain and the US within it, that it is standard English of the kind which is associated with these nations that is the principal reference for this form. It seems relevant to ask, then, whether a terminal crisis of the capitalist system could lead to its displacement. Here is Marx again:

> Hence the highest development of productive power together with the greatest expansion of existing wealth will coincide with depreciation of capital, degradation of the labourer, and a most straitened exhaustion of his vital powers. These contradictions lead to explosions, cataclysms, crises, in which by momentaneous suspension of labour and annihilation of a great portion of capital the latter is violently reduced to the point where it can go on. . . . Yet, these regularly recurring catastrophes lead to their repetition on a higher scale, and finally to its violent overthrow.
>
> (Marx, 1973: 750)

Throughout the history and movement of capitalism, as this book has documented, crisis has been ever-present. During the past one hundred years of the US hegemony, one dimension of this has been the role of English as the language of capitalist crisis management and its resolution. But that capitalism should end someday and transition to something else has been expected as inevitable by many, and not only by Marx. Much less certain has been the how of that process and when it might happen. In the above passage Marx reminds us that he did not imagine that the transition would be a smooth one, and that it would involve many explosions, cataclysms and catastrophes along the way. In *Capital Volume I* he notes how capitalism is marked by repeated 'decennial' cycles of prosperity, over-production, crisis and stagnation (Marx, 1976 [1867]: 785). Modern liberal political economists refer to this as 'the cyclical churn of the global economy' (Sharma, 2020: 71). During the past fifty years the US-directed global economy has quite closely followed this pattern: the 1960s were a boom decade, to be followed by a marked slowdown in the 1970s and early 1980s, resurgence again in the 1990s, hyper-financialization running into catastrophe in the 2000s, and austerity and market recapitalization in the 2010s. Until the global pandemic of 2020–1, the markets had been on a strong upward trend since 2010, and the US had even increased its share of global GDP from 23 per cent to 25 per cent (ibid). That the 2010s, from the perspective of the markets, were a 'good' decade for the United States [even if they were not for anyone else] suggested to investors that a secular downturn for the 2020s was already expected, regardless of the shock of the coronavirus, which was entirely unforeseen [in the moment in which it occurred]. Factors of concern were China's reluctance to instigate domestic reform in the way the markets and the US wanted, ongoing regional tensions in the Middle East and Asia, the sustainability of China's growth, the US trade war with China, and the enormous volume of public debt the US was carrying. But despite these concerns, the markets maintained their upward M-M' trajectory. This was all wiped out by the declaration of the WHO in March 2020 that the coronavirus was a global pandemic.[1] Stock markets around the world plummeted, and nationwide lockdowns were imposed which brought global economic activity, and the normal circulation of capital, almost to a standstill. The IMF subsequently predicted that the world-economy would experience the worst recession since the Great Depression (IMF World Economic Outlook, April 2020).[2]

A pandemic was not the kind of event Marx was envisaging when he spoke of 'regularly occurring catastrophes', although there seems little doubt that it was capitalism which was the root cause by creating and condoning an economic market in wild animal meat and related products. The

---

1 www.euro.who.int/en/health-topics/health-emergencies/coronavirus-covid-19/news/news/2020/3/who-announces-covid-19-outbreak-a-pandemic Accessed April 25, 2020.
2 www.imf.org/en/Publications/WEO/Issues/2020/04/14/weo-april-2020 Accessed April 25, 2020.

propensity of capital to induce concentration and specialization of production in the interests of M' was responsible for encouraging the ever more intense exploitation of wild animal habitats and a fatal disturbance of the balance between the fictional market of capital and the real natural world. If capital was going to treat nature as 'a vast store of potential use values' (Harvey, 2014: 250; see also Nichols, 2015), at some point nature was going to strike back, and this is what it did. Capital has always managed through innovation and scientific advances somehow to compensate for the imbalances it creates with nature, but the time may be coming when that imbalance can no longer be redressed. It is to be hoped, for example, that a vaccine can be found for COVID-19, but no meaningful efforts are being made to tackle the climate catastrophe which awaits, and it may already be too late. Whatever remedies are found for coronavirus or for global warming will also be subject to the diktats of capital, which will seek to acquire commercial rights to vaccines, and also to any carbon-reducing or 'atmosphere-cleansing' technology, which can then be sold at a market price. This seems likely unless – and I admit to a certain pessimism about this – an alternative social contract between humanity and nature can be forged, that is, one that is not based on capital (see Harvey, 2014: 294–297, for what this might look like). But even as capitalism leads the world into another catastrophe of its own making, the response to it, despite its present mass discordance and inter-state 'beggar-thy-neighbour' policies, is being mediated by normative English, through the WHO, the IMF, the World Bank, the WTO, the G20 and a broad range of pan-regional institutions, including the world's financial markets and its transnational corporations (see also Chapters 1 and 5). There is no doubt that alternative Englishes, translingualisms, transspatial assemblages and translanguaged practices utilizing English all play their part as well, but from the linguistically mediated responses which these global organizations produce for dissemination and public consumption, it seems evident that it is the normative grammar which is being recognized and followed, and not something else. This is likely to continue until such a time as there is a hegemonic transfer which sees the eclipse of the United States and with it English, or the capitalist world-system itself comes to end.

Immiseration, inequality and anti-systemic assimilation

The history of the capitalist world-system since it began in the sixteenth century has been one of endless brutality, exploitation and suffering for countless billions of people who have lived through it, involving dispossession, exploitation, discrimination, destruction, poverty, famine, terror, violence, cruelty and greed. Its secular rhythm has also ensured massive and enduring inequality between peoples and, in the modern era, between geopolitically defined nations too. Even as the world has advanced in education, literacy, technology and health, enormous economic and social inequality persists. The wholesale relocation of capitalist production processes from the first world to the developing world as capital has gone in search of cheaper labour costs also shows that the essential exploitative dynamic which Marx identified for Western capitalism has not abated. As services have replaced factory production in the north, so that there are fewer people forced to labour with their hands, in Africa, Asia, Latin America, the Caribbean, Russia and the Middle East, capitalism still has a systematically exploited labouring proletariat, many of whose members live and work in conditions which are every bit as degrading as anything Marx described more than one hundred and fifty years ago. They include the migrant roadworkers of Dubai, the shipyard breakers of Alang in India, and the toxic waste scavengers of Agbogbloshie in Ghana. They continue to bear witness to Marx's general law of capitalist accumulation, whereby

> Accumulation of wealth at one pole is . . . at the same time accumulation of misery, the torment of labour, slavery, ignorance, brutalization and moral degradation at the opposite pole, i.e. on the side of the class that produces its own product of capital.
>
> (Marx, 1976 [1867]: 799)

As yet, immiseration has not proved a sufficient basis for the overthrow of the capitalist world-system, at least not on its own. Part of the reason is that just as capitalism has managed to find solutions to the imbalances it creates with the natural world, so it has also sought to assimilate and neutralize anti-systemic movements and other existential social threats where they arise, principally through the political mechanism of legislation. In many capitalist societies this has brought recognition in matters such as race, ethnicity, religion, sexuality, civic freedoms, public healthcare and workers' rights.

Deeply rooted in the culture of capitalism and its ideological legitimacy has been the idea since the mid-nineteenth century that a combination of science and social inclusion will solve society's ills (Wallerstein, 2000 [1989]: 287). Since the 1960s, particularly in the capitalisms of Europe and the United States, there has been an increasing disillusionment with science because of what its technological advances – driven by a *disembedding capital*[3] – have done to the planet (Polanyi, 2001 [1944]: 76), and also with inclusion, as the promises which legislation was supposed to bring forth have not materialized, or only inadequately so. I am thinking here, for example, of issues around societal racism, religious intolerance, indigenous rights, gender inequality, LGBTQI politics and social welfare. In all these areas anti-systemic groups have found themselves distracted by internal

---

3 Capital seeks to 'disembed' the economy from the necessity of state administration and regulation. But this is a fiction. The more nature is left to the market, the more nature is destroyed and defiled (Polanyi, 2001 [1944]: 75–77).

division and mutual antipathies and unable to coordinate their anti-systemic interests. This has enabled capitalism and its advocates to play them off against one another, while also making efforts at assimilation through legal adjustments which accord piecemeal recognition to their various wants. For example, until quite recently, same-sex marriage had no legal basis in any society in the world. Now it is common, particularly in the West. At bottom, there is still great store placed in the supposed ideological rationalism of capitalism, and this translates as an ambivalence concerning the desirability of its overthrow:

> As long as the anti-systemic movements remain at the level of tactical ambivalence about the guiding ideological values of our world-system . . . we can say that they are in no position to fight a war of position with the forces that defend the inequalities of the world.
> (Wallerstein, 2000 [1989]: 287)

Within the capitalist world-system there are various kinds of anti-systemic movements. They include socialist, or 'old left', movements of the kind personified by politicians like Jeremy Corbyn in the UK and Bernie Sanders in the US; social movements which represent ethnic minority rights, women's rights, LGBTQI rights, human rights, indigenous rights, and the rights of the environmental commons etc.; in the global South there are anti-systemic 'leftist' movements, either in power or in opposition, in for example Mexico, Colombia, Cuba, Venezuela and Bolivia; and in many parts of the world, including the Western world, there are anti-systemic religionist movements which reject modernity altogether. Some of these anti-systemic movements, such as the religionist ones, are entirely incompatible with the others. If not that, then they have conflicting agendas and struggle to find common cause. Also included in anti-systemic movements are those which campaign on a range of issues under the heading of linguistic rights, such as the protection of endangered languages (e.g. Phillipson, 2008; Skutnabb-Kangas & Phillipson, 2010), and also a looser configuration which advocate a principled opposition to standard English, such as World Englishes, ELF, language commodification, and translingualism. Heller and McElhinny, for example, from the perspective of linguistic anthropology, advocate a politics of refusal. This consists in a refusal 'to respect the heavily policed boundaries among languages that so many missionaries, administrators, teachers, linguists, and anthropologists have devoted so much work to producing; [and] *a similar refusal to respect the conventions of standardized language*' (Heller & McElhinny, 2017: 21; emphasis added). The authors are themselves instinctive expert users of this form, and so such a refusal does not seem to be within their capacity to produce. In addition, like many of those whom they single out – who are like them also workers in a capitalist world-system – they unfortunately find themselves in the position of endlessly (re)producing these conventions themselves. As Marx puts it with a slightly different emphasis, 'This incessant reproduction, this perpetuation of the worker, is the absolutely necessary condition for capitalist production' (Marx, 1976 [1867]: 716). In our context, this incessant reproduction is what makes the standardized language what it is. Capital also shows no sign of taking heed of linguistic refusal, or even of opting for a policy of inclusion. This is because language as a normative written grammar is an elemental capitalist distinction which separates the language of capital from the 'lesser' and more diverse linguistic practices of the 'multitude' (Gramsci, 1975; Bourdieu, 1984; Hardt & Negri, 2000). The 'English Only Movement' in the United States, the 'Speak Good English Movement' in Singapore and the standard English prescriptivists in the United Kingdom are good examples, not only of the values of elitism and supposed educatedness which are associated with this form, but also of its link to capital, and of our complicity, including my own, as the instruments of its domination.

Ideological endism and the collapse of capitalism

If China seems unlikely to displace the United States as the next global hegemon, and so also to dislodge English from the dominant position it finds itself in, then what is the likelihood that capitalism through its predicted near-term demise will perform that role instead? One of the most fascinating if also unsettling aspects of the present era is the conflict between the belief that we are in living in a permanent present and the belief that capitalism as we know it is soon to come to an end. Capitalism triumphant after 1991 passed into a new phase; one of *endism*. This is 'the view that history, once real, has come to an end in the present' (Bhaskar, 2016: 183). The period since then is one of 'everlasting posthistory' (ibid): the future proceeds, but there is no alternative to the present. No new ideologies of qualitative institutional or social change appear; only endless market fundamentalism remains (Hartwig, 2011). We see this starkly after the 2007–8 financial crisis when the neoliberal world, unable to contemplate another path, sought refuge in the present through the bailing out of the banks and a resetting of accumulation through the imposition of austerity. This worked to reassure the markets, and a 'fat' decade of capital expansion followed.[4] The failure of capitalism in 2007–8 was repackaged as a failure of public probity, and by 2010 business resumed as before, with the losses of the financial sector absorbed by the state. In 2020, the coronavirus struck and such was the shock that many voices were raised to the effect that there must now be meaningful institutional and social change because the virus and the number of deaths that followed exposed the extreme poverty and insincerity of the neoliberal social contract. Just at the moment when a coordinated state response was most needed to deal with the crisis, many

---

4 www.ft.com/content/cb398952-e6c9-11e5-bc31-138df2ae9ee6 Accessed May 1, 2020.

nations, especially those in the wealthy hyper-neoliberal North, discovered that the services that were most critical to public wellbeing had been so severely denuded and fragmented by neoliberal cuts and competitive outsourcing that they were – through no fault of their own – unable to respond effectively or coherently, and many thousands needlessly died. Despite the mounting death toll, a rising swell of right-wing capitalist opinion in the US and in Europe called for a swift end to state-imposed national lockdowns so that economic activity and accumulation could resume. The clamour was for a return to capitalist economic arrangements as they had been before the pandemic. Adam Tooze has described this as 'an irrepressible impulse that insists we satisfy its demands regardless of the cost, a symptom not of realism but derangement' (Tooze, 2020: 6). It is as yet unclear what the fallout of the virus will mean for neoliberal political economy, but the sclerotic and ineffectual responses of the United States and the United Kingdom, as well as the deaths which followed, stand as terrible indictments of the system. In spite of these ongoing failures, there is in the capitalist world order still no serious contemplation of an alternative path to be followed, only the overriding impulse to return to the everlasting posthistory of remorseless accumulation.

The blind retreat into capitalist endism is already widely acknowledged as unsustainable, not least for the reasons of the climate catastrophe that awaits. It is quite bad enough that the most ardent climate change deniers, such as those behind Trump in the United States, refuse to accept that there is a problem. But even amongst those who do realize this, there are many disincentives to doing anything very decisive about it since that would require fundamental political, economic and social change, and many populations have no appetite for what that would entail. There are also few politicians who wish to sell it to them. Their hopes, and the hopes of the politicians, are instead pinned upon a *deus ex machina* that will save the day, ideally sometime after they are all no longer around. We are nevertheless considered to be in a time of transition in the world-system, if not from one hegemon to another, then from capitalism into something else. Xi Jinping's China is a reluctant world hegemon. In addition to lacking hegemonic preparedness, it is not seriously interested in assuming any of the responsibilities or risks that being the hegemonic power would bring (see Chapter 6). But it does want to be a regional hegemon as well as a global power of high standing, and to be acknowledged as such by the United States and by the rest of the world. Its concern for the present is to avoid not only the middle income trap mentioned in the previous chapter, but also what Graham Allison has referred to as 'Thucydides' trap' (*Financial Times*, August 21, 2012).[5] Thucydides' trap is what befalls a declining hegemon as it finds itself inexorably dragged into war with a competing rising hegemon. In the fifth century BC, Athens

---

5 www.ft.com/content/5d695b5a-ead3-11e1-984b-00144feab49a Accessed April 30, 2020.

rose to challenge Sparta; in the seventeenth century Britain rose to challenge the United Provinces; and at the end of the nineteenth century Germany rose to challenge Britain. All three challenges ended in war. Most do. Peaceful outcomes are achievable, but these require 'huge adjustments in the attitudes and actions of the governments and the societies of both countries involved' (ibid). A war between the US and China in Asia is unlikely to be a limited war and would destabilize the world-economy even more dramatically than the coronavirus pandemic. However, it is now increasingly acknowledged that with the tensions in the South and East China Seas acting as a catalyst, the US and China risk drifting towards Thucydides' trap. Some argue that to avoid this the US needs to make concessions to China in Asia and should make greater efforts to avoid confrontation (Campbell & Sullivan, 2019; Wertheim, 2020). Others believe that increased US assertiveness and visible war preparedness is needed in order that China is contained (Colby & Mitchell, 2020; see also Tooze, 2019). A common theme is US hegemonic decline. World-systems analysis sees nothing recent in this: the US hegemony has been in decline since the early 1970s, and in accelerated decline since the early 2000s (Arrighi, 2010; Wallerstein, 2000 [1983], 2000 [1992], 2000 [1994], 2011d; Wallerstein et al., 2013). This either will lead to Thucydides' trap as the competing hegemons fight it out or, if that is avoided, could lead – if sense does not prevail – to structural crisis and a complete breakdown of the world-system through a combination of the stress factors affecting the system as a whole.

Foremost among these stress factors are the persistent inegalitarianism of the world-system and continued high levels of systemic risk. The two feed off one another in potentially destructive ways. Global inequality has not abated. A minority in the developed world live at income levels far higher than those in the rest of the world. Not that this has statistically changed very much in the last thirty years. According to the Gini index,[6] between 1990 and 2015 global income inequality on average remained largely the same.[7] In some regions, such as North America and Europe, income inequality increased as neoliberalism and then austerity became more prevalent, while in other parts of the world, in Latin America and sub-Saharan Africa for example, inequality levels have remained fairly constant. Elsewhere, for example in India, China, Indonesia and Tanzania, inequality has risen. In Eastern Europe as a whole inequality has also increased as the countries of this region have transitioned from state-planned to market-led economies.

---

6 The Gini index measures the degree of inequality in the distribution of family income in a country. The more egalitarian a country is, the closer its Gini index is to zero. The more inegalitarian it is, the closer it is to 100. Sweden had a Gini index of 24.9 in 2015 for example. Chile's index by comparison was 50.5. www.cia.gov/library/publications/the-world-factbook/rankorder/2172rank.html Accessed May 1, 2020.

7 Is income inequality rising around the world? Joe Hasell, November 19, 2018. https://ourworldindata.org/income-inequality Accessed May 1, 2020.

All told, inequality remains a major global problem, which despite greater international consciousness of it has barely shifted in any sense that would make a meaningful difference to most people living in the developing world. Western Europe, North America, Australasia and the oil-rich Middle East are at least three to four times wealthier than the most economically productive nations of Latin America and Africa, and around seventy times wealthier than the poorest.[8]

By remaining constant, these polarizations in income and in life prospects have been given heightened resonance for those at the sharp end of that experience, who have either witnessed no meaningful improvement in their or their children's life chances, or have seen them deteriorate still further in the face of developmentalist structural adjustment programmes and neoliberal 'free market' economics. In these societies, child mortality, life expectancy, education and income are very difficult to ameliorate. Countries where GDP per capita is under $1000 and most people live in extreme poverty, such as in parts of Central and West Africa, stand abandoned on the extremes of the capitalist periphery and have no development prospects at all.[9] Grinding poverty and persistent deprivation, in combination with natural disasters and regional conflicts, have seen an explosion in northward migration, especially to Europe and the United States. US culpability in fomenting increased regional destabilization since 2000 and the first world's continued insistence on the developmentalist fallacy (see Chapters 1 and 4) have only exacerbated migratory pressures as populations have been displaced and economic prospects have either stagnated or gone into reverse, in which one side effect has been increased translingualism amongst those displaced or forced to migrate (Barrera, 2017; Georgiou, 2018). Since 2015, the West has moved more emphatically to a fortress mentality on inward migration which has been accompanied, and encouraged, by a rise in protectionist xenophobic nationalism, nowhere more so than in the US and Europe. The Trump administration even threatened Mexico with punitive tariffs, despite the USMCA free trade accord (see Chapter 6), if it did not stem the tide of migrants trying reach the US from the poorer Central American nations to its south. The vast levels of debt which exist in the United States and Europe also spell further falling living standards and increased deprivation for those on low incomes or in marginalized groups.

In keeping with endism (see earlier), a new round of economic austerity is already being predicted, with 'financial repression and higher levels of taxation' but also poor prospects for renewed growth (*Financial Times*, April 25, 2020).[10] Austerity is in contradiction with stimulus since it slashes demand to which the only answer is more stimulus and increased debt. Stimulus

---

8 https://ourworldindata.org/grapher/gdp-per-capita-worldbank Accessed May 1, 2020.
9 https://ourworldindata.org/income-inequality-since-1990 Accessed May 1, 2020.
10 www.ft.com/content/e0705292-c9cb-4d4e-8586-4f1174665e83 Accessed May 1, 2020.

will also hit US bondholders as the US government uses up bond repayment money on the stimulus. It is also inflationary, so reducing further the value of the government bonds. The tension between financial probity in the markets and falling bond values and market incomes is likely to put still greater pressure on governments to police the markets less closely. This could lead to the renewed assertion of 'vulture-capitalist' risk. The levels of debt leverage and the pressures this places upon the international monetary system are bad news for the United States, which is not accustomed to being anything other than the global hegemon. It is also bad news for China, where its public debt is three times the size of its GDP. If the US were to lose the trust of market credit, which seems unlikely just now,[11] the dollar would no longer be the international currency of reserve, and the US would be unable to service its debts. A mercantilist financial contagion would follow in which China would lose its largest overseas market and all of its growth – and the rule of the CCP would be put to the question. Around the world, those who are unable to migrate to the north will find themselves locked into increasingly authoritarian and unstable regimes so further exacerbating internal and regional population displacements. Without any global leadership or coordination through international governance organizations such as the UN and the G20 [the dominant nation in these groupings having opted for 'great power suicide' and vacated the stage (Arrighi, 2010: 384)], nuclear proliferation could spiral out of control leading to nuclear confrontations and wars. These would most likely be driven as much, if not more, by clashing ideological and nationalist fundamentalisms as by any geopolitical considerations. Global environmental destruction and economic inequality would also be greatly compounded as the planet took a poor second place to the everyday struggle for survival. There would be nothing remotely Schumpeterian about any of it.

Capitalist disintegration and the end of the English hegemony

In such a future dystopia, it seems unlikely that capital-centric normative English would continue to have any relevance or meaning for the world, except as a historical linguistic artefact of the era of accumulation. Somewhat prophetically, Wallerstein was predicting thirty years ago,

> Somewhere down the line, in 2025 or 2050, the day of reckoning will arrive. And the United States [but not it alone] will face the same kind of choice then that it has today, but on a world scale. Either the world-system will move toward a repressive restructuring or it will move toward an egalitarian restructuring.
>
> (Wallerstein, 2000 [1992]: 413)

---

11 www.foreignaffairs.com/articles/2020-05-19/future-dollar Accessed August 23, 2020.

He hoped for an egalitarian restructuring. But now in the 2020s, in Europe and North America, for the first time since the 1930s, Western nations [and many others too] have been opting for isolationism and populist crypto-fascism over inclusiveness and egalitarianism. This includes the past and present hegemons of the capitalist world-system, Britain and the United States. In both nations, the old nineteenth-century imperialist alliance between 'capital and mob' (Arendt, 1968: 35) has been resurrected and re-applied to an isolationist age. In this world it is once more legitimate to be racist, to beggar-thy-neighbour, and to fall in with ideological extremism and narrow mercantilism.[12] The British right-wing establishment, wishing to cling to the mythical vestiges of past imperial glories and backed by deeply disaffected elements of the dispossessed [and not so dispossessed] White working class, has thrown its lot in with a Trumpian United States which rails at the narrowing of its economic advantage and is lashing out [at least for now].

But what Wallerstein observed in the 1990s still applies today: 'Unless [the US] realizes that there is no salvation that is not the salvation of all human-kind, neither it nor the rest of the world will surmount the structural crisis of our world system' (Wallerstein, 2000 [1992]: 414). And if the US cannot realize this and is unable find its way out of the Trumpian crypto-fascist labyrinth it finds itself in,[13] then with structural crisis and the collapse of the world-system, the historical era of normative standard English will also come to an end. And with that, 'The modern world system will have seen its definitive demise, ceding place to a successor or successors yet unknown, unknowable, and whose characteristics we cannot yet sketch' (ibid, 2011d: xvii). Whatever English in the world might have become by then, it will not be as the pre-eminent *lingua franca* of the world-system that it will be known. This connection will be finished because the dialectical relation of normative English to capital [as M^E-C^E-M'^E and M^E-M'^E] will have been severed, and in the absence of any unifying hegemony to sustain it, its fetish nature will be swept away. It may well survive in pockets amongst the *ancien régime* of US clientelist elites and their hangers on, as they retreat into isolation and out of the dollar into gold. It will also have its place for those who know no other form of English. In English-medium academic research, in literature and in English-language education too, there will be spaces where it will still linger. But normative standard English will no longer hold the same allure or Weberian 'iron cage' natural necessity that it once did. Instead, it may be that for the first time we really will be able to dismiss the modernist notion of language and can talk more

---

12 The international relations scholar Barry Buzan, arguing that the 1930s could not be repeated in the modern world-system, reached precisely the opposite conclusion in a lecture given in London in 2012 when he declared that ideological racism and economic nationalism were things of the past. See Buzan, B. (2012). *No more superpowers* [YouTube TEDx Talk]. Retrieved from www.youtube.com/watch?v=JC27GMQoM08
13 Even with the election of Biden, the route out for the US is far from clear.

meaningfully, without the distraction of capital and capitalism, of 'the communicative practices of transnational groups that interact using different languages and communicative codes simultaneously present in a range of communicative channels, both local and distant' (Jacquemet, 2005: 265, cited in Pennycook, 2010c: 683). Normative English will not matter in the way that it once did, so allowing superdiverse translingualism to emerge from its shadow as the 'practical constitutive activity' that Raymond Williams and Marx once spoke of, one which is unburdened by the constraints of capital.

We can but hope that the world into which English-inflected translingualisms will emerge will be less unremittingly inegalitarian, alienating and fixated upon capital than the one which preceded it, but the indications are not promising. The bifurcation point that world-systems analysis warned us of is fast approaching, and at the moment it seems that the world in the hands of the United States and China, and abetted by a slew of reactionary governments across Europe, Latin America, Africa, the Middle East and Asia, is opting for regressive ideological fundamentalism and irrealism as its preferred destination. If humankind has the wherewithal to act, a new social contract might be achieved, but this requires sustained collective action and a critically conscious *revolutionism* (Fanon, 1967; Gramsci, 1971; Habermas, 1987; Vogler, 2013; Harvey, 2014; Holborow, 2015; Bhaskar, 2016); that is, one which rejects the capitalist alienation of nature and of all living things and purposefully seeks the essence of humanity not in the inevitable conversion of use values into exchange values but in 'an absolute humanism of history' (Gramsci, 1971: 465). In such a revolutionism, neither hope on its own nor cumulative individuated resistances will suffice; for the point, as Marx so keenly reminds us, is that we exist not only to interpret the world, but also to change it (Marx, 1998 [1845]: 571). Let us hope that it is not already too late, because an unalienated, sustainable, humanitarian and linguistically diverse postmodernity which has been absented of the endless accumulation of capital is one that is worth fighting for.

FINIS.

References

Adamson, B. (2002). Barbarian as a foreign language: English in China's schools. *World Englishes*, 21(2), 231–243.
Adamson, B. (2004). *China's English: A History of English in Chinese Education*. Hong Kong: Hong Kong University Press.
Adamson, L. (2020). *Negotiating Language and Learning: An Ethnographic Study of Students' Experiences in Two Tanzanian Secondary Schools* (PhD). University College London, London, UK.
Akram, T. (2019). The Japanese economy: Stagnation, recovery, and challenges. *Journal of Economic Issues*, 53(2), 403–410.
Albaugh, E. A. (2009). The colonial image reversed: Language preferences and policy outcomes in African education. *International Studies Quarterly*, 53, 389–420.
Alim, S. H. (2006). *Roc the Mic Right. The Language of Hip Hop Culture*. New York: Routledge.
Alsagoff, L. (2008). The commodification of Malay: Trading in futures. In P. Tan & R. Rubdy (Eds.), *Language as Commodity: Global Structure, Local Marketplaces* (pp. 44–56). London: Continuum.
Althusser, L. (1971). *Lenin and Philosophy*. New York: Monthly Review Press.
Althusser, L. (1996 [1965]). *For Marx*. London: Verso.
Ambrose, S. E. (1993). *Rise to Globalism: American Foreign Policy Since 1938*. New York: Penguin.
Amin, S. (1977). *Imperialism and Unequal Development*. New York: Monthly Review Press.
Appadurai, A. (1990). Disjuncture and difference in the global cultural economy. In M. Featherstone (Ed.), *Global Culture: Nationalism, Globalization and Modernity* (pp. 295–310). Thousand Oaks: Sage.
Arendt, H. (1968). *Imperialism: Part Two of the Origins of Totalitarianism*. San Diego: Harvest.
Arnaut, K., & Spotti, M. (2014). Superdiversity discourse. *Working Papers in Urban Languages and Literacies*, 122, 1–11.
Arrighi, G. (2010). *The Long Twentieth Century: Money, Power and the Origins of our Times*. London: Verso.
Ashkanasy, N. M., Trevor-Roberts, E., & Earnshaw, L. (2002). The Anglo-cluster: Legacy of the British empire. *Journal of World Business*, 37, 28–39.
Avineri, S. (1969). Introduction. In S. Avineri (Ed.), *Karl Marx on Colonialism and Modernization* (pp. 1–34). New York: Anchor.

Bailey, R. W. (2017). Standard American English. In A. Bergs & L. J. Brinton (Eds.), *The History of English* (Vol. 5: Varieties of English, pp. 9–30). Berlin and Boston: De Gruyter.

Baker, A. (2006). *The Group of Seven: Finance Ministries, Central Banks and Global Financial Governance*. London: Routledge.

Bakhtin, M. M. (1981). *The Dialogic Imagination*. Austin: University of Texas Press.

Bamgbose, A. (1991). *Language and the Nation: The Language Question in Sub-Saharan Africa*. Edinburgh: Edinburgh University Press.

Barakos, E. W., & Unger, J. (Eds.). (2016). *Discursive Approaches to Language Policy*. London: Palgrave Macmillan.

Barber, N. (1965). *The Black Hole of Calcutta: A Reconstruction*. London: Collins.

Barrera, T. E. (2017). Salvaging the mother tongue in exile. *Comparative Critical Studies*, 14(2–3), 187–204.

Battelle, J. (2018, February 25). The end of democratic capitalism? *Medium*. Retrieved from https://medium.com/newco/the-end-of-democratic-capitalism-358cf992931e

Bauman, Z. (2000). *Liquid Modernity*. Cambridge: Polity Press.

Baynham, M. (1995). *Literacy Practices: Investigating Literacy in Social Contexts*. London: Longman.

Beasley, W. G. (1951). *Great Britain and the Opening of Japan 1834–1858*. London: Luzac & Company.

Becker, G. (1993). *Human Capital: A Theoretical and Empirical Analysis, with Special Reference to Education* (3rd ed.). Chicago: University of Chicago Press.

Bennui, P., & Hashim, A. (2014). English in Thailand: Development of English in a non-postcolonial context. *Asian Englishes*, 16(3), 209–228.

Bentley, R. S., & Grebstein, S. (1956). English – Tomorrow's international language. *The English Journal*, 45(7), 395–399.

Benton, L. (2002). *Law and Colonial Cultures: Legal Regimes in World History, 1400–1900*. Cambridge: Cambridge University Press.

Bernstein, B. (1971). *Class, Codes and Control* (Vol. 1). London: Routledge.

Betta, C. (2000). Marginal Westerners in Shanghai: The Baghdadi Jewish community, 1845–1931. In R. Bickers & C. Henriot (Eds.), *New Frontiers: Imperialism's New Communities in East Asia, 1842–1953* (pp. 38–54). Manchester: Manchester University Press.

Bevins, V. (2020). *The Jakarta Method. Washington's Anticommunist Crusade & the Mass Murder Program that Shaped Our World*. New York: Public Affairs.

Bhaskar, R. (1998). *The Possibility of Naturalism: A Philosophical Critique of the Contemporary Human Sciences*. London: Routledge.

Bhaskar, R. (2002). *Reflections on Meta-Reality: Transcendence, Emancipation and Everyday Life*. New Delhi and London: Thousand Oaks and Sage.

Bhaskar, R. (2008 [1975]). *A Realist Theory of Science*. London: Verso.

Bhaskar, R. (2016). *Enlightened Common Sense: The Philosophy of Critical Realism*. London: Routledge.

Bhatt, R. M. (1995). Prescriptivism, creativity and World Englishes. *World Englishes*, 14(2), 247–259.

Bhatt, R. M. (2001). World Englishes. *Annual Review of Anthropology*, 30, 527–550.

Bickers, R. (1998). Shanghailanders: The formation and identity of the British settler community in Shanghai. *Past and Present*, 159, 179–180.

Bickers, R. (2000). Who were the Shanghai Municipal Police, and why were they there? The recruits of 1919. In R. Bickers & C. Henriot (Eds.), *New Frontiers: Imperialism's New Communities in East Asia, 1842–1953* (pp. 170–191). Manchester: Manchester University Press.

Bickers, R. (Ed.). (2010a). *Settlers and Expatriates: Britons Over the Seas*. Oxford: Oxford University Press.

Bickers, R. (2010b). Shanghailanders and others: British communities in China, 1842–1957. In R. Bickers (Ed.), *Settlers and Expatriates: Britons Over the Seas* (pp. 269–301). Oxford: Oxford University Press.

Block, D. (2012a). Economising globalisation and identity in applied linguistics in neoliberal times. In D. Block, J. Gray, & M. Holborow (Eds.), *Neoliberalism and Applied Linguistics*. London: Routledge.

Block, D. (2012b). Commentary: Transnational South Korea as a site for a sociolinguistics of globalization and the distinction of global elites. *Journal of Sociolinguistics*, 16(2), 277–282.

Block, D. (2013). The structure and agency dilemma in identity and intercultural communication research. *Language and Intercultural Communication*, 13(2), 126–147.

Block, D. (2014). *Social Class in Applied Linguistics*. London: Routledge.

Block, D. (2017a). Political economy in applied linguistics research. *Language Teaching*, 50(1), 32–64.

Block, D. (2017b). What is language commodification? In S. Breidbach, L. Küster, & B. Schmenk (Eds.), *Sloganizations in Language Education Discourse* (pp. 121–141). Bristol: Multilingual Matters.

Block, D. (2018a). Inequality and class in language policy and planning. In J. W. Tollefson & M. Pérez-Milans (Eds.), *The Oxford Handbook of Language Policy and Planning* (pp. 568–590). Oxford: Oxford University Press.

Block, D. (2018b). The political economy of language education research (or the lack thereof): Nancy Fraser and the case of translanguaging. *Critical Inquiry in Language Studies*, 15(4), 237–257.

Block, D. (2018c). *Political Economy and Sociolinguistics: Neoliberalism, Inequality and Social Class*. London: Bloomsbury.

Block, D. (2019). *Post-Truth and Political Discourse*. London: Palgrave Macmillan.

Block, D., Gray, J., & Holborow, M. (2012). *Neoliberalism and Applied Linguistics*. London: Routledge.

Blommaert, J. (2009). A market of accents. *Language Policy*, 8, 243–259.

Blommaert, J. (2010). *The Sociolinguistics of Globalization*. Cambridge: Cambridge University Press.

Blommaert, J. (2013). *Ethnography, Superdiversity and Linguistic Landscapes: Chronicles of Complexity*. Bristol: Multilingual Matters.

Blommaert, J. (2015). Chronotopes, scales, and complexity in the study of language in society. *Annual Review of Anthropology*, 44(1), 105–116.

Blommaert, J. (2016). Superdiversity and the neoliberal conspiracy. *Ctrl+Alt+Dem*. Retrieved from http://alternative-democracy-research.org/2016/03/03/superdiversity-and-the-neoliberal-conspiracy/

Blommaert, J., Collins, J., & Slembrouck, S. (2005). Spaces of multilingualism. *Language and Communication*, 25(3), 197–216.

Blommaert, J., & Rampton, B. (2012). Language and superdiversity. *MMG Working Paper, Max Planck Institute for the Study of Religious and Ethnic Diversity, 12–05*, 7–30.

Blum, W. (2014). *Killing Hope: US Military and CIA Interventions Since World War II*. London: Zed Books.

Blustein, P. (2005). *And the Money Kept Rolling In (and Out): Wall Street, the IMF and the Bankrupting of Argentina*. New York: Public Affairs.

Bobda, A. S. (2010). Local networks in the formation and development of West African English. In M. Saxena & T. Omoniyi (Eds.), *Contending with Globalization in World Englishes*. Clevedon: Multilingual Matters.

Bolton, K. (2003). *Chinese Englishes: A Sociolinguistic History*. Cambridge: Cambridge University Press.

Bolton, K. (2013). World Englishes, globalization and language worlds. In N. L. Johannesson & G. Melcher (Eds.), *Of Butterflies and Birds, of Dialects and Genres: Essays in Honour of Philip Shaw* (pp. 227–252). Stockholm: Acta Universitatis Stockholmiensis.

Borjian, M. (2013). *English in Post-Revolutionary Iran: From Indigenization to Internationalization*. Bristol: Multilingual Matters.

Bottomore, T. (1991). Finance capital. In T. Bottomore (Ed.), *A Dictionary of Marxist Thought* (2nd ed., pp. 198). London: Blackwell.

Bourdieu, P. (1977). The economics of linguistic exchanges. *Social Science Information, 16*(6), 645–668.

Bourdieu, P. (1982). *Ce que parler veut dire*. Paris: Seuil.

Bourdieu, P. (1984). *Distinction: A Social Critique of the Judgement of Taste*. London: Routledge.

Bourdieu, P. (1986). The forms of capital. In J. Richardson (Ed.), *Handbook of Theory and Research for the Sociology of Education* (pp. 241–258). New York: Greenwood.

Bourdieu, P. (1991). *Language and Symbolic Power*. Oxford: Polity Press.

Boutet, J. (2012). Language workers: Emblematic figures of late capitalism. In A. Duchêne & M. Heller (Eds.), *Language in Late Capitalism: Pride and Profit* (pp. 207–220). London: Routledge.

Bown, C. P., & Irwin, D. A. (2019). Trump's assault on the trading system. And why decoupling will change everything. *Foreign Affairs, 98*(5), 125–136.

Braibanti, J. D. (1949). Administration of military government in Japan at the prefectural level. *The American Political Science Review, 43*(2), 250–274.

Braine, G. (Ed.). (2005). *Teaching English to the World: History, Curriculum, and Practice*. Mahwah: Lawrence Erlbaum.

Braudel, F. (1980 [1958]). *On History* (S. Matthews, Trans.). Chicago: University of Chicago Press.

Braudel, F. (2012 [1958]). History and the social sciences: The longue durée (I. Wallerstein, Trans.). In R. E. Lee (Ed.), *The Longue Durée* (pp. 241–246). Albany: State University of New York Press.

Brennan, S. C. (2018). Advocating commodification: An ethnographic look at the policing of Irish as a commercial asset. *Language Policy, 17*(2), 157–177.

Brenner, R. (1977). The origins of capitalist development: A critique of neo-Smithian Marxism. *New Left Review, 104*, 25–92.

Brewer, A. (1990). *Marxist Theories of Imperialism: A Critical Survey* (2nd ed.). London: Routledge.

Bruthiaux, P. (2008). Dimensions of globalization and applied linguistics. In R. Rubdy & P. K. W. Tan (Eds.), *Language as Commodity: Global Structures: Local Marketplaces* (pp. 1–30). London: Continuum.

Brutt-Griffler, J. (2002). *World English: A Study of its Development*. Clevedon: Multilingual Matters.

Budach, G., & de Saint-Georges, I. (2017). Superdiversity and language. In S. Canagarajah (Ed.), *The Routledge Handbook of Migration and Language* (pp. 63–78). London: Routledge.

Bukharin, N. (1972 [1925–6]). Imperialism and the accumulation of capital. In K. J. Tarbuck (Ed.), *Imperialism and the Accumulation of Capital* (pp. 153–270). London: Penguin.

Bukharin, N. (1987 [1915]). *Imperialism and World Economy*. London: Merlin Press.

Buzan, B., & Little, R. (2000). *International Systems in World History: Remaking the Study of International Relations*. Oxford: Oxford University Press.

Cain, P. J., & Hopkins, A. G. (1980). The political economy of British expansion overseas, 1750–1914. *The Economic History Review*, 33(4), 463–490.

Cain, P. J., & Hopkins, A. G. (1986). Gentlemanly capitalism and British expansion overseas I. The Old Colonial System, 1688–1850. *The Economic History Review*, 39(4), 501–525.

Cain, P. J., & Hopkins, A. G. (1987). Gentlemanly capitalism and British expansion overseas II: New Imperialism, 1850–1945. *The Economic History Review*, 40(1), 1–26.

Cain, P. J., & Hopkins, A. G. (2013). *British Imperialism 1688–2000* (2nd ed.). London: Routledge.

Callinicos, A. (2009). *Imperialism and Global Political Economy*. Cambridge: Polity Press.

Calvet, L.-J. (1998). *Language Wars: Language Policies and Globalization*. Retrieved from https://nanovic.nd.edu/assets/8706/calvetpaper.pdf

Cameron, D. (2000). Styling the worker: Gender and the commodification of language in the globalized service economy. *Journal of Sociolinguistics*, 4, 323–427.

Cameron, D. (2012). The commodification of language: English as a global commodity. In T. Nevalainen & E. C. Traugott (Eds.), *The Oxford Handbook of the History of English* (pp. 352–361). Oxford: Oxford University Press.

Campbell, K. M., & Sullivan, J. (2019). Competition without catastrophe. How America can both challenge and coexist with China. *Foreign Affairs*, 98(5), 96–111.

Canagarajah, S. (1999). *Resisting Linguistic Imperialism in English Teaching*. Oxford: Oxford University Press.

Canagarajah, S. (2006). Negotiating the local in English as a Lingua Franca. *Annual Review of Applied Linguistics*, 26, 197–218.

Canagarajah, S. (2013). *Translingual Practice: Global Englishes and Cosmopolitan Relations*. London: Routledge.

Canagarajah, S. (2018). Translingual practice as spatial repertoires: Expanding the paradigm beyond structuralist orientations. *Applied Linguistics*, 39, 31–54.

Canagarajah, S., & Dovchin, S. (2019). The everyday politics of translingualism as a resistant practice. *International Journal of Multilingualism*, 16(2), 127–144.

Carrington, C. E. (1968). *The British Overseas: Exploits of a Nation of Shopkeepers* (Vol. 1, 2nd ed.). Cambridge: Cambridge University Press.

Castells, M. (2006). Globalisation and identity: A comparative perspective. *Journal of Contemporary Culture, 1*, 56–66.

Cavanaugh, J. R. (2018). Linguistic economies: Commentary on language policy special issue 'Policing for commodification: Turning communicative resources into commodities'. *Language Policy, 17*, 261–263.

Cavanaugh, J. R., & Shankar, S. (2014). Producing authenticity in global capitalism: Language, materiality, and value. *American Anthropologist, 116*(1), 51–64.

Chang, J. (2016). The ideology of American English as standard English in Taiwan. *Arab World English Journal, 7*(4), 80–96.

Chen, S.-C. (2006). Simultaneous promotion of indigenization and internationalization: New language-in-education policy in Taiwan. *Language and Education, 20*(4), 322–337.

Choi, E. K. (2002). Trade and the adoption of a universal language. *International Review of Economics and Finance, 11*, 265–275.

Chomsky, N. (2001). The United States is a leading terrorist state: An interview with Noam Chomsky by David Barsamian. *Monthly Review, 53*(6).

Chouliaraki, L., & Fairclough, N. (1999). *Discourse in Late Modernity: Rethinking Critical Discourse Analysis*. Edinburgh: Edinburgh University Press.

Chowdhury, R., & Kabir, A. (2014). Language wars: English education policy and practice in Bangladesh. *Multilingual Education, 4*(1), 1–16.

Chowdhury, R., & Phan, L. H. (2014). *Desiring TESOL and International Education: Market Abuse and Exploitation*. Cleveland: Multilingual Matters.

Chun, C. W. (2017). *The Discourses of Capitalism: Everyday Economists and the Production of Common Sense*. London: Routledge.

Clarence-Smith, W. G. (1994). The organization of consent in West Africa, 1820s to 1860s. In D. Engels & S. Marks (Eds.), *Contesting Colonial Hegemony: State and Society in Africa and India* (pp. 55–78). London: British Academic Press.

Clough, R. (1991). Taiwan under Nationalist rule, 1949–1982. In R. MacFarquhar & J. Fairbank (Eds.), *The Cambridge History of China* (pp. 813–874). Cambridge: Cambridge University Press.

Codó, E. (2018). Language policy and planning, institutions, and neoliberalisation. In M. Pérez-Milans & J. W. Tollefson (Eds.), *The Oxford Handbook of Language Policy and Planning* (pp. 467–484). Oxford: Oxford University Press.

Cogo, A., & Dewey, M. (2012). *Analysing English as a Lingua Franca: A Corpus-driven Investigation*. London: Continuum.

Colby, E. A., & Mitchell, A. W. (2020). The age of great-power competition. How the Trump administration refashioned American strategy. *Foreign Affairs, 99*(1), 118–130.

Coleman, T. (1965). *The Railway Navvies: A History of the Men Who Made the Railways*. London: Hutchinson & Co Ltd.

Cook, G. (2000). *Language Play, Language Learning*. Oxford: Oxford University Press.

Cooper, R. N. (2014). Book review: The Bretton Woods transcripts by Kurt Schuler and Andrew Rosenberg. *Journal of Economic Literature, 52*(1), 234–236.

Coupland, N., & Jaworski, A. (Eds.). (1999). *The Discourse Reader*. London: Routledge.

Cox, R. W. (1987). *Production, Power, and World Order: Social Forces in the Making of History*. New York: Columbia University Press.
Cox, R. W. (1992). Global Perestroika. In R. Miliband & L. Panitch (Eds.), *Socialist Register 1992*. London: Merlin.
Cranmer-Byng, J. L. (1965). Linguists at Canton. *Ch'ing-shih wen-t'i, 1*(2), 5–6.
Creese, A., Blackledge, A., & Hu, R. (2018). Translanguaging and translation: The construction of social difference across city spaces. *International Journal of Bilingual Education and Bilingualism, 21*(7), 841–852.
Crow, C. (1921). *Handbook for China* (3rd ed.). New York: Dodd, Mead & Co.
Crystal, D. (2017). The future of new Euro-Englishes. *World Englishes, 36*(3), 330–335.
Cui, A. (2018). Building the belt and road: The overlooked unveiling of China's boldest. *Harvard International Review, 39*(1), 16–18.
Darwent, C. E. (1920). *Shanghai: A Handbook for Travellers and Residents to the Chief Objects of Interest in and Around the Foreign Settlements and Native City*. Shanghai: Kelly & Walsh, Limited.
Darwin, J. (2009). *The Empire Project: The Rise and Fall of the British World System, 1830–1970*. Cambridge: Cambridge University Press.
Da Silva, E., McLaughlin, M., & Richards, M. (2007). Bilingualism and the globalized new economy: The commodification of language and identity. In M. Heller (Ed.), *Bilingualism: A Social Approach* (pp. 183–206). London: Palgrave Macmillan.
Davey, B. (1975). *The Economic Development of India*. London: Spokesman Books.
Davies, W. (2013). When is a market not a market? *Theory, Culture and Society, 30*(2), 32–59.
Davis, C. B. (1991). Railway Imperialism in China, 1895–1939. In C. B. Davis, K. E. Wilburn, & R. E. Robinson (Eds.), *Railway Imperialism* (pp. 155–174). Westport: Greenwood Press.
Davis, C. B., Wilburn, K. E., & Robinson, R. E. (Eds.). (1991). *Railway Imperialism*. New York: Greenwood Press.
Davuluy, M. (2012). War, peace and languages in the Canadian navy. In M. Heller & A. Duchêne (Eds.), *Language in Late Capitalism: Pride and Profit* (pp. 142–160). London: Routledge.
DeCorse, C. (2016). Tools of empire: Trade, slaves, and the British forts of West Africa. In D. Maudlin & B. L. Herman (Eds.), *Building the British Atlantic World: Spaces, Places, and Material Culture, 1600–1850* (pp. 165–187). Chapel Hill: University of North Carolina Press.
De Costa, P. (2010). Language ideologies and standard English language policy in Singapore: Responses of a 'designer immigrant' student. *Language Policy, 9*(3), 217–239.
De Costa, P., Park, J. S.-Y., & Wee, L. (2016). Language learning as linguistic entrepreneurship: Implications for language education. *The Asia-Pacific Education Researcher, 25*(5–6), 695–702.
De Costa, P., Park, J. S.-Y., & Wee, L. (2019). Linguistic entrepreneurship as affective regime: Organizations, audit culture, and second/foreign language education policy. *Language Policy*, 387–406.
Deleuze, G., & Guattari, F. (1988). *A Thousand Plateaus: Capitalism and Schizophrenia*. London: The Athlone Press Ltd.

Del Percio, A. (2018). Engineering commodifiable workers: Language, migration and the governmentality of the self. *Language Policy, 17*(2), 239–259.

Del Percio, A., & Duchêne, A. (2012). Commodification of pride and resistance to profit language practices as terrain of struggle in a Swiss football stadium. In A. Duchêne & M. Heller (Eds.), *Language in Late Capitalism: Pride and Profit* (pp. 43–72). London: Routledge.

Del Percio, A., Flubacher, M.-C., & Duchêne, A. (2017). Language and political economy. In O. García, N. Flores, & M. Spotti (Eds.), *The Oxford Handbook of Language and Society* (pp. 1–24): Oxford University Press.

De Man, P. (1979). *Allegories of Reading*. Yale: Yale University Press.

Derrida, J. (1973). *Speech and Phenomena and Other Essays on Husserl's Theory of Signs*. Evanston: Northwestern University Press.

Derrida, J. (1975). The purveyor of truth. *Yale French Studies, 52*, 31–113.

Derrida, J. (1976). *Of Grammatology*. Baltimore: John Hopkins University Press.

Derrida, J. (1994). *Specters of Marx*. New York: Routledge.

Derrida, J. (1995). *Points: Interviews, 1974–1994*. Stanford: Stanford University Press.

De Swann, A. (2001). *Words of the World*. Cambridge: Polity Press.

Dian, M. (2016, Winter). Does China have structural power? Rethinking Chinese power and its consequences for the international order. *The Journal of Northeast Asian History, 2*, 121–157.

Dixon, R. (1997). *The Rise and Fall of Languages*. Cambridge: Cambridge University Press.

Dobb, M. (1963). *Studies in the Development of Capitalism*. London: Routledge.

Domingo, M. (2014). Transnational language flows in digital platforms: A study of urban youth and their multimodal text making. *Pedagogies: An International Journal, 9*(1), 7–25.

Donnelly, J. S. (2002). *The Great Irish Potato Famine*. Cheltenham: The History Press.

Dreyfus, H. L., & Rabinow, P. (1982). *Michel Foucault: Beyond Structuralism and Hermeneutics*. Chicago: University of Chicago Press.

Duchêne, A. (2009). Marketing, management and performance: Multilingualism as a commodity in a tourism call center. *Language Policy, 8*(1), 27–50.

Duchêne, A., & Heller, M. (Eds.). (2012). *Language in Late Capitalism: Pride and Profit*. London: Routledge.

Dufva, H., Suni, S., Aro, M., & Salo, O.-P. (2011). Languages as objects of learning: Language learning as a case of multilingualism. *Journal of Applied Language Studies, 5*(1), 109–124.

Duménil, G., & Lévy, D. (2011). *The Crisis of Neoliberalism*. Cambridge, MA: Harvard University Press.

Dunn, B. (2014). *The Political Economy of Global Capitalism and Crisis*. London: Routledge.

Dussel, E. (1996). *The Underside of Modernity: Apel, Ricoeur, Rorty, Taylor and the Philosophy of Liberation* (E. Mendieta, Trans.). Amherst, MA: Humanity Books.

Dyer-Ball, J. (1903). *Things Chinese*. Hong Kong and Shanghai: Kelly & Walsh, Limited.

Emmanuel, A. (1972). *Unequal Exchange: A Study of the Imperialism of Trade*. London: New Left Books.

Engels, F. (1981 [1894]). *Preface to K. Marx, Capital: A Critique of Political Economy* (Vol. III). London: Penguin.
Engels, F. (1981 [1895]). *Supplement and Addendum to K. Marx, Capital: A Critique of Political Economy* (Vol. III). London: Penguin.
Eno, J. N. (1918). English as an international language. *The Journal of Education*, 87(3), 68–69.
Epstein, I. (1956). *From Opium War to Liberation*. Peking: New World Press.
Evans, S. (2002). Macaulay's minute revisited: Colonial language policy in nineteenth-century India. *Journal of Multilingual and Multicultural Development*, 23(4), 260–281.
Fairbank, J. K., Bruner, K. F., & Matheson, E. M. (Eds.). (1975). *The I. G. in Peking: Letters of Robert Hart, Chinese Maritime Customs 1868–1907*. Cambridge, MA: Belknap Press of Harvard University Press.
Fairclough, N. (1992). *Discourse and Social Change*. Cambridge: Polity Press.
Fairclough, N. (2003). *Analysing Discourse: Textual Analysis for Social Research*. London: Routledge.
Fairclough, N. (2006). *Language and Globalization*. London: Routledge.
Fairclough, N. (2010). A dialectical-relational approach to critical discourse analysis in social research. In N. Fairclough (Ed.), *Critical Discourse Analysis: The Critical Study of Language* (pp. 230–254). London: Longman.
Fanon, F. (1967). *The Wretched of the Earth*. Harmondsworth: Penguin.
Feng, A., & Adamson, B. (2019). Language policies in education in the People's Republic of China. In A. Kirkpatrick (Ed.), *The Routledge International Handbook of Language Education Policy in Asia* (pp. 45–59). London: Routledge.
Ferguson, N. (2003). *Empire*. London: Penguin.
Fernando, M. C. (2012). Colonialism and education: English language education in Sri Lanka. *Mediterranean Journal of Social Sciences*, 3(14), 73–79.
Ferri, G. (2018). *Intercultural Communication: Critical Approaches and Future Challenges*. London: Palgrave Macmillan.
Fine, B. (1978, May–June). On the origins of capitalist development. *New Left Review*, 109, 88–95.
Firth, A. (1996). The discursive accomplishment of normality: On 'lingua franca' English and conversation analysis. *Journal of Pragmatics*, 26(2), 117–135.
Fishman, J. A. (1998–9, Winter). The new linguistic order. *Foreign Policy*, 113, 26–32, 34–40.
Fleming, P. (1959). *The Siege at Peking*. Oxford: Oxford University Press.
Flores, N. (2013). The unexamined relationship between neoliberalism and plurilingualism: A cautionary tale. *TESOL Quarterly*, 47(3), 500–520.
Flubacher, M.-C., & Del Percio, A. (Eds.). (2017). *Language, Education and Neoliberalism: Critical Studies in Sociolinguistics*. Bristol: Multilingual Matters.
Fong, E. T. Y. (2009). English in China: Some thoughts after the Beijing Olympics. *English Today*, 25(1), 44–49.
Fontaine, P. (2014). Free riding. *Journal of the History of Economic Thought*, 36(3), 359–376.
Forche, C. (2012). On the emergence of Euro-English as a potential European variety of English – attitudes and interpretations. *Jezikoslovlje*, XIII(2), 447–478.
Foucault, M. (1980). *Power/Knowledge: Selected Interviews and Other Writings*. Brighton: Harvester.

Foucault, M. (1981). *The History of Sexuality* (Vol. 1). Harmondsworth: Penguin.
Foucault, M. (1989). *The Archaeology of Knowledge*. London: Tavistock Publications.
Foucault, M. (1991). *Discipline and Punish*. Harmondsworth: Penguin.
Foucault, M. (2003). *"Society Must Be Defended", Lectures at the Collège de France, 1975–76* (D. Macey, Trans.). London: Penguin.
Foucault, M. (2008 [1979]). *The Birth of Biopolitics: Lectures at the Collège de France 1978–1979*. New York: Palgrave Macmillan.
Fox, D. M. (1870). *Description of the Line and Works of the São Paulo Railway in the Empire of Brazil: With an Abstract of the Discussion Upon the Paper (Excerpt Minutes of Proceedings of the Institution of Civil Engineers)*. London: William Clowes & Sons.
Frank, A. G. (1969a [1967]). *Capitalism and Underdevelopment in Latin America: Historical Studies of Chile and Brazil*. New York: Monthly Review Press.
Frank, A. G. (1969b). *Latin America: Underdevelopment or Revolution*. New York: Monthly Review Press.
Fraser, N. (1995). From redistribution to recognition? Dilemmas of justice in a 'post-socialist' age. *New Left Review*, 1(212), 68–93.
Friedberg, A. L. (2011). *A Contest for Supremacy: China, America, and the Struggle for Mastery in Asia*. New York: W. W. Norton & Company.
Friedman, M. (1962). *Capitalism and Freedom*. Chicago: University of Chicago Press.
Friedrich, P. (2000). English in Brazil: Functions and attitudes. *World Englishes*, 19(2), 215–223.
Friedrich, P., & Berns, M. (2003). Introduction: English in South America, the other forgotten continent. *World Englishes*, 22(2), 83–90.
Fuchs, C. (2014). *Digital Labour and Karl Marx*. London: Routledge.
Fuchs, C. (2015). *Culture and Economy in the Age of Social Media*. London: Routledge.
Fujita, S. (1981). Exercises in the Yokohama dialect 所謂ピジアンイング リッシュと横浜用語. *Historical English Studies in Japan*, 1982(14), 53–62.
Fukuyama, F. (1992). *End of History and the Last Man*. New York: Free Press.
Gal, S. (1989). Language and political economy. *Annual Review of Anthropology*, 18, 345–367.
Gal, S. (2016). Language and political economy: An afterword. *Journal of Ethnographic Theory*, 6(3), 331–335.
Gal, S., & Irvine, J. (1995). The boundaries of languages and disciplines: How ideologies construct differences. *Social Research*, 62(4), 967.
Gallagher, J., & Robinson, R. (1953). The imperialism of free trade. *The Economic History Review*, 6(1), 1–15.
Gao, Y. (2018). China's fluctuating English education policy discourses and perpetuating ambivalences in identity construction. In A. Curtis & R. Sussex (Eds.), *Intercultural Communication in Asia: Education, Language and Values* (Vol. 24, pp. 241–261). Cham: Springer.
García, O., & Li, W. (2014). *Translanguaging: Language, Bilingualism and Education*. London: Palgrave Macmillan.
Gardner, R. N. (1956). *Sterling-Dollar Diplomacy: Anglo-American Collaboration in the Reconstruction of Multinational Trade*. New York: Colombia University Press.

Garrido, M. R. (2017). Multilingualism and cosmopolitanism in the construction of a humanitarian elite. *Social Semiotics, 27*(3), 359–369.
Gazzola, M., Grin, F., & Vaillancourt, F. (2020). Evaluating language policy and planning: An introduction to the economic approach. In C. Vigouroux & S. Mufwene (Eds.), *Bridging Linguistics and Economics* (pp. 109–139). Cambridge: Cambridge University Press.
Gee, J. P. (1991). *Social Linguistics and Literacies: Ideology in Discourses*. Basingstoke: The Falmer Press.
Georgiou, A. (2017). Language ideology and the global dominance of English. *Bellaterra Journal of Teaching & Learning Language & Literature, 10*(2), 97–104.
Georgiou, A. (2018). An ethnographic study of the linguistic practices of newly arrived migrant children in a Cypriot primary school. In J. Mackay, M. Birello, & D. Xerri (Eds.), *ELT Research in Action* (pp. 99–104). Faversham, Kent: IATEFL.
Giddens, A. (1990). *The Consequences of Modernity*. Cambridge: Polity Press.
Giddens, A. (2002). *Runaway World: How Globalization is Shaping our Lives* (2nd ed.). London: Profile Books.
Gilpin, R. (1975). *U.S. Power and the Multinational Corporation*. New York Basic Books.
Gilpin, R. (2001). *Global Political Economy: Understanding the International Economic Order*. Princeton: Princeton University Press.
Gindin, S., & Panitch, L. (2017). The informal empire of the United States. In F. Ilkowski (Ed.), *Capitalist Imperialism in Contemporary Theoretical Frameworks* (pp. 79–93). Frankfurt am Main: Peter Lang.
Go, J. (2000). Chains of empire, projects of state: Political education and U.S. colonial rule in Puerto Rico and the Philippines. *Comparative Studies in Society and History, 42*(2), 333–362.
Goldstein, A. (2007). Power transitions, institutions, and China's rise in East Asia: Theoretical expectations and evidence. *The Journal of Strategic Studies, 30*(4), 639–682.
Goodrich, N. H. (2020). English in Iran: A sociolinguistic profile. *World Englishes, 39*(3), 482–499.
Graddol, D. (2006). *English Next: Why Global English May Mean the End of English as a Foreign Language*. British Council. Retrieved from http://britishcouncil.org/learning-research-english-next.pdf
Graeber, D. (2011). *Debt, the First 5000 Years*. New York: Melville House.
Graham, R. (1976). Robinson and Gallagher in Latin America: The meaning of informal imperialism. In Wm. R. Louis (Ed.), *Imperialism: The Robinson and Gallagher Controversy* (pp. 217–220). New York: New Viewpoints.
Gramsci, A. (1971). *Selections from the Prison Notebooks* (Q. Hoare & G. Nowell Smith, Eds.). London: Lawrence and Wishart.
Gramsci, A. (1975). *Quaderni del Carcere*. Turin: Einaudi.
Gramsci, A. (1999). *The Antonio Gramsci Reader* (D. Forgacs, Ed.). London: Lawrence and Wishart.
Gray, J. (2016). TESOL and the discipline of English. In A. Hewings, L. Prescott, & P. Seargeant (Eds.), *Futures for English Studies: Teaching Language, Literature and Creative Writing in Higher Education* (pp. 81–98). Basingstoke: Palgrave Macmillan.
Greenberg, M. (1951). *British Trade and the Opening of China, 1800–1842*. New York: Monthly Review Press.
Grin, F. (2001). English as economic value: Facts and fallacies. *World Englishes, 20*(1), 65–78.

Grin, F. (2018). On some fashionable terms in multilingualism research: Critical assessment and implications for language policy. In P. A. Kraus & F. Grin (Eds.), *The Politics of Multilingualism: Europeanisation, Globalisation and Linguistic Governance* (pp. 247–274). Amsterdam, The Netherlands: John Benjamins.

Guardiola-Rivera, O. (2013). *Story of a Death Foretold: Pinochet, the CIA and the Coup against Salvador Allende*. London: Bloomsbury.

Habermas, J. (1987). *The Philosophical Discourse of Modernity*. Oxford: Polity Press.

Hall, S. (1996). Race, articulation, and societies structured in dominance. In M. Diawara, H. A. Baker, & R. H. Lindeborg (Eds.), *Black British Cultural Studies* (pp. 16–60). Chicago: University of Chicago Press.

Hannerz, U. (1990). Cosmopolitans and locals in world culture. In M. Featherstone (Ed.), *Global Culture* (pp. 237–251). London: Sage.

Hannerz, U. (2006). Two faces of cosmopolitanism: Culture and politics. *Documentos CIDOB, Dinámicas Interculturales*, 7, 3–29.

Haraway, D. (1988). Situated knowledges: The science question in feminism and the privilege of partial perspective. *Feminist Studies*, 14(3), 575–599.

Hardt, M., & Negri, A. (2000). *Empire*. Cambridge, MA: Harvard University Press.

Harris, R. (2006). *New Ethnicities and Language Use*. London: Palgrave Macmillan.

Hartwig, M. (2011). Bhaskar's critique of the philosophical discourse of modernity. *Journal of Critical Realism*, 10(4), 485–510.

Harvey, D. (1990). *The Condition of Postmodernity*. Oxford: Blackwell.

Harvey, D. (1996). *Justice, Nature and the Geography of Difference*. Oxford: Blackwell.

Harvey, D. (2003). *The New Imperialism*. Oxford: Oxford University Press.

Harvey, D. (2004). The 'new' imperialism: Accumulation by dispossession. In L. Panitch & C. Leys (Eds.), *Socialist Register 2004: The New Imperial Challenge* (Vol. 40, pp. 63–87). New York: Monthly Review Press.

Harvey, D. (2005). *A Brief History of Neoliberalism*. Oxford: Oxford University Press.

Harvey, D. (2010). *Companion to Marx's Capital, Volume 1*. London: Verso.

Harvey, D. (2013). *Companion to Marx's Capital, Volume 2*. London: Verso.

Harvey, D. (2014). *Seventeen Contradictions and the End of Capitalism*. London: Profile Books.

Haslam, J. (2005). *The Nixon Administration and the Death of Allende's Chile: A Case of Assisted Suicide*. London: Verso.

Hawks Pott, F. L. (1928). *A Short History of Shanghai*. Shanghai: Kelly & Walsh, Limited.

Hayek, F. A. (1944). *The Road to Serfdom*. Chicago: University of Chicago Press.

Headrick, D., & Griset, P. (2001). Submarine cables: The business and politics, 1838–1939. *Business History Review*, 75, 543–578.

Hegel, G. W. F. (1956 [1837]). *The Philosophy of History*. New York: Dover Publications.

Held, D., McGrew, A., Goldblatt, D., & Perraton, J. (1999). *Global Transformations: Politics, Economics and Culture*. Stanford: Stanford University Press.

Helleiner, E. (2006). Below the state: Micro-level monetary power. In D. M. Andrews (Ed.), *International Monetary Power* (pp. 72–90). Ithaca and London: Cornell University Press.

Heller, M. (2003). Globalization, the new economy and the commodification of language. *Journal of Sociolinguistics*, 7(4), 473–492.
Heller, M. (2010). The commodification of language. *Annual Review of Anthropology*, 39(1), 101–114.
Heller, M., & Duchêne, A. (2012). Pride and profit, changing discourses of language, capital and nation state. In A. Duchêne & M. Heller (Eds.), *Language in Late Capitalism: Pride and Profit* (pp. 1–21). London: Routledge.
Heller, M., & Duchêne, A. (2016). Treating language as an economic resource: Discourse, data and debate. In N. Coupland (Ed.), *Sociolinguistics: Theoretical Debates* (pp. 139–156). Cambridge: Cambridge University Press.
Heller, M., & McElhinny, B. (2017). *Language, Capitalism, Colonialism: Toward a Critical History*. Toronto: University of Toronto Press.
Heller, M., Pujolar, J., & Duchêne, A. (2014). Linguistic commodification in tourism. *Journal of Sociolinguistics*, 18(4), 539–566.
Heng Hartse, J., & Kubota, R. (2014). Pluralizing English? Variation in high-stakes academic texts and challenges of copyediting. *Journal of Second Language Writing*, 24(1), 71–82.
Herranz-Loncan, A. (2011). The contribution of railways to economic growth in Latin America before 1914: A growth accounting approach. *Munich Personal RePEc Archive, Paper No. 33578*, n/a.
Heyd, T., & Schneider, B. (2019). The sociolinguistics of late modern publics. *Journal of Sociolinguistics*, 23(5), 435–449.
Hickey, M. (2018). Thailand's 'English fever', migrant teachers and cosmopolitan aspirations in an interconnected Asia. *Discourse (Abingdon, England)*, 39(5), 738–751.
Higgins, C. (2009). *English as a Local Language*. Bristol: Multilingual Matters.
Higgins, C. (2015). Earning capital in Hawai'i's linguistic landscape. In R. Tupas (Ed.), *Unequal Englishes: The Politics of Englishes Today* (pp. 145–162). London: Palgrave Macmillan.
Highet, K. (2021). *Becoming English Speakers: A Critical Sociolinguistic Ethnography of English, Inequality and Social Mobility in Delhi* (PhD). University College London, London, UK.
Hilferding, R. (1981 [1910]). *Finance Capital: A Study of the Latest Phase of Capitalist Development*. London: Routledge.
Hindley, R. (1990). *The Death of the Irish Language*. London: Routledge.
Hobsbawm, E. (1991). *Nations and Nationalism since 1780: Programme, Myth, Reality*. Cambridge: Cambridge University Press.
Hobsbawm, E. (1995). *The Age of Extremes, 1914–1991*. London: Abacus.
Hobsbawm, E. (1997). *The Age of Capital, 1848–1875*. London: Abacus.
Hobson, J. A. (2011 [1902]). *Imperialism*. London: Spokesman Books.
Holborow, M. (1999). *The Politics of English: A Marxist View of Language*. London: Sage.
Holborow, M. (2015). *The Language of Neoliberalism*. London: Routledge.
Holliday, A., & MacDonald, M. N. (2020). Researching the intercultural: Intersubjectivity and the problem with postpositivism. *Applied Linguistics*, 41(5), 621–639.
Horkheimer, M., & Adorno, T. W. (1997 [1944]). *Dialectic of Enlightenment*. London: Verso.

Hoshiyama, S. (1978). A general Survey of TEFL in postwar Japan. In I. Koike (Ed.), *The Teaching of English in Japan* (pp. 104–114). Tokyo: Eichosha.

Howard, M. C., & King, J. E. (1985). *The Political Economy of Marx* (2nd ed.). London: Longman.

Howatt, A. P. R., & Smith, R. (2014). The history of teaching English as a foreign language, from a British and European perspective. *Language & History*, 57(1), 75–95.

Hubbert, J. (2019). *China in the World: An Anthropology of Confucius Institutes, Soft Power, and Globalization*. Hawaii: University of Hawaii Press.

Huber, M. (1999). *Ghana Pidgin English in its West African Context: A Sociohistorical and Structural Analysis*. Amsterdam, The Netherlands: John Benjamins.

Hughes, D., & Main, P. (Eds.). (2012). *The Degenerated Revolution: The Rise and Fall of the Stalinist States*. London: Prinkipo.

Hurd, D. (1967). *The Arrow War: An Anglo-Chinese Confusion*. London: Collins.

Hymes, D. (1974). Ways of speaking. In R. Bauman & J. Sherzer (Eds.), *Explorations in the Ethnography of Speaking* (pp. 433–451). Cambridge: Cambridge University Press.

Inoue, A. (2006). Grammatical features of Yokohama pidgin Japanese: Common characteristics of restricted pidgins. In N. McGloin & J. Mori (Eds.), *Japanese/Korean Linguistics, 15* (pp. 55–66). Chicago: Chicago University Press.

Irvine, J. (1989). When talk isn't cheap: Language and political economy. *American Ethnologist*, 16(2), 248–267.

Islam, M., & Hashim, A. (2019). Historical evolution of English in Bangladesh. *Journal of Language Teaching and Research*, 10(2), 247–255.

Ito, H., & McCauley, R. N. (2019). The currency composition of foreign exchange reserves. *BIS Working Papers, No 828*.

Ives, P. (1998). A grammatical introduction to Gramsci's political theory. *Rethinking Marxism*, 10(1), 34–51.

Ives, P. (2006). "Global English": Linguistic imperialism or practical lingua franca? *Studies in Language and Capitalism*, 1, 121–141.

Ives, P. (2010). Cosmopolitanism and global English: Language politics in globalization debates. *Political Studies*, 58(3), 516–535.

Ives, P. (2015). Global English and inequality: The contested ground of linguistic power. In R. Tupas (Ed.), *Unequal Englishes: The Politics of Englishes Today* (pp. 74–91). London: Palgrave Macmillan.

Ives, P. (2019). Gramsci and "global English". *Rethinking Marxism*, 31(1), 58–71.

Jacquemet, M. (2005). Transidiomatic practices: Language and power in the age of globalization. *Language and Communication*, 25(3), 257–277.

James, L. (1997). *Raj: The Making and Unmaking of British India*. London: Little, Brown and Company.

Jameson, F. (1984). *Postmodernism, or, the Cultural Logic of Late Capitalism*. London: Verso.

Jaspers, J. (2018). The transformative limits of translanguaging. *Language & Communication*, 58, 1–10.

Jay, M. (1973). *The Dialectical Imagination*. Berkeley and Los Angeles: University of California Press.

Jayaweera, P. M. (2019). *A Critical Analysis of the ESP Teaching/Learning Scenario at the Faculty of Agriculture, University of Peradeniya, Sri Lanka* (MPhil). University of Peradeniya, Peradeniya, Sri Lanka.

Jenkins, J. (2006). Current perspectives on teaching world Englishes and English as a Lingua Franca. *TESOL Quarterly, 40*(1), 157–181.
Jenkins, J. (2007). *English as a Lingua Franca: Attitude and Identity*. Oxford: Oxford University Press.
Jenkins, J. (2009). English as a Lingua Franca: Interpretations and attitudes. *World Englishes, 28*(2), 200–207.
Jenkins, J. (2011). Accommodating (to) ELF in the international university. *Journal of Pragmatics, 43*(4), 926–936.
Jenkins, J. (2017). The future of English as a Lingua Franca. In J. Jenkins, A. Baker, & M. Dewey (Eds.), *The Routledge Handbook of English as a Lingua Franca*. London: Routledge.
Jenkins, J., Cogo, A., & Dewey, M. (2011). Review of developments into research into English as a Lingua Franca. *Language Teaching, 44*(3), 281–315.
Jenks, C. (2017). *Race, Ethnicity and English Language Teaching, Korea in Focus*. Bristol: Multilingual Matters.
Johnson, R. (2013). "True to their salt" – Mechanisms for recruiting and managing military labour in the army of the East India Company during the Carnatic wars in India. In E. J. Zürcher (Ed.), *Fighting for a Living: A Comparative History of Military Labour* (pp. 267–290). Amsterdam, The Netherlands: Amsterdam University Press.
Johnstone, I. (2007). *Social States: China in International Institutions, 1980–2000*. Princeton: Princeton University Press.
Jordan, J. (2015). Material translingual ecologies. *College English, 77*(4), 364–382.
Jørgensen, J. N. (2008). Polylingual languaging around and among children and adolescents. *International Journal of Multilingualism, 5*(3), 161–176.
Kachru, B. B. (1985). Standards, codification and sociolinguistic realism: The English language in the outer circle. In R. Quirk & H. G. Widdowson (Eds.), *English in the World: Teaching and Learning the Language and Literatures* (pp. 11–30). Cambridge: Cambridge University Press.
Kachru, B. B. (1990). World Englishes and applied linguistics. *World Englishes, 9*(1), 3–20.
Kachru, B. B. (1996). World Englishes: Agony and ecstasy. *Journal of Aesthetic Education, 30*(2), 135–155.
Kang, H.-S. (2020). Changes in English language policy in Kim Jong-un's North Korea. *English Today, 36*(1), 30–36.
Kanno, Y. (2008). *Language and Education in Japan: Unequal Access to Bilingualism*. London: Palgrave Macmillan.
Karlin, M. (2019, May 8). Why does Trump like communist Vietnam? Because it's capitalist. *Truthout*. Retrieved from https://truthout.org/articles/why-does-trump-like-communist-vietnam-because-its-capitalist/
Kayaoglu, T. (2010). *Legal Imperialism: Sovereignty and Extraterritoriality in Japan, the Ottoman Empire, and China*. Cambridge: Cambridge University Press.
Kee, R. (1976). *The Green Flag* (Vol. I: *The Most Distressful Country*). London: Quartet Books.
Kelly-Holmes, H. (2016). Theorising the market in sociolinguistics. In N. Coupland (Ed.), *Sociolinguistics: Theoretical Debates* (pp. 157–172).
Kennan, G. F. (1947). The sources of Soviet conduct. *Foreign Affairs. An American Quarterly Review, 4*(25), 566–582 (Reprint 2000 by the Council on Foreign Relations, Inc.)

Kent, A. (2013 [2001]). China's participation in international organisations. In G. Austin & Y. Zhang (Eds.), *Power and Responsibility in Chinese Foreign Policy* (pp. 132–166). Canberra: ANU Press.

Kerr, I. J. (1995). *Building the Railways of the Raj, 1850–1900*. New Delhi: Oxford University Press.

Keynes, J. M. (1936). *The General Theory of Employment, Interest and Money*. London: Palgrave Macmillan.

Kiernan, V. G. (1964). Farewells to empire. *The Socialist Register (New York, 1964)*, 259–279.

Kim, E. G. (2011). English educational policies of the U.S. army military government in Korea from 1945 to 1948 and their effects on the development of English language teaching in Korea. *Language Policy*, 10, 193–220.

Kim, M., Liu, A. H., Tuxhorn, K.-L., Brown, D. S., & Leblang, D. (2014). Lingua mercatoria: Language and foreign direct investment. *International Studies Quarterly*, 1–14.

Kim, Y.-M. (2002). Collective neurosis of English fever. *Education Review*, 9, 56–64.

Kirkpatrick, A. (Ed.). (2010a). *The Routledge Handbook of World Englishes*. London: Routledge.

Kirkpatrick, A. (2010b). *English as a Lingua Franca in ASEAN: A Multilingual Model*. Hong Kong: Hong Kong University Press.

Kitao, S. K., Kitao, K., Nozawa, K., & Yamamoto, M. (1985). Teaching English in Japan. In K. Kitao (Ed.), *TEFL in Japan* (pp. 127–138). JALT 10th Anniversary Collected Papers. Retrieved from https://files.eric.ed.gov/fulltext/ED265741.pdf

Kramsch, C. (2018). Trans-spatial utopias. *Applied Linguistics*, 30(1), 108–115.

Kress, G. R. (2010). *Multimodality: A Social Semiotic Approach to Contemporary Communication*. London: Routledge.

Kubota, R. (1998). Ideologies of English in Japan. *World Englishes*, 17(3), 295–306.

Kubota, R. (2015). Inequalities of Englishes, English speakers, and languages: A critical perspective on pluralist approaches to English. In R. Tupas (Ed.), *Unequal Englishes: The Politics of Englishes Today* (pp. 21–41). London: Palgrave Macmillan.

Kubota, R. (2016). The multi/plural turn, postcolonial theory, and neoliberal multiculturalism: Complicities and implications for Applied Linguistics. *Applied Linguistics*, 37(4), 474–494.

Kumaravadivelu, B. (2008). *Cultural Globalization and Language Education*. New Haven: Yale University Press.

Laclau, E. (1979 [1977]). *Politics and Ideology in Marxist Theory*. London: Verso.

Lacoste, V., Leimgruber, J., & Breyer, T. (2014). Authenticity: A view from inside and outside sociolinguistics. In V. Lacoste, J. Leimgruber, & T. Breyer (Eds.), *Indexing Authenticity: Sociolinguistic Perspectives* (Vol. 39, pp. 1–13). Berlin and Boston: De Gruyter.

Lamounier, L. (2000). The 'labour question' in nineteenth century Brazil: Railways, export agriculture and labour scarcity. *Department of Economic History Working Papers No 59/00*. Retrieved from http://www.lse.ac.uk/economicHistory/pdf/wp5900.pdf

Langer, W. L. (1935). *The Diplomacy of Imperialism, 1890–1902*. New York: Alfred A. Knopf.

Lash, S., & Urry, J. (1987). *The End of Organized Capitalism*. Cambridge: Cambridge University Press.

Lather, P. (1993). Fertile obsession: Validity after poststructuralism. *Sociological Quarterly, 34,* 673–693.

Lave, J., & Wenger, E. (1991). *Situated Learning: Legitimate Peripheral Participation.* Cambridge: Cambridge University Press.

LeClerc, J. (2011). *L'aménagement linguistique dans le monde.* Retrieved from www.axl.cefan.ulaval.ca

Lee, R. E. (Ed.). (2012). *The Longue Durée and World-Systems Analysis.* Albany: State University of New York Press.

Lee, T. V. (1995). 'Introduction', 'Coping with Shanghai: Means to survival and success in the early twentieth century – a symposium'. *Journal of Asian Studies, 54,* 7.

Lehman, K. D. (2016). Completing the revolution? The United States and Bolivia's long revolution. *Bolivian Studies, 22,* 4–35.

Lemberg, D. (2018). "The universal language of the future": Decolonization, development, and the American embrace of global English, 1945–1965. *Modern Intellectual History, 15*(2), 561–592.

Lenin, V. I. (1975 [1917]). *Imperialism, the Highest Stage of Capitalism.* Peking: Foreign Languages Press.

Lewis, C. M. (1983). *British Railways in Argentina 1857–1914: A Case Study in Foreign Investment.* London: The Athlone Press Ltd.

Lewis, W. A. (1949). *Economic Survey, 1919–39.* London: Allen & Unwin.

Li, W. (2016). New Chinglish and the post-multilingualism challenge: Translanguaging ELF in China. *Journal of English as a Lingua Franca, 5*(1), 1–25.

Li, W. (2018a). Translanguaging as a practical theory of language. *Applied Linguistics, 39*(1), 9–30.

Li, W. (2018b). Linguistic (super)diversity, post-multilingualism and Translanguaging moments. In A. Creese & A. Blackledge (Eds.), *The Routledge Handbook of Language and Superdiversity: An Interdisciplinary Perspective* (pp. 16–29). London: Routledge.

Li, W., & Zhu, H. (2013). Translanguaging identities and ideologies: Creating transnational space through flexible multilingual practices amongst Chinese university students in the UK. *Applied Linguistics, 34,* 516–535.

Lin, A., Wang, W., Akamatsu, N., & Riazi, A. M. (2002). Appropriating English, expanding identities, and re-visioning the field: From TESOL to teaching for glocalized communication (TEGCOM) *Journal of Language, Identity and Education, 1*(4), 295–316.

Lin, H.-Y. (2012). Local responses to global English: Perceptions of English in Taiwan: Personal responses toward the spread of global English and its impact in Taiwan. *English Today, 28*(3), 67–72.

Lin, J. Y. (2011). China and the global economy. *China Economic Journal, 4*(1), 1–14.

Little, L. K. (1975). Introduction. In J. K. Fairbank, K. F. Bruner, & E. M. Matheson (Eds.), *The I. G. in Peking: Letters of Robert Hart, Chinese Maritime Customs 1868–1907* (Vol. 1, pp. 1–38). Cambridge, MA: Belknap Press of Harvard University Press.

Livingstone, G. (2009). *America's Backyard.* London and New York: Zed Books.

Llewellyn-Jones, R. (2007). *The Great Uprising 1857–58, Untold Stories, Indian and British.* London: Boydell & Brewer.

Lo Bianco, J., Orton, J., & Gao, Y. (Eds.). (2009). *China and English: Globalisation and the Dilemmas of Identity.* Bristol: Multilingual Matters.

Lopes Cardozo, M. (2012). Decolonising Bolivian education: Ideology versus reality. In T. G. Griffiths & Z. Millei (Eds.), *Logics of Socialist Education: Engaging with Crisis, Insecurity and Uncertainty* (pp. 21–35). Dordrecht, The Netherlands: Springer.

López-Gopar, M. E. (2016). *Decolonizing Primary English Language Teaching*. Bristol: Multilingual Matters.

Lorente, B. P. (2012). The making of "workers of the world": Language and the labor brokerage state. In A. Duchêne & M. Heller (Eds.), *Language in Late Capitalism: Pride and Profit* (pp. 183–206). London: Routledge.

Louis, Wm. R. (Ed.). (1976). *Imperialism: The Robinson and Gallagher Controversy*. New York: New Viewpoints.

Loveman, B. (1988). *Chile: The Legacy of Hispanic Capitalism* (2nd ed.). Oxford: Oxford University Press.

Luxemburg, R. (1951 [1913]). *The Accumulation of Capital*. London: Routledge & Kegan Paul.

Luxemburg, R. (1972 [1921]). The accumulation of capital – An anti-critique. In K. J. Tarbuck (Ed.), *Imperialism and the Accumulation of Capital* (pp. 47–150). London: Penguin.

Lyotard, J. (1986 [1979]). *The Postmodern Condition: A Report on Knowledge*. Manchester: Manchester University Press.

Mahan, A. T. (2010 [1890]). *The Influence of Sea Power Upon History, 1660–1783*. Cambridge: Cambridge University Press.

Makoni, S., & Pennycook, A. (2005). Disinventing and (re)constituting languages. *Critical Inquiry in Language Studies*, 2(2), 137–156.

Manchester, A. K. (1964). *British Preeminence in Brazil: A Study in European Expansion*. New York: Octagon Books.

Manthorpe, J. (2005). *Forbidden Nation: A History of Taiwan*. New York: Palgrave Macmillan.

Marschan-Piekkari, R., Welch, D., & Welch, L. (1999). In the shadow: The impact of language on structure, power and communication in the multinational. *International Business Review*, 8, 421–440.

Marx, K. (1951). *Marx on China*. London: Lawrence & Wishart.

Marx, K. (1964 [1844]). *The Economic & Philosophic Manuscripts of 1844*. New York: International Publishers.

Marx, K. (1969 [1853]). The future results of British rule in India. In A. Avineri (Ed.), *Karl Marx on Colonialism and Modernization* (pp. 132–139). New York: Anchor Books.

Marx, K. (1970 [1859]). *A Contribution to the Critique of Political Economy*. Moscow: Progress Publishers.

Marx, K. (1973). *Grundrisse*. London: Penguin.

Marx, K. (1976 [1859]). *Preface and Introduction to 'A Contribution to the Critique of Political Economy'*. Peking: Foreign Languages Press.

Marx, K. (1976 [1867]). *Capital: A Critique of Political Economy* (Vol. I). London: Penguin.

Marx, K. (1976 [1873]). *Postface to the Second Edition of Capital* (Vol. I). London: Penguin.

Marx, K. (1978 [1843]). For a ruthless criticism of everything existing. In R. C. Tucker (Ed.), *The Marx-Engels Reader* (pp. 12–15). New York: W. W. Norton & Company.

Marx, K. (1978 [1852]). The eighteenth Brumaire of Louis Bonaparte. In R. C. Tucker (Ed.), *The Marx-Engels Reader* (pp. 594–617). New York: W. W. Norton & Company.

Marx, K. (1978 [1884]). *Capital: A Critique of Political Economy* (Vol. II). London: Penguin.

Marx, K. (1991 [1894]). *Capital: A Critique of Political Economy* (Vol. III). London: Penguin.

Marx, K. (1998 [1845]). *Theses on Feuerbach*. In K. Marx & F. Engels, *The German Ideology* (pp. 569–575). New York: Prometheus Books.

Marx, K., & Engels, F. (1948 [1848]). *Manifesto of the Communist Party*. New York: International Publishers.

Marx, K., & Engels, F. (1998 [1845]). *The German Ideology*. New York: Prometheus Books.

Matear, A. (2008). English language learning and education policy in Chile: Can English really open doors for all? *Asia Pacific Journal of Education*, 28(2), 131–147.

Mauranen, A. (2012). *Exploring ELF: Academic English Shaped by Non-native Speakers*. Cambridge: Cambridge University Press.

Mauranen, A. (2015). What is going on in academic ELF? Findings and implications. In P. Vettorel (Ed.), *New Frontiers in Teaching and Learning* (pp. 31–54). Newcastle upon Tyne: Cambridge Scholars Publishing.

Mauranen, A., & Ranta, E. (Eds.). (2009). *English as a Lingua Franca: Studies and Findings*. Newcastle upon Tyne: Cambridge Scholars Publishing.

May, C. (1996). Strange fruit: Susan Strange's theory of structural power in the international political economy. *Global Society*, 10(2), 167–189.

May, G. A. (1980). *Social Engineering in the Philippines: The Aims, Execution, and Impact of American Colonial Policy, 1900–1913*. Westport: Greenwood Press.

Mayers, W. F., Dennys, N. B., & King, C. (1977 [1867]). *The Treaty Ports of China and Japan. A Complete Guide to the Open Ports of those Countries, Together with Peking, Yedo, Hongkong and Macao*. San Francisco: Chinese Materials Centre, Inc.

Mazrui, A. M. (2004). *English in Africa after the Cold War*. Clevedon: Multilingual Matters.

Mazrui, A. M. (2016). *The Cultural Politics of Translation: East Africa in a Global Context*. London: Routledge.

McArthur, T., Lam-McArthur, J., & Fontaine, L. (Eds.). (2018). *The Oxford Companion to the English Language* (2nd ed.). Oxford: Oxford University Press.

McGill, K. (2013). Political economy and language. *Journal of Linguistic Anthropology*, 23(2), 84–101.

McGregor, R. (2019). Party man: Xi Jinping's quest to dominate China. *Foreign Affairs*, 98(5), 18–25.

McKay, S. (2002). Teaching English as an international language: The Chilean context. *English Language Teaching Journal*, 57(2), 139–148.

McKinley, J. (2019). English L2 writing in international higher education. In G. Barkhuizen (Ed.), *Qualitative Research Topics in Language Teacher Education* (pp. 104–109). New York: Routledge.

McKinley, J., & Rose, H. (2019). Standards of English in academic writing: The authors respond. *Journal of Second Language Writing*, 44, 114–116.

McLellan, J. (2010). Mixed codes or varieties of English. In A. Kirkpatrick (Ed.), *The Routledge Handbook of World Englishes* (pp. 425–441). London: Routledge.

McNamara, T. (2011). Multilingualism in education: A poststructuralist critique. *Modern Language Journal, 95*, 430–441.

McNamara, T. (2019). *Language and Subjectivity*. Cambridge: Cambridge University Press.

Mearsheimer, J. (2001). *The Tragedy of Great Power Politics*. New York: W. W. Norton & Company.

Mearsheimer, J. (2006). China's unpeaceful rise. *Current History, 105*(690), 160–162.

Menon, J. (2008). Cambodia's persistent dollarization: Causes and policy options. *Working Paper Series on Regional Economic Integration, 19*.

Mertz, E. (1985). Beyond symbolic anthropology: Introducing semiotic mediation. In E. Mertz & R. J. Parmentier (Eds.), *Semiotic Mediation: Sociocultural and Psychological Perspectives* (pp. 1–22). London: Academic Press Inc.

Michael, J. (2017). Highbrow culture for high-potentials? Cultural orientations of a business elite in the making. *Poetics, 61*, 39–52.

Michieka, M. M. (2005). English in Kenya: A sociolinguistic profile. *World Englishes, 24*(2), 173–186.

Milanovic, B. (2020). The clash of capitalisms: The real fight for the global economy's future. *Foreign Affairs, 99*(1), 10–21.

Milroy, J. (2000). Historical description and the ideology of the standard language. In L. Wright (Ed.), *The Development of Standard English, 1300–1800: Theories, Descriptions, Conflicts* (pp. 11–28). Cambridge: Cambridge University Press.

Mirowski, P. (2014). *Never Let a Serious Crisis Go to Waste: How Neoliberalism Survived the Financial Meltdown*. London: Verso.

Modiano, M. (2017). English in a post-Brexit European Union. *World Englishes, 36*(3), 313–327.

Modiano, M., Seidlhofer, B., & Jenkins, J. (2001). Euro-English: A new variety of English; Towards making 'Euro-English' a linguistic reality; 'Euro-English' accents. *English Today, 17*(4), 13.

Mogi-Hein, Y. (1999). *Higher Education Reform under the American Occupation, 1945–1952: The Rise of a Japanese Meritocracy* (PhD). Columbia University, Ann Arbor, MI.

Montessori, N. M. (2009). *A Discursive Analysis of a Struggle for Hegemony in Mexico: The Zapatista Movement versus President Salinas de Gortari*. Riga: VDM Verlag.

Moody, T. (1974). *The Ulster Question 1603–1973*. Dublin: Mercier Press.

Moon, P. T. (1926). *Imperialism and World Politics*. New York: Palgrave Macmillan.

Morgan, B. (2007). Poststructuralism and applied linguistics. In J. Cummins & C. Davison (Eds.), *International Handbook of English Language Teaching* (pp. 949–968). London: Springer.

Morgan, H. (1994). An unwelcome heritage: Ireland's role in British empire building. *History of European Ideas, 19*(4–6), 619–625.

Mori, J., & Sanuth, K. K. (2017). Navigating between a monolingual utopia and translingual realities: Experiences of American learners of Yorùbá as an additional language. *Applied Linguistics, 39*, 78–98.

Morse, H. B. (1913). *The Trade and Administration of China*. Shanghai: Kelly & Walsh, Limited.

Mufwene, S. S. (2008). *Language Evolution: Contact, Competition and Change*. London: Continuum.

Mufwene, S. S. (2011). La Francophonie: An ecological history of language expansion and contraction since the European colonial expansion. *Rutgers Central African Studies Newsletters, Spring*, 13–14.

Mufwene, S. S. (2014). Globalisation économique mondiale des XVIIe–XVIIIe siècles, émergence des Créoles, et vitalité langagière. In A. Carpooran (Ed.), *Langues Créoles, Mondialisation et Éducation* (pp. 23–79). St. Louis, Mauritius: Creole Speaking Unit.

Mufwene, S. S. (2015). Pidgin and Creole languages. In J. D. Wright (Ed.), *International Encyclopedia of the Social & Behavioral Sciences* (2nd ed., pp. 133–145). Amsterdam, The Netherlands: Elsevier.

Mukherji, P. (1918). *Indian Constitutional Documents (1600–1918)* (Vol. 1). Calcutta: Thacker, Spink & Co.

Murata, K., & Jenkins, J. (Eds.). (2009). *Global Englishes in Asian Contexts*. London: Palgrave Macmillan.

Mustafa, S. G. (1964). *The British in the Sub-Continent*. Lahorre: Ferozsons Ltd.

Muth, S., & Del Percio, A. (2018). Policing for commodification: Turning communicative resources into commodities. *Language Policy, 17*, 129–135.

Myers, M. (2018). China's belt and road initiative: What role for Latin America? *Journal of Latin American Geography, 17*(2), 239–243.

Myers Jaffe, A. (2004). United States and the Middle East: Policies and dilemmas. In *Bipartisan Policy Center, Ending the Energy Stalemate* (pp. 1–2). Washington, DC: National Commission on Energy Policy.

Myers-Scotton, C. (1993). Elite closure as a powerful language strategy: The African case. *International Journal of the Sociology of Language, 103*(1), 149–164.

Nederveen Pieterse, J. (2009). *Globalization and Culture* (2nd ed.). Lanham, MD: Rowman & Littlefield.

Nederveen Pieterse, J. (2010). *Development Theory* (2nd ed.). London: Sage.

Nguyen, N. T. (2017). Thirty years of English language and English education in Vietnam. *English Today, 33*(129), 33–35.

Nichols, R. (2015). Disaggregating primitive accumulation. *Radical Philosophy, 194*, 18–28.

Nicolaus, M. (1973). Foreword. In K. Marx, *Grundrisse: Foundations of the Critique of Political Economy (Rough Draft)* (pp. 7–64). London: Penguin.

Nield, R. (2010). *The China Coast: Trade and the First Treaty Ports*. Hong Kong: Joint Publishing.

Niño-Murcia, M. (2003). "English is like the dollar": Hard currency ideology and the status of English in Peru. *World Englishes, 22*(2), 121–141.

Nkwetisama, C. (2017). Rethinking and reconfiguring English language education: Averting linguistic genocide in Cameroon. *International Journal of Applied Linguistics & English Literature, 6*(6), 106–114.

Norton, B. (1997). Language, identity and the ownership of English. *TESOL Quarterly, 31*(3), 409–429.

Nye, J. S. (2004). *Soft Power: The Means to Success in World Politics*. New York: Public Affairs.

Nye, J. S. (2016). China's soft power deficit. In D. Shambaugh (Ed.), *The China Reader: Rising Power* (pp. 305–306). Oxford: Oxford University Press.

Ochieng, D. (2015). The revival of the status of English in Tanzania. *English Today, 31*(2), 25–31.

Olsen, M. (1965). *The Logic of Collective Action: Public Groups and the Theory of Groups*. Cambridge, MA and London: Harvard University Press.

O'Regan, J. P. (2014). English as a Lingua Franca: An immanent critique. *Applied Linguistics*, 35(5), 533–552.

O'Regan, J. P. (2015). On anti-intellectualism, cultism, and one-sided thinking. *Applied Linguistics*, 36(1), 128–132.

O'Regan, J. P. (2016). Intercultural communication and the possibility of English as a Lingua Franca. In P. Holmes & F. Dervin (Eds.), *The Cultural and Intercultural Dimensions of English as a Lingua Franca* (pp. 203–217). Bristol: Multilingual Matters.

O'Regan, J. P. (2021). Capital and the hegemony of English in a capitalist world-system. In R. Rubdy & R. Tupas (Eds.), *Bloomsbury World Englishes Volume 2: Ideologies*. London: Bloomsbury.

O'Regan, J. P., & Betzel, A. (2016). Critical discourse analysis: A sample study of extremism. In H. Zhu (Ed.), *Research Methods in Intercultural Communication: A Practical Guide* (pp. 281–296). Malden, MA: Wiley-Blackwell.

O'Regan, J. P., & Gray, J. (2018). The bureaucratic distortion of academic work: A transdisciplinary analysis of the UK Research Excellence Framework in the age of neoliberalism. *Language and Intercultural Communication*, 18(5), 533–548.

Orton, J. (2009). English and the Chinese quest. In J. Lo Bianco, J. Orton, & Y. Gao (Eds.), *China and English: Globalisation and the Dilemmas of Identity* (pp. 79–100). Bristol: Multilingual Matters.

Osa, O. (1986). English in Nigeria: 1914–1985. *English Journal*, 75(3), 38–40.

Ostrower, F. (1998). The arts as cultural capital among elites: Bourdieu's theory reconsidered. *Poetics*, 26(1), 43–53.

Otsuji, E., & Pennycook, A. (2010). Metrolingualism: Fixity, fluidity and language in flux. *International Journal of Multilingualism*, 7(3), 240–254.

Otsuji, E., & Pennycook, A. (2015). *Metrolingualism: Language in the City*. London: Routledge.

Otte, T. G., & Neilson, K. (2006). *Railways and International Politics: Paths of Empire, 1848–1945*. London: Routledge.

Ouedraogo, R. M. (2000). *Language Planning and Language Policies in Some Selected West African Countries*. Addis Ababa: UNESCO International Institute for Capacity Building in Africa.

Paik, K. (2018). The English language in Korea: Its history and vision. *Asian Englishes*, 20(2), 122–133.

Pan, L. (2010). Dissecting multilingual Beijing: The space and scale of vernacular globalization. *Visual Communication*, 9(1), 67–90.

Pan, L. (2011). English language ideologies in the Chinese foreign language education policies: A world-system perspective. *Language Policy*, 10, 245–263.

Pan, L. (2015). *English as a Global Language in China*. Cham: Springer.

Pan, Z. (2015). *An Exploration of English Language Ideologies Held by Chinese University Members on the English Used by Chinese People in Relation to Inner-Circle Englishes* (PhD). University College London, London, UK.

Panitch, L., & Gindin, S. (2012). *The Making of Global Capitalism: The Political Economy of Global Empire*. London: Verso.

Parakrama, A. (2012). The malchemy of English in Sri Lanka: Reinforcing inequality through imposing extra-linguistic value. In V. Rapatahana & P. Bunce (Eds.),

English Language as Hydra: Its Impacts on Non-English Language Cultures (pp. 107–132). Bristol: Multilingual Matters.
Parboni, R. (1981). *The Dollar and its Rivals*. London: Verso.
Park, J.-K. (2009). 'English fever' in South Korea: Its history and symptoms. *English Today*, 25(1), 50–57.
Park, J. S.-Y. (2010). The promise of English: Linguistic capital and the neoliberal worker in the South Korean job market. *International Journal of Bilingual Education and Bilingualism*, 14(4), 443–455.
Park, J. S.-Y., & Wee, L. (2012). *Markets of English: Linguistic Capital and Language Policy in a Globalizing World*. London: Routledge.
Park, J. S.-Y., & Wee, L. (2013). Linguistic baptism and the disintegration of ELF. *Applied Linguistics Review*, 4(2), 343–363.
Park, L. E. (2021). *Writing on the Margins and Engaging in Teacher-Student Dialogue: An Autoethnography of a Korean-American TESOL Educator in South Korea (PhD)*. London: University College London.
Pavlenko, A. (2017). Superdiversity and why it isn't: Reflections on terminological innovation and academic branding. In S. Breidbach, L. Küster, & B. Schmenk (Eds.), *Sloganizations in Language Education Discourse* (pp. 142–168). Bristol: Multilingual Matters.
Peck, J. (2010). *Constructions of Neoliberal Reason*. Oxford: Oxford University Press.
Pei, M. (2020). China's coming upheaval. Competition, the coronavirus, and the weakness of Xi Jinping. *Foreign Affairs*, 99(3), 82–95.
Pelcovits, N. A. (1948). *Old China Hands*. New York: Vail-Ballou Press.
Pennycook, A. (1994). *The Cultural Politics of English as an International Language*. London: Longman.
Pennycook, A. (1998). *English and the Discourses of Colonialism*. London: Routledge.
Pennycook, A. (2001). *Critical Applied Linguistics: A Critical Introduction*. Mahwah: Lawrence Erlbaum.
Pennycook, A. (2007). *Global Englishes and Transcultural Flows*. London: Routledge.
Pennycook, A. (2009). Plurilithic Englishes: Towards a 3D model. In K. Murata & J. Jenkins (Eds.), *Global Englishes in Asian Contexts* (pp. 194–207). London: Palgrave Macmillan.
Pennycook, A. (2010a). *Language as a Local Practice*. London: Routledge.
Pennycook, A. (2010b). Critical and alternative directions in applied linguistics. *Australian Review of Applied Linguistics*, 33(2), 16.11–16.16.
Pennycook, A. (2010c). The future of Englishes. In A. Kirkpatrick (Ed.), *The Routledge Handbook of World Englishes* (pp. 673–687). London: Routledge.
Pennycook, A. (2017). Translanguaging and semiotic assemblages. *International Journal of Multilingualism*, 14(2), 1–14.
Pennycook, A. (2018). *Posthumanist Applied Linguistics*. London: Routledge.
Pennycook, A. (2020). Translingual entanglements of English. *World Englishes*, 39(2), 222–235.
Pennycook, A., & Otsuji, E. (2015). *Metrolingualism: Language in the City*. London: Routledge.
Perez-Milans, M. (2015). Language education policy in late modernity: Insights from situated approaches. *Language Policy*, 14(2), 99–197.

Peters, P. (2017). Standard British English. In A. Bergs & L. J. Brinton (Eds.), *The History of English. Vol. 5: Varieties of English* (pp. 96–120). Berlin and Boston: De Gruyter.
Phan, L. H. (2015). Unequal Englishes in imagined intercultural interactions. In R. Tupas (Ed.), *Unequal Englishes: The Politics of Englishes Today* (pp. 223–243). London: Palgrave Macmillan.
Phan, L. H. (2017). *Transnational Education Crossing 'Asia' and 'the West': Adjusted Desire, Transformative Mediocrity, Neo-colonial Disguise*. London and New York: Routledge.
Phillipson, R. (1992). *Linguistic Imperialism*. Oxford: Oxford University Press.
Phillipson, R. (2008). The linguistic imperialism of neoliberal empire. *Critical Inquiry in Language Studies*, 5(1), 1–43.
Phillipson, R. (2017). Myths and realities of 'global' English. *Language Policy*, 16(313–331).
Phillipson, R. (2018). Language challenges in global and regional integration. *Sustainable Multilingualism*, 12, 14–35.
Phillipson, R., & Skutnabb-Kangas, T. (1996). Linguicide and linguicism. In H. Goebl, P. H. Nelde, S. Zdenek, & W. Wölck (Eds.), *Contact Linguistics. Linguistique de Contact. Ein Internationales Handbuch Zeitgenössiger Forschung. An International Handbook of Contemporary Research. Manuel International des Recherches Contemporaines* (Vol. I, pp. 667–675). Amsterdam, The Netherlands: Walter de Gruyter.
Piller, I., & Cho, J. (2014). Neoliberalism as language policy. *Language in Society*, 42(1), 23–44.
Piller, I., & Takahashi, K. (2006). A passion for English: Desire and the language market. In A. Pavlenko (Ed.), *Bilingual Minds: Emotional Experience, Expression and Representation* (pp. 59–83). Clevedon: Multilingual Matters.
Pivetti, M. (2015). Marx and the development of critical political economy. *Review of Political Economy*, 27(2), 134–153.
Polanyi, K. (2001 [1944]). *The Great Transformation*. Boston: Beacon Press.
Porto, M. (2014). The role and status of English in Spanish-speaking Argentina and its education system: Nationalism or imperialism? *Sage Open*, 1–14.
Powis, J. (1984). *Aristocracy*. London: Blackwell.
Pradella, L. (2015). *Globalization and the Critique of Political Economy*. London: Routledge.
Preece, S. (2019). Elite bilingual identities in higher education in the Anglophone world: The stratification of linguistic diversity and reproduction of socio-economic inequalities in the multilingual student population. *Journal of Multilingual and Multicultural Development: Special Issue: Elite Multilingualism: Discourses, Practices, and Debates*, 40(5), 404–420.
Price, G. (2014). English for all? Neoliberalism, globalization, and language policy in Taiwan. *Language in Society*, 43(5), 567–589.
Puga, R. M. (2014). Early British presence in China: The first Anglo-Portuguese voyage to Macao. In C. X. G. Wei (Ed.), *Macao – The Formation of a Global City* (pp. 107–120). London: Routledge.
Pujolar, J. (2018). Post-nationalism and language commodification. In J. W. Tollefson & M. Pérez-Milans (Eds.), *The Oxford Handbook of Language Policy and Planning* (pp. 485–504). Oxford: Oxford University Press.

Pujolar, J., & Jones, K. (2012). Literary tourism: New appropriations of landscape and territory in Catalonia. In A. Duchêne & M. Heller (Eds.), *Language in Late Capitalism: Pride and Profit* (pp. 103–125). London: Routledge.
Quirk, R. (1989/1990). Language varieties and standard language. *JALT Journal*, 11(1), 14–25.
Rabe, S. L. (2012). *The Killing Zone: The United States Wages Cold War in Latin America*. Oxford: Oxford University Press.
Rahimi, S. (2017). *Language Teacher (De)motivation: Hearing the Voice of Experienced EFL Teachers in a Language Institute in Iran* (MA dissertation). University College London, London, UK.
Rahman, T. (2009). Language ideology, identity and the commodification of language in the call centers of Pakistan. *Language in Society*, 38(2), 233–258.
Rahman, T. (2015). The development of English in Pakistan. In G. Leitner, A. Hashim, & H.-G. Wolf (Eds.), *Communicating with Asia: The Future of English as a Global Language* (pp. 13–27). Cambridge: Cambridge University Press.
Rajagopalan, K. (2004). The concept of 'world English' and its implications for ELT. *ELT Journal*, 58(2), 111–117.
Rajagopalan, K. (2012). 'World English' or 'world Englishes'? Does it make any difference? *International Journal of Applied Linguistics*, 22(3), 374–391.
Rampton, B. (1995). *Crossing: Language and Ethnicity Among Adolescents*. London: Longman.
Rampton, B. (2006). *Language in Late Modernity*. Cambridge: Cambridge University Press.
Rampton, M. B. H. (1990). Displacing the "native speaker": Expertise, affiliation, and inheritance. *ELT Journal*, 44, 97–101.
Rassool, N. (2007). *Global Issues in Language, Education and Development: Perspectives from Postcolonial Countries*. Clevedon: Multilingual Matters.
Reksulak, M., Shughart, W. F., & Tollison, R. D. (2004). Economics and English: Language growth in economic perspective. *Southern Economic Journal*, 71(2), 232–259.
Ricento, T. (Ed.). (2015a). *Language Policy & Political Economy: English in a Global Context*. Oxford: Oxford University Press.
Ricento, T. (2015b). Political economy and English as a "global" language. In T. Ricento (Ed.), *Language Policy and Political Economy* (pp. 27–47). Oxford: Oxford University Press.
Ricento, T. (2018). The promise and pitfalls of global English. In P. A. Kraus & F. Grin (Eds.), *The Politics of Multilingualism: Europeanisation, Globalisation and Linguistic Governance* (pp. 201–222). Amsterdam, The Netherlands: John Benjamins.
Rini, J. E. (2014). English in Indonesia. *Beyond Words*, 2(2), 19–39.
Ritzer, G. (1993). *The McDonaldization of Society*. London: Sage.
Robinson, B. (2015). *They All Love Jack: Busting the Ripper*. London: 4th Estate.
Robinson, R. (1976 [1972]). Non-European foundations of European imperialism: Sketch for a theory of collaboration. In Wm. R. Louis (Ed.), *Imperialism: The Robinson and Gallagher Controversy* (pp. 74–128). New York: New Viewpoints.
Robinson, R., & Gallagher, J. (1961). *Africa and the Victorians: The Official Mind of Imperialism*. London: Palgrave Macmillan.

Robinson, R., & Gallagher, J. (1976 [1962]). The partition of Africa. In Wm. R. Louis (Ed.), *Imperialism: The Robinson and Gallagher Controversy* (pp. 54–73). New York: New Viewpoints.

Robinson, R. E. (1991). Introduction: Railway imperialism. In C. B. Davis, K. E. Wilburn, & R. E. Robinson (Eds.), *Railway Imperialism* (pp. 1–6). New York: Greenwood Press.

Robinson, W. I. (2007). Theories of globalization. In G. Ritzer (Ed.), *The Blackwell Companion to Globalization* (pp. 125–143). London: Blackwell.

Robinson Sirkin, N., & Sirkin, G. (1971). The battle of Indian education: Macaulay's opening salvo newly discovered. *Victorian Studies*, 14(4), 407–428.

Rodney, W. (2012 [1972]). *How Europe Underdeveloped Africa*. Baltimore: Black Classic Press.

Rosenberg, E. S. (1982). *Spreading the American Dream: American Economic and Cultural Expansion, 1890–1945*. New York: Hill & Wang.

Rosenberg, J. (2005). Globalization theory: A post mortem. *International Politics*, 42, 2–74.

Rosenberg, J. (2006). Why is there no historical sociology? *European Journal of International Relations*, 12(3), 307–340.

Rösler, D. (2017). The only turn worth watching in the 20th century is Tina Turner's: How the sloganization of foreign language research can impede the furthering of knowledge and make life difficult for practitioners. In B. Schmenk, S. Breidbach, & L. Küster (Eds.), *Sloganization in Language Education Discourse*. Bristol: Multilingual Matters.

Rostow, W. W. (1966). *The Stages of Economic Growth: A Non-Communist Manifesto*. Cambridge: Cambridge University Press.

Roy, M. (1993). The Englishing of India: Class formation and social privilege. *Social Scientist*, 21(5/6), 36–62.

Roy, M. (1994). "Englishing" India: Reinstituting class and social privilege in nineteenth-century India. *Social Text*, 39, 83–109.

Rubdy, R. (2015). Unequal Englishes, the native speaker, and decolonization in TESOL. In R. Tupas (Ed.), *Unequal Englishes: The Politics of English Today* (pp. 42–58). London: Palgrave Macmillan.

Sachs, J. (1986). Managing the LDC debt crisis. *Brookings Papers on Economic Activity*, 2, 397–440.

Sadeghpour, M. (2019). *Englishes in English Language Teaching*. London: Routledge.

Said, E. W. (1978). *Orientalism*. Harmondsworth: Penguin.

Saraceni, M. (2009). Relocating English: Towards a new paradigm for English in the world. *Language and Intercultural Communication*, 9(3), 175–186.

Saraceni, M. (2015). *World Englishes: A Critical Analysis*. London: Bloomsbury.

Sato, T. (2019). *Vernacular Cosmopolitanism in the Context of Neoliberalism: The Case of Plurilingual Asian Students in Japanese Higher Education* (PhD). University College London, London, UK.

Saxena, M., & Omoniyi, T. (2010). *Contending with Globalization in World Englishes*. Bristol: Multilingual Matters.

Sayer, P. (2018). Does English really open doors? Social class and English teaching in public primary schools in Mexico. *System (Linköping)*, 73, 58–70.

Schedel, S. S. (2018). Turning local bilingualism into a touristic experience. *Language Policy*, 17, 137–155.

Schneider, E. W. (2003). The dynamics of new Englishes: From identity construction to dialect birth. *Language, 79*(2), 233–281.

Schneider, E. W. (2007). *Postcolonial English: Varieties Around the World.* Cambridge: Cambridge University Press.

Schneider, E. W. (2014). New reflections on the evolutionary dynamics of World Englishes. *World Englishes, 33*(1), 9–32.

Schuler, K., & Rosenberg, A. (2013). *The Bretton Woods Transcripts.* New York: Centre for Financial Stability.

Schumpeter, J. (2010 [1943]). *Capitalism, Socialism and Democracy.* London and New York: Routledge.

Schuyler, R. L. (1945). *The Fall of the Old Colonial System.* New York: Oxford University Press.

Seargeant, P. (2009). *The Idea of English in Japan: Ideology and the Evolution of a Global Language.* Bristol: Multilingual Matters.

Seargeant, P. (2012). *Exploring World Englishes.* London: Routledge.

Seargeant, P., & Erling, E. J. (2011). The discourse of 'English as a language for international development': Policy assumptions and practical challenges. In H. Coleman (Ed.), *Dreams and Realities: Developing Countries and the English Language.* London: British Council.

Seargeant, P., Erling, E. J., Solly, M., Chowdhury, Q. H., & Rahman, S. (2017). Analysing perceptions of English in rural Bangladesh. *World Englishes, 36*(4), 631–644.

Seidlhofer, B. (2001). Closing a conceptual gap: The case for the description of English as a Lingua Franca. *International Journal of Applied Linguistics, 11*(2), 133–158.

Seidlhofer, B. (2007). English as a Lingua Franca and communities of practice. In S. Volk-Birke & J. Lippert (Eds.), *Halle 2006 Proceedings* (pp. 307–318). Trier: Wissenschaftlicher Verlag.

Seidlhofer, B. (2009). Common ground and different realities: World Englishes and English as a Lingua Franca. *World Englishes, 28*(2), 236–245.

Seidlhofer, B. (2012a). Anglophone-centric attitudes and the globalization of English. *Journal of English as a Lingua Franca, 1*(1), 393–407.

Seidlhofer, B. (2012b). Corpora and English as a Lingua Franca. In K. Hyland, C. M. Huat, & M. Handford (Eds.), *Corpus Applications in Applied Linguistics* (pp. 135–149). London: Continuum.

Seidlhofer, B., & Jenkins, J. (2003). English as a Lingua Franca and the politics of property. In C. Mair (Ed.), *The Politics of English as a World Language: New Horizons in Postcolonial Cultural Studies* (pp. 139–154). New York: Rodopi.

Sethia, T. (1991). Railways, Raj, and the Indian states: Policy of collaboration and coercion in Hyderabad. In B. Davey, K. E. Wilburn, & R. E. Robinson (Eds.), *Railway Imperialism* (pp. 103–120). Westport: Greenwood Press.

Shambaugh, D. (2016a). The complexities of a rising China. In D. Shambaugh (Ed.), *The China Reader: Rising Power* (pp. 1–4). Oxford: Oxford University Press.

Shambaugh, D. (2016b). The illusion of Chinese power. In D. Shambaugh (Ed.), *The China Reader: Rising Power* (6th ed., pp. 26–33). Oxford: Oxford University Press.

Sharma, R. (2020). The comeback nation. US economic supremacy has repeatedly proved declinists wrong. *Foreign Affairs, 99*(3), 70–81.

Shaw, M. (2011). Britain and genocide: Historical and contemporary parameters of national responsibility. *Review of International Studies*, 37, 2417–2438.

Shibata, M. (2008). Japan and Germany under the U.S. occupation: A comparative analysis of the post-war education reform. (reprint, 2005). *Reference and Research Book News [0887–3763]*, 23(3), n/a.

Si, J. J. (2006). *The Circulation of English in China, 1840–1940: Historical Texts, Personal Activities, and a New Linguistic Landscape* (PhD). Pennsylvania: University of Pennsylvania.

Si, J. J. (2013). Treaty-port English in nineteenth-century Shanghai: Speakers, voices, and images. *Cross-Currents: East Asian History and Culture Review*, 6, 38–66.

Silverstein, M. (1985). Language and the culture of gender. In E. Mertz & R. J. Parmentier (Eds.), *Semiotic Mediation: Sociocultural and Psychological Perspectives* (pp. 219–259). Cambridge, MA: Academic Press.

Simpson, W. (2017). An instrumental tool held at arm's length: English as a vehicle of cultural imperialism in China. *Chinese Journal of Applied Linguistics*, 40(3), 333–348.

Simpson, W. (2020). *Commodity, Capital, and Commercial ELT: A Political Economy of Eikaiwa English Language Teaching* (PhD). University College London, London, UK.

Simpson, W., & O'Regan, J. P. (2018). Fetishism and the language commodity: A materialist critique. *Language Sciences*, 70, 155–166.

Simpson, W., & O'Regan, J. P. (2021). Confronting language fetishism in practice. In J. E. Petrovic & B. Yazan (Eds.), *The Commodification of Language: Conceptual Concerns and Empirical Manifestations* (pp. 7–23). London: Taylor and Francis.

Singh, M., & Han, J. (2008). The commoditization of English and the Bologna process. In P. Tan & R. Rubdy (Eds.), *Language as Commodity: Global Structures, Local Marketplaces* (pp. 204–224). London: Continuum.

Skidelsky, R. (2003). *John Maynard Keynes 1883–1946: Economist, Philosopher, Statesman*. London: Palgrave Macmillan.

Skutnabb-Kangas, T. (2000). *Linguistic Genocide in Education – or Worldwide Diversity and Human Rights?* Mahwah: Lawrence Erlbaum.

Skutnabb-Kangas, T. (2012). Linguistic human rights. In L. M. Solan & P. M. Tiersma (Eds.), *The Oxford Handbook of Language and Law* (pp. 1–12). Oxford: Oxford University Press.

Skutnabb-Kangas, T., & Phillipson, R. (2010). The global politics of language: Markets, maintenance, marginalization, or murder? In N. Coupland (Ed.), *Blackwell Handbooks in Linguistics, The Handbook of Language and Globalization, Global Multilingualism, World Languages, and Language Systems* (pp. 77–100). Oxford: Blackwell.

Smith, A. (1999a [1776]). *The Wealth of Nations. Books I–III*. London: Penguin.

Smith, A. (1999b [1776]). *The Wealth of Nations. Books IV–V*. London: Penguin.

Smith, L. E. (2016). Familiar issues from a World Englishes perspective. *Polylinguality and Transcultural Practices*, 1, 14–18.

Smith, R. (1974). The Lagos Consulate, 1851–1861: An outline. *The Journal of African History*, 15(3), 393–416.

Soederberg, S. (2002). The new international financial architecture: Imposed leadership and "emerging markets". In L. Panitch & C. Leys (Eds.), *Socialist Register 2002: A World of Contradictions* (pp. 175–192). London: Merlin Press.

Soherwordi, S. H. S. (2010). 'Punjabisation' in the British Indian army 1857–1947 and the advent of military rule in Pakistan. *Edinburgh Papers in South Asian Studies*, 24, 1–34.

Song, J. J. (2011). English as an official language in South Korea: Global English or social malady? *Language Problems & Language Planning*, 35(1), 35–55.

Sonntag, S. K. (2009). Linguistic globalization and the call center industry: Imperialism, hegemony or cosmopolitanism. *Language Policy*, 8, 5–25.

Sowden, C. (2012). ELF on a mushroom: The overnight growth in English as a Lingua Franca. *ELT Journal*, 66(1), 89–96.

Spence, J. (1990). *The Search for Modern China*. London: Hutchinson.

Spivak, G. C. (1976). Translator's preface. In J. Derrida (Ed.), *Of Grammatology* (pp. ix–lxxxvii). Baltimore: John Hopkins University Press.

Sridhar, S. N. (2019, June 21). *The Curious Dynamics of Center and Periphery in World Englishes*. Keynote lecture presented at the 24th Conference of the International Association for World Englishes, University of Limerick, Ireland.

Sridhar, S. N., & Sridhar, K. K. (2018). Coda 2 A bridge half-built: Toward a holistic theory of second language acquisition and world Englishes. *World Englishes*, 37(1), 127–139.

Stedman-Jones, D. (2012). *Masters of the Universe: Hayek, Friedman, and the Birth of Neoliberal Politics*. Princeton and Oxford: Princeton University Press.

Stein, D. (1993). Sorting out the variants: Standardization and social factors in the English language 1600–1800. In D. Stein & I. Tieken-Boon van Ostade (Eds.), *Towards a Standard English: 1600–1800* (pp. 1–18). Berlin and Boston: De Gruyter.

Storey, R. (1960). *A History of Modern Japan*. Harmondsworth: Penguin.

Strange, S. (1989). Toward a theory of transnational empire. In E. O. Czempiel & J. N. Rosenau (Eds.), *Global Changes and Theoretical Challenges: Approaches to World Politics for the 1990s* (pp. 161–176). Lexington, MA: Lexington Books.

Sweezy, P. M. (1972). *Modern Capitalism and Other Essays*. New York and London: Monthly Review Press.

Tan, P., & Rubdy, R. (Eds.). (2008). *Language as Commodity: Global Structures, Local Marketplaces*. London: Continuum.

Tarbuck, K. J. (Ed.). (1972). *Imperialism and the Accumulation of Capital*. London: Penguin.

Taylor, P. J. (1996). What's modern about the modern world system? Introducing ordinary modernity through world hegemony. *Review of International Political Economy*, 3(2), 260–286.

Teng, S.-Y., & Fairbank, J. K. (1954). *China's Response to the West: A Documentary Survey*. Harvard: Harvard University Press.

Thérien, J.-P. (1993). Co-operation and conflict in La Francophonie. *Ethnic Tension & Nationalism*, 48(3), 492–526.

Thiong'o, N. w. (1987). *Decolonizing the Mind. The Politics of Language in African Literature*. London: James Currey Ltd.

Thiong'o, N. w. (1991). Moving the centre: Towards a pluralism of cultures. *The Journal of Commonwealth Literature*, 26(1), 198–206.

Thompson, J. (1984). *Studies in the Theory of Ideology*. Cambridge: Polity Press.

Thrift, N. J. (2007). *Non-Representational Theory: Space, Politics, Affect*. London: Routledge.

Tollefson, J. W., & Pérez-Milans, M. (Eds.). (2018). *The Oxford Handbook of Language Policy and Planning*. Oxford: Oxford University Press.

Tooze, A. (2019). Is this the end of the American century? *London Review of Books*, 41(7), 3–7.

Tooze, A. (2020). The world goes bust. *London Review of Books*, 42(8), 3–6.

Trakulkasemsuk, W. (2018). English in Thailand: Looking back to the past, at the present and towards the future. *Asian Englishes*, 20(2), 96–105.

Tsuda, Y. (2010). Speaking against the hegemony of English: Problems, ideologies, and solutions. In T. K. Nakayama & R. T. Halualani (Eds.), *The Handbook of Critical Intercultural Communication* (pp. 248–269). London: Blackwell.

Tuck, R. (2008). *Free Riding*. Cambridge, MA: Harvard University Press.

Tupas, R. (2003). History, language planners, and strategies of forgetting: The problem of consciousness in the Philippines. *Language Problems and Language Planning*, 27(1), 1–25.

Tupas, R. (2008). Anatomies of linguistic commodification: The case of English in the Philippines via-à-vis other languages. In P. Tan & R. Rubdy (Eds.), *Language as Commodity: Global Structures, Local Marketplaces* (pp. 106–121). London: Continuum.

Tupas, R. (Ed.). (2015). *Unequal Englishes: The Politics of Englishes Today*. London: Palgrave Macmillan.

Tupas, R. (2019). Entanglements of colonialism, social class, and unequal Englishes. *Journal of Sociolinguistics*, 23(5), 529–542.

Tupas, R., & Rubdy, R. (2015). Introduction: From world Englishes to unequal Englishes. In R. Tupas (Ed.), *Unequal Englishes: The Politics of Englishes Today* (pp. 1–17). London: Palgrave Macmillan.

Ukers, W. H. (1935). *All about Tea* (Vol. I). New York: The Tea and Coffee Trade Journal Company.

Urciuoli, B. (2008). Skills and selves in the new workplace. *American Ethnologist*, 35(2), 211–228.

Ustinova, I. (2005). English in Russia. *World Englishes*, 24(2), 239–251.

Vandrick, S. (1995). Privileged ESL university students. *TESOL Quarterly*, 29(2), 357–381.

Vandrick, S. (2011). Students of the new global elite. *TESOL Quarterly*, 45(1), 160–169.

Vandrick, S. (2014). The role of social class in English language education. *Journal of Language, Identity and Education*, 13(2), 85–91.

Van Dyke, P. A. (2005). *The Canton Trade: Life and Enterprise on the China Coast, 1750–1845*. Hong Kong: Hong Kong University Press.

Van Dyke, P. A. (2017). The Canton linguists of the 1730s: Managers of the margins of trade. *Journal of the Royal Asiatic Society Hong Kong Branch*, 57, 7–35.

Van Hoof, S. (2018). Civilization versus commerce: On the sociolinguistic effects of the deregulation of the TV market on Flemish public service broadcasting. *Language Policy*, 17.

Velez-Rendon, G. (2003). English in Colombia: A sociolinguistic profile. *World Englishes*, 22(2), 185–198.

Vertovec, S. (2007). Super-diversity and its implications. *Ethnic and Racial Studies*, 30(6), 1024–1054.

Viebrok, B. (2017). Just another prefix? From inter- to transcultural foreign language learning and beyond. In *Sloganization in Language Education Discourse* (pp. 72–93). Bristol: Multilingual Matters.

Vigouroux, C. B. (2013). Francophonie. *Annual Review of Anthropology*, 42, 379–397.
Vogler, J. (2013). Mainstream theories. Realism, rationalism and revolutionism. In P. G. Harris (Ed.), *Routledge Handbook of Global Environmental Politics*. London: Routledge.
Vološinov, V. N. (1973). *Marxism and the Philosophy of Language*. Cambridge, MA: Harvard University Press.
Wade, R., & Veneroso, F. (1998). The Asian crisis: The high debt model versus the Wall Street-Treasury-IMF Complex. *New Left Review*, 3–22.
Wall, R. F. (1964). Japan's century: An interpretation of Japanese history since the eighteen-fifties. *The Historical Association*, 56, 3–44.
Wallerstein, I. (1976, December). From feudalism to capitalism: Transition or transitions? *Social Forces*, LV, 273–281.
Wallerstein, I. (1983). *Historical Capitalism*. London: Verso.
Wallerstein, I. (2000). *The Essential Wallerstein*. New York: The New Press.
Wallerstein, I. (2000 [1973]). Africa in a capitalist world. In I. Wallerstein (Ed.), *The Essential Wallerstein* (pp. 39–68). New York: The New Press.
Wallerstein, I. (2000 [1974]). The rise and future demise of the world capitalist system: Concepts for comparative analysis. In I. Wallerstein (Ed.), *The Essential Wallerstein* (pp. 71–105). New York: The New Press.
Wallerstein, I. (2000 [1975]). Class formation in the capitalist world-economy. In I. Wallerstein (Ed.), *The Essential Wallerstein* (pp. 315–323). New York: The New Press.
Wallerstein, I. (2000 [1983]). The three instances of hegemony in the capitalist world-system. In I. Wallerstein (Ed.), *The Essential Wallerstein* (pp. 253–263). New York: The New Press.
Wallerstein, I. (2000 [1988]). 1968, revolution and the world-system: Theses and queries. In I. Wallerstein (Ed.), *The Essential Wallerstein* (pp. 355–373). New York: The New Press.
Wallerstein, I. (2000 [1989]). Culture as the ideological battleground of the modern world-system. In I. Wallerstein (Ed.), *The Essential Wallerstein* (pp. 264–289). New York: The New Press.
Wallerstein, I. (2000 [1992]). America and the world: Today, yesterday and tomorrow. In I. Wallerstein (Ed.), *The Essential Wallerstein* (pp. 387–415). New York: The New Press.
Wallerstein, I. (2000 [1994]). Peace, stability and legitimacy, 1990–2025/2050. In I. Wallerstein (Ed.), *The Essential Wallerstein* (pp. 435–453). New York: The New Press.
Wallerstein, I. (2004). *World-Systems Analysis: An Introduction*. Durham and London: Duke University Press.
Wallerstein, I. (2011a). *The Modern World-System I: Capitalist Agriculture and the Origins of the European World-Economy in the Sixteenth Century*. Berkeley and Los Angeles: University of California Press.
Wallerstein, I. (2011b). *The Modern World-System II: Mercantilism and Consolidation of the European World-Economy, 1600–1750*. Berkeley and Los Angeles: University of California Press.
Wallerstein, I. (2011c). *The Modern World-System III: The Second Era of Great Expansion of the Capitalist World-Economy, 1730s-1840s*. Berkeley and Los Angeles: University of California Press.

Wallerstein, I. (2011d). *The Modern World System IV: Centrist Liberalism Triumphant, 1789–1914*. Berkeley and Los Angeles: University of California Press.

Wallerstein, I. (2013). Structural crisis or why capitalists may no longer find capitalism rewarding. In I. Wallerstein, R. Collins, M. Mann, G. Derlugian, & C. Calhoun (Eds.), *Does Capitalism Have a Future?* (pp. 9–36). Oxford: Oxford University Press.

Wallerstein, I., Collins, R., Mann, M., Derlugian, G., & Calhoun, C. (2013). *Does Capitalism Have a Future?* Oxford: Oxford University Press.

Walter, A. (1991). *World Power and World Money: The Role of Hegemony and International Monetary Order*. New York: Academic Press.

Weber, M. (1978). *Economy and Society: An Outline of Interpretive Sociology*. Berkeley: University of California Press.

Wee, L., Pakir, A., & Lim, L. (Eds.). (2010). *English in Singapore: Modernity and Management*. Hong Kong: Hong Kong University Press.

Weedon, C. (1987). *Feminist Practice and Poststructuralist Theory*. London: Wiley.

Wertheim, S. (2020). The peace of primacy. Why America shouldn't dominate the world. *Foreign Affairs*, 99(2), 19–29.

Westad, O. A. (2019). The sources of the Chinese conduct. *Foreign Affairs*, 98(5), 86–95.

Whitehead, C. (1995). The medium of instruction in British colonial education: A case of cultural imperialism or enlightened paternalism? *History of Education*, 24(1), 1–15.

Widdowson, H. G. (1994). The ownership of English. *TESOL Quarterly*, 28(2), 377–389.

Widdowson, H. G. (1997). EIL, ESL, EFL: Global issues and local interests. *World Englishes*, 16(1), 146–153.

Williams, E. (1994 [1944]). *Capitalism and Slavery*. Chapel Hill: The University of North Carolina Press.

Williams, R. (1977). *Marxism and Literature*. Oxford: Oxford University Press.

Woo, W. T. (2012). China meets the middle-income trap: The large potholes in the road to catching-up. *Journal of Chinese Economic and Business Studies: China's Economic Dynamics: Challenges for A New Paradigm in The Making*, 10(4), 313–336.

Woodruff, W. (1966). *Impact of Western Man: A Study of Europe's Role in the World Economy 1750–1960*. London: Palgrave Macmillan.

Woolf, L. (n.d.). *Empire and Commerce in Africa*. London: George Allen & Unwin.

Wright, L. (2000). *The Development of Standard English, 1300–1800: Theories, Descriptions, Conflicts*. Cambridge: Cambridge University Press.

Wright, W. R. (1974). *British-Owned Railways in Argentina: Their Effect on Economic Nationalism*. Austin and London: University of Texas Press.

Zacek, N. A. (2010). *Settler Society in the English Leeward Islands, 1670–1776*. Cambridge: Cambridge University Press.

Zakaria, F. (2019). The self-destruction of American power: Washington squandered the unipolar moment. *Foreign Affairs*, 98(4), 10–16.

Zakaria, F. (2020). The new China scare: Why America shouldn't panic about its latest challenger. *Foreign Affairs*, 99(1), 52–69.

Zein, S. (2019). English, multilingualism and globalisation in Indonesia: A love triangle: Why Indonesia should move towards multilingual education. *English Today*, 35(1), 48–53.

Žižek, S. (2012). How did Marx invent the symptom? In S. Žižek (Ed.), *Mapping Ideology* (pp. 296–331). London: Verso.
Zoellick, R. (2005). Whither China: From membership to responsibility? *NBR Analysis, 16*(4), 5–15.
Zucchi, K. (2019, June 25). Did derivatives cause the recession? *Investopedia*. Retrieved from www.investopedia.com/financial-edge/0210/did-derivatives-cause-the-recession.aspx

Index

academic labour 184, 188; and reproduction of standard English 184n4, 188–189, 198
accumulation by dispossession 26, 36–38, 178, 190, 206–207, 211; *see also* capital, accumulation of; capital, overaccumulation of; linguistic capital, dispossession; primitive accumulation
Accumulation of Capital, The (1913) 22–23
Acheson, Dean 118
Adamson, B. 95, 159–160, 175
Adamson, L. 128
Adorno, T. W. 24
Africa 1850–1900 84–89; *see also* 'Scramble for Africa'
African pidgins and creoles 88
alienation 18, 220; alienableness of English 193–195, 201
Alim, S. H. 185
Allende, Salvador: death of 139
Althusser, L. 5–6, 20
Ambrose, S. E. 118
Amin, S. 25
Anglo-cluster 72; anglophone core 2
annihilation of space through time 71
anti-systemic movements 43, 211–214; and assimilation of 212
applied linguistics 2, 8, 35, 182, 188, 191, 204, 204n16
Arendt, H. 36–37, 206, 219
Argentina: 1890s financial crisis 73; debt 133, 137–138, 141; investments in 103; and middle-income trap 161; railways 90
Argentinean crisis 2001–2 143–144, 146; and English 146
arms trade: and English 174

Arrighi, G. 39, 106–114, 122–138, 216–218
ASEAN 148, 174n36
Asian crisis 1997–98 143–145, 147; and English 145
Asian Infrastructure Investment Bank (AIIB) 169–170, 174; and English 170
Asian 'Tiger' economies 18, 125
assemblage(s) 21, 35, 43, 195–198, 200, 204, 211
atomic bomb: Hiroshima and Nagasaki 114
austerity 65, 135, 144, 151, 165, 210, 214, 216
Australia *see* White settlement colonies
authenticity 6, 154, 201; reproduction of 6
autocentrism 39, 40; *see also* extroversion

Baker, A. 131
Baker Plan 136; *see also* Latin American debt crisis
Bakhtin, M. M. 6
Bakufu 72; *see also* Yedo
Bandung Conference 1955 121, 121n23
Bank of England: the Bank 59, 98, 116, 207; and corruption 59; and English financial revolution 59
Bank of International Settlements (BIS) 142, 148, 174n36
barbarian (*yi*, 夷): prohibition of use 95
Barrera, T. E. 217
Baudrillard, J. 182
Bauman, Z. 181
Beasley, W. G. 72
Becker, G. 191, 191n10
Belt and Road Initiative (BRI) 163–164, 169, 174, 178; and English 163–164; *see also* China

Index 255

Bentley, R. S. 110, 122, 122n26
Benton, L. 81
Berlin Wall: fall of 134, 139, 181
Bernstein, B. 155
Betta, C. 79, 80, 82
Betzel, A. 55n10
Bevins, V. 114
Bhaskar, R. 7, 29n22, 55, 153–156, 182, 194, 199, 200, 214, 220; accumulation 29n22; causal powers/mechanisms 7, 194, 196, 200; dialectic 156; endism 43, 214–218; epistemic fallacy 194; implicit ontology 199; philosophical discourse of modernity 29n22; power 155; *presentism* 182, 214; the real 200; revolutionism 220; structure and agency 154–156; theory free knowledge 55; TINA 153; *see also* Hartwig, M.
Bickers, R. 79–80, 79n6, 81n12, 82–83, 109
Biden, Joe 33n27, 168n18, 172n27, 176n38, 219n13
Block, D. 2–3, 36, 148, 151, 182, 189, 193, 202n14
Blommaert, J. 3–4, 34, 154, 156, 175, 185, 197, 200, 205
Blum, W. 107n7, 114–120, 139, 141, 143
Boer Wars 84n13, 85n18
Bolivar, Simon 65
Borjian, M. 141
Bottomore, T. 22
Bourdieu, P. 40, 41, 56, 184–185, 202, 202n14; capitals 6, 56, 138, 179, 184; linguistic market 41, 195, 201; misrecognition 40, 185, 188, 206, 209; phonocentrism 202; *see also* capital; fetish/fetishism
Bown, C. P. 169, 171
Boxer Rebellion 1898–1901 97–98, 99n24; *see also* China
Brady Plan 136, 138, 138n1; *see also* Latin American debt crisis
Braudel, F. 3, 8, 35
Brazil: 1974 oil crisis 133; 1980s debt crisis 136–137; 1999 banking crisis 146; Brazilian capitalism 25; British dominance in 66; investments in 103; railways 90; *see also* Latin American Debt Crisis
Bretton Woods trading system 42, 110–113, 123–125, 127–132, 166, 170; collapse 1971 127–132; and English 111, 113, 123, 125; founding 1944 110–113; *see also* gold standard; Keynes, John Maynard
Brewer, A. 8, 22–23, 26, 28, 53
BRICS nations 167, 167n12, 174n36
BRICS New Development Bank (NDB) 169–170; and English 170
Britain: 1815–1850 62–68; 1850–1914 69–101; 1918–1939 106–109; British decline 1870–1918 42, 48, 54n9, 69–70, 85, 100, 102–105; British empire 29, 30n24, 44–45, 49, 109–110, 128; imperial expansion 1688–1815 58–62; imperialism 41, 49, 54; *Pax Britannica* 69; *see also* empire
British East Africa Association 87–88; and Imperial British East Africa Company (IBEAC) 86–89
British South Africa Company (BSAC) 85–86, 85n19
Brown, D. S. 130
Bruner, K. F. 96
Bruthiaux, P. 3
Buffett, Warren 149
Bukharin, N. 22–23, 23n20; *see also* imperialism
Bush, George W. 150–151, 151n7, 161, 165
Buzan, B. 219n12

Cain, P. J. 54–73, 83–87, 93–94, 98, 101–103, 107
call centres 201, 204; *see also* language commodification; phone sex
Calvet, L.-J. 5
Campbell, K. M. 216
Canada 2, 61, 64, 69, 72, 81n11, 89, 105, 109, 131, 143, 169, 171, 171n26; *see also* White settlement colonies
Canagarajah, S. 155, 175, 182n1, 196, 197, 198, 199, 200, 204, 204n16
Canning, George 65–66, 73
Canton Pidgin English (CPE) 31, 72, 95; Canton 'jargon' 83
Canton Trade: and Canton linguists 31
Cape Colony 64, 84–85, 84n16; *see also* BRICS; South Africa
capital: accumulation of 4, 7, 8–9, 9n7, 11–12, 16, 22, 26, 28–30, 36–39, 41, 52–53, 84, 91, 109, 113, 121, 123–126, 136, 141, 143,

156, 190, 206, 220; antediluvian 15, 47; capital flight 108, 143–144; circulating 10, 12, 18; circulation of 9–12, 12n10 16–18, 44, 101, 210; commercial 15, 22, 30; commodity 13–14; as a dialectical process 18–22; disembedding 212, 212n3; finance/financial 5, 15–16, 16n15, 22–23, 30–31, 45, 54, 66; fixed 10; industrial 14, 15, 30, 47, 57; linguistic 39, 130; merchants' 14–15, 47; merging with linguistic capital 130; mobile/mobility of 10–12, 45–47, 58, 136; money 13–14, 87, 11, 126, 130; overaccumulation of 12, 16, 23–24; as a social relation 6; superfluous 36–37; surplus 12; symbolic 6–7, 15, 140, 184, 190, 201–202, 206; usurers' 15; *see also* capital circulation; free riding; global capital flows

capital-centric English 6, 42, 135–157, 185, 189, 209, 218

capital circulation: as M-C-M' 12–17, 14n15, 37, 39, 96, 104, 192, 200; as M-M' 14–15, 14n11, 39, 57, 88, 96, 104, 126, 131, 142, 200, 210; *see also* surplus value

Capital: A Critique of Political Economy Vol. I (1867) 9, 12, 17, 21, 210; Vol. II (1884) 132n31; Vol. III (1894) 15

capitalism: agricultural 47, 54; demise and disintegration of 209–211, 214–220; diagonal 166; economic cycles of 210; industrial 47n4, 56, 57; mode(s) of production 17n16, 19–23, 25, 29n22, 30, 36, 48, 123, 136, 192, 207; origins 4–8, 17–18, 28, 30n24, 36, 47, 211; periodization/periodicity of 30, 47–48, 53–54, 54n9; vertical 166, 177; *see also* late capitalism

capital networks 31, 36, 42, 45–47, 53, 68, 101, 106–109, 123–126, 148; reproduction of 189

Carter, Jimmy 135

Cavanaugh, J. R. 202

Chiang Kai-shek 115–116, 120–121

Chile 65, 70, 80, 90, 103, 107, 114, 128, 138, 216n6; 1973 coup 139; 1980s debt crisis 138; death of Allende 139; English 80, 114, 128; railways 90; *see also* CIA; dirty wars

China: 1750–1850 31, 50, 61, 65; 1850–1912 72–73, 79–84, 92–100; 1912–1949 109–118; 1949–2020 158–180; 1949 revolution 80, 116, 118, 120; accession to WTO 2001 144, 159, 174; Beijing Olympics 2008 144, 159; Belt and Road Initiative (BRI) 163–164, 169, 174, 176, 178; Boxer Rebellion 1898–1901 97–98, 99n24; collapse of the Qing 99–100; communications in English 95; concessions 79–80, 79n6, 94–95, 97; currency centrality of renminbi (RMB) 170, 173, 175; English language policy 160, 175; English learning in 95–97, 159; ethnic minorities in 162, 166–167, 179; FDI and clientelist states 178; foreign legations in Peking 92, 96, 98; global structural power 160–164, 175–176; hegemonic unpreparedness 177–180, 215; Hong Kong security law 2020 177; indemnity loans 93–95, 97–98; lack of the 'trust of credit' 179; membership of intergovernmental organizations 174, 174n36; middle classes in 159, 169, 176–177; military expansion 167–168; military power 169, 173, 176, 179; Opium Wars 50, 61, 72, 92, 95; overtaking of US as world's largest economy 160, 172; post-1978 'open door' policy 27, 43, 140, 160, 168, 174; public debt 176; railway imperialism in 92–100; resistance to internal market reform 159, 162, 166; response to COVID-19 178–179; rivalry with US 168–171; Scramble for China 24, 94, 97; secretiveness 179; state totalitarianism 177; subsidies to state sector 167; Taiping Rebellion 1850–1864 105n5; tensions in South China Sea 167, 173; Thucydides' trap 215–216; treaty ports 61, 61n17, 79n6, 81, 92–93, 96–97; unequal treaties 92, 92n20, 175; use of English as a global *lingua franca* 163–164, 168, 170, 174–175, 179–180; *see also* Hong Kong; Mandarin Chinese; Taiwan; Xi Jinping

Chinese capitalism 177–78; middle-income trap 161; *see also* socialism with Chinese characteristics

Chinese Civil War 1945–49 114–116; Nationalists and Communists 115, 116, 120–121; *see also* Chiang Kai-shek; Mao Zedong
Chinese Communist Party (CCP) 140, 162–163, 169, 173, 176–177, 179, 218; and corruption 162–163, 165, 178; and fear of dissent 162, 176–177; *see also* US-China trade war
Chinese diplomacy: and risk aversion of 178
Choi, E. K. 5
Chomsky, N. 155n10, 179
Chouliaraki, L. 181
chronotope 200
Chun, C. W. 20
CIA (Central Intelligence Agency) 122, 125n28, 139; *see also* dirty wars
City of London 16, 30, 53–61, 67–73, 83–85, 90, 101, 108, 111, 126, 131, 148
Cixi, Dowager Empress 99
Clarence-Smith, W. G. 88
class 11, 20n18, 22, 40–41, 51, 52, 55, 57, 57n11, 60, 64–67, 74–75, 81–82, 98, 129, 144, 148, 150–151, 154, 165–166, 184, 206–207, 212, 219; class struggle 20n18; *see also* clientelism; elites, and elite cosmopolitanism; gentlemanly capitalism; Old Corruption
clientelism 39, 53, 73, 91, 109, 124, 142, 158, 189, 219; and transnational bourgeoisie 137; *see also* corruption; elites, and elite cosmopolitanism
climate change 177–179, 211, 215
Clive, Sir Robert 45–46, 61, 73
Clooney, Rosemary 122; *see also* jazz
Colby, E. A. 167, 216
Cold War 31, 33, 42, 45, 103, 113–118, 122, 124–125, 141, 145, 166; and US containment 117, 118–122; *see also* dirty wars
Coleman, T. 91
colonialism 2, 22, 23, 29, 36–50, 58, 84, 104, 115, 121n23, 178; and colonial acquisition 24, 38, 41–42, 44, 47, 49–50, 63, 71; and colonization 38, 47, 66–67, 103; *see also* Derrida, J.; phallogocentrism, and economic penetration/intercourse
commodities 12–19, 17n16, 192–194; circulation of 12–13, 17; as imaginary 193, 195; *see also* capital; fetish/fetishism; language commodification
communications: and communication networks 4, 35, 68, 70, 90–91, 106–109, 177, 189, 190
communism 34, 42, 113, 116–118, 121, 127, 135, 140, 141n2
Confucius Institutes 175–176; *see also* soft power
containment *see* Cold War; debt crises
Contribution to the Critique of Political Economy, A (1859) 9
coolie slave trade 97; *see also* slave trade
Cooper, R. N. 111
Corbyn, Jeremy 213
core/periphery 26–29, 39, 52–53, 57–58, 91, 143, 148, 150, 183, 191, 217; semi-periphery 27–28, 39; *see also* Wallerstein, I.; world-systems analysis
coronavirus *see* COVID-19
corruption 53, 55, 59, 67, 74, 99, 116n17, 162–163, 165, 178; *see also* gentlemanly capitalism; Old Corruption
cosmopolitanism *see* clientelism; elites, and elite cosmopolitanism
Coupland, N. 181
COVID-19/coronavirus pandemic 35, 160, 165, 170n24, 172–173, 176, 178–179, 205, 206n18, 208, 210–211, 215–216
Cox, R. W. 140
creative destruction 12, 37, 206; *see also* Schumpeter, J.
critical realism 194; *see also* Bhaskar, R.
Cuba: 24, 45n1, 90, 104, 114, 125, 159, 213; as anti-systemic 213; as degenerated workers' state 24; Guantanamo Bay 45n1; outside US world-economy 114, 125, 159; railways 90; US occupation 1899–1902 45n1; as US protectorate 104
Cui, A. 163

Darwent, C. E. 64, 79, 83
Darwin, J. 79, 83, 100
Da Silva, E. 190
Davey, B. 74
Davies, W. 152
debt crisis 42, 133, 136, 138–139; and crisis containment 142, 145; *see also* Argentinean crisis; Asian crisis;

258   Index

Brazil; Latin American debt crisis; Mexico
debt structuring in the world-economy 132–134; and English 133; *see also* structural adjustment programmes (SAPs)
declinism 32, 32n25; *see also* hegemony; United States
DeCorse, C. 84
degenerated socialist states 24; *see also* socialism in one country
Deleuze, G. 182, 196
Del Percio, A. 190, 193–195, 201, 206
Deng Xiaoping 140, 161–162
dependency theory 8, 24–27, 30; and development of underdevelopment 25–27
deregulation 38, 42, 145, 151, 161, 165; *see also* neoliberalism
derivatives 142, 148–153, 156; credit default swaps (CDSs) 149–150
Derrida, J. 20n17, 53n7, 182, 203, 203n16, 205; and phallogocentrism of colonialist discourse 53n7; privileging of speech over writing 202–205; and de Saussure 203–205; *see also* metaphysics of presence; phonocentrism
developmentalism 27, 113, 217; and developmentalist fallacy 27, 217
dialectic(s) 19–20, 156; *see also* capital
Dian, M. 159, 173
dirty wars 43, 114, 139, 166; *see also* Cold War
discourse 25, 29n22, 36, 55n10, 181, 185, 191, 199; order of discourse 185; philosophical discourse of modernity 29n22; *see also* ideology
disembedding of the economy 212; *see also* capital; Polanyi, K.
Dobb, M. 107
dollar *see* US dollar
dollar centrality 127; *see also* seignorage; US dollar, as international reserve currency
dollarization 129–130; and 'pegging' 129, 173; *see also* US dollar
Domingo, M. 185
Donnelly, J. S. 59, 63
Dovchin, S. 196, 200
Duchêne, A. 19, 190, 201–204
Dunn, B. 127
Dussel, E. 27
Dyer-Ball, J. 93

East Africa 72, 78, 83, 85–90; *see also* Kenya; Tanzania; Uganda
East Asia: 1850–1900 79–84, 92–100; 1945–1973 113–123; reintroduction of English 121–122; Westernization of dress 122; *see also* China; Japan; Shanghai; South Korea; Taiwan
East India Company (EIC) 45–46, 62, 73–79, 74n1; corruption 74; EIC army 76; Indian Civil Service 75, 75n2; Royal Charter 46, 74n1; underinvestment in Indian public utilities 74; *see also* India; Indian Mutiny
Economic and Philosophic Manuscripts (1844) 9, 12
economic nationalism 24, 124, 168–171, 219n12; *see also* mercantilism
edge see hegemony; structural power
Egypt: British occupation of 1882 52, 73, 84–85
elites 24, 26, 40, 51, 53, 66, 105, 124–125, 128–129, 137–148, 159, 169, 179, 189, 219; and elite cosmopolitanism 40, 70, 183; *see also* gentlemanly capitalism
empire: formal 48, 50–52, 69–73, 81n11, 90; informal 25, 44–54, 60–68, 100, 103; world-empire 29; *see also* Britain; United States
endism 43, 214–218; *see also* Bhaskar, R., *presentism*; Fukuyama, F.
Engels, F. 10–13, 14n11, 21, 47; letter to Bloch 20n18
English: commodification of 3, 43, 175, 189–195, 197, 200–204, 213; diffusion of 73–84, 89, 93, 95, 105; hegemony of 5, 53, 133, 183, 204, 208, 209–220; historiography of 3–4; ideological dominance of 2, 5, 6, 39, 139, 170, 175, 183, 186, 190, 200, 206, 209; invisibleness of 100–101; as a network good 5, 109; ownership of 43, 184n4, 186–189, 190, 193, 195, 197; periodization of 54n9; pluricentricity of 183, 196n13; political economy of 1–43, 102–134, 200; registers of 200; structuration/structuring of 42, 123, 130, 135–141, 185, 200–201; as a *transactional lingua franca* 15, 156; transnationalization of 126–132; as a vehicular language 5, 6, 42,

102; *see also* capital-centric English; normative English
English as a Lingua Franca (ELF) 1, 35, 40, 43, 182, 186–189, 196–197, 196n13, 200–205, 202n15; *see also* superdiverse translingualism
English fever: and desire for English 144, 148, 193
Eno, J. N. 105
epistemic fallacy 194; *see also* Bhaskar, R.
Epstein, I. 72, 115
Eri, Chiemi 122; *see also* jazz
Eurodollars 126–132; *see also* petrodollars; US dollar
Europe: transfer of US institutional and sociocultural systems to 109, 123
European Union (EU) 148, 158, 164–166, 171n26, 189
Evans, S. 74–75
exchange value *see* value
exploitation 11, 17, 19, 22n19, 25, 27, 29n22, 74, 90, 194–195, 204, 207, 211–212; *see also* alienation; immiseration
extraterritoriality 34, 38, 45n1, 52, 61, 61n17, 64, 80n10, 81, 81n12, 97, 104–109, 124, 163, 178
extremism: ideological 172, 219; Islamist 161; populist 33, 120, 151, 219; *see also* war on Islamist extremism
extroversion 39; *see also* autocentrism

Fairbank, J. K. 96, 175
Fairclough, N. 3, 181, 194
Fanon, F. 220
FDI: and correlation with language policy 130–131
Federal Reserve (the Fed): crisis management 136–137, 141–142; interest rate policy 33, 108, 150; and management of international monetary system 33, 38, 106, 111, 122, 125, 127, 131, 173; *see also* structural adjustment programmes (SAPs); Volcker, Paul, and 'Volcker shock'
Feng, A. 160, 175
Ferguson, N. 45–46
Ferri, G. 199
fetish/fetishism 19, 142, 149–150, 154, 156, 188, 192, 194, 204n16, 207, 219; *see also* Bourdieu, P.; language commodification; Marx, K.; misrecognition
finance capital *see* capital
financial crash 2007–8: 31, 35, 42–43, 145, 149, 151, 153–157, 161, 165, 214; and English 156–157; and Keynesian correction 152; sub-prime debt 148–150
financialization: of the global economy 39, 139, 190, 210; *see also* vulture capitalist risk
First Hundred Years' War 1337–1453 62n
First World War *see* World War I
Fishman, J. A. 128, 140
Fleming, P. 97
Flores, N. 199
Flubacher, M.-C. 19
Fong, E. T. Y. 159
Fontaine, P. 5, 7
Formosa *see* Taiwan
Foucault, M. 21, 25, 55n10, 153–155, 182, 185, 191, 195n12, 206; *see also* discourse; *homo economicus*; human capital theory
Fox, D. M. 91
France: defeat by Britain 1815 31, 62, 71–72; French Indo-China/Vietnam 118, 125, 128; German East Africa 87–88; and hegemonic rivalry with England 31, 164; Imperial Maritime Customs [Shanghai] 96; India 73; military power of 174; overseas investments and world trade 1860–1914 45, 102–103; railway imperialism 89, 92, 99; 'Scramble for Africa' 71, 86; Treaty of Versailles 1919 and German reparations 106; unequal treaties [with China] 92, 92n20, 94; *see also* Francophonie; French [language]
Francophonie, La: and Africa 128; *see also* French
Frank, A. G. 16, 25–30, 53, 66, 124, 124n26; *see also* dependency theory; development of underdevelopment
Fraser, N. 184, 187–188, 199–200; *see also* politics of recognition; politics of redistribution
free rider/free riding 5–9, 12–16, 30, 36, 40–41, 139, 142, 148, 156, 171
free trade 23–24, 30, 49–54, 62–68, 71–73, 83, 86, 88–89, 106, 113, 152, 171–172, 217

French [language]: and challenge of English [Africa] 125, [Vietnam] 128; *see also* Francophonie
French Revolution 1789 59
Friedman, M. 142, 191n9
Friedrich, P. 143
Frondizi, Arturo 124
Fujita, S. 72
Fukuyama, F. 141, 141n2; *see also* endism

G20 145, 156, 161, 170n24, 189, 207, 211, 218
G7 131, 139, 145–146, 156, 189, 207
Gal, S. 19, 206
Gallagher, J. 48–58, 73, 84; and imperialism of free trade, 49–50; official mind 51–52, 57
Gao, Y. 4, 144, 159–160, 175, 183
García, O. 196–197
Gardner, R. N. 111
Garrido, M. R. 183
Gazzola, M. 191n10
General Agreement on Tariffs and Trade (GATT) 113–114, 144, 159; *see also* World Trade Organization (WTO)
General Theory of Employment, Interest and Money, The (1936) 112
gentlemanly capitalism 24, 41, 54–58, 63, 65–68, 72, 84, 86–87, 98, 112n13, 207; *see also* class
Germany: 1919 reparations 106–107; African colonies [Tanganyika, Kamarun, Togoland] 88, 106; defeat by allies 1918/1945 31; and economic nationalism of Trump; German East Africa 88; and hegemonic transition 164; loss of colonies 106; military power 174; overseas investments and world trade 1860–1914 102–103; post-1919 US conditionality loans to 107; post-1945 recovery/resurgence 158; railway imperialism 92, 99; rise of Nazism 107; rivalry with Britain 31, 70, 102–103, 164; 'Scramble for Africa' 71, 86, 88; Thucydides' trap 216; Treaty of Versailles 1919 and reparations 106–107; unequal treaties [with China] 92, 92n20
Georgiou, A. 55n10, 200, 217
German Ideology, The 9–12
Gilpin, R. 3–4, 126–132

Gindin, S. 27, 104–111, 123–132, 135–146, 150, 190
Gini Index *see* global income inequality
Gladstone, W. E. 53, 53n8
Glasnost 140
global capital flows 40, 46, 69–71, 103, 114, 122, 124, 126, 130, 163, *see also* capital
global English *see* capital-centric English; English; normative English; standard English
global income inequality; and Gini Index 216–217
globalization 2–4, 4n2, 11, 27, 38, 139, 181; and *presentism* 3, 182; and recentness debate 3–4; *see also* endism
global North 43, 156; and migration to 156, 217
global South 27, 156, 213
Glorious Revolution 1688 58
gold standard 106, 106n6, 108–112, 126–127, 158, 207; UK gold standard 1918–1931 108–109; US gold standard 1944–1971 127, 158; *see also* sterling; US dollar
Goodrich, N. H. 141
Gorbachev, M. 140
Graeber, D. 142
Graham, R. 53
grammar: normative grammar 5–6, 6n5, 40, 56, 183, 188, 209, 211; spontaneous *vs.* immanent 6, 183; *see also* English; Gramsci, A.; normative English; writing
Gramsci, A. 5–6, 6n5, 25, 25n21, 32–34, 156, 183, 209, 214, 220; and grammar 5–6, 6n5, 183, 209; *see also* normative English; Ives, P.
Gray, J. 34, 193, 195n12
Great Depression 1930s 112, 112n11, 123, 210
Great Navigation Act 1851 46, 46n2, 59; *see also* Navigation Acts
Grebstein, S. 110, 122, 122n25
Grin, F. 193, 207
Grundrisse (1973) 9, 9n7, 17
Guantanamo Bay prison complex 45n1
Guardiola-Rivera, O. 139
Guatemala 53, 139
Guattari, F. 196
Gulf War 1990–1 141

Habermas, J. 220
Hall, S. 5
Hannerz, U. 183
Haraway, D. 55, 181
Hardt, M. 214
Hart, Sir Robert 96–97; see also Imperial Maritime Customs
Hartwig, M. 27, 29n22, 153, 182, 214
Harvey, D. 3, 12, 15–16, 19–21, 24, 26–27, 29, 36–38, 108, 111, 112n11, 113, 132n31, 133, 136–139, 142–143, 147–148, 152, 190, 199, 211, 220; see also accumulation by dispossession; dialectic(s); 'moments'; overaccumulation; overdetermination
Haslam, J. 139
Hawks Pott, F. L. 64, 96
Hayek, F. A. 142, 191n9
Hegel, G. W. F. 18, 141, 141n2, 169
hegemony 5–6, 5n4, 25n21, 31–32, 32n26, 35, 43, 54n9; 'edge' 7, 31–32, 34, 40; great power suicide 218; hegemonic transition/decline 30, 32, 35, 42–43, 48, 54n9, 69, 100, 102–103, 133n32, 158–160, 164–168, 208, 215–216; and Thucydides' trap 215–216; see also Britain; China; United States
Heller, M. 3, 19, 182, 190–193, 200–206, 213
Heng Hartse, J. 199
Herranz-Loncan, A. 90
Highet, K. 185, 188
Hilferding, R. 8, 16n15, 22–23, 30, 104n4, 107; see also capital; finance capital; imperialism
Hindley, R. 59, 59n15, 63
hip hop: and rap 185
Hiroshima: dropping of atomic bomb on 114
historical materialism 19, 55; see also Marx, K., base/superstructure
Hobsbawm, E. 108, 122–126, 132–133
Hobson, J. A. 23–24, 49; see also imperialism
Holborow, M. 1–3, 20, 55n10, 193, 220
Holliday, A. 194
homo economicus 191, 206; see also Foucault, M.; human capital theory
Hong Kong: 1842–1945 38, 44, 49–50, 61, 63–64, 69–71, 79, 82–85, 92, 92n20, 95–96, 104; diagonal capitalism 166; disturbances in 177, 179; English of Carrie Lam 147n3; Hong Kong security law 2020 177; as 'offshore' tax haven 126; pegging to US dollar 129; post-1945 115, 118, 126, 129, 147n3, 160, 166, 177, 179; restoration of colonial administration 1945 115, 118; transport system 160; and Treaty of Nanking 1842 79, 92, 92n20, 95–96, 100; and Treaty of Tientsin 1858 92, 92n20, 95; see also China, communications in English; China, Opium Wars; China, unequal treaties
Hopkins, A. G. 54–73, 83–87, 93–94, 98, 101–103, 107
Horkheimer, M. 24
Howatt, A. P. R. 54n9, 68
Hubbert, J. 176
Hughes, D. 24
human capital theory 191, 191n10, 206; 'worker-self-as-skills-bundle' 191; see also homo economicus
human rights 213; see also linguistic rights
Hurd, D. 72

IBRD (International Bank for Reconstruction and Development) 110, 174
ideology 21, 29n22, 39, 41, 43, 53, 55, 55n10, 67, 110–111, 113, 116, 118, 124, 139–140, 150–153, 161–163, 172, 186, 190, 196, 199–200, 206, 212–214, 218–219; see also discourse; fetish/fetishism; misrecognition
IMF (International Monetary Fund) 33, 38, 40, 107–132, 136–148, 166, 173–174, 174n36, 183, 189, 207, 210–211; and conditionality 38, 107–108; and English 107, 112, 136–137, 139, 144–148, 156, 174, 183, 189, 207, 211; see also structural adjustment programmes (SAPs); Wall Street [Wall Street-Treasury-IMF Complex]
immanent critique 25
immiseration 211–214
imperialism 22–25, 36–42, 163; and gentlemanly capitalism 54–58, 67; and imperialism of free trade 49–53; linguistic imperialism 146, 186; and new imperialism 49; railway imperialism 89–100; see

also accumulation by dispossession; capital, accumulation of; capital, overaccumulation
Imperialism and World Economy (1915) 23
Imperial Maritime Customs 94–98, 207; *see also* Shanghai
implicit ontology 199, 204; *see also* Bhaskar, R.; normative English
import substitution industrialization (ISI); in Latin America 123
indexical scale 185, 206
India: 1600–1850 73–76; 1850–1918 76–79, 83, 103, 105; post-1945 109–110, 121n23, 125–128, 167n12, 216; English in 75–79, 128; language policy 128; language riots 128; opium export 61–62; postcolonial nationalism 127–128; railway imperialism 89–91; *see also* EIC
Indian labourers overseas 89; *see also* Indian troops; Shanghai Municipal Police (SMP)
Indian Mutiny 1857–58 71, 74n1, 76–78, 77n5; and British atrocities 77n5
Indian Official Languages (Amendment) Act 1967 128
Indian troops: and service overseas 78–79, 83, 105, 109–110; *see also* Indian labourers overseas
Indonesia 121, 139, 144; Ford Foundation donations to 121n24; *see also* Asian crisis; dirty wars
industrial revolution 46, 48, 54, 70
inner circle 2, 139, 154, 183, 187, 189, 209
Inoue, A. 72
international political economy (IPE) 7, 31–36, 41, 183
international trading system 158; US destabilization of 170–174, 177; *see also* Bretton Woods; World Trade Organization (WTO)
Iran: 1953 coup 125n28; 1979 Islamic Revolution 125n28; deal on nuclear proliferation 172; English in 125n28; hostage crisis 1979–80 172; Iran-Iraq War 1980–8 141; Mohammed Mosaddegh 125n28; Shah Mohammed Reza Pahlavi 125n28, 133n32, 141; *see also* dirty wars; CIA
Ireland: Act of Union with England 1801 5; Battle of the Boyne 1690 58n14; colonization 46; Cromwellian invasion 46n2; genocide in 46n2; Irish language 59, 59n15, 63; Irish railway navvies 91; potato famine 1845–9 59n15, 63; role of Irish in British empire 5, 82; Scots plantation and clearances 58n13, 59; *see also* Shanghai Municipal Police [multiculturalism in]
Irvine, J. 193, 200
Irwin, D. A. 169, 171
Islamism *see* extremism
Ito, H. 160
Ives, P. 1–3, 4n2, 34, 137, 156, 183, 188, 209; *see also* Gramsci, A.

Jack the Ripper 57; *see also* class
Jacquemet, M. 220
James, L. 76, 77n5
Jameson, F. 181
Japan: 1850–1945 72, 80–81, 80n10, 89–90, 92–94, 92n20, 94n22, 97, 103, 110, 112, 115, 115n15; 1945 surrender 114–116, 120; annexation of Korea 1911 114; annexation of Manchuria 1931 115; Asian crisis 144–145; British investments in 80n10, 103; challenge to US hegemony 158, 165; China 92–94, 92n20, 94n22, 97, 115, 115n15; diagonal capitalism 166; English in 121–122; extraterritoriality in 81; foreign concessions in 64, 72, 80; holding of US debt 151n7; Japan-China-Republic of Korea Trilateral Summit 168–170; Japanese Settlement in Shanghai 80, 80n8; military power of 174; post-1945 34, 42, 110–111, 114–116, 118–119, 119n21, 121–122, 144, 158, 165–166, 168–172, 174; railways 103; recession 158; Russo-Japanese War 1904–5 103; Sino-Japanese War 1894–5 93, 97, 114; Treaty of Shimonoseki 1895 and session of Taiwan, 93, 114; and Trump's economic nationalism 171; US aid to 112; US containment 118–119; US occupation of 118–119, 119n21; US cultural influence 122; *see also* Asian crisis; Cold War, and containment; East Asia; Korea; Taiwan
Japan-China-Republic of Korea Trilateral Summit; and English 168, 170

Japanese Constitution: English scripting of 119, 119n20
Jaspers, J. 188
Jaworski, A. 181
Jay, M. 25
Jayaweera, P. M. 128
jazz 122
Jenkins, J. 154, 186–188, 189n7, 201
Johnson, R. 76
Johnstone, I. 159
Jordan, J. 184

Kachru, B. B. 2, 28, 186
Kayaoglu, T. 61n17, 80n10, 81
Kee, R. 46n2, 58n13
Kelly-Holmes, H. 204
Kennan, George. F. 117–118; *see also* NSC 68
Kent, A. 174
Kenya: and BRI 163; and English 129
Kerr, I. J. 89
Keynes, John Maynard 111–112, 111n10, 112n13; demand management 112; elitism of 112n13
Keynesianism 133, 191n9
Kiernan, V. G. 52
Kim, E. G. 119, 122
Kim, M. 130, 131, 207
Kim, Y.-M. 144
Kim Il-sung 119
Kobe 64, 80
Korea: annexation by Japan 1911 114; Korean War 1950–3 118–119; Treaty of Shimonoseki 1895 93–94, 114; US occupation 115–116; *see also* North Korea; South Korea
Kress, G. R. 196
Kubota, R. 2, 121, 182–184, 199, 205
Kuomintang 115–116, 121

labour power 191–192; *see also* power
Laclau, E. 26, 182
Lagos: and British acquisition 49, 71, 84–85, 85n17
Lamounier, L. 91
language: as alienable 190, 193–195, 211; as bounded 155, 197; as desire 193; as a dialectical relation 154, 206–207, 219; phonocentrism of 200–205; as a practical consciousness 21, 153–158, 206; as property 187; as skill 191; as socialization 155; as a social relation of capital 6, 184, 205–209; as symbolic capital 15, 184–185, 202; as territorialized/essentialized 197; as trait 187; as transformative 199; as transgression 199–200; as unbounded/distributed 155, 196; *see also* superdiverse translingualism
language accreditation: IELTS, TOEFL, TOEIC 194; language credentials 195
language commodification 3, 189–195; as discursive 191, 193; as fetish 193, 204n16; *see also* superdiverse translingualism
language endangerment 213
language ideologies 199–200; 'native-speakerism' 2
language policy 133; and correlation with FDI 130–131, 207
late capitalism 182, 190, 202; *see also* capital; capitalism; globalization; modernism
Latin America: 1600–1900 25, 29n23, 53, 59–68, 69–72, 80n10, 81; 1900–1945 103–108, 113, 117; 1945–1980 123–124, 130; BRI and China 163–164; extraterritoriality 80n10, 81 (*see also* railway imperialism); Europeanness and *nostalgia in absentia* 66, 72; foreign investment in 69–72; import substitution industrialization (ISI) 123; independence struggle 65; inequality in 216; inward migration 65; *latifundism* 66; post 1980 133, 136–139, 151, 163–164, 171n26, 212; racialism 66; *see also* clientelism; dependency; development of underdevelopment
Latin American debt crisis 1980s 33, 133, 136–139; and debt peonage 42, 142–143
League of Nations 106, 166, 207
Leblang, D. 130
LeClerc, J. 130
Lee, R. E. 35
Lee, T. V. 82
Lehman Bros. 145, 150
Lehman, K. D. 29n23
Lemberg, D. 5, 102, 104, 108, 121, 121n24, 125, 156
Lenin, V. I. 8, 22–23, 49–50; *see also* imperialism
Lewis, W. A. 70
LGBTQI 212–213; *see also* anti-systemic movements

Li, W. 6, 184, 186, 194, 196–197, 200, 204; *see also* translanguaging
Lin, J. Y. 160
Lindley, E. K. 121–122, 122n25
linguistic anthropology 191, 204n16, 213
linguistic capital 39, 130; and dispossession 39; *see also* accumulation by dispossession; capital
linguistic imperialism 22, 39, 146, 186; *see also* imperialism; Phillipson, R.
linguistic rights 219; *see also* human rights
Little, L. K. 96
Liu, A. H. 130
Livingstone, G. 139
Llewellyn-Jones, R. 75n2, 77n5
Lo Bianco, J. 144
London Stock Exchange 59
longue durée 8, 35, 41–43, 44, 100–101, 206; *see also* Braudel, F.
López-Gopar, M. E. 143
Louis, Wm. R. 51–52, 52n6, 86
Loveman, B. 66, 139
Luxemburg, R. 4, 8, 22–24, 23n20, 37, 66, 74, 76; death of 23n20; *see also* imperialism
Lyotard, J. 181

Macao 1, 97
MacArthur, General Douglas 119
Macaulay, Lord: 1834 Minute of 76–77
MacDonald, M. N. 194
Mackinnon, William 87–90; and Lake Victoria to Mombasa railway 89; *see also* British East Africa Association
Mahan, A. T. 59
Main, P. 24
Malaysia 28, 125, 167, 171
Manchester, A. K. 81
Manchuria 94, 95n23, 115, 115n14; and Japanese occupation of 115, 115n
Mandarin Chinese: and challenge to English 40, 43, 157, 168, 170, 173–175, 177; *see also* soft power
Manifesto of the Communist Party, The (1848) 9, 11–12
Manthorpe, J. 120n22, 121
Mao Zedong 115–116, 120–121, 140, 162; and Maoism 117, 160
Marshall Plan 112–113, 123–124, 143, 163, 207; and English 113, 123

Marx, K. 4–37, 47–48, 58–59, 62, 64, 64n19, 65, 70–71, 81n11, 89–90, 97, 132n31, 133, 142, 149, 152–154, 176–177, 184–185, 189, 191–195, 191n10, 192n11, 206, 209–213, 220; base/superstructure 19–21, 20n17, 153–154, 185; and collapse of capitalism 209–212; dialectical method 18–22, 156; economic determinism 19–21, 206; and Engels 10–11, 21; fetish 19, 149, 194; imaginary prices 193, 195; immiseration thesis 113, 212; language as a practical consciousness 21, 153–157; 'moments' 19, 36; primitive accumulation 22, 36–37, 206–207; reproduction of the worker 213–214; revolutionism 220; socially necessary labour time 192–193, 192n11; stadial interpretation of history 9, 19, 37; surplus value 13, 17–18, 22, 26, 47; unfamiliarity of scholars with 19–20; *see also* capital; *Capital: A Critique of Political Economy* (1867); fetish/fetishism
Marxism 20n17, 26; Marxist(s) 1, 4, 8, 16, 18, 22–25, 27, 44, 49, 52, 54, 55n10, 57, 138, 143; Marxism-Leninism 117
Matear, A. 114
Matheson, E. M. 96
Mauranen, A. 155, 185
May, C. 32, 133
McCarthy, Joseph R. 116, 165; McCarthyism 116
McCauley, R. N. 160
McElhinny, B. 19, 182, 206, 213
McGill, K. 3, 193
McGregor, R. 162
McKinley, J. 183
Mearsheimer, J. 159
Menon, J. 129
mercantilism 30–31, 63–68, 219; *see also* economic nationalism
MERCOSUR 148
Mertz, E. 6
metaphysics of presence 203, 204n16; *see also* Derrida, J.; phonocentrism
Mexico: 1800–1914 53, 65, 70; 1994 crisis 142–143, 146, 161; Latin American debt crisis 136–138; and leftist movements 213; NAFTA 171; post-1945 133, 135; and railways 90; USMCA 171, 217; *see also* anti-

Index   265

systemic movements; Volcker, Paul, and 'Volcker shock'
Michael, J. 183
micro-physical techniques *see* resistance
Middle East: 1850–1914 73, 80, 80n10, 83, 108; and 9/11 attacks 161; extremism in 172; oil 125, 217; post-1945 109, 123–125, 171–172, 210, 217; reactionism in 220; *see also* 1974 oil crisis
middle-income trap *see* Argentina; Chinese capitalism
migration: from global South 156, 217
Milanovic, B. 159, 162–163, 169, 176, 178
Milroy, J. 56
Mirowski, P. 27, 152, 190, 191n9
misrecognition 40, 185, 188, 206, 209; *see also* Bourdieu, P.; fetish/fetishism; ideology
Mitchell, A. W. 167, 216
modernism 29n22; *see also* structuralism; postmodernism; poststructuralism
Modiano, M. 189n8
moments 3, 19, 21–22, 164; *see also* Harvey, D.
money capital: merging with linguistic capital 130; *see also* capital
Montessori, N. M. 143
Moody, T. 58n13, 59
Morgan, H. 5
Morse, H. B. 94, 97
Mukherji, P. 46
multimodality 196
multinational corporations (MNCs) 4, 126, 130–132, 148; inter/trans-nationalization of 126, 132; *see also* transnational corporations (TNCs)
Multi-Party Interim Appeal Arbitration Arrangement (MPIA) 171n26
multi/plural turn 2, 43, 181–186; *see also* social turn
Mustafa, S. G. 74, 74n1, 75–77
Muth, S. 195, 201
Myers, M. 163
Myers Jaffe, A. 125

NAFTA (North American Free Trade Association) 143, 148, 171; *see also* USMCA (United States, Mexico and Canada Agreement)
Nagasaki: dropping of atomic bomb on 114; foreign concession at 64, 80

Napoleon Bonaparte: defeat of 46, 62
native-speakerism 139, 154, 186, 189, 190; *see also* language ideologies
Navigation Acts 59–60, 63, 67; and English 60; *see also* Great Navigation Act 1651
Nederveen Pieterse, J. 4, 27, 38, 137, 143
Negri, A. 214
neoliberalism 3, 27, 30, 55, 139, 142–144, 147, 150–153, 161–166, 182, 190, 191n9, 199, 206, 214–217
New Deal 108, 112
New Zealand *see* White settlement colonies
Nguyen, N. T. 145
Nicaragua: Sandinistas and 'Contras' 139; US protectorate 104; *see also* Reagan, Ronald
Nichols, R. 4, 19, 47–48, 211
Nicolaus, M. 9, 9n7, 17, 19, 192
Nixon, Richard M. 127, 165
normative English 41–43, 144, 148, 157, 211, 218–220; as a governing stratum 5, 209; as an implicit ontology 204; normative form(s) 5, 43, 153, 155, 160, 180, 181–186, 200, 205–209; persistence of 181–186; reproduction of 6, 41, 142, 151n7, 155, 213–14; as a social relation of capital 205–208; as a truncated repertoire 175; *see also* capital-centric English; English; grammar; language; misrecognition
normative grammar *see* grammar
North American colonies 58–59, 61
North Korea 24, 119, 159, 178–179; as ally of China 179; as degenerated workers' state 24; outside US world-economy 159; *see also* Korean War; South Korea
NSC 68 117–118, 117n18, 121, 125, 127; *see also* Cold War; Kennan, George. F.
Nye, J. S. 163, 178; *see also* 'soft power'

Obama, Barack 151–152, 165, 168n18, 172
Ochieng, D. 129
OECD (Organization of Economic Cooperation and Development) 133, 148, 189
offshore centres 126, 132
O'Higgins, Bernardo 65

266 Index

oil crisis 1974 132–133, 133n32, 135, 140; and petrodollars 132, 136, 140
Old Corruption 55, 67; see also class
Olsen, M. 5
OPEC (Organization of Petroleum Exporting Countries) 132
open door agreements 72, 104; see also China
opium 93, 97
Opium Wars see China
O'Regan, J. P. 3, 20, 34, 55n10, 182, 184, 187–188, 193–195, 199, 200, 204n16
Orientalism 74, 128, 169; see also Said, E. W.
Orton, J. 144, 159
Ostrower, F. 183
Otsuji, E. 185, 194, 197–198
overaccumulation 12, 16, 23–24
overdetermination 20–21, 184; see also dialectic(s)
ownership of English see English

Paik, K. 114
Palmerston, Lord 64–67, 84
Pan, L. 159–160, 175
Pan, Z. 160, 175
Panama: and Panama Canal Zone 45n1, 104, 104n3, 105; see also dollarization
pandemic see COVID-19
Panitch, L. 27, 103–111, 123–132, 135–146, 150, 190
Parboni, R. 127
Park, J.-K. 128, 144
Park, J. S.-Y. 34, 102, 128, 144, 156, 190, 193–194, 201
Pax Americana 110, 125, 152
Pax Britannica 69
Peck, J. 142
pegging see dollarization
Pei, M. 167, 169, 176
Pelcovits, N. A. 93–94
Pennycook, A. 2–3, 38, 55n10, 155, 181–182, 185, 194, 196–200, 207, 220
People's Liberation Army (PLA) 140, 177
Perestroika 140
periodization/periodicity 29–30, 47, 53
Peru 90, 103, 107, 133, 138, 171; debt crisis 138
Peters, P. 34
petrodollars see 1974 oil crisis

phallogocentrism: and economic penetration/intercourse 53n7; see also Derrida, J.
Phan, L. H. 130, 183, 189, 193
Philippines 45n1, 103–104; and Latin American debt crisis 138; as US colony 1898–1946 45n1, 104, 106; post-1946 118, 120, 138, 148; and US containment 118; and US postcolonial incorporation 120
Phillipson, R. 1–3, 22, 39, 53, 102, 108, 132, 137, 146, 156, 200, 213; see also linguistic imperialism
philosophical discourse of modernity 29n22; see also Bhaskar, R.; discourse; Hartwig, M.
phone sex 191; see also call centres; sex
phonocentrism 200–205; see also Derrida, J.; language; superdiverse translingualism
Pivetti, M. 113; see also immiseration
Plassey, Battle of 1757 45–46, 48, 61, 74
pluricentricity: and English 183; see also English
Polanyi, K. 27, 106–107, 212, 212n3
political economy: 1688–1850 44–68; 1850–1914 69–101; 1919–2008 102–134, 135–158; and applied linguistics 3; and COVID-19 173, 211; definition of 3; and developmentalism 113; and free riding 7; and ideology 113; and link to global English 8, 100, 109, 183; post-2008 158–220; and structural power 31–36, 200; see also capital; capitalism; developmentalism; international political economy; structural power
politics of recognition 187, 189, 199–200; see also Fraser, N.
politics of redistribution 199; see also Fraser, N.
Pompeo, Mike 168
Ponzi scheme 149, 149n4
Poor Law 1834 65
populism see extremism
port life 60, 71, 80
Porto, M. 146
postcolonialism 1, 124, 183–184, 186; and linguistic diversity 183; and local elites 128–129; postcolonial nationalism 127–128; and resistance to English 128; see also French

Index   267

postmodernism 181–182, 220; *see also* multi/plural turn; social turn; modernism
poststructuralism 20n17, 197; *see also* multi/plural turn; social turn; structuralism
post-truth *see* truth
pound *see* sterling
power: concept of 17, 21, 25–27, 31–36, 40–41, 153–155, 157, 158, 164, 196, 202; as misrecognition 40; *see also* Bourdieu, P.; Foucault, M.; hegemony; labour power; soft power; structural power; symbolic power
Powis, J. 56
Pradella, L. 9n8, 16
praxis as process 154; *see also* Bhaskar, R., structure and agency
Preece, S. 183
Preface to *A Contribution to the Critique of Political Economy* (1859) 19–20
primitive accumulation 22, 36–37; *see also* accumulation by dispossession; theft
Puga, R. M. 46
Pujolar, J. 191
Puyi, last Emperor of China 99

Quirk, R. 2

Rabe, S. L. 103, 114, 139, 143
Rahimi, S. 4
Rahman, T. 191
railway imperialism [in Latin America, India, Africa and Asia] 42, 83, 85n19, 88, 89–100, 104
Rampton, M. B. H. 186
Reagan, Ronald 33–34, 139, 151, 165; and support for Contras in Nicaragua 139
recognition: politics of *see* Fraser, N.
redistribution: politics of *see* Fraser, N.
registers 200; *see also* Blommaert, J.
Reksulak, M. 5, 15, 109
renminbi (RMB): and for denominating international loans 175; rivalry with US dollar 170, 173, 175; RMB and dollar as trade currencies 173
resistance [to standard English] 43, 195–200; as micro-physical techniques/acts 180, 195–196; as refusal 213–214; *see also* superdiverse translingualism

revolutionism 220
Rhee, Dr Syngman 119–120
Rhodes, Cecil J. 85, 85n19, 89–90
Ricento, T. 2–3, 128, 133, 207
Richards, M. 170
Robinson, B. 57n11
Robinson, R. 5, 16, 48–58, 66, 73, 84; and imperialism of free trade, 49–50; official mind 51–52, 57
Robinson, R. E. 89, 91, 100
Rodney, W. 89
Roosevelt, Franklin, D. 108, 112, 114
Rose, H. 183
Rosenberg, A. 111, 123
Rosenberg, E. S. 43, 108–109, 112–113
Rostow, W. W. 27
Roy, M. 75–76
Royal Niger Company 86, 88
Rubdy, R. 187–188
rule of law: international English-scripted 104; respect for 166
Russia: financial crisis 1998 142; and transition to capitalism 140
Russian 114, 122, 149
Russian Revolution 1917 107, 107n7

Sachs, J. 138
Saddam Hussein 45n1, 141
Said, E. W. 138
Sanders, Bernie 213
Saraceni, M. 3
Sato, T. 183
Schneider, E. W. 200, 204
Schuler, K. 111
Schumpeter, J. 12, 37, 206, 218
'Scramble for Africa' 24, 37, 49, 54n9, 70–71
Scramble for China 84, 97
Seargeant, P. 3
Second Hundred Years' War 1689/1714–1815 62, 62n18
Second World War *see* World War II
Seidlhofer, B. 186, 188, 189n8
seignorage: currency 33, 127, 129, 158, 170; dollar 127, 129, 151, 170; and English 42; linguistic 42, 126–132; *see also* gold standard; sterling; US dollar
Sethia, T. 89
sex 60, 71; *see also* port life
Shambaugh, D. 174, 176, 178–179
Shanghai: English in 79–84; International Settlement 79–82; *see*

also Imperial Maritime Customs; Shanghai Municipal Council (SMC); Shanghai Municipal Police (SMP)
Shanghai Municipal Council (SMC) 81–83; *see also* Shanghai
Shanghai Municipal Police (SMP); and multiculturalism [Sikh, British, Irish, Chinese] 82
Sharma, R. 32n25, 35, 173, 176–177, 179, 210
Shibata, M. 123
Shughart, W. F. 5
Si, J. J. 31, 81–82
Siam and 'open door' agreements 72
Sierra Leone 49, 64, 84, 84n15, 88; and Creole resistance to sickness 88
Silverstein, M. 185, 197
Simpson, W. 3, 15n13, 20, 128, 144, 175, 184, 187–188, 193–195
Singapore 63, 115, 125–126, 148, 160, 166; diagonal capitalism 166; as 'offshore' tax haven 126; 'Speak Good English Movement' 214; as 'Tiger' economy 125, 148
Sino-Japanese War 1894–5 93, 97; and Treaty of Shimonoseki 1895 93, 114
Skidelsky, R. 107, 111–112, 112n12
Skutnabb-Kangas, T. 38, 213
slave trade 46, 58, 65, 84, 97; slavery 18, 47, 84n13, 212
Smith, A. 9, 10, 191n9
Smith, L. E. 197
Smith, R. 54n9, 68
social being 20, 29n22, 190
social change 154, 195, 214–215; and possibility of 154, 195; *see also* resistance
socialism in one country 118, 140
socialism with Chinese characteristics 140, 162; *see also* China
social turn 181–182; *see also* multi/ plural turn; poststructuralism
sociolinguistics 3, 8, 183
Sociolinguistics of Globalization, The (2010) 3
Soederberg, S. 136–137
soft power: and China 163, 173–175; *see also* Mandarin Chinese
Soherwordi, S. H. S. 78
Song, J. J. 128, 144
Song Mei-ling (Madam Chiang) 115, 120
South Africa *see* BRICS; Cape Colony; White settlement colonies

South Korea 18, 34, 45n1, 112, 114, 116, 119–120, 148, 165–166, 174; and Asian crisis 144–145; economic development of 112, 148, 165; and containment 118–122; diagonal capitalism 166; and dictatorship 119–120, 128; and US cultural influence 122; US occupation of 45n1, 116, 119; *see also* Cold War, and containment; Korea; Korean War; North Korea; Rhee, Dr Syngman
Soviet Union/USSR: collapse of 3–4, 30, 33, 43, 107n7, 134, 139–141, 158, 181; and Eastern Europe 140; entry into World War II 115; global ambitions of 118; and occupation of North Korea 115; and postcolonial nationalism 124; rivalry with US 31; and US containment 33, 114, 117–118; *see also* Cold War; NSC 68; socialism in one country
Sowden, C. 138, 202n15
spatial repertoires 196–198; as semioticized resources 198
speech *see* Derrida, J.; phonocentrism; writing
Spence, J. 93, 95–97, 99, 140
Spivak, G. C. 203
spontaneous/immanent grammar *see* grammar; Gramsci, A.
Sridhar, S. N. 183–185, 197
standard English *see* normative English
Stedman-Jones, D. 142, 152, 190
sterling [as international reserve currency] 69, 106–107, 106n6, 173; *see also* seignorage
Storey, R. 80n9, 119
Straits Settlements [Ultra Gangetic Territory] 63, 69
Strange, S. 32–36, 45, 133, 172–173
structural adjustment programmes (SAPs) [English-meditated]: 27, 42, 107, 124, 133, 136–138, 142, 145–146, 166, 217; and debt restructuring 137
structuralism 196–197, 199, 203–204; and anti-structuralism 196–197, 199, 204; *see also* modernism; postmodernism; poststructuralism; superdiverse translingualism
structuration effects [of English] 42, 123, 135–141, 200

structural power [production, credit, knowledge, security, language]: 31–36, 40–41, 43, 133, 139–140, 148, 160, 163, 169–170, 172, 175–176, 184, 207; see also China; hegemony; United States
structure and agency 7, 32–33, 39, 154–156, 199–200, 202, 202n14; see also Bhaskar, R.; Marx, K., base/superstructure
sub-prime debt see 2007–8 financial crisis
submarine cable 70
Sudan conflict 1881–99 85, 89
Suez Canal 52, 72, 87; Suez Crisis 1956 30
Sullivan, J. 216
Sun Yat-sen 99, 99n24
superdiverse translingualism: 43, 181–209, 220; and anti-structuralism of 204; and phonocentrism of 200–205; and resistance [to standard English] 195–200; see also English as a Lingua Franca (ELF); language commodification; language; resistance; poststructuralism; superdiversity; translanguaging; translingualism; trans-spatial assemblage; World Englishes
superdiversity 1, 3, 35, 43, 182, 182n1, 195, 197, 204; see also superdiverse translingualism
superfluous capital 36–37; see also accumulation by dispossession; overaccumulation
surplus value see value; capital
Swartz, Aaron: death of 35
Sweezy, P. M. 4, 8, 18
symbolic capital see Bourdieu, P.; language

Taiping Rebellion 1850–64 105n5; see also China
Taiwan (Formosa): 1860–1895 92–93, 112, 114–116; English fever in 144; English in 121–122; influence of Song Mei-ling (Madam Chiang) 115, 120; post-1949 18, 34, 42, 45, 116, 118, 120–122, 144, 167–168; pro-US stance of Chiang Kai-shek 116, 120–121; retreat of Kuomintang armies to 116; session to Japan in Treaty of Shimonoseki 1895 93, 114; tensions with China 167–168; treaty ports in 92; US advisors in 122; US aid to 112, 122; and US containment 34, 42, 118–121; US incorporation 18, 42, 122; see also Cold War, andcontainment; East Asia; Japan; South Korea
Tanzania 85–86, 88, 128–129, 216; English in 128–129; inequality in 216
Tarbuck, K. J. 22
Taylor, P. J. 5, 27, 142
tea 1, 62, 73; tea house 71
Tea Party 165
Teng, S.-Y. 175
Thailand: Asian crisis 144–145, 161; English fever 144
thick description 195
Thompson, J. 55n10
Thrift, N. J. 200
Thucydides' trap 215–216; see also hegemony
Tibet see China [ethnic minorities]; Xi Jinping [autonomous regions]
Tollefson, J. W. 133
Tollison, R. D. 5
Tongmenghui 99, 99n24
Tooze, A. 32n25, 35, 40, 160–161, 172, 215–216
translanguaging 1, 3, 35, 43, 182, 182n1, 195, 197, 204; see also superdiverse translingualism
translingualism 1, 3, 35, 43, 182, 182n1, 195, 197, 204; see also superdiverse translingualism
transnational corporations (TNCs) 33–36, 40, 131, 207, 211; see also multinational corporations (MNCs)
trans-spatial assemblage(s) 35, 43, 195–198, 200, 204, 211; see also spatial repertoires; superdiverse translingualism
Treaty of Nanking 1842 see Hong Kong
Treaty of Shimonoseki 1895 see Japan; Korea
Treaty of Tientsin 1858 see Hong Kong
treaty ports see China
Truman, Harry S. 114–116, 118, 120–121
Truman Doctrine 113
Trump, Donald: 2016 election 35, 152, 165–166; 2020 defeat 33n27, 168n18, 176n38; America first policy 166; attitude to China 169, 169n19; attitude to Iran 169n19; climate

270 *Index*

change 178–179, 215; demagoguery 40, 151, 176; destabilization of international trading system 168, 170–172; economic nationalism 170, 217; egomania 176; free riding 7n6, 171; response to COVID-19 165, 206n18, 215; rivalry with Xi Jinping 176, 179; trade war with China 33, 168–169; WHO 172; withdrawal from Trans-Pacific-Partnership (TPP) 177; wrecking of Iran nuclear non-proliferation deal 172; WTO 170; *see also* United States [*passim*]
truncated multilingualism 197, 205
truncated repertoire *see* normative English
truth 55n10; and post-truth 151
Tsungli Yamen 97
Tuck, R. 5
Tupas, R. 104, 148, 184, 188
Tuxhorn, K.-L. 130
Twin Towers attacks 9/11 151, 151n7, 161

Uganda 78, 85, 87–90, 129, 138
Uighurs 167; *see also* China; Xinjiang
Ukers, W. H. 1
UN (United Nations) 118, 148, 167, 174, 174n36, 178, 218
underconsumption 23–24, 37; *see also* capital, overaccumulation of
unequal English(es) 188
unequal treaties *see* China; Hong Kong
United States (US): 1870–1918 101, 102–106; 1919–1945 106–109; 1945–1979 109–126; 1979–2020 135–157; capital flows/networks 40, 42, 109, 123–126, 189; climate change 178–179, 215; collapse 218–220; conditionality loans and SAPs 107–108, 136–138, 145; continued 'trust of credit' 179; COVID-19 172, 206, 215; cultural influence 121–122; debt 217–218; debt structuring and SAPs 132–134, 135–141; decline/declinism 32, 32n25, 35, 43, 133n32, 158–180, 208, 216; derivatives 148–153, 156; destabilization of world-system 171–174; economic expansion 31, 42, 69–70, 102–103, 214; empire 44–45; extraterritoriality 38, 104, 107, 114, 125; foreign assets 1920s 107; Foreign Direct Investment (FDI) 124–125, 128, 130–131, 136, 140, 145, 159, 207; gold standard 106, 106n6, 108, 110–112, 158; and hegemonic transition 164–165; informal empire 103–104, 179; imperialism 2, 40; protectionism/economic nationalism 107, 168–174; railway imperialism of 92, 99; resilience of US structural power 172–174, 176; rivalry with China 158–174; Russian Revolution 107n7; structural power 32–39, 43, 133, 139–140, 158, 170, 172, 174–176, 184, 207; territorial acquisition/formal empire 45n1, 45–46, 104, 116, 118; Thucydides' trap 215–216; trade war with China 33, 168–169; unequal treaties with China 92n20; US world-economy 30, 30n24, 44, 68, 103, 114, 122–123, 127, 139–141, 147, 162, 170
Urciuoli, B. 191; *see also homo economicus*; human capital theory
Uruguay: British investments 103; extraterritoriality 80, 80n10; independence 1830 65; Latin American debt crisis 138; railways 90; Uruguayan Civil War 1840s 67
US Army Military Governments 115, 118; *see also* Japan; Korea
US-China trade war 33, 168–169; and 'market-distorting practices' 167; *see also* Trump; United States, rivalry/trade war with China
US dollar: hoarding of [in response to COVID-19] 173; as international reserve currency 33, 40, 106, 127, 129, 132, 158–159, 170, 173, 218; rivalry with renminbi (RMB) 170, 173; *see also* dollarization; Eurodollars; gold standard; petrodollars; *seignorage*; United States, continued 'trust of credit'
use value *see* value
US Federal Reserve *see* Federal Reserve
US-Korea Free Trade Agreement (KORUS) 172
USMCA (United States Mexico and Canada Agreement) 171, 217; *see also* NAFTA (North American Free Trade Association)
Ustinova, I. 140
US Treasury 111, 133, 136–137, 139, 142–150, 183; *see also* Wall Street

Vaillancourt, F. 207
value: exchange value(s) 13, 17, 192, 220; surplus value 13, 17–18, 22, 26, 47; symbolic value 140, 206; use value(s) 13, 17, 192, 211, 220; *see also* circulating capital; Marx, K., imaginary prices
Van Dyke, P. A. 31
Vandrick, S. 183
Veneroso, F. 143, 145, 147
Versailles, Treaty of 1919 30, 107; Treaty of 1783 84
vertical capitalism: and China 166
Vietnam: containment 117; as degenerated workers' state 24; English fever in 144; and French Indo-China 118; outside US world-economy 114, 125, 159; Paris Peace Accords 1973 122; tensions in South China Sea 167; Vietnam War 1950–1973 32, 122, 127, 139, 141
Vogler, J. 220
Volcker, Paul 131, 135–137, 139; and 'Volcker shock' 135, 139
Vološinov, V. N. 207
vulture capitalist risk 218

Wade, R. 143, 145, 147
Wall, R. F. 103
Wallerstein, I. 3–5, 8, 16, 25–31, 32n26, 39, 44, 47–48, 53, 62n18, 106, 113, 125, 130, 132, 133n32, 160, 164–165, 169, 177, 184, 207, 212–213, 216, 218–219; *see also* Braudel, F.; core/periphery; *longue durée*; world-systems analysis
Wall Street 30, 131, 145, 156; and Wall Street-Treasury-IMF Complex 143, 145, 147, 183
Walter, A. 131
war on Islamist extremism: 'War on Terror' 161
Wealth of Nations [1776] 9
Weber, M. 56, 206; and 'Iron Cage' 219
Wee, L. 34, 102, 128, 144, 156, 190, 193–194, 201
Wertheim, S. 216
Westad, O. A. 167–168
West Africa: British forts in 84
Whitehead, C. 75, 77
White settlement colonies [Australia, Canada, South Africa, New Zealand] 69, 72–73, 105, 109; *see also* Anglo-cluster

Widdowson, H. G. 154, 184, 186–188
William of Orange 58, 60; and Battle of the Boyne 1690 58n14
Williams, E. 61
Williams, R. 20–21, 20n18, 47, 153; and language as a practical consciousness 206, 220; *see also* language; Marx, K.
Woo, W. T. 161–162, 177
Woodruff, W. 89–90, 93, 102–103
World Bank 27, 33, 38, 40, 110–114, 125, 133, 136–137, 139, 142, 148, 156, 169, 173–174, 189, 207, 211; *see also* IMF, and conditionality; IMF, and English; structural adjustment programmes (SAPs)
world-economy: British 5, 8, 28–30, 30n24, 34, 38, 40, 42, 44, 46, 48, 58, 68, 83–86, 89, 100; US 103, 109–111, 113–114, 122–123, 125, 127, 130–133, 135, 139–142, 145, 147, 148, 151–152, 154, 156–157, 159, 162, 166, 168, 170–171, 176, 189–191, 206–208, 210, 216; incorporation of East European states into 133, 139–140, 216; reproduction of 157, 189; transnationalization of 125–126, 131–132. 205
world-empire *see* empire
World Englishes 1, 35, 40, 43, 182, 186, 188, 196–197, 200, 202, 204, 213; *see also* superdiverse translingualism
world market 4, 10–11, 14, 22, 29, 33, 40, 48, 136, 138, 159
world-systems analysis 8, 24, 32, 41, 50, 53, 216, 220; *see also* capitalism, collapse of; core/periphery; globalization, and recentness debate; hegemony; *longue durée*; structural power; Wallerstein, I.; world-economy; world-empire
World War I 41–42, 101, 103, 105n5, 166; and English 105
World War II 45n1, 104, 108–110, 110n9, 123, 130, 132; and African Americans 110n9; and English 109–110; and Native Americans 110n9
writing [and normative standard English]: 6, 35, 95, 111, 147, 164, 183–184, 188, 197–198, 204–205, 214; and Belt and Road

155; and Bretton Woods 111; and Chinese international bodies [AIIB; NDB] 169–170; and international diplomacy/politics/finance 147; and other international English-medium contexts [higher education; high culture; English language policies, etc.] 183–184; and unequal treaties 95; and Wall Street-Treasury-IMF Complex 147; writing as the 'speech of capital' 204–205; *see also* Derrida, J.; phonocentrism

WTO (World Trade Organization) 144–145, 148, 159, 171, 174, 174n36, 189, 211; and Trump 171; *see also* GATT (General Agreement on Tariffs and Trade)

Xi Jinping: autocracy and centralization of power 33, 162, 169, 176–177; and autonomous regions [Tibet, Xinjiang] 162, 167, 177; abolition of two-term limit 162; 'China Dream' 162; corruption purge 163; global leadership initiatives 177–79; Hong Kong 177; patriotic nationalism 177–179; public image 176; resistance to internal market reform 166, 169; rivalry with Trump 168–169, 176; support for state sector 162–163; US-China trade war 33, 168–169, 179; Xi Jinping thought 162; *see also* China [*passim*]

Xinjiang 162, 167, 177

Yedo 72, 80; *see also Bakufu*
Yokohama settlement 64; Yokohama Pidgin 72
Yom Kippur War 1973 132
Yuan Shih-kai 99

Zacek, N. A. 60
Zakaria, F. 160–161, 167–168, 172
Zanzibar: and British interests in 85–88; *see also* British East Africa Association
Zapatista uprising 1994 143
Zein, S. 148
Žižek, S. 188
Zoellick, R. 159
Zucchi, K. 150